# The Nazi Dictatorship

# The Nazi Dictatorship

## Problems and Perspectives of Interpretation

*Second edition*

**Ian Kershaw**

Edward Arnold
A division of Hodder & Stoughton
LONDON   NEW YORK   MELBOURNE   AUCKLAND

© 1985, 1989 Ian Kershaw

First published in Great Britain 1985
Second edition published 1989
Reprinted 1989, 1990 (twice)

Distributed in the USA by Routledge, Chapman and Hall, Inc.
29 West 35th Street, New York, NY 10001

*British Library Cataloguing in Publication Data*

Kershaw, Ian, *1943–*
   The Nazi dictatorship: problems and
   perspectives of interpretation.—2nd ed.
   1. Germany, 1933–1945.
   I. Title.
   943.086

   ISBN 0–340–49008–X

*Library of Congress Cataloging-in-Publication Data*

Kershaw, Ian.
   The Nazi dictatorship.

   Bibliography: p.
   Includes index.
   1. National socialism—History.   2. Germany
—Politics and government—1933–1945.
I. Title.
DD256.5.K47   1989      321.9'4'0943   88–33350
ISBN 0–340–49008–X

Typeset in 10/11 pt Times
by Colset Private Limited, Singapore
Printed and bound in Great Britain for Edward Arnold,
a division of Hodder and Stoughton Limited,
Mill Road, Dunton Green, Sevenoaks, Kent TN13 2YA
by Clays Ltd, St Ives plc

# Contents

# Preface

The idea for this book grew out of the 'Special Subject' on 'The Nazi Dictatorship' which I have taught for a number of years to final-year undergraduates at Manchester University. Even students with good German have difficulty finding their way around an immense literature and grappling with some complex theoretical problems of interpretation. This prompted me to think that a book which attempted to single out the key interpretational problems related to the Nazi Dictatorship, to provide a concise guide to why there is a problem and how historians of different persuasion have tackled it, and then, on the basis of the most recent research, to attempt a clear evaluation of the positions, might have some uses. Since I first had the idea, I am happy to have been 'upstaged' in part by the publications of Pierre Ayçoberry, Klaus Hildebrand, and John Hiden and John Farquharson (see 'Suggestions for Further Reading' for references). However, valuable though these works are, they are more in the nature of broad historiographical surveys than deep analyses, and the need I originally sensed has, I think, still not been completely met. My book differs, therefore, in conception, approach, format, and – not least – interpretation from each of them. In narrowing down my own analysis to a concentrated treatment of a number of selected 'problem areas', I have confined myself to the period of the Dictatorship itself. Contentious and important issues relating to the origins and rise of Nazism, such as whether there was a German 'special path' of development leading to the Third Reich, or relations between 'big business' and Nazism before 1933, or the social composition of the Nazi movement demand extensive analysis of their own, and I have only alluded to them here as background problems to the ones I have considered. Even for the Third Reich itself, I decided – reluctantly – to omit a systematic discussion of the problem of 'resistance' to Nazism. The social bases of consent and opposition to the Nazi regime are an area at the centre of much current research, with interpretations still to some extent in a state of flux. To have dealt here with the problem would have required far more space than I had at my disposal. However, I am not avoiding the issue. It forms a focus of another book, which I am currently working on, on 'the German People under Hitler – a social history of the Third Reich'. Despite these limitations, I hope the present book has something to offer students and scholars who are tackling such a fundamentally important phenomenon in twentieth-century development as the Nazi Dictatorship.

It is a great pleasure for me to record my thanks here to all those friends and colleagues who have contributed directly to the making of this book. On a clear 'primacy of economics' principle, my first debt is to the Leverhulme

Foundation for granting me a Fellowship which allowed me to spend six months of 1982 working on the book in Germany, mainly at the excellent library of the Institut für Zeitgeschichte in Munich. I am grateful, too, to the British Academy and the Akademie der Wissenschaften der DDR which, between them, funded a stay of several weeks in autumn 1981 at the Zentralinstitut für Geschichte in East Berlin, where I profited from detailed discussion with a number of leading historians of the German Democratic Republic. My debt to a number of West German historians will be clear from the text and footnotes which follow, but I would single out a personal as well as intellectual debt of gratitude to Hans Mommsen and Martin Broszat. Special thanks, too, are owing to Bernd Weisbrod and Elisabeth Domansky, who influenced my thinking on a number of points while I had the good fortune to be working closely with them during a Semester at the Ruhr-Universität Bochum in 1983–4. In England, I exploited good friendship as well as great expertise in prevailing upon John Breuilly, Jeremy Noakes, and Bill Carr to read the typescript and offer valuable comment and criticism, while Dick Geary (courtesy of Boddington's Ales), Alan Milward, and Tim Mason have now as before given me great stimulation and encouragement, not least through their own outstanding work. They will have been unable to save me from all the pitfalls involved in tackling such thorny issues, but I'm happy to carry the can for what is left. Finally, I would like most sincerely to thank successive generations of 'Special Subject' students at Manchester as well as, more recently, my students at Bochum on whom I inflicted my own interpretations of the Third Reich and who helped to sharpen these interpretations through their own lively engagement and perceptive criticism.

Ian Kershaw
Manchester, September 1984

# Preface to the Second Edition

Things move quickly in the historiography of the Third Reich. Since this book was first published, the historical profession in West Germany has been preoccupied with controversy about 'revised' approaches to the Nazi past in the so-called '*Historikerstreit*' ('historians' dispute').

Closely tied in with this have been debates about how to write the history of the Third Reich, and whether that history can now be 'historicized', that is, treated in genuine historical fashion, as a 'normal' part of Germany's past. For the second edition, I have added two new chapters which try to explain why these issues are so contentious, and to evaluate the development and outcome of the debates. I have also attempted to revise thoroughly and bring up to date the other chapters, together with the suggestions for further reading. My thinking on the two new chapters, especially, has profited from a fruitful dialogue with Otto Dov Kulka (Jerusalem), and I am most grateful for his advice and encouragement. Now as before, my editor at Edward Arnold has provided invaluable guidance and support, for which I would like to offer sincere thanks.

I.K.
Nottingham, July 1988

# Abbreviations

AfS     *Archiv für Sozialgeschichte*
AHR     *American Historical Review*
APZ     *Aus Politik und Zeitgeschichte (Beilage zur Wochenzeitung 'das Parlament')*
BAK     Bundesarchiv, Koblenz
CEH     *Central European History*
EcHR     *Economic History Review*
GG     *Geschichte und Gesellschaft*
GWU     *Geschichte in Wissenschaft und Unterricht*
HWJ     *History Workshop Journal*
HZ     *Historische Zeitschrift*
JCH     *Journal of Contemporary History*
JMH     *Journal of Modern History*
MGM     *Militärgeschichtliche Mitteilungen*
NPL     *Neue Politische Literatur*
PVS     *Politische Vierteljahresschrift*
VfZ     *Vierteljahrshefte für Zeitgeschichte*

# 1

## Historians and the Problem of Explaining Nazism

More than four decades after the destruction of the Third Reich, leading historians are far from agreement on some of the most fundamental problems of interpreting and explaining Nazism. Of course, great progress has been made since the historical writing of the immediate post-war era, when historians were attempting to write 'contemporary history' even before the dust had begun to settle on the wreckage of Hitler's Europe in a climate determined by the horrific disclosures of the Nuremberg Trials and the full realization of the bestiality of the regime. In such a climate, it is hardly surprising that recrimination from the Allied side and a proneness to apologetics from the German side featured strongly in writing on the immediate past. The lengthier time perspective and a vast outpouring of high-class scholarly research by a new generation of historians – especially from the 1960s on, following the opening up of the captured German records which in the meantime had been returned to Germany – brought major advances in knowledge of many vital aspects of Nazi rule. But as soon as the detailed scholarly monographs are placed in the context of overarching interpretative questions about Nazism, the limits of consensus are rapidly reached. A synthesis of polarized interpretations, often advocated and pleaded for, is nowhere in sight. The debate continues unabated, conducted with great vigour and frequently, too, with a rancour going beyond the bounds of conventional historical controversy. This has recently been most vividly illustrated by the explosion of feeling which accompanied the '*Historikerstreit*' (or 'historians' dispute') – a major public controversy about the place of the Third Reich in German history involving Germany's leading historians. The significance of the dispute is assessed in chapter 9 below.

Of course, debate and controversy are the very essence of historical study, the pre-requisite for progress in historical research. However, Nazism raises questions of historical interpretation which either have a flavour of their own or highlight in marked fashion wider issues of historical explanation. The special features of historians' fundamental disagreements about interpreting Nazism are framed, in my view, by the inevitable merging of three dimensions – a historical–philosophical, a political–ideological, and a moral dimension – which are inseparable both from the historian's subject matter and from the historian's understanding of his present-day role and task in studying and writing about Nazism. These special features are, I would further argue, conditioned by and a reflection of a central element in the political consciousness of both post-war German states: mastering the Nazi past – *Vergangenheitsbewältigung*, coming to grips with and learning from Germany's recent history.

The radically different approaches to the Nazi past in East and West Germany have naturally lent a peculiar colouring to historical writing about Nazism. But since the problem of facing the past has been tackled in a less unilinear fashion in the Federal Republic than in the German Democratic Republic, the controversies about interpreting Nazism have above all been West German controversies. To say this is, of course, in no sense to underestimate the major, often path-breaking, contribution made to German history by non-German historians. Often it has been, in fact, the very detachment (with correspondingly different perspective) of foreign historians both from the burden of 'mastering the past' and from the intellectual currents of West German society which has provided the springboard for fresh impulses and new methods. The important mark of international scholarship will be clearly apparent in the following chapters. Nevertheless, it is a basic contention of this book that the contours of the debates have generally been established by German historians, especially of the Federal Republic, and have been shaped in great measure by West German historians' perception of their task in helping to shape 'political consciousness' and thereby overcome the past.

It has been said of the Federal Republic that it is even more than Israel or South Vietnam 'a State born of contemporary history, a product of catastrophe erected to overcome the catastrophe'.[1] In such a society, the historian of the recent past clearly has a much more overtly *political* role than, for example, in Britain. It is not going too far to say that through his interpretation of the recent past the historian is seen, and sees himself, in certain ways as the guardian or the critic of the present. The inseparability of historical research on Nazism from 'political education' contributes in part to the latent feeling of some historians that, above all in grasping the essence of the Nazi system, there *ought* to be clarity. This feeling was expressed by the (then) Chancellor of the Federal Republic, Helmut Schmidt, when he addressed the German Historians' Annual Conference in 1978 and complained that a surfeit of theory had produced for many present-day Germans a picture of Nazism still lacking 'a clear contour'.[2] The same argument marks the tone – a mixture of anger and sorrow – of some historians, whose interpretation dominated the 1950s and 1960s, in reacting to a 'revisionist' challenge to established orthodoxy which goes so far as to subject to radical questioning 'basic scholarly findings which had been taken to be certain, indeed uncontested'.[3]

The connection between the changing perspective of historical research and the shaping of current political consciousness is recognized as an explicit one – by 'traditionalists' and 'revisionists' alike.[4] As the '*Historikerstreit*' has again clearly demonstrated, conflicting interpretations of Nazism are part of a continuing reappraisal of West Germany's political identity and political future. The contemporary historian and his work are public property. This

---

[1] Ernst Nolte, *Marxismus, Faschismus, Kalter Krieg* (Stuttgart, 1977), p. 217.
[2] Cited in Walther Hofer, '50 Jahre danach. Über den wissenschaftlichen Umgang mit dem Dritten Reich', *GWU* 34 (1983), p. 2.
[3] Hofer, p. 2.
[4] 'Revisionism' is not only a 'dirty' word, but also a shifting and confusing one. Thus some of those who in the 1970s criticized the 'revisionists' have, in the recent '*Historikerstreit*', found themselves decried as 'revisionists'.

forms the basic framework and colours the nature of the historical controversies we shall be appraising.


The extent of the literature on Nazism is so vast that even experts have difficulty
in coping. And it is clear to see that students specializing in modern German
history are frequently unable to assimilate the complex historiography of
Nazism and to follow interpretational controversies carried out for the most
part in the pages of German scholarly journals or in scholarly monographs.
My book was written with this in mind. It offers no description of the
development of historiography, no history of the history of Nazism, so to
say.[5] Rather, it is an attempt to examine the nature of a number of central
problems of interpretation, relating specifically to the period of the Dictatorship itself, which confront present-day historians of Nazi Germany.[6]
   The structure of the book is largely pre-shaped by the interlocking and
interrelated themes which form the basis of the controversies. The following
chapter seeks to analyse the wide-ranging and sharply opposed interpretations of the nature of Nazism: whether it can be most satisfactorily
viewed as a form of fascism, as a brand of totalitarianism, or as a unique
product of recent German history – a political phenomenon 'of its own
kind'. Directly related to the fascism debate is the heated controversy about
Nazism and capitalism, in particular over the role of German industry,
which forms the subject of the subsequent chapter. The key issue which has
emerged in recent years has been how to interpret the position, role, and
significance of Hitler himself in the Nazi system of rule, a complex problem
explored below in three separate chapters on the power structure of the Third
Reich and the framing of anti-Jewish and foreign policy. The focus is then
moved from the government of the Third Reich to society under Nazi rule,
seeking to examine the extent to which Nazism altered, even revolutionized,
German society. This is followed by an analysis of the important recent
debate which has developed about the 'historicization' of the Third Reich –
whether the Nazi era can be dealt with at all like other periods of the past, as
'history'. Finally, I turn to the implications of the open confrontation of
German historians on the problems of interpreting Nazism – the '*Historikerstreit*'. Within each chapter I try to summarize adequately the differing
interpretations and the current state of research, and then offer an evaluation. I have not seen it as my task to attempt to sit on the fence and adopt a
neutral stance in reviewing the controversies – in any case an impossibility. I
hope to represent the views I am summarizing as fairly as I can, but also to
participate in the debate, not 'referee' it, advancing my own position in each
case.

[5] For a good, if often rather agnostic, historiographical survey, see Pierre Ayçoberry, *The Nazi
Question* (London, 1981).
[6] For recent discussions of the literature and state of research on Nazism, see Klaus Hildebrand,
*Das Dritte Reich* (Munich/Vienna, 1979), Engl. trans. *The Third Reich* (London, 1984);
Andreas Hillgruber, *Endlich genug über den Nationalsozialismus und Zweiten Weltkrieg?
Forschungsstand und Literatur* (Düsseldorf, 1982); and John Hiden and John Farquharson,
*Explaining Hitler's Germany. Historians and the Third Reich* (London, 1983). Gerhard
Schreiber's *Hitler. Interpretationen* (Darmstadt, 1984) offers an exhaustive historiographical
survey of works on Hitler.

The varied approaches to the history of the Third Reich encountered in this book share a common aim: to offer an adequate *explanation* of Nazism. To explain the past is the task of all historians, but the daunting nature and complexity of this task in the case of Nazism will become apparent in the pages which follow. Arguably, indeed, an *adequate* explanation of Nazism is an intellectual impossibility. In Nazism, we have a phenomenon which seems scarcely capable of subjection to rational analysis. Under a leader who talked in apocalyptic tones of world power or destruction and a regime founded on an utterly repulsive ideology of race-hatred, one of the most culturally and economically advanced countries in Europe planned for war, launched a world conflagration which killed around 50 million people, and perpetrated atrocities – culminating in the mechanized mass murder of millions of Jews – of a nature and scale as to defy imagination. Faced with Auschwitz, the explanatory powers of the historian seem puny indeed. How can he hope to write adequately and 'objectively' about a system of government which produced horror of such monumentality? How is he to go about his task? He can hardly confine himself in neo-Rankean terms to recovering from the sources the story of 'what it was actually like'. And can he hope to 'understand' (in the historicist tradition) such a criminal regime and its inhumane leader? Or is his task to lay bare the evil of Nazism to provide witness for the present and warning for the future? If so, how is this to be done? Can or should the historian strive to attain the 'detachment' from his subject matter which is usually taken to be the very essence of 'objective' historical writing? Simply to pose such questions suggests some of the reasons why no explanation of Nazism can be intellectually wholly satisfying. Ultimately, nevertheless, the merit of any interpretational approach must rest in the extent to which it might be seen to *contribute* towards a potentially improved explanation of Nazism. The aim of this book will have been served if its evaluation of varying interpretations of the Nazi Dictatorship suggests which approaches have a better potential than others (or differently expressed: are less inadequate than others) to offer an explanation of the processes of dynamic radicalization in the Third Reich which led to war and genocide on an unparalleled scale.

Before considering the historical–philosophical, political–ideological, and moral dimensions underlying the controversies which we shall be examining, a final preliminary point must be made. It is an obvious enough point, but bears repeating nevertheless: the inadequacies of the source materials. For, despite the vastness of surviving archival relics of the Third Reich, the documentation is patchy in the extreme and serious problems of interpretation are in part linked to fundamental deficiencies in the nature of the sources. Much crucial documentation was, of course, deliberately destroyed by the Nazis towards the end of the war, or lost through bombing raids. But the problem extends beyond the mere physical loss of record material. It reaches to the huge gaps in the documentary sources at the most critical and sensitive points, which themselves are an inevitable product of the way the Nazi system of government functioned. Nowhere are the gaps more apparent or more frustrating than those surrounding Hitler himself and his role in the government of the Third Reich. Thus, the increasing breakdown of any formalized central government machinery in the Third Reich, together with Hitler's extraordinarily unbureaucratic style of rule where decisions were seldom formally registered, has left a huge void in the documentation of the sphere of central decision-making. The immense bureaucratic remnants of the Third Reich stop, therefore, short of Hitler. It is difficult to know what material from the government was even reaching Hitler, let alone whether he read it and how he reacted to it. As Dictator of Germany, Hitler is for the historian largely unreachable, cocooned in the silence of the sources. For this very reason, fundamental conflicts of interpretation about Hitler's place in the Nazi system of rule can neither be avoided nor conclusively resolved on the basis of the available evidence.

The deficiencies of the sources form a relatively minor part of the problem of interpreting Nazism. A more significant role in shaping the character of the controversies over the Nazi Dictatorship has been played by historians' divergent, often quite contradictory, conceptions and methods of historical writing, when applied to the study of Nazism.

## The Historical–Philosophical Dimension

Two points can be made at the outset. The first is, that the differences in historical approach, method, and philosophy are by no means peculiar to the study of Nazism, though the problems involved in interpreting Nazism bring out these issues of historical philosophy in particularly forceful fashion. The second point is, that the intensity and rigour of the debate on historical method stems from the specifically German tradition of historical writing and the challenge to this tradition, applied to the terrain of the Third Reich. Though non-German historians have often made significant contributions, the debate on historical method is largely and characteristically a West German affair. In what follows, therefore, we need to turn our attention to the course and nature of German historiography, and to the radically opposed views on the form and purpose of historical writing advanced by current leading West German historians.

The contours of post-war German historiography have been shaped by a number of specific factors distinguishing Germany from the historiographical development of other countries. Underpinning the whole process has been the need to come to terms with the Nazi past. This has been fundamental in shaping the particularly close connection in post-war German historical scholarship between the problems of interpreting the course and character of recent German history and far-reaching questions of historical method and philosophy. Broadly speaking, the development since the war of historical studies in West Germany – the GDR has to be excluded from this categorization – can be divided into three phases: a period of continued and partly refurbished historicism, lasting until the early 1960s; a transitional phase of transformation, extending into the mid 1970s; and a phase continuing to the present time, despite some stiff challenges and certain regressive tendencies, in which new forms of structurally based 'social history' aligned to the social sciences and closely interwoven with parallel developments in international scholarship, can be said to have established themselves.[7]

The historicist tradition had exerted a dominance over historical philosophy and writing in Germany since the time of Ranke incomparably greater than that of any philosophy of history in any other country.[8] It rested on an idealistic – in the philosophical sense – concept of history as cultural development formed by men's 'ideas' as revealed through their actions, from which their intentions, motives, and 'self-reflection' could be deduced. Historical writing concentrated on the task of trying to explain actions by 'understanding' intuitively the intentions which lay behind them. In practice, this led to a heavy emphasis on the uniqueness of historical events and personages, on the overwhelming importance of will and intention in the historical process, and on the power of the State as an end in itself (and consequently the elevation of the Prussian–German national State).

For a historical profession which had concentrated heavily upon the nature and role of the State as a 'positive' factor in history, it was an extreme shock after 1945 to have to deal 'not only with the break-up of a State . . . but with the break-up of a State burdened with State crimes of inconceivable extent'.[9] Nevertheless, the collapse of the Third Reich brought no fundamental change in the historicist tradition and dominance in historical writing. As in 1918 and 1933, continuity was the essential hallmark. The two foremost historians of post-war Germany, Friedrich Meinecke and Gerhard Ritter, had both been reared and had written in the historicist tradition, and their ideas were deeply embedded in the German idealistic tradition of historical and political thought. Neither had been a Nazi. In fact, both had had their brushes with the Nazis: Meinecke had been removed from his post as editor of the *Historische Zeitschrift* in 1935; Ritter was, as an associate of Carl Goerdeler, imprisoned in 1944 following the attempt on Hitler's life. Meinecke's influential book, *Die deutsche Katastrophe*, which appeared in 1946, and Ritter's more strongly apologetic *Europa und die deutsche Frage*, published in 1948, formed in essence attempts to justify German idealism and the national political tradition. According to such a view, Nazism had emerged from a sort of parasitic sub-growth, traceable to the negative forces which had first come to the fore in the French Revolution, and existing alongside the generally healthy and positive development of the German State. Though there were menacing signs in the late nineteenth century, it was above all a disastrous series of events triggered by the First World War which brought in the whole of Europe and not just in Germany a collapse of moral and religious values, the dominance of materialism, the growth of

---

[7] For this periodization, see Jörn Rüsen, 'Theory of History in the Development of West German Historical Studies: A Reconstruction and Outlook', *German Studies Review* 7 (1984), pp. 14–18. I am indebted to Prof. Rüsen for his comments and suggestions on this section and profited, too, from the excellent essay of Bernd Faulenbach, 'Deutsche Geschichtswissenschaft nach 1945', *Tijdschrift voor Geschiednis* 94 (1981), pp. 29–57. See also, Georg G. Iggers, *Deutsche Geschichtswissenschaft* (Munich, 1971), ch. 8 (revised and extended from his *The German Conception of History* (Middletown, Connect., 1968)), and Wolfgang J. Mommsen, 'Gegenwärtige Tendenzen in der Geschichtsschreibung der Bundesrepublik', *GG* 7 (1981), pp. 149–88.
[8] Iggers, p. 11.
[9] The comment of Manfred Schlenke, cited in Iggers, pp. 356–7.

barbarism, and the corruption of politics as machiavellianism and demagogy. Nazism was, therefore, according to such an interpretation, the terrible outcome of European, not specifically German, trends; it marked a decisive break with the 'healthy' German past rather than being a product of it. Meinecke spoke of 'the history of the degeneration of German mankind'.[10] Ritter found it 'almost unbearable' to think that 'the will of a single madman' had driven Germany into the Second World War.[11] Nazism was, therefore, more or less an accident in an otherwise commendable development. And the disaster which had befallen Germany could in no small measure be attributed to the 'demon' Hitler. (Such defensive attempts to interpret Nazism as part of a European disease were of course the direct counter to the crude interpretation of Anglo-American writers after the war, that Nazism could only be seen as the culmination of centuries of German cultural and political misdevelopment reaching back to Luther and beyond.[12])

The beginning of a rapid decline in the influence of historicism and a transformation in historical thinking was ushered in by the 'Fischer Controversy' of the early 1960s. By using wholly traditional methods of research, Fritz Fischer, in his *Griff nach der Weltmacht*, published in 1961, demonstrated the aggressive, expansionist war aims of Germany's élites in the First World War, and in so doing knocked the bottom out of the argument that a hitherto basically healthy development had somehow 'gone off the rails' *after* the war. Unwittingly, too, Fischer had opened up new areas of concern for historical research – especially the role of the 'traditional' élites and the continuities in social structures and domestic as well as foreign policy linking the Imperial with the Nazi era. The furore which Fischer's work provoked reflected plainly the extent of the culture shock for the older historical establishment.[13] The transformation process partly unleashed by the 'Fischer Controversy' was greatly furthered by the weakening of old rigidities through the expansion of the university system, challenges to the historical profession arising from the advances being made by the social sciences, and by the changes in the political and intellectual climate which accompanied the end of a long spell of conservative rule and the 'students' movement' of the late 1960s.[14]

---

10 Friedrich Meineke, *Die deutsche Katastrophe* (Weisbaden, 1946), p. 28.

11 Gerhard Ritter, *Das deutsche Problem. Grundfragen deutschen Staatslebens gestern und heute* (Munich, 1962), p. 198. This was a new edition, with added introduction and conclusion, of Ritter's *Europa und die deutsche Frage. Betrachtungen über die geschichtliche Eigenart des deutschen Staatsdenkens* (Munich, 1948).

12 Classics of the genre are Rohan O'Butler, *The Roots of National Socialism* (London, 1941), and William Montgomery McGovern, *From Luther to Hitler. The History of Nazi-Fascist Philosophy* (London, 1946). Such anti-German distortions were massively popularized in William Shirer's bestseller, *The Rise and Fall of the Third Reich* (New York, 1960).

13 Fritz Fischer, *Griff nach der Weltmacht* (Düsseldorf, 1961), Engl. trans. *Germany's Aims in the First World War* (London, 1966). For the 'Fischer controversy' see the collections of essays in Hans W. Koch ed., *The Origins of the First World War* (London, 1972), and, more recently, especially Volker Berghahn, 'Die Fischerkontroverse – 15 Jahre danach', *GG* 6 (1980), pp. 403–19.

14 Rüsen, 'Theory of History', p. 16; see also, Hans-Ulrich Wehler, 'Geschichtswissenschaft heute', in Jürgen Habermas, ed., *Stichworte zur 'Geistigen Situation der Zeit'* (2 vols., Frankfurt am Main, 1979), vol. 2, pp. 739–42, Engl. trans., *Observations on 'The Spiritual Situation of the Age'* (Cambridge, Mass., 1984).

Denuded of its historicist isolation, and in a political context where close cultural relations with other European countries and with the USA were actively and intensively promoted, German historical scholarship moved into the outside world. Structural history concepts, derived in particular from the French *Annales* school, and the influence of American political and social science began to transform historical approaches in West Germany.

New, more theoretical approaches to historical scholarship leaning heavily upon transatlantic developments in social and political science fought to establish themselves for the first time in German universities. The 'new social history' or 'historical–social science' approach, arguing for a theoretically based integrative discipline to build a structural analysis of the 'history of society', upturned the traditional emphasis in German historical scholarship by asserting that the concept of 'politics' needed to be subordinated to the concept of 'society', so that 'political history', while important in itself, could not alone provide a key to historical understanding and needed to be rooted in a wider (and theoretical) context.[15] The foundation of two new journals – *Geschichte und Gesellschaft* in 1975, and *Geschichtsdidaktik* in 1976 – embodying the methodology and publishing the research findings of these new approaches, could be said to reflect the fact that 'history as social science', innovative in the mid 1960s, had become established and institutionalized a decade later.

This progress was not, of course, unchallenged. The gauntlet laid down by representatives of the 'new social history' approach was taken up by leading historians who, though now divorced from classical historicism, still held fast to conventional historical method and spheres of interest. The debates about historical method between exponents of the two – seemingly irreconcilable – sides were at times fierce. And they have a direct relevance to the nature of the controversies about Nazism.

The leading protagonist of the 'history of society' approach, Hans-Ulrich Wehler, is not generally regarded as a specialist on Nazism, though his studies of Imperial Germany were expressly related to the question of continuity in the structures of German society between 1870 and 1945.[16] Among the foremost assailants of the 'new social history' and defenders of the merits of conventional political history – with heavy emphasis upon foreign and diplomatic history, the importance of the individual and his will and intention as against structural determinants, and the value of the traditional historical method of empirical research – are Andreas Hillgruber and Klaus Hildebrand, both renowned experts on the foreign policy of Nazi Germany.[17]

15 See, for example, Hans-Ulrich Wehler, 'Anwendung von Theorien in der Geschichtswissenschaft', in Jürgen Kocka and Thomas Nipperdey, eds., *Theorie der Geschichte. Beiträge zur Historik* (Munich, 1979), vol. 3, pp. 17–39; Jürgen Kocka, 'Theorien in der Sozial- und Gesellschaftsgeschichte', *GG* 1 (1975), pp. 9–42; and the critical (untitled) review essay of K.G. Faber in *History and Theory* 16 (1977), pp. 51–66.
16 Best known of all his works is Hans-Ulrich Wehler, *Das Kaiserreich, 1871–1918* (Göttingen, 1973), Engl. trans. *The German Empire, 1871–1918* (Leamington Spa, 1984). See also the penetrating critique by Thomas Nipperdey, 'Wehlers Kaiserreich', *GG* 1 (1975).
17 Prominent among their many works: Andreas Hillgruber, *Hitlers Strategie, Politik und Kriegführung 1940–1941* (Frankfurt am Main, 1965), and his collected essays, *Deutsche Großmacht und Weltpolitik im 19. und 20. Jahrhundert* (Düsseldorf, 1977); Klaus Hildebrand, *Vom Reich zum Weltreich. Hitler, NSDAP und koloniale Frage 1919–1945* (Munich, 1969), and *The Foreign Policy of the Third Reich* (London, 1973).

In a key-note article in 1973, Hillgruber made a plea for a return to a central emphasis on modern political history.[18] He fiercely attacked the 'exaggerated and modish claims of "social history" ', in which models replaced concrete evidence. The new social history approaches were in his view simply not suited to cast light on the international system and the still crucial determinant of the 'balance of power' in international affairs. He rejected the oversimplicity of theories of 'imperialism' or 'fascism', and ended with a broadside against the notion that there is no such thing as 'value-free scholarship', reasserting his view that the work of the scholar must remain independent of his political engagement. Hildebrand's line of attack was similar, though he was even more forthright in tone.[19] He hit out at the application of theory, since political action must be sought in the sources and in source criticism, in the evaluation of the particular situation, individual aspirations, decisions, accidental and surprising events. He denied that international relations could be regarded as a derivate of social developments, and argued that, compared with 'hegemony' and 'balance of power', the concepts of the 'new social history' were of limited value. The only legitimate procedure for the historian is to work from the particular to the general, not the other way round. The application of theory he found methodologically dubious, potentially excluding much of the many-faceted reality, and he concluded by reasserting the view that the past is autonomous and not there to inform or instruct the present.

Wehler's replies argued that Hillgruber's approach, too, needed theoretical and conceptual underpinning, and that his reliance upon the aims of leadership groups, political ideas, and intentions led inexorably towards a political history of ideas which opened up no new vistas. Wehler emphasized the limitations of concentrating on archival sources alone for analysis of foreign-policy decision-making.[20] His response to Hildebrand was more sharply couched, accusing him of rhetorical exaggeration, straw-man attacks, and seeming in one place even to imply deliberate misquoting.[21] He saw Hildebrand's insistence on moving from the particular to the general as insufficient even for Hildebrand's own research on Nazism. In a later broadside, he attacked the approach to the history of Nazism as featured in Hildebrand's work as a 'weedy and mangled historicism'.[22] Hildebrand in return claimed that Wehler's comments demonstrated just how the relationship of society and Hitler, of structure and personality in the Third Reich, 'can be distorted and simplistically described through prejudice and lack of knowledge', claiming that Wehler's article lay outside the bounds of serious scholarship, simply accumulated statements of political opinion and personal

---

[18] Andreas Hillgruber, 'Politische Geschichte in moderner Sicht', *HZ* 216 (1973), pp. 529–52.

[19] Klaus Hildebrand, 'Geschichte oder "Gesellschaftsgeschichte"? Die Notwendigkeiten einer politischen Geschichtsschreibung von den internationalen Beziehungen', *HZ* 223 (1976), pp. 328–57.

[20] Hans-Ulrich Wehler, 'Moderne Politik-geschichte oder "Große Politik der Kabinette"?', *GG* 1 (1975), pp. 344–69.

[21] Hans-Ulrich Wehler, 'Kritik und kritische Antikritik', *HZ* 225 (1977), pp. 347–84.

[22] Wehler, 'Geschichtswissenschaft heute', p. 745.

insult, and had no use in the context of serious academic discussion.[23]

These uncompromising exchanges on theoretical approaches and method-ological questions have a direct bearing on the nature of some of the key interpretative controversies about Nazism. They indicate the theoretical dif-ficulties in reconciling a 'structural' approach to the history of Nazism with a personalistic one – a key problem in interpreting the role and place of Hitler in the Nazi system of government. Secondly, they point to some of the difficulties of the relationship of the historian to his sources – how he should approach and read his sources. Thirdly, they raise the complex question of the political stance of the historian, his relationship to the political circum-stances in which he lives and works, and the relationship between theoretical–methodological and political–ideological positions.

On the first point, Wehler's theoretical, conceptual approach prompts an instinctive methodological preference and sympathy for the work of so-called 'revisionist' historians of Nazism such as Hans Mommsen, Martin Broszat, and Wolfgang Schieder, who, for the most part working without the conscious application of a great theoretical encumbrance, have approached complex problems such as the interrelationship of domestic and foreign policy in the Nazi State, the structure of the State machinery and decision-making processes, and not least the place and function of Hitler in the Nazis system, in what can loosely be described as a 'structural-functionalist' way. Correspondingly, the limitations are strongly emphasized of explanations resting heavily upon Hitler's conscious inten-tions and individual role in forming Nazi policy.[24]

On the second point, the dispute about historical method has highlighted the problem of how the historian builds his explanation from the sources. Quite apart from the deficiencies in the source materials on Nazism which we noted earlier, sources can often (as Tim Mason pointed out with express reference to Hitler's intentions and aims) 'be read in very different ways, depending upon the different kinds of other historical knowledge which is brought to bear upon these texts', and should not necessarily be read solely in what appears to be the literal 'common-sense' way.[25] Hence, some of the controversies (particularly those surrounding Hitler) are between historians using precisely the same documentary sources but, starting from different premises and conceptions – not only about what the Third Reich was like but also what writing history is about – and reading them in radically differ-ent fashion.

The third point, the influence of political–ideological considerations on the historiography of Nazism, raises a separate and important issue, to which I now want to turn.

[23] Klaus Hildebrand, 'Monokratie oder Polykratie? Hitlers Herrschaft und das Dritte Reich', in Gerhard Hirschfeld and Lothar Kettenacker, eds., *Der 'Führerstaat': Mythos und Realität* (Stuttgart, 1981), p. 95 n. 74. The polemical debate is summarized in W.J. Mommsen, 'Gegenwärtige Tendenzen', pp. 165–8. For a more recent attack on Wehler's 'critical history' approach, ending in the suggestion that the 'search for national identity' might be a legitimate new theme which could help further a 'change of paradigm' in German historical scholarship, see Irmline Veit-Brause, 'Zur Kritik an der "Kritischen Geschichtswissenschaft": Tendenzwende oder Paradigmawechsel?', *GWU* 35 (1984), pp. 1–24.
[24] Wehler, 'Geschichtswissenschaft heute', pp. 731–2.
[25] Tim Mason, 'Intention and Explanation: A Current Controversy about the Interpretation of National Socialism', in Hirschfeld and Kettenacker, pp. 23–42, here p. 31.

## The Political-Ideological Dimension

Two separate, though related, areas need consideration: first, the ways in which the division of Germany has moulded the political–ideological premises of interpreting Nazism on both sides of the Wall; and second, the ways in which political–ideological differences have shaped the changing patterns of writing on Nazism within the Federal Republic itself.

In the German Democratic Republic, anchored in marxist–leninist principles, anti-fascism has been from the beginning an indispensable cornerstone of the state's ideology and legitimacy. Historical work on 'Hitler–Fascism', therefore, has always had a direct political relevance. And since fascism is taken to be an intrinsic product of capitalism, and the neighbouring West German state was founded on the capitalist principles of the Western Allies, historical research on fascism has the task not merely of educating East German citizens about the horrors and evil of the past, but even more so of the dangers and evil of the present and future – of the potential fascism built into western capitalist imperialism, especially in the Federal Republic.

The understanding of Nazism in the German Democratic Republic rested on the long tradition in the Communist International of wrestling with the problem of fascism in the 1920s and 1930s, culminating in Georgi Dimitroff's famous formulation, definitively established at the Seventh Congress of the Comintern in 1935, that fascism was 'the open terroristic dictatorship of the most reactionary, most chauvinist, and most imperialist elements of finance capital'.[26] The 'unmastered past' of the West German state – not least the survival in prominent places in the economy and in political life of persons with a more than dubious past in the Third Reich scarcely behind them – simply underlined for East German scholars the present-day relevance and political purpose of their historical scholarship. The introduction to the most recent collection of essays summarizing the results of historical research in the German Democratic Republic on Nazism, states categorically: 'The aim and concern of the book will have been satisfied if, as a first step on the way to comprehensive research on the historical and current political problems of fascism, it provides scholarly material for the present-day struggle against fascism and imperialism'.[27] And a contributor to the volume further emphasized: the attempt by capitalists to prop up their power with new methods – those of fascism – is a truth which 'has been taken to heart by marxist historians, who, with their research into the history of fascism, want to make a contribution to combating the reactionary forces which are ever reappearing in new guise and, on the basis of their historical experience, proceed from the standpoint that the anti-fascist struggle can only be carried to victory through the complete removal from power and overcoming of monopoly capital'.[28] One of the

---

[26] Georgi Dimitroff, *Gegen Faschismus und Krieg. Ausgewählte Reden und Schriften* (Reclam edn., Leipzig, 1982), p. 50. The definition had already been formulated at the 13th Plenum of the Executive Committee of the Comintern in December 1933.

[27] Dietrich Eichholz and Kurt Gossweiler, eds., *Faschismusforschung. Positionen, Probleme, Polemik* (Berlin (East), 1980), p. 18.

[28] Wolfgang Ruge, 'Monopolbourgeoisie, faschistische Massenbasis und NS-Programmatik', in Eichholz and Gossweiler, pp. 125–55, here p. 155.

foremost GDR historians precisely summed up the point: 'For us, research on fascism means participation in the current class struggle'.[29]

The ideological framework within which historical research operated in West Germany was less openly stated, but was none the less apparent. The main aim in the formulation of the West German Constitution (the 'Basic Law') was to eliminate the potential for the creation of a 'totalitarian' system, not only such as had existed in the Third Reich, but as continued to exist in the Soviet Union and in the Soviet Zone of Germany. The constitution was intentionally both anti-fascist and anti-communist. As has been pointed out, 'the theory of totalitarianism which compares and even equates fascism and communism can therefore be seen as the dominant idea behind the basic constitutional law and even to some extent as the official ideology of the Federal Republic'.[30] The 'totalitarian' premise was thus implicitly widely accepted in Western Germany, even among Social Democrats, before the scholarly writings of German emigrants in the USA, notably Hannah Arendt and Carl Friedrich, established totalitarianism as the central concept in interpreting Nazism.[31] The 'totalitarian' approach dominated research on 'contemporary history' in the Federal Republic in the 1950s and early 1960s. The seminal works of Karl Dietrich Bracher on the end of the Weimar Republic and on the Nazi 'seizure of power' are among the most prominent examples.[32] The central journal of 'contemporary history', the *Vierteljahrshefte für Zeitgeschichte*, first published in 1953, also saw its task residing not only in studying Nazism, but in undertaking research on totalitarian movements in general, including of course communism.[33]

The challenge to the dominant totalitarian theory and the revival of fascist theories in West Germany in the 1960s was carried out on two planes, those of academic scholarship and of ideological–political polemic. But, as always, there was an intrinsic connection between the two levels, which could never be completely separated. Slotting into the first major challenge to the dominant values of the conservative state run by the Christian Democrats in the mid 1960s and the growing crisis within German universities which broke in 1968, academic discussion of fascism and the scholarly rehabilitation of fascist theories of the inter-war years was quickly turned into political sloganizing by segments of the Left, while the shocked over-reaction of the Liberal and Conservative Right ensured the place of debate about fascism or totalitarianism as part of current political dialogue and conflict. We will go into the theories and criticisms of them in the next chapter. Here, it is a matter of illustrating the clear political overtones which the academic controversies carry. Moreover, not only the repercussions of the year of turmoil in 1968, but also the far more overt politicization of university faculties

[29] Kurt Gossweiler, 'Stand und Probleme der Faschismusforschung in der DDR', *Bulletin des Arbeitskreises 'Zweiter Weltkrieg'* 1 (1976), p. 13.
[30] Wolfgang Wippermann, 'The Post-War German Left and Fascism', *JCH* 11 (1976), p. 192.
[31] Hannah Arendt, *The Origins of Totalitarianism* (New York, 1951); Carl Joachim Friedrich and Zbigniew Brzezinski, *Totalitarian Dictatorship and Autocracy* (Cambridge, Mass., 1956).
[32] Karl Dietrich Bracher, *Die Auflösung der Weimarer Republik* (Stuttgart, 1955); Karl Dietrich Bracher, Wolfgang Sauer, and Gerhard Schulz, *Die nationalsozialistische Machtergreifung. Studien zur Errichtung des totalitären Herrschaftssystems in Deutschland 1933–34* (Cologne/Opladen, 1960).
[33] See Iggers, p. 357.

themselves in West Germany have helped to delineate the contours of the debates. And whereas in the 1960s and early 1970s the expansion of universities on the whole promoted a sense of challenge to orthodoxy and establishment positions, the restrictions in growth in higher education and the *Berufsverbot* have contributed towards a changed climate.[34] The dominance – supported by prolific, highly influential publications – of the conservative-liberal establishment in the historical profession has been in no small measure re-asserted. The tone of the conflict is well represented in the comments of two of the leading 'liberal–conservative' historians of Nazism, Karl Dietrich Bracher and Andreas Hillgruber.

In a short, widely-read textbook on post-war German history, published in the mid 1970s,[35] Andreas Hillgruber speaks of radical criticism in universities growing increasingly dependant upon 'the forces of doctrinaire marxism–leninism' orientated towards the model of the German Democratic Republic, and of a search among the 'New Left' for ideology and indoctrination (which, in labelling 'need for theory', he implicitly associated with the 'progressive' side of the theoretical–methodological debates within the historical discipline). He saw the 'primacy of domestic politics' hypothesis, which Wehler and others had derived from the work of Eckhart Kehr and deployed mainly as a heuristic device, as providing an 'apparent scholarly legitimation' of the alleged conviction of the 'New Left' that radical social change and even revolution was the only concern of the present.

The most eminent of all West German historians of the Third Reich, Karl Dietrich Bracher, also made his views absolutely clear on the changing nature of writing on 'contemporary history'.[36] The lively discussion of the 1960s, he wrote, had been stimulated, but also overshadowed and often distorted, by the politicization and institutional upheavals in German universities and higher education. Research tendencies towards interdisciplinary and comparative approaches had also made their contribution, especially the widening of historical method and the demand for a social-science base to historical writing. A 'marxist renaissance' of the 'New Left' had increased the complexity and confusion of concepts, especially in the 'vehemently voiced demands for theory' and in the 'radical attack on previous patterns of interpretation which had essentially arisen from the effort at mastering the past after the catastrophes of 1933 and 1945'. As the approaches shaped by the experience of the Third Reich faded, they had been replaced by social-critical approaches and concepts which had placed the former interpretations under a cross-fire frequently carried out 'with crude weapons'. Previous research achievements were ignored or distorted, and there was a resort to political agitation in which 'the ideological struggle was

[34] See Wehler, 'Geschichtswissenschaft heute', pp. 745 ff. Veit-Brause (pp. 1–3) argues that the shift in political climate towards conservatism is only a minor part of the revision of paradigms in West German historical writing, which she attributes in far greater extent to new intellectual insights putting the 'critical history' approach in question.

[35] Andreas Hillgruber, *Deutsche Geschichte 1945–1972* (Berlin, 1974), pp. 162–4. See Wehler's comments in 'Geschichtswissenschaft heute', pp. 747–8 and 'Moderne Politik-geschichte', p. 355.

[36] Karl Dietrich Bracher, 'Zeitgeschichte im Wandel der Interpretationen', *HZ* 225 (1977), pp. 635–55, here esp., pp. 635–8, 648–51, 654–5.

carried out on the back and in the name of scholarship'. Under the demand for theory and revision, previous scholarly standards were also distorted. At its most obvious, the attack on liberal–democratic values had been articulated in the bitter assaults on the totalitarianism concept and in the boundless expansion of the general theory of fascism, which had rapidly degenerated from new scholarly approaches (such as those of Ernst Nolte) into marxist–communist agitatory formulations revamping those of the 1920s and 1930s, attacking the Western concept of democracy as 'late bourgeois' and 'late capitalist', and the liberal–democratic West German parliamentary state as simply 'restorative'. Ideological monocausal explanations had replaced the earlier openness of historical and political science. Non-marxist writers, too, had under the impetus of socio-economic methods and the 'sociologization of contemporary history' contributed to a changed language and style of interpretation. All in all, the tapping of new sources and the intensification of empirical research had widened the base for solid, specialized work. But this stood in an uneasy relationship to the 'tendency, through theorizing and ideologizing alienation from the history of persons and events, to show and put into effect as the dominant leading theme the contemporary criticism of capitalism and democracy'.

The controversies which we shall be exploring have arisen in this climate, overlain with political and ideological considerations. In a state which has not had a dominant marxist historiographical school, most of the debates we shall consider are controversies between historians of different kinds of liberal-democratic persuasion. The politicization of the debate is here more latent than overt. In so far as it comes into the open at all, it is darkly reflected in philosophical disputes about the relevance of present-day social and political values to the historian's writing, and whether these should be banished in the interests of a 'value-free' and 'objective' history.[37] There is general agreement on the historian's task of 'enlightenment' in the values of reason, freedom, and 'emancipation', but such a vague commitment to virtue not sin naturally leaves room for a multitude of often only semi-concealed ideological positions. And, as the above comments demonstrate, it also does not prevent the occurrence of slights and slurs as the accompaniment to scholarly controversy. One manifestation of this is the allegation that, in their attempted 'revision' of established interpretations of Nazism, historians are 'trivializing' the evil nature of the Nazi regime. This strikingly indicates the prominence, also, of the moral dimension, inescapable in writing on Nazism.

## The Moral Dimension

The moral content of early post-war writing on Nazism was explicit. Historians of the victorious powers were only too anxious to find in Nazism a confirmation of all the worst traits in Germans present throughout the centuries, and from the evident mass support for Hitler in the 1930s deduced

---

[37] See e.g., Thomas Nipperdey, 'Geschichte als Aufklärung', in M. Zöller, ed., *Aufklärung heute. Bedingungen unserer Freiheit* (Zurich, 1980), pp. 50–62; Jürgen Kocka, 'Legende, Aufklärung und Objektivität in der Geschichtswissenschaft', *GG* 6 (1980), pp. 449–55; and Jörn Rüsen, 'Geschichte als Aufklärung?', *GG* 7 (1981), pp. 189–218.

a peculiarly 'German disease' and an easy equation of Germans and Nazis. We have already noted the moral tone of the defence against this crude allegation in the works of Meinecke and Ritter, which reflected the not unnatural apologetic character of German historical writing in the post-war era. The emphasis on 'the other Germany' and the resistance plot of 1944 – as, for instance, in Gerhard Ritter's biography of Goerdeler – again indicates the dominance of the moral dimension in early German post-war writing on the Third Reich.[38]

Though more recent scholarship has totally departed from the indignation and resentment, condemnation and apology, which characterized the post-war era, a strong moral element remains as a latent presence. All serious scholars (Germans above all) demonstrate even by the very language they employ – as in the frequent use of terms such as 'criminality' or 'barbarity' in connection with the Nazi regime – their moral detestation for Nazism. This raises a point which numerous commentators have noted as a difficulty about interpreting Nazism. Whereas historians traditionally try to eschew moral judgement (with varying degrees of success) in attempting to reach a sympathetic 'understanding' (*Verstehen*) of their subject matter, this is clearly an impossibility in the case of Nazism and Hitler. Wolfgang Sauer put the dilemma in the following way: 'In Nazism, the historian faces a phenomenon that leaves him no way but rejection, whatever his individual position. There is literally no voice worth considering that disagrees on this matter. . . . Does not such fundamental rejection imply a fundamental lack of understanding? And if we do not understand, how can we write history? The term "understanding" has, certainly, an ambivalent meaning; we can reject and still "understand". And yet, our intellectual, and psychological, capacities reach, in the case of Nazism, a border undreamed of by Wilhelm Dilthey. We can work out explanatory theories, but, if we face the facts directly, all explanations appear weak'.[39] It may be that the problem is in practice less serious than Sauer imagined. After all, historians of many other political regimes and their leaders often have little enough chance to show 'sympathetic understanding' for the object of their studies.

Even so, the problem could not be highlighted more plainly than in the case of Hitler's Germany, although the universal moral condemnation of Nazism makes it all the more surprising that the question of its implicit moral trivialization in recent historical writing has been raised at all. Karl Dietrich Bracher appears to have started it, and his comments show that the allegation is not unconnected with the questions of historical method and

[38] See Gerhard Ritter, *Carl Goerdeler und die deutsche Widerstandsbewegung* (Munich, 1955) and Hans Rothfels, *The German Opposition to Hitler* (Chicago, 1948). See also Iggers, pp. 344–7. For surveys of more recent trends in the historiography of 'resistance', see Hildebrand, *Das Dritte Reich*, pp. 181–6, and Reinhard Mann, 'Widerstand gegen den Nationalsozialismus', *Neue politische Literatur* 22 (1977), pp. 425–42. For a comprehensive statement of the present state of research, see Jürgen Schmädeke and Peter Steinbach, eds., *Der Widerstand gegen den Nationalsozialismus. Die deutsche Gesellschaft und der Widerstand gegen Hitler* (Munich, 1985). Problems of interpreting the 'resistance' to Hitler will always remain thorny ones, not least because of the normative political and moral connotations of the term 'resistance' (*Widerstand*), which is at the same time used as a concept of scholarly analysis.
[39] Wolfgang Sauer, 'National Socialism: Totalitarianism or Fascism?', *AHR* 73 (1967–8), p. 408. See also Klaus Hildebrand, 'Der "Fall" Hitler', *NPL* 14 (1969), p. 379.

political–ideological overtones which we discussed earlier. Bracher claimed that recent marxist and 'New Left' approaches – but also those of some well-established liberal 'bourgeois' (or, as he calls them, 'relativist') historians – amounted to a gross underestimation of the reality of Nazism. Accordingly, 'the ideological and totalitarian dimension of National Socialism shrinks to such an extent that the barbarism of 1933–45 disappears as a moral phenomenon'. As a result, 'it could well appear as if a new wave of trivialization or even apologetics was beginning'.[40] In similar vein, Klaus Hildebrand criticized those who 'theoretically fixed, are vainly concerned with functional explanations of the autonomous force in history and as a result frequently contribute towards its trivialization'.[41] The most forthright rejection of such allegations has been voiced by Tim Mason, within the context of debates on Nazism: 'The debate has reached such a pitch of intensity that some historians are now accusing other historians of "trivializing" National Socialism in their work, of implicitly, unwittingly, furnishing an apologia for the Nazi Regime. This is perhaps the most serious charge which can be made against serious historians of the subject', raising 'fundamental questions about the moral and political responsibility of the historian'.[42]

The interpretations which have given rise to these allegations of trivialization will concern us later in the book. It suffices for now to point out that the charge has been made in order to illustrate the inevitable moral undertones to any discussion about Nazism, particularly among German historians. In actual fact, though Bracher has some grounds for his charge in the more trite productions of the 'New Left' which see no essential difference between fascism and other forms of 'bourgeois domination', it seems to me that it is a wholly unnecessary and unjustified slur when extended to serious historians of Nazism.

However, the charge of 'trivialization' does raise pointedly the question of a moral purpose in writing about Nazism. Is the aim to learn the evil of Nazism by 'understanding' it? Is it a matter of condemning a uniquely evil phenomenon which by the nature of its uniqueness can never repeat itself and is gone for ever? Is it to draw lessons from this horror of the past about the fragility of modern democracy and the need to maintain a constant guard against the threat to liberal democracy from Right and Left? Is it to provide strategies for the recognition and prevention of the re-emergence of fascism? Is it to carry out simultaneously an act of remembrance and warning cast through hatred and anger? The latter seems to be the position of Lucy Dawidowicz in a book solely about the morality of historical writing on the holocaust.[43] She speaks there of Nazism as 'the essence of evil, the daemon let loose in society, Cain in a corporate embodiment'. She holds that 'nothing but the most lucid consciousness of the horror that happened can help avoid it for the future'. And she cites

---

[40] Karl Dietrich Bracher, *Zeitgeschichtliche Kontroversen. Um Faschismus, Totalitarismus, Demokratie* (Munich, 1976), pp. 62–3.

[41] Hildebrand, 'Geschichte oder "Gesellschaftsgeschichte"?', p. 355.

[42] Mason, 'Intention and Explanation', p. 23.

[43] Lucy Dawidowicz, *The Holocaust and the Historians* (Cambridge, Mass., 1981). See the sharply critical reviews by Richard Bessel, *Times Higher Education Supplement*, 19 March 1982, p. 14, and Geoff Eley, 'Holocaust History', *London Review of Books*, 3–17 March 1982, p. 6.

approvingly the words of Karl Jaspers: 'That which has happened is a warning. To forget it is guilt. It must be continually remembered. It was possible for this to happen, and it remains possible for it to happen again at any minute. Only in knowledge can it be prevented'.[44] At the same time, her distaste for the methods of marxist and structuralist historians (who are again accused of abdicating their professional responsibility) and her predilection for personalized history – for the 'attribution of human responsibility for the occurrence of historic events . . . to the movers and shakers who made events happen'[45] – raises once more in striking fashion the problem of how the historical method she favours can produce the ends she desires.

We are back again to the interrelationship of the historian's method, the moral nature of his professional obligation, and the political–ideological framework in which this obligation is carried out.

44 Dawidowicz, *Holocaust*, pp. 20–1.
45 Dawidowicz, *Holocaust*, p. 146.

# 2

## The Essence of Nazism: Form of Fascism, Brand of Totalitarianism, or Unique Phenomenon?

There has been debate since the 1920s about the nature and character of the Nazi phenomenon – how it ought to be located in the context of the strikingly new political movements which, since the Bolshevik Revolution of 1917 and five years later Mussolini's 'March on Rome', had been recasting the shape of Europe. While Comintern theorists were already in the 1920s categorizing Nazism as a form of fascism engendered by capitalism in crisis, bourgeois writers were only little later beginning to associate Right and Left as the combined totalitarian enemies of democracy. The debates were, of course, considerably broadened during the years of Nazi rule: on the one hand through the finalizing of the Comintern definition of fascism in 1935 and through analyses of fascism by left-wing theorists exiled in the West; and on the other hand through a growing readiness in the western democracies and in the USA to view Nazism and Soviet Communism as two sides of the same totalitarian coin – a view seemingly confirmed by the Nazi–Soviet Non-Aggression Pact of 1939. Though this line was naturally played down from 1941 onwards, it re-emerged all the more strongly with the onset of the Cold War in the later 1940s. During the Cold War era, left-wing interpretations of Nazism as a form of fascism lost their influence, while totalitarianism theories enjoyed their hey-day and came gradually under fire – crumbling beneath the weight of accumulating detailed research – only in the period of growing detente, increasing introspection and criticism of western society and governments, and then the upheavals in universities and intellectual currents in the later 1960s. Revival of interest in fascism as a generic problem was reflected in a burgeoning output of studies not only from the Left but also from liberal writers, setting the 'totalitarianism' theorists on the defensive, though there was some retrenchment in the 1970s as some weaknesses of the comparative fascism approach became increasingly visible. The debate about whether Nazism can best be regarded as a type of fascism, or whether it should be seen as a prominent form of totalitarian rule has still not subsided, least of all in West German historiography.

The debate about fascism and totalitarianism has been kept alive, too, by its relationship to a third strand of interpretation which, in recent years, has proved highly influential: that Nazism can only be explained as a product of the peculiarities of Prussian–German development over the previous century or so. Such an interpretation has, however, itself been advanced in two quite distinct and opposed forms.

Social historians, concentrating on the *causes* of Nazism, have emphasized a specific path of modernization in Germany in which, far more so than was the case in western societies, pre-industrial, pre-capitalist, and pre-bourgeois authoritarian and feudal traditions survived in a society which was never truly bourgeois, existing in a relationship of tension with a modern, dynamic capitalist economy and finally exploding into violent protest when that economy collapsed in crisis. Less the nature of German capitalism than the strength of pre-modern forces in German society determined the road to Nazi victory in 1933. Though stressing the peculiarities of the German development, exponents of such an interpretation point to obvious parallels in other societies, for instance in Italy, and regard Nazism, for all its singular characteristics, as a form of fascism in terms of its socio-economic origins and formation, seeing also no necessary incompatibility with elements of the totalitarianism theory in terms of certain components of rule.[1]

This emphasis upon a 'failed bourgeois revolution' and the dominance of pre-industrial, neo-feudal structures in explaining a German 'special path' of development has recently been subjected to a frontal attack.[2] The alternative position stresses in contrast the *bourgeois* character of late-nineteenth-century German society and politics and – implicitly rather than explicitly – the need to explain Nazism not through 'German peculiarities' but through the particular instabilities of the form of capitalism and capitalist state which existed in Germany. It might be thought that this line of argument – whatever its merits – only brought one back to a slightly different set of questions about 'peculiarities' in order to answer the obvious problem about why Germany alone of all the highly advanced industrial capitalist economies – Italy, though making great advances in industrialization before the War, could not rank with the major industrial economies – produced a fully-blown 'fascist' dictatorship. The recent heated (if somewhat artificial) debate on the 'special path' of Germany's development is concerned more with interpreting the Imperial period than the Third Reich. Despite its obvious connotations for understanding the origins of Nazism, it need occupy us no longer here – not least because historians on both sides of the debate fully accept that, for all its singular characteristics, Nazism belongs to

---

[1] Representative of this line of argument is Jürgen Kocka, 'Ursachen des National-sozialismus', *APZ* (21 June 1980), pp. 3–15.

[2] See David Blackbourn and Geoff Eley, *Mythen deutscher Geschichtsschreibung* (Frankfurt am Main/Berlin/Vienna, 1980), Engl. trans. *The Peculiarities of Germans History* (Oxford, 1984). For the sharp and polemical debate unleashed by this book, see e.g. the reviews by Hans-Ulrich Wehler, ' "Deutscher Sonderweg" oder allgemeine Probleme des westlichen Kapitalismus?', *Merkur* 5 (1981), pp. 478–87; Hans-Jürgen Puhle, 'Deutscher Sonderweg. Kontroverse um eine vermeintliche Legende', *Journal für Geschichte*, Heft 4 (1981), pp. 44–5; Wolfgang J. Mommsen, in *Bulletin of the German Historical Institute*, London 4 (1980), pp. 19–26; and the discussion forum *Deutscher Sonderweg – Mythos oder Realität* (Kolloquien des Instituts für Zeitgeschichte, Munich/Vienna, 1982). Directly relating this to the causes of fascism, and partly in reply to Kocka's article (see note 1), see also Geoff Eley, 'What produces Fascism: Preindustrial Traditions or a Crisis of the Capitalist State?', *Politics and Society* 12 (1983), pp. 53–82. Jürgen Kocka, 'German History before Hitler: The Debate about the German *Sonderweg'*, *JCH* 23 (1988), pp. 3–16, provides an excellent critique of the pros and cons of the *Sonderweg* argument. He concludes that while the term '*Sonderweg*' is itself misleading and dispensable, the notion of a divergence from the pattern of development of other 'advanced' western countries retains its value in explaining why Germany offered so few barriers to the fascist challenge.

a wider category of political movements which we call 'fascist'. The German 'peculiarities' under question in this controversy are those which set Germany apart from western parliamentary democracies, not from Italian or other manifestations of fascism.

A different and more exclusive emphasis upon the singularity of Nazism as the product of recent Prussian–German history is an important focus of the interpretation of some of the leading West German political historians in their analyses of the character and nature of Nazi rule. According to such an interpretation, Nazism was *sui generis* – altogether a unique phenomenon, emerging from the peculiar legacy of the Prusso-German authoritarian state and German ideological development, but owing its uniqueness above all to the person of Hitler, a factor of overriding importance in the history of Nazism and one which is incapable of being ignored, played-down, or substituted. So singular was Hitler's ideological and political contribution to the shaping and direction of the Nazi movement and then the Nazi State that any attempt to label National Socialism as 'fascism', thus placing it in comparison with other 'similar' movements, is meaningless and implies, moreover, the 'trivialization' of Hitler and Nazism. Rather, so completely interwoven was National Socialism with the rise, fall, political aims, and destructive ideology of this unique personality, that it is legitimate to speak of Nazism as 'Hitlerism'. Though excluding vehemently any possibility of regarding 'Hitlerism' as a type of fascism, exponents of this interpretation nevertheless attach one important strand of comparison, arguing that the form and nature of Nazi rule make it essential to regard Nazism as a brand of totalitarianism alongside Soviet Communism (in particular Stalinism).[3]

In this chapter I shall first summarize briefly the stages of development and the main variants of interpretation within the 'totalitarianism' and 'fascism' approaches. There is by now a wide literature examining and describing these approaches in detail, so that I shall offer as brief an outline as possible for purposes of orientation. Secondly, I shall attempt to evaluate the strengths and weaknesses of the concepts in their application to Nazism. Finally, in the light of discussion of totalitarianism and fascism I shall return to consider the argument for the singularity of Nazism in the context of the 'peculiarity' of German development.

## Totalitarianism

It is mistaken to regard the totalitarianism concept as simply a product of the Cold War, though that was indeed the period of its full flourishing. Its usage is in fact almost as old as that of fascism, dating back to the 1920s. And though slightly later on the scene than fascist theorems, the totalitarianism approach came earlier to gain general acceptance as an 'established' and 'establishment' theory before being subjected to damaging challenge in the 1960s. I shall deal, therefore, with totalitarianism first.

The term was coined in Italy as early as May 1923 and used initially as an

---

[3] See the essays by Karl Dietrich Bracher in his *Zeitg. Kontrov.*, Part I, and his 'The Role of Hitler: Perspectives of Interpretation', in Walter Laqueur, ed., *Fascism. A Reader's Guide* (Harmondsworth, 1979), pp. 193–212; Hildebrand, *Das Dritte Reich*, pp. 132ff., 187 ff.; and Hillgruber, *Endlich genug?*, pp. 38–42.

anti-fascist term of abuse. In order to turn the tables on his opponents, Mussolini usurped the term in June 1925, speaking of the 'fierce totalitarian will' of his Movement. Thereafter, it was used in positive self-depiction by Mussolini and other Italian fascists, then later by German legalists and by the Nazis. Gentile, the chief ideologue of Italian fascism, also employed the term on numerous occasions, though in a more étatist sense, implying an all-embracing state which would overcome the state–society divide of weak pluralist democracies. The two notions, this étatist one and Mussolini's implication of the dynamic revolutionary will of the Movement, existed side by side. The German usage was somewhat different, but related and with the same dual approach. Ernst Jünger was one of a number of writers already coining the notion of 'total war' and 'total mobilization' in the 1920s – a term with dynamic, revolutionary implications. Around the same time Carl Schmitt, Germany's foremost legal theorist, was developing the concept of power politics based on a friend–foe relationship, into which he fitted, as the historical antithesis to the liberal pluralization of the state, the 'total state of identity of state and society'. Both forms, therefore, the 'actionist' and the 'étatist', existed before the Nazis came to power and were incorporated into Nazi usage (though the word 'totalitarian' was, in fact, seldom used by the Nazi leadership).[4]

First usage of the word 'totalitarianism' to bracket together fascist and communist states seems to have been in England in 1929, although several years earlier Nitti, the former prime minister of Italy, was among those making structural comparisons between Italian fascism and bolshevism. In the 1930s and 1940s the concept was also applied by notable left-wing analysts of fascism such as Borkenau, Löwenthal, Hilferding, and Franz Neumann as a tool for characterizing what they saw as the new and specific in fascism (or Nazism) alone, without the comparative element of extension to Soviet Communism. Franz Neumann, for example, built his application of the term in his masterly *Behemoth* on the contemporary fascist self-stylization and the notion of the collapse into chaos of the Schmitt 'total state' under the 'totalitarian' drive of the Nazi movement.[5] At the same time the dominant usage of the adjective 'totalitarian' to link fascism and Nazism with communism was already gaining ground in Anglo-Saxon countries in the 1930s, boosted by German exile writing, the Stalinist terror, and the Nazi–Soviet Pact. The way was being paved for the emergence of the fully-

---

[4] For the developing usage of the 'totalitarianism' concept, see Walter Schlangen, *Die Totalitarismus-Theorie. Entwicklung and Probleme* (Stuttgart/Berlin/Cologne/Mainz, 1976), chs. 1–3. For guidance on the early Italian usage, I am indebted to Professor Meir Michaelis (Univ, of Haifa). See his informative paper: 'Anmerkungen zum italienischen Totalitarismusbegriff. Zur Kritik der Thesen Hannah Arendts und Renzo de Felices', *Quellen und Forschungen aus italienischen Archiven und Bibliotheken* (published by the German Historical Institute in Rome) 62 (1982) pp. 270–302, esp. pp. 292–7.

[5] Franz Neumann, *Behemoth. The Structure and Practice of National Socialism* (London, 1942). The German edition (Cologne/Frankfurt am Main, 1977, based on the extended 1944 English edition) has a valuable 'Nachwort' by the editor, Gert Schäfer. See also Richard Saage, 'Das sozio-politische Herrschaftssystem des Nationalsozialismus. Reflexionen zu Franz Neumanns "Behemoth" ', *Jahrbuch des Instituts für Deutsche Geschichte, Tel Aviv* 10 (1981), pp. 342–62.

fledged totalitarian model of the early post-war era, popularized in different ways above all by Hannah Arendt and Carl Friedrich.

Hannah Arendt's *Origins of Totalitarianism* is a passionate and moving denunciation of inhumanity and terror – depersonalized and rationalized as the execution of objective laws of history. Her emphasis on the radicalizing, dynamic, and structure-destroying inbuilt characteristics of Nazism has been amply borne out by later research. However, the book is less satisfactory on Stalinism than on Nazi Germany. Moreover, it offers no clear theory or satisfactory concept of totalitarian systems. And its basic argument explaining the growth of totalitarianism – the replacement of classes by masses and the emergence of a 'mass society' – is clearly flawed.[6]

Carl Friedrich's publications, written from a standpoint of constitutional theory, were even more influential than Hannah Arendt's. Every subsequent writer on totalitarianism has had to confront Friedrich's work, and especially his famous 'six-point syndrome' highlighting what he saw as the central characteristics of totalitarian systems (an official ideology, a single mass party, terroristic police control, monopoly control over the media, a monopoly of arms, and central control of the economy). The main weaknesses of the Friedrich model have frequently been pointed out. It is above all a static model, allowing little room for change and development in the inner dynamics of a system, and it rests on the exaggerated assumption of the essentially monolithic nature of 'totalitarian regimes'. His model has, therefore, come largely to be rejected even by those scholars still operating with a totalitarianism approach.[7]

Since the stabilization of the USSR in the post-Stalin era, totalitarianism theorists have tended to concentrate attention far more on current eastern-bloc regimes rather than on the dead Nazi system, and have divided into those who broadened the totalitarianism concept to include all manifestations of communist rule and those who limited it in the main to Stalinism. In both cases, however, the comparison with fascist systems was at least implicitly preserved.[8]

In the meantime, totalitarianism had been adopted in the 1950s as the fundamental prop of leading scholarly interpretations of Nazism, as in the classic pioneering works of Karl Dietrich Bracher. A political scientist himself, Bracher has pointed out the caution needed in developing a general theory of totalitarianism through constitutional or sociological categories resting on all too meagre empirical historical research. Such research was vital, in his view, to reveal the many varied forms of totalitarian rule, but would confirm the essential similarity in the techniques of rule of the Bolshevik/communist and Nazi/fascist systems. Bracher was unwilling to tie himself to the static, constitutive, and insufficiently differentiated features of the Friedrich model which could do scant justice to the 'revolutionary dynamic' which he saw as the 'core princi-

[6] Arendt, *Origins* (see above ch. 1 note 31). See the remarks of Klaus Hildebrand, 'Stufen der Totalitarismus-Forschung', *PVS* 9 (1968), pp. 406–8; Martin Kitchen, *Fascism* (London, 1976), pp. 30–1; and Aycoberry, pp. 130–3.
[7] Friedrich first advanced his model in his essay, 'The Unique Character of Totalitarian Society' in the volume he edited, *Totalitarianism* (Cambridge, Mass., 1954), and extended it in Friedrich and Brzezinski, *Totalitarian Dictatorship and Autocracy*. For criticism from within the 'totalitarianism' approach and a revised model, see Leonard Schapiro, *Totalitarianism* (London, 1973).
[8] See Schlangen, ch. 4.

ple' distinguishing totalitarian from other forms of authoritarian rule. The decisive character of totalitarianism lies for him in the total claim to rule, the leadership principle, the exclusive ideology, and the fiction of identity of rulers and ruled. It represents a basic distinction between an 'open' and a 'closed' understanding of politics.[9] The fundamental value of the totalitarianism concept resides therefore in its ability to recognize the primary distinction between democracy and dictatorship. Though Bracher sees that, as in all political and social theories which go beyond simple description, totalitarianism theories have their weaknesses, he claims that now as before, even after Hitler and Stalin, there is 'the phenomenon of totalitarian claims to rule and the tendency to the totalitarian . . . temptation' (which in this context he goes on to associate with the New Left among German intellectuals and also with the growth of terrorism of Left and Right in the Federal Republic in the 1970s).[10] In his view, the primary question of the totalitarian character of political systems cannot be shirked either in the interest of scholarly clarity and objectivity, or in view of the political and human consequences of such dictatorships and the tendencies towards totalitarianism in present-day society.

Though other eminent scholars have applied and continue to apply the concept of totalitarianism to characterize what they see as the essence of the Nazi system, it suffices here to summarize Bracher's use of the concept. Not only has he been at the pinnacle of scholarship on Nazism for 30 years, but he has also consistently argued the case for totalitarianism within the framework of understanding different models of political domination and has more than any other historian been instrumental in the retention and even current revival of the totalitarianism concept in its application to Nazism. However, doubts must remain about Bracher's employment of a rather undifferentiated divide between 'open' and 'closed' understandings of politics as a key ordering principle for defining totalitarianism, about his lack of clear distinction between totalitarianism as a tendency and as a system of rule, about the arguable value of the concept of 'revolutionary dynamic' when applied to various societies which Bracher would regard as 'totalitarian', and, fundamentally, about the attribution of relatively superficial common characteristics to regimes revealing many significant differences of organization and aim.

We can turn now to a brief outline of opposed interpretations locating Nazism in the family of inter-war European fascisms, rejecting at the same time the comparison with Soviet Communism inherent in the totalitarianism approach.

## Fascism

A new wave of interest in fascism as a phenomenon experienced in most countries of inter-war Europe was prompted in no small measure in the 1960s

---

[9] For a succinct recent statement of his position of 'totalitarianism', see *Totalitarismus und Faschismus. Eine wissenschaftliche und politische Begriffskontroverse* (Munich/Vienna, 1980), pp. 10–17, 53–4, 69–70.
[10] Karl Dietrich Bracher, *Schlüsselwörter in der Geschichte* (Düsseldorf, 1978), pp. 109–10, 121–3.

by the appearance of Ernst Nolte's highly influential book *Der Faschismus in seiner Epoche* in 1963.[11] Within five years several major international conferences had been held, numerous anthologies were in print containing studies of the nature and manifestation of fascist movements throughout Europe, and a considerable scholarly literature had built up.[12] Scholarly interest in comparative fascism merged with, and was then in part overtaken by, political interest on the Left in the later 1960s during the period of the 'New Left' challenge to the values of contemporary liberal–bourgeois society. The political conditions of the 1960s spurred and steered, therefore, a revival of marxist theories of fascism derived from the writings of contemporary marxist analysts of the fascist phenomenon alongside the proliferation of non-marxist interpretations of fascism.[13] In the case of both marxist and non-marxist interpretations, it can generally be said that, as with totalitarianism, most of the strands of the debate reach back practically as far as the phenomenon of fascism itself.

## Marxist Theories

The first serious attempt to explain fascism in theoretical terms was undertaken by the Comintern in the 1920s. The Comintern understanding, initially of Italian fascism, was founded on the notion of a close instrumental relationship between capitalism and fascism. Derived from the Leninist theory of imperialism, the theory held that the coming inevitable collapse of capitalism fostered an increased need on the part of the most reactionary and powerful groups within the now highly-concentrated finance capital to secure their imperialist aims by manipulating a mass movement capable of

[11] Ernst Nolte, *Der Faschismus in seiner Epoche* (Munich, 1963), Engl. trans. *The Three Faces of Fascism* (London, 1965, subsequent references to Mentor edn., New York/Toronto, 1969).

[12] E.g. Eugene Weber, *Varieties of Fascism* (New York, 1964); 'International Fascism, 1920-1945', *JCH* 1 (1) (1966); Ernst Nolte, *Die faschistischen Bewegungen* (Munich, 1966); Francis L. Carsten, *The Rise of Fascism* (London, 1967); Stuart J. Woolf, ed., *European Fascism* (London, 1968), and *The Nature of Fascism* (London, 1968); Wolfgang Schieder, 'Faschismus', in C.D. Hernig, ed., *Sowjetsystem und demokratische Gesellschaft. Eine vergleichende Enzyklopädie* (7 vols., Freiburg/Basel/Vienna, 1966-72), vol. 2 (1968), columns 438-77; Renzo de Felice, *Interpretations of Fascism* (Cambridge, Mass., 1977, first Italian edn. 1969). For useful later anthologies and surveys of the literature, see Wolfgang Wippermann, *Faschismustheorien* (Darmstadt, 1972); Wolfgang Schieder, ed., *Faschismus als soziale Bewegung* (Hamburg, 1976); Hans-Ulrich Thamer and Wolfgang Wippermann, *Faschistische und neofaschistische Bewegungen* (Darmstadt, 1977); Walter Laqueur, ed., *Fascism. A Reader's Guide* (Harmondsworth, 1979); Stanley Payne, *Fascism: Comparison and Definition* (Madison, Wisconsin, 1980); Stein Ugelvik Larsen et al., *Who were the Fascists? Social Roots of European Fascism* (Bergen, 1980); Wolfgang Wippermann, *Europäischer Faschismus im Vergleich, 1922-1982* (Frankfurt am Main, 1983); and Detlef Mühlberger, ed., *The Social Basis of European Fascist Movements* (London/Sydney, 1987).

[13] E.g. Ernst Nolte, ed., *Theorien über den Faschismus* (Cologne, 1967); Wolfgang Abendroth, ed., *Faschismus und Kapitalismus. Theorien über die sozialen Ursprünge und die Funktion des Faschismus* (Frankfurt am Main/Vienna, 1967); Reinhard Kühnl, ed., *Texte zur Faschismusdiskussion l. Positionen und Kontroversen* (Reinbek bei Hamburg, 1974); Reinhard Kühnl, *Formen bürgerlicher Herrschaft* (Reinbek bei Hamburg, 1971); Manfred Clemenz, *Gesellschaftliche Ursprünge des Faschismus* (Frankfurt am Main, 1972). A cross-section of 'New Left' work of the 1960s can be seen in *Das Argument* 1-6 (1964-70). For a sharp critique, see Heinrich August Winkler, *Revolution, Staat, Faschismus* (Göttingen, 1978), ch. 3.

destroying the revolutionary working class and therefore of safeguarding in the short-term capitalist interests and profits to be achieved through expansion and war. Fascism was thus the necessary form and final stage of bourgeois–capitalist rule. According to this interpretation, therefore, politics was a direct function of economics and wholly subordinated to it; the fascist mass movements were a product of capitalist manipulation; fascist rule served the function of bolstering profit; fascist leaders were thereby the 'agents' of the capitalist ruling class. The key question to be asked was: in whose advantage did the system work? And the answer left no doubt as to the intrinsic link between the fascist lackeys and the capitalist rulers. Though a short summary can do scant justice to the debates within the Comintern and to the varied glosses and interpretations which were advanced (the most far-sighted and nuanced by Clara Zetkin), it can be said that the view just described prevailed in essence to be encapsulated at the thirteenth plenary meeting of the Executive Committee of the Communist International in December 1933, and in its final form in the Dimitroff definition of 1935, mentioned in chapter 1. It has remained the basis of Soviet and East German writing on Nazism to the present.[14]

The contemporary dominance of the 'orthodox' Comintern thinking meant that 'nonconformist' marxist interpretations often received less attention than they merited at the time. The subtle interpretations, for example, of the KPD 'renegade' August Thalheimer, excluded from the Communist Party in 1928, and the Austrian theorist Otto Bauer received due recognition only during the revival of fascist studies in the 1960s and 1970s, though their influence on recent western marxist interpretations of fascism has generally been greater than the Comintern formulation.

Thalheimer, in a series of essays published in 1930 but gaining full recognition only in the late 1960s, and Bauer, in an essay printed in 1924 and elaborated upon in a chapter of a book written in 1936, both based their understanding of fascism on Marx's writings on Bonapartism, in particular his *Eighteenth Brumaire of Louis Bonaparte*, written immediately after the *coup d'état* of 2 December 1851. Though neither equated Bonapartism with fascism (which at the time of their original publications remained chiefly in its Italian manifestation), both saw in Marx's interpretation of the French *coup d'état* a significant pointer to understanding the mechanics of the fascist relation to the capitalist ruling class. Marx's work had rested on his assertion that the mutual neutralization of the social classes in the struggle for power in France had enabled Louis Bonaparte, supported by the lumpenproletariat and the mass of a-political peasant small-holders, to build the executive authority of the State into a relatively independent power. Applying Marx's analysis to fascism allowed Thalheimer and Bauer to distinguish between the social and political domination of the capitalist ruling class, to give weight to the autonomous importance of the fascist mass backing, to see fascism as only one of a number of possible ways out of the crisis of capitalism and by no means the equivalent of the final stage of capitalism *en route* to socialism, and, finally, to give weight to the relative

[14] For a summary of the latest GDR research by some of its foremost historians, see Eichholtz and Gossweiler, *Faschismusforschung* (see above ch. 1 note 27).

autonomy of the fascist executive once in power. In each case, this interpretation brought them into direct conflict with the 'orthodox' Leninist line
(though in his last writings in 1938 Bauer played down Bonapartism and
came much closer to a Leninist analysis of imperialism). The crucial point
was the dialectical relationship between the economic rule of the 'big bourgeoisie' and the political supremacy of the fascist 'ruling caste', financially
supported by capitalists but not created by them. Though petty bourgeois in
composition, the fascist party in power was bound, however, to become the
instrument of the economic ruling class, especially its more warlike elements,
but the inner contradictions within the system which would result in clashes
of interest between the fascist caste and the capitalist ruling class could only
be soluble through war.[15]

While the Comintern theory remains operational in the GDR as the key to
an understanding of fascism, variants of the Bonapartist approach (such as
can also be seen in Trotsky's perceptive writings on fascism[16]) have greatly
influenced the theoretical writings of western marxists since the 1960s. In
recent years, however, writing on fascism on the Left has been significantly
affected by a third major strain of marxist fascism interpretation, derived
from Gramsci's work (in particular his concept of 'bourgeois hegemony')
and articulated by Nicos Poulantzas, whose interpretation we will consider
more closely in chapter 3.[17] The neo-Gramscian approach lays far more
emphasis than other marxist interpretations on the conditions of *political*
crisis, arising when the state can no longer organize the political unity of the
dominant class and has lost popular legitimacy, and which make fascism
attractive as a radical populist solution to the problem of restoring the
dominant class's 'hegemony'. Marxist interpretations of fascism, briefly
described here, will concern us in the following chapter when we deal with
the relationship of politics to economics in the Nazi system of rule.

## Non-Marxist Interpretations

While, as I have indicated, most recent marxist interpretations of fascism
have adopted or built upon theories which were current in the 1920s and
1930s, early 'bourgeois' or non-marxist interpretations – few if any of them
actually amounting to a *theory* of fascism – have generally been found seriously wanting by later scholarship. The 'moral crisis of European society'
view, for instance, favoured by Croce, Meinecke, Ritter, and later Golo
Mann, has had only the most indirect impact upon later non-marxist fas-

[15] On Thalheimer, Bauer, and 'Bonapartism', see esp. Gerhard Botz, 'Austro-Marxist Interpretations of Fascism', in 'Theories of Fascism', *JCH* 11 (4) (1976), pp. 129–56, esp.
pp. 131–47; Jost Dülffer, 'Bonapartism, Fascism, and National Socialism', in *JCH* 11 (1976),
pp. 109–28; and most recently Hans-Gerd Jaschke, *Soziale Basis und soziale Funktion des
Nationalsozialismus. Studien zur Bonapartismustheorie* (Opladen, 1982). See also Kitchen,
ch. 7; Aycoberry, pp. 57–64; and Hildebrand, *Das Dritte Reich*, pp. 125–6. Winkler, *Revolution*, ch. 2 and pp. 83 ff. offers a critique. And for an excellent evaluation of interwar marxist
analyses of fascism ('orthodox' and 'deviant'), together with a selection of the most important
texts, see David Beetham, *Marxism in Face of Fascism* (Manchester, 1983).
[16] Leon Trotsky, *The Struggle against Fascism* (New York, 1971). Trotsky regarded the presi-
dential cabinets of Brüning, von Papen, and Schleicher, not Fascism itself, as 'Bonapartism'.
See Robert S. Wistrich, 'Leon Trotsky's Theory of Fascism', *JCH* 11 (1976), pp. 170–1.
[17] Nicos Poulantzas, *Fascism and Dictatorship* (London, 1974).

cism interpretation. Wilhelm Reich's attempt to combine marxism and freudianism in interpreting fascism as a consequence of sexual repression, and Erich Fromm's collective psychology approach arguing for an 'escape from freedom' to take refuge in submission, have also provided little methodological impetus for current analysis of fascism. Only Talcott Parsons's approach through the 'anomie' of modern social structures and the conflict-laden coexistence of traditional, archaic value-systems and modern social processes can be said to have 'left an indelible imprint' on later non-marxist analyses of fascism linked to theories of modernization.[18] Non-marxist scholarship on comparative fascism, since its revival in the 1960s, found its drive chiefly from three different directions: from the 'phenomenological' history of ideas approach emanating from Ernst Nolte's work; from a number of varied 'structural-modernization' approaches; and from 'sociological' interpretations of the social composition and class base of fascist movements and voters.

Nolte's self-proclaimed 'phenomenological method' seems to amount in practice to little more than taking the self-depiction of a phenomenon seriously – in this case the writings of fascist leaders. Biting critics have suggested that it turns out 'to be essentially Dilthey's good, old method of empathy', or 'little more than historicism in fancy dress'.[19] Nolte gives little serious consideration to the social foundations of fascism, since he finds socio-economic explanations of fascism inadequate. Rather, his analysis of the development of fascist ideas brings him to what he rather grandiosely calls a 'metapolitical' conception of fascism as a generic and autonomous force. In a somewhat mystical and mystifying conclusion, he sees fascism as 'practical and violent resistance to transcendence'. By 'transcendence' he understands a twofold process of mankind's quest for emancipation and progress (which he terms 'practical transcendence'), and of man's search beyond this world for salvation, 'reaching out of the mind beyond what exists and what can exist toward an absolute whole' – i.e. belief in God and an after-life (which he calls 'theoretical transcendence'). Fascism is in essence, therefore, anti-modernist; but in the emphasis on the notion of 'violent resistance to transcendence', Nolte distinguishes fascism from mere 'reaction' and sees it as a European movement which was both anti-traditional and anti-modern, which, in rejecting first and foremost its mirror image of communism, at the same time threatened also the existence of bourgeois society. Finally, in his stress on 'fascism in its epoch' (the original German title of his major work), Nolte is claiming that fascism was historically time-bound, that 'it would not be possible for the "same" sociological configuration in a different period and under other world conditions to produce an historically relevant phenomenon that can qualify as fascism, at least not . . . in the form of European national fascism'.[20]

---

[18] See Talcott Parsons, 'Democracy and Social Structure in Pre-Nazi Germany', and 'Some Sociological Aspects of the Fascist Movements', in his *Essays in Sociological Theory* (London/Toronto, 1949). The quotation is from Geoff Eley, 'The Wilhelmine Right: How it Changed', in Richard J. Evans, ed., *Society and Politics in Wilhelmine Germany* (London, 1978), p. 115.

[19] Sauer, p. 414 (ch. 1 note 39); Kitchen, p. 40.

[20] Nolte, *Three Faces*, pp. 529, 537 ff., 566-7. The quotation is from Ernst Nolte, 'The Problem of Fascism in Recent Scholarship', in Henry A. Turner, ed., *Reappraisals of Fascism* (New York, 1975), p. 30.

Nolte's was an important book and, as mentioned earlier, stirred up interest in the problem of generic fascism more than any other single work of the 1960s. But it is difficult to see that either methodologically or in terms of its conclusions it has gained a wide following. Other writers on comparative fascism, also working from the self-image of the fascists, have argued that fascism was revolutionary rather than backward-looking, that it 'looks much like the Jacobinism of our time'.[21] Secondly, the omission of detailed analysis of the nature and dynamics of the socio-economic foundation of fascist movements is a significant limitation of Nolte's work. Finally, from a different perspective it has been questioned whether Nolte has done more than describe similar manifestations of a type of political system which he calls 'fascism', but which showed vitally different degrees of intensity throughout Europe, in other words missing the point that the differences outweigh the similarities, which would call into question the very existence of the phenomenon itself.[22]

The second major non-marxist *group* of approaches (for they contain many varied nuances and differences of emphasis) is that linked to modernization theories, in which fascism is seen as one of a number of different paths along the route to modern society. In one variant of the modernization approach, which Klaus Hildebrand has dubbed the 'structural–functional theory', fascism is regarded as 'a special form of rule in societies which find themselves in a critical phase of the process of social transformation to industrial society and at the same time objectively or in the eyes of the ruling strata are threatened by the possibility of a communist upheaval'.[23] Fascism gains its chief impetus, in this view, from the resistance of residual élites to the egalitarian tendencies of industrial society. Other approaches see fascism as a form of developmental dictatorship (Gregor), as primarily a phenomenon encountered in agrarian societies in a particular phase of their transition to modernization (Organski), as a product of the road to modernism of an agrarian society which has encountered only 'revolution from above', resulting in revolutionary unrest – with temporary modernizing force – of a thoroughly reactionary class (the peasantry) which is doomed to extinction (Barrington Moore).[24]

The main problem of the 'structural–functionalist' approach seems to lie in its over-emphasis on the resistance of the ruling élites to change at the expense of the weight to be attached to the autonomous dynamism of the fascist mass movements themselves. Coupled with this is the difficulty of establishing which states afflicted by fascism were precisely in this process of transition to a pluralistic industrial society. At best this seems to apply to Italy and Germany, though the degree of the transition was so different in the two countries that doubts remain about the value of the 'model'.[25] The chief difficulty with those

---

[21]   Weber, *Varieties*, p. 139.

[22]   Hildebrand, *Das Dritte Reich*, p. 136.

[23]   Wolfgang J. Mommsen, 'Gesellschaftliche Bedingtheit und gesellschaftliche Relevanz historischer Aussagen', in Eberhard Jäckel and Ernst Weymar, eds., *Die Funktion der Geschichte in unserer Zeit* (Stuttgart, 1975), pp. 219–20; Hildebrand, *Das Dritte Reich*, p. 136.

[24]   A.J. Gregor, *The Ideology of Fascism* (New York, 1969); A.F.K. Organski, 'Fascism and Modernization', in Woolf, ed., *The Nature of Fascism*, pp. 19–41; Barrington Moore Jr., *Social Origins of Dictatorship and Democracy* (London, 1967).

[25]   Pointed out in Hildebrand, *Das Dritte Reich*, pp. 137–8.

modernizing theories which place fascism chiefly in an agrarian context is that they seem scarcely to apply to the German case, where Nazism developed in a highly-industrialized society. Significantly, Organski – one of the most prominent exponents of this approach – leaves Germany out of his model, while Barrington Moore's stimulating and wide-ranging analysis of different patterns of modernizing development rooted in the varied nature of the power base of the landed élites greatly over-emphasizes the importance of feudal traditions to the success of fascism, correspondingly underrating significantly the relationship to the dynamics of a fully-fledged capitalist economy and bourgeois society. Such modernization approaches as concentrate specifically upon Germany (e.g. the works of Dahrendorf and Schoenbaum[26]) are not concerned with a theory of fascism, but rather with the modernizing impact (if largely unintended) of Nazism itself. These interpretations are evaluated in the final chapter below.

A third influential non-marxist approach to fascism has been Seymour Lipset's 'sociological' interpretation of fascism as lower-middle-class radicalism – the 'extremism of the centre', as he dubbed it.[27] According to this view, fascism arose when mounting economic distress and a perceived threat both from big capital and organized labour forced middle-class strata which had previously supported centrist liberal parties to turn to the extreme Right. Such an interpretation has in recent years come under fire from various directions. First, it has been shown that the lower-middle-class vote in Germany before the rise of Nazism – and Lipset's argument was heavily based upon the German case – went to parties which in no sense could be regarded as 'liberal' or moderate centrist parties, but were distinctly rightist (authoritarian, nationalist, and often racist) in complexion. A vote for a fascist party was in fact the end of a long process of gradual rightwards shift in voting patterns.[28] Secondly, the Nazi Party received its main voter support in large cities – as has recently been demonstrated – from well-to-do districts representing the established upper bourgeoisie not the precariously placed or declining lower-middle-class social groups of the classic Lipset theory, while at the other end of the social scale the Nazis gained a higher level of backing from the working class (if not making serious inroads into 'organized' labour) than had been presumed.[29] Finally, it has been objected, exclusive concentration on the

---

[26] Ralf Dahrendorf, *Society and Democracy in Germany* (London, 1968); David Schoenbaum, *Hitler's Social Revolution* (London, 1966; all subsequent references to Anchor Books edn., New York, 1967).

[27] Seymour Martin Lipset, *Political Man. The Social Bases of Politics* (New York, 1960), ch. 5.

[28] See Heinrich August Winkler, 'Extremismus der Mitte? Sozialgeschichtliche Aspekte der nationalsozialistischen Machtergreifung', *VfZ* 20 (1972), pp. 175–91; and Thomas Childers,- *The Nazi Voter. The Social Foundations of Fascism in Germany, 1919–1933* (Chapel Hill/ London, 1983).

[29] For the big city vote, see Richard F. Hamilton, *Who voted for Hitler?* (Princeton, 1982). The wide social spectrum of Nazi support is emphasized by Childers, Jürgen W. Falter, 'Wer verhalf der NSDAP zum Sieg?', *APZ* (14 July 1979), pp. 3–21, and Heinrich August Winkler, 'Mittelstandsbewegung oder Volkspartei? Zur sozialen Basis der NSDAP', in Schieder, ed., *Faschismus als soziale Bewegung*, pp. 97–118. For the social structure of the party membership, see Michael Kater, *The Nazi Party. A Social Profile of Members and Leaders, 1919–1945* (Oxford, 1983). A good survey of the literature on the social composition of Nazi support, in

political behaviour of the lower middle class ignores completely both the role of the élites in bringing fascism to power and also the obvious subordination of lower-middle-class interests to those of big capitalism during the regime phase of fascism.[30]

It has not been my intention to attempt a full critique of the widely differing interpretations of fascism, but rather to illustrate the fact that, despite considerable advances in developing sophisticated typologies of fascist movements, there is no prospect in view of any theory of fascism which might win universal approval. No single marxist theory can command general acceptance even among marxist scholars, while some of the weaknesses and criticisms of 'bourgeois' interpretations have been indicated. Finally, as mentioned earlier, some leading scholars – whether favouring a 'totalitarianism' approach or not – question the whole basis of studies of comparative fascism, arguing that profound differences between the 'fascist' movements render any concept of generic fascism meaningless.

Following this brief description of the stages of development of the concepts of totalitarianism and fascism, we can now turn to consider critically whether either model type satisfactorily embraces the phenomenon of Nazism.

## General Reflections on the Concepts of 'Totalitarianism' and 'Fascism'

Neither 'totalitarianism' nor 'fascism' is a 'clean' scholarly concept. Both terms have, from the beginning of their usage, served a double function: as an ideological instrument of negative political categorization, often serving in common parlance as little more than 'boo-words'; and as a heuristic scholarly device used in an attempt to order and classify political systems. It is as good as impossible to treat them as 'neutral' scholarly analytical tools, detached from political connotations. Scholarly debate about the use of the terms illustrates above all the closeness of the mesh of history, politics, and language.[31] This is reflected, too, in the lack of agreement about precise definitions as well as usages of the terms.

Furthermore, there is often less than clarity about the link between concept and theory. If 'theory' is taken to be a system of interrelated statements,

---

particular the vexed questions of the nature and extent of working-class backing for Nazism and whether the SA had a more 'middle-class' or 'proletarian' character, can be found in Mathilde Jamin, *Zwischen den Klassen. Zur Sozialstruktur der SA-Führerschaft* (Wuppertal, 1984), pp. 11–45.

[30] Bernt Hagtvet and Reinhard Kühnl, 'Contemporary Approaches to Fascism: A Survey of Paradigms', in Larsen *et al.*, pp. 26–51, here p. 31. This is a perceptive analysis of the problems of comparative fascism. From a different perspective, see also Juan J. Linz, 'Some Notes towards a Comparative Study of Fascism in Sociological Historical Perspective', in Laqueur, pp. 13–78.

[31] See Karl Dietrich Bracher, 'Betrachtung: Terrorismus und Totalitarismus', in his *Schlüsselwörter*, pp. 103–23 (a lecture given in 1977 at a CDU conference on the causes of terrorism), and the comments of Bracher and Martin Broszat in *Total. und Fasch.*, pp. 10–11, 32–3.

deriving from and based upon each other, with general explanatory power, and 'concept' as an abstract linguistic short-cut, without independent standing and offering no systematic explanation, then it could be argued that in the case of totalitarianism Friedrich produced a conceptual definition, but one which does not provide a genuine theory of totalitarianism. In the case of fascism, most non-marxist approaches, as mentioned earlier, are essentially descriptive and rest on no clearly-defined theoretical premises, while marxist approaches derive from theoretical positions but the applied theory is not always based upon a clear conceptual definition and sometimes even upon what comes close to a tautological one.[32]

Though both 'fascism' and 'totalitarianism' approaches seek to provide typologies of political systems, these are of quite a different kind. The emphasis in fascism 'theories' is upon fascist *movements* – upon the conditions of growth, aims, and function of these movements as distinct from all other forms of political organization. (Though this is also true of the Comintern theory and its later application, much more emphasis has generally here been attached to the nature of fascist dictatorship rather than to the 'movement' phase.) Totalitarianism models, on the other hand, are practically by definition largely uninterested in the pre-power phase, except in so far as it betrays 'totalitarian' ambitions. The focus is rather on *systems* and *techniques of rule*. Many questions, therefore, of vital importance to the analyst of fascist movements – regarding, for instance, the socio-economic 'causes' of fascism, the social composition of fascist parties, and the relationship of fascist movements to the existing 'ruling class' – are of little importance to the totalitarianism theorist. Significant concerns in the totalitarianism approach, on the other hand, such as the existence of a single monopoly party, plebiscitary legitimation of rule, or the dominance of an official ideology, are usually regarded as secondary by analysts of fascism, who stress rather the major differences in the aims, social base, and economic structures of fascist and communist regimes.

Both 'fascism' and 'totalitarianism' are concepts extending beyond single systems of rule to 'generic types'. As such, they both demand rigorous comparative method. Yet in practice, thorough comparative analysis has often been lacking, particularly so in the totalitarianism model, and both approaches have traditionally been top-heavy in their reliance on the case of Nazi Germany.[33] Valuable systematic comparative research has been undertaken in recent years into the structure of fascist movements,[34] but much comparative work remains to be done on the character of fascist institutions in power. From the totalitarianism perspective, research into Stalinist government and society has reached nowhere near the level of penetration of that into the Nazi Regime, and comparisons are in practice often highly superficial.

---

[32] Uwe Dietrich Adam, 'Anmerkungen zu methodischen Fragen in den Sozialwissenschaften: Das Beispiel Faschismus und Totalitarismus', *PVS* 16 (1975), pp. 55–88, here esp. pp. 75–6.
[33] Examples for fascism are the books of Clemenz (note 13), Richard Saage, *Faschismus theorien* (Munich, 1976), and Niels Kadritzke, *Faschismus und Krise* (Frankfurt am Main/New York, 1976), and, for totalitarianism, Hans Buchheim, *Totalitäre Herrschaft. Wesen und Merkmale* (Munich, 1962).
[34] There is an excellent summary of up-to-date findings in Larsen *et al.* (note 12).

Despite the fact that the concepts are politically irreconcilable – protagonists of a general fascism concept rest their position upon the view that right-wing dictatorships are *fundamentally different* from left-wing dictatorships, while protagonists of a totalitarian approach begin with the premise that fascist and communist dictatorships are *basically similar* – prominent German scholars have recently claimed the indispensability of both concepts in analysing modern political structures and have argued that it is possible to apply both approaches in different ways in examining Nazism.[35] This seems to attract the difficulty of applying *comparative* concepts to a single phenomenon while leaving unresolved the problem of whether the comparative concept itself is a valid one. Nevertheless, that each of the concepts undeniably contains political overtones does not in itself disqualify them from having scholarly value and intellectual validity. Hence, there remains the need to test the explanatory value of each of the terms as vehicles for assessing the essential character of Nazism.

## Nazism as Totalitarianism?

Critics of the totalitarianism concept fall into two main categories: *(a)* those who reject categorically any deployment of a concept or theory of totalitarianism; and *(b)* those who are prepared to concede it some theoretical validity, but who regard its practical deployment as a tool of analysis as limited in potential. The arguments in favour of the second position are, in my view, more convincing.

*(a)* Categorical rejection of totalitarianism as a wholly worthless concept is usually pressed on the following grounds:[36]

*(i)* Totalitarianism is no more than a Cold War ideology, devised and deployed by western capitalist states in the 1940s and 1950s as an anti-communist instrument of political integration, and continuing to be used as such to the present day. Apart from the fact that, as we have seen, the concept and its application existed long before the Cold War, the undoubted and usually crude political use to which it was put in the Cold War and which in the post-detente period is again finding such resonance of itself no more deprives totalitarianism of potential value as a scholarly analytical tool than the often equally crude political exploitation of the term 'fascism' robs theories of fascism of any validity.

*(ii)* The totalitarianism concept treats the form – the outward shape of the systems of rule – as content, as their essence. As a result, it fully ignores the completely different aims and intentions of Nazism and Bolshevism – aims which were wholly inhumane and negative in the former case and ultimately humane and positive in the latter case. The objection is not altogether convincing. As Adam has pointed out,[37] the argument is based upon a deduction from the future (neither verifiable nor falsifiable) to the present, a procedure

---

[35] Kocka, 'Ursachen', pp. 14–15, and the comments of Kocka, Broszat, Schieder, and Nolte, in *Total. und Fasch.*, pp. 32–53.
[36] Kitchen, ch. 2, comes close to this position.
[37] Adam, 'Anmerkungen', pp. 64–7.

which in strict logic is not permissible. There is also a presumption that form and content can be so dissociated from each other that a comment on the form says nothing about the content – a point rejected even by materialist dialectics. Furthermore, the emphasis upon the ultimate humanity of Bolshevism contrasted with the inhumanity of Nazism correlates a presumed idealistic intention of the one system with the known reality of the other, and shirks the question of possible actual similarities in techniques of domination between the Stalinist and Hitler regimes. The purely functional point that communist terror was 'positive' because it was 'directed towards a complete and radical change in society', whereas 'fascist (i.e. Nazi) terror reached its highest point with the destruction of the Jews' and 'made no attempt to alter human behaviour or build a genuinely new society'[38] is, apart from the debatable assertion in the last phrase, a cynical value judgement on the horrors of the Stalinist terror.

*(b)* Four substantial criticisms are raised by those who do not reject the totalitarianism model out of hand, but see its application as very limited:

*(i)* The concept of totalitarianism, however defined, can only unsatisfactorily grasp the peculiarities of the systems it attempts to classify. Broszat pointed out, for instance, in the introductory remarks to his masterly analysis of the 'Hitler State', the difficulty of locating the amorphous structurelessness of the Nazi system in any typology of rule.[39] The totalitarianism concept can, in fact, only speak in a generalized and limited fashion about the similarities of systems, which on closer inspection are so differently structured that comparisons are forced to remain highly superficial. Hans Mommsen has indicated, for example, how different the Nazi Party and the Soviet Communist Party were from each other in structure and function, and how little it says, therefore, simply to refer to both Nazi Germany and Soviet Russia (even confining the treatment to the Stalinist period) as 'one-party states'.[40] Equally significant were the major differences in the essential character of leadership in the two states, so that the roles of Hitler and Stalin can only with difficulty be typified as those of 'totalitarian dictators'. And the fundamental contrasts in the control of the Nazi and Soviet economies are an even more striking example of highly misleading generalizations emanating from the totalitarianism approach – in this instance about centralized 'totalitarian' economies.

*(ii)* The totalitarianism concept cannot cope adequately with change within the communist system. The extension of the concept to post-Stalinist USSR and other eastern-bloc states is forced to see the essence of totalitarianism as lying elsewhere than in the specific features of Stalinism usually taken to be comparable with Nazism (e.g. terror, leadership cult etc.). Still retaining the implicit (if not explicit) linkage with Nazism and other 'right-wing dictatorships', such attempts often rapidly widen into outright absurdity.

*(iii)* The decisive disadvantage of totalitarianism as a concept is that it says nothing about socio-economic conditions, functions, and political aims of a

---

[38] Kitchen, p. 31.
[39] Martin Broszat, *Der Staat Hitlers* (Munich, 1969), p. 9, not included in the Engl. transl., *The Hitler State* (London, 1981).
[40] Hans Mommsen, in *Total. und Fasch.*, pp. 18–27.

system, but is content to rely solely upon emphasis of techniques and overt forms of rule (exclusivity of ideology, tendency to comprehensive mobilization etc.).[41] Since one of the most obvious and striking differences between the Nazi and the Soviet systems lies in the socio-economic sphere, it has been pointed out that 'the value of an analysis which ignores the relations of production and the resulting social structure of the two systems is strictly limited'.[42]

*(iv)* The legitimacy of the totalitarianism concept rests upon the upholding of the values of western 'liberal democracy' and the distinction between 'open' and 'closed' government, between 'shared' and 'unified' power. There is, however, built into the totalitarianism concept an ambivalence between describing historically real systems of rule (Nazism, 'Stalinism') and being widened out into a 'tendency' which extends to so many modern dictatorships and even to sections of society within western democracies that the concept loses much of its analytical value.[43]

These criticisms are generally advanced by those who nevertheless would not wish altogether to discard the concept of totalitarianism. They claim – and I would agree with their argument – that it is in itself a wholly legitimate exercise, whatever essential differences existed in ideology and socio-economic structures, to compare the forms and techniques of rule in Germany under Hitler and the Soviet Union under Stalin; and that a new scale and concept of the development of force in governmental systems, in attempted comprehensiveness of control and manipulation, in methods (based on modern technology) of dynamic plebiscitary mobilization of the population behind its rulers, and a radical intolerance of any focus of co-existing alternative loyalties or any form of institutional 'living space' except under the regime's own terms, corresponding therefore to the *attempted* politicization of all facets of social experience, can justifiably be seen in both systems. The spectrum of dissent ranging to 'resistance' in Nazi Germany (and *pari passu*, though so far little analysed, in Stalin's Russia) can in fact only be understood in the light of the relationship to the demands of a regime which made a 'total claim' on behaviour and manifestations of outward conformity, hence creating nonconformist and oppositional behaviour which even in other authoritarian systems would not have been politicized and turned, thereby, into political dissent.[44] If the redundant echoes of 'atomized mass society' theories can be dispensed with, then it may indeed be at the social rather than the institutional level that, if not the full-blown, politically loaded, concept of totalitarianism, then the more modest notion of the 'total claim' of a regime on its subjects could prove heuristically useful in a comparative analysis of behavioural patterns – acclamatory and oppositional – in quite differently structured societies and political systems.[45]

---

[41] Jürgen Kocka, in *Total. und Fasch.*, pp. 39–44.
[42] Kitchen, p. 31.
[43] Martin Broszat, in *Total. und Fasch.*, pp. 32–8.
[44] See Ian Kershaw, *Popular Opinion and Political Dissent in the Third Reich. Bavaria 1933–1945* (Oxford, 1983), esp. pp. 374 ff.
[45] For a recent perceptive assessment of the impact of Nazism on German society, see Detlev Peukert, *Volksgenossen und Gemeinschaftsfremde* (Cologne, 1982). Engl. transl. *Inside Nazi Germany. Conformity and Opposition in Everday Life* (London, 1987).

Even the posing of an extreme 'total claim' might then be seen as symptomatic of the 'crisis management' of regimes in transitory, unstable periods rather than as lasting characteristics of rule.

Beyond this, it seems to me that depictions of Nazism as a 'totalitarian system' are best avoided, not simply because of the inescapable political colouring attached to the label 'totalitarianism', but because of the weighty conceptual problems which the term poses and which have been outlined above. There remains a final possibility of deploying the concept in a non-comparative sense, restricting its usage to Nazi/fascist systems alone and reverting to something like its earlier usage by Franz Neumann and others in distinguishing phases of development in the impact of a dynamic mass movement with 'total' claims upon the legislative and executive structures of the state. Broszat's analysis of the Nazi state, for instance, uses the adjective 'totalitarian' divorced from comparison with the USSR to distinguish the more radical phase of Nazi government after 1937–8 from the earlier merely 'authoritarian' phase.[46] Quite apart from the question of attaching distinctive labels to the periods of the Third Reich before and after 1937–8, and of ridding 'totalitarianism' of its usual comparative connotations with the USSR, it might be seriously doubted whether, in dealing with the Nazi state alone, the adjective 'totalitarian' is needed at all simply as a synonym for progressively radicalizing negative dynamism. Others, developing the same line of interpretation, find the term wholly redundant.[47]

All in all, the value of the totalitarianism concept seems extremely limited, and the disadvantages of its deployment greatly outweigh its possible advantages in attempting to characterize the essential nature of the Nazi Regime.

## Nazism as Fascism or Unique Phenomenon?

Opponents of the use of a generic concept of fascism advance two principal and serious objections to the ranking of Nazism as fascism: firstly – an objection I find justified – that the concept is often extended in inflationary fashion to a wide variety of movements and regimes of wholly disparate character and significance; and secondly, but in my view less persuasive, that the concept is unable satisfactorily to embrace the singular characteristics of Nazism, and that the differences between Italian fascism and German National Socialism significantly outweigh whatever superficial similarities they might appear to possess.

*(a)* The first criticism pertains particularly, though not solely, to marxist interpretations of fascism. The intrinsic relationship between fascism and capitalism in the marxist–leninist version of fascism theory, for instance, extends the notion of 'fascist dictatorship' to cover numerous kinds of repressive regime, and no fundamental distinction is drawn between military

---

[46] Broszat, *The Hitler State*, pp. ix–xiv, 346 ff. In his later work, Franz Neumann came to deploy the 'totalitarianism' concept in its conventional 'Cold War' usage. See his *The Democratic and the Authoritarian State* (New York, 1957).

[47] E.g. Hans Mommsen, in *Total. und Fasch.*, p. 65, where he states: 'The totalitarianism theory is the myth which stands in the way of any *real* social historical explanation [of Nazism]', particularly because of its teleological tendency to take the end product for granted before examining the conditions of its growth.

dictatorships and mass-party dictatorships in terms of the essence of rule. Since, according to this view, the mass base of a fascist party is a manipulated product of the ruling capitalist class without any autonomous force, the importance of the mass movement (which most non-marxist analysts would regard as a significant difference between military authoritarian regimes and fascist regimes) recedes. Hence, GDR scholars class such disparate regimes as existed in Poland, Bulgaria, and Hungary in the inter-war period, in Portugal under Salazar and Caetano and Spain under Franco, in Greece under the Colonels, Argentina under the Generals, and present-day Chile and other South American dictatorships, as 'fascist' alongside 'Hitler Fascism'.[48] Decisive for GDR historians is not the outward form of the dictatorship, but its essence as the weapon of the most aggressive elements of finance capital. Nevertheless, the latest GDR scholarship does distinguish very clearly between two basic types of fascist dictatorship: the 'normal' form – usually a military dictatorship – in countries with relatively unadvanced capitalist economies; and the *exceptional* form – mass-party fascism – of which only the two examples of Italy and Germany have so far been experienced, both arising in highly unusual conditions within the framework of a complete national crisis.[49] Consideration of the relationship between capitalism and Nazism, on which this theory rests, will have to wait until the following chapter. It suffices here to say that, however unconvincing the underlying principles are, GDR interpretations compare very favourably with the writings of parts of the 'New Left' in the Federal Republic, where the concept of fascism is extended to any form of 'repressive' government which serves to uphold the domination of economic power-groups, thus allowing western capitalist systems – and the Federal Republic in particular – to be dubbed 'fascist' or at least 'fascistoid' or 'proto-fascist'.[50] In such cases, where the fascism concept is widened in hopelessly nebulous fashion, it seems perfectly correct to speak of a trivialization of the horror of Nazism.

*(b)* The second, related, criticism claims that no theory or concept of generic fascism can possibly do justice to the peculiarities and unique characteristics of Nazism. While movements calling themselves fascist or national socialist existed in most European countries outside the Soviet Union in the inter-war period, it is widely accepted that fully-fledged, self-sustaining fascist dictatorships deriving their impetus from mass parties consolidated power only in Italy and Germany (leaving aside puppet or quisling governments of the war years). A comparison of fascism in all its stages can accordingly be made only for the systems in these two countries.[51] Yet in the eyes of some leading authorities, the differences between the two regimes were so profound that the term 'fascism' should be reserved for the Italian system

[48] E.g. Manfred Weißbecker, 'Der Faschismus in der Gegenwart', in Eichholz and Gossweiler, pp. 217 ff.; Kurt Gossweiler, *Faschismus und antifaschistischer Kampf* (Antifaschistische Arbeitshefte, Röderberg Verlag, Frankfurt am Main, 1978), pp. 18–23.
[49] Kurt Gossweiler, *Kapital, Reichswehr und NSDAP, 1919–1924* (East Berlin, 1982), ch. 1 provides a thoughtful discussion.
[50] See the theoretical remarks of Adam, 'Anmerkungen', pp. 70–6; and Winkler, *Revolution*, pp. 108 ff.
[51] See the comments of Schieder, in *Total. und Fasch.*, pp. 45–9. MacGregor Knox, 'Conquest, Foreign and Domestic, in Fascist Italy and Nazi Germany', *JMH* 56 (1984), pp. 1–57 provides an interesting comparative essay on the Mussolini and Hitler regimes.

under Mussolini, while Nazism should be called 'National Socialism' and regarded as a unique phenomenon (though, interestingly enough, falling in terms of techniques of rule within the category of 'totalitarian systems'). Since, in this view, the generic concept of fascism does not even apply to the two leading species within the genus, it had better be discarded altogether. The central differences emphasized in this argument focus on the dynamic nature of the Nazi race ideology, which had no exact parallel in Italian fascism; on the discrepancy between the Nazi elevation of the *Volk* over the state, contrasted with Italian fascist étatism; on the anti-modern, archaic aims and ideology of Nazism compared with the modernizing tendencies of Italian fascism; on the totality of the Nazi conquest of state and society as against the far more limited penetration of the established order by the Italian fascists; and, not least, on the contrast between a relatively 'traditional' imperialistic policy on the part of Italy, and a qualitatively different drive for racial domination, eventually of the whole world, by the Nazi regime. And since this last and most crucial distinction is, according to such interpretations, attributable directly to Hitler himself, it is claimed that 'the case of Hitler' was unique, and cannot be subjected to the generalizations of comparative fascism, not even to a comparison limited to Italy and Germany.[52]

These criticisms cannot be lightly passed over. Indeed, examination of two central issues – the relationship between capitalism and Nazism, and the personal role of Hitler in the Nazi system – form the direct subject of later chapters. There is space here only for a number of general observations about the criticisms of the generic fascism approach, related to the alternative possibility of emphasizing the uniqueness of Nazism.

A number of the supposed major differences between Nazism and Italian fascism are open to debate. This would apply, for instance, to the stress on the 'backward-looking' nature of Nazism in distinction to the 'modernizing' pressures of fascism in Italy. Recent research is calling such a distinction increasingly into question, as chapter 7 below indicates.[53] Quite apart from such qualification, the uniqueness of specific features of Nazism would not of itself prevent the location of Nazism in a wider genus of political systems. It might well be claimed that Nazism and Italian fascism were separate species within the same genus, without any implicit assumption that the two species ought to be well-nigh identical. Ernst Nolte has stated that the differences could easily be reconciled by employing a term such as 'radical fascism'

[52] Hildebrand, *Das Dritte Reich*, pp. 139–42; Hillgruber, *Endlich genug?*, pp. 17, 38, 42; Bracher, *Zeitg. Kontrov.*, chs. 1–4, and in *Total. und Fasch.*, pp. 14–17; Henry A. Turner, 'Fascism and Modernization', in Turner, *Reappraisals*, pp. 132–3; see also De Felice, p. ix (introductory comments of Charles F. Delzell) and pp. 10–12, 180.

[53] For modern traits in Nazism, see e.g. Peukert, pp. 42–7; Tim W. Mason, 'Zur Entstehung des Gesetzes zur Ordnung der nationalen Arbeit, vom 20. Januar 1934: Ein Versuch über das Verhältnis "archaischer" und "moderner" Momente in der neuesten deutschen Geschichte', in Hans Mommsen *et al.*, eds., *Industrielles System und politische Entwicklung in der Weimarer Republik* (Düsseldorf, 1974), pp. 322–51; Horst Matzerath and Heinrich Volkmann, 'Modernisierungstheorie und Nationalsozialismus', in Jürgen Kocka, ed., *Theorien in der Praxis des Historikers* (Göttingen, 1977), pp. 95–7; Hans-Dieter Schäfer, *Das gespaltene Bewußtsein. Deutsche Kultur und Lebenswirklichkeit 1933–1945* (Munich/Vienna, 1981), pp. 114–62; Martin Broszat, 'Zur Struktur der NS-Massenbewegung', *VfZ* 31 (1983), pp. 52–76.

for Nazism.[54] Winkler has indicated that for him Nazism was 'also but not only "German fascism" ',[55] while Linz regarded it as a 'distinctive branch grafted on the fascist tree'.[56] Jürgen Kocka, in a recent subtle essay on the causes of Nazism, again sees no incompatibility between the unique features of National Socialism in Germany and its attribution to a broader class of generic fascism, indispensable for putting the Nazi phenomenon in a wider than purely national perspective and understanding the social and political contexts in which such a movement could arise and take power.[57] Such approaches rightly stress the significant similarities between Nazism and the many movements (above all the Italian one) which called themselves fascist. Such similarities included: extreme chauvinistic nationalism with pronounced imperialistic, expansionist tendencies; an anti-socialist, anti-marxist thrust aimed at the destruction of working-class organizations and their marxist political philosophy; the basis in a mass party drawing from all sectors of society, though with pronounced support in the middle class and proving attractive to the peasantry and to various uprooted or highly unstable sectors of the population; fixation on a charismatic, plebiscitarily legitimized leader; extreme intolerance towards all oppositional and presumed oppositional groups, expressed through vicious terror, open violence, and ruthless repression; glorification of militarism and war, heightened by the backlash to the comprehensive socio-political crisis in Europe arising from the First World War; dependence upon an 'alliance' with existing élites – industrial, agrarian, military, and bureaucratic – for their political breakthrough; and at least an initial function – despite a populist-revolutionary, anti-establishment rhetoric – in the stabilization or restoration of social order and capitalist structures.[58]

The establishment of fundamental generic characteristics linking Nazism to movements in other parts of Europe allows further consideration on a comparative basis of the reasons why such movements were able to become a real political danger and gain power in Italy and Germany, whereas in other European countries they mainly remained an unpleasant, but transitory irritant. Among other things, one would undoubtedly have to lay stress on features prominent, though in different strengths, in both Italy and Germany before the First World War and massively accentuated through the traumatic consequences of the War itself. Common to both countries were the powerful imperialist–expansionist strains pronounced among the ruling élites and bolstered by the widespread extreme chauvinism in the bourgeois classes of these new states – self-perceived 'have-not nations'; the co-existence and conflict of highly modern strands of development and powerful remnants of archaic social structures and value-systems in societies simultaneously undergoing the processes of national integration, transition to a

[54] Nolte, in *Total, und Fasch.*, pp. 77–8, and in *Three Faces*, pp. 529, 569–77.
[55] Winkler, *Revolution*, p. 66.
[56] Linz (note 30), p. 24.
[57] Kocka, 'Ursachen', esp. p. 15.
[58] See Kocka, 'Ursachen', p. 15, and in *Total. und Fasch.*, pp. 39, 44. See also Winkler, *Revolution*, p. 66.

bourgeois constitutional state, and rapid industrialization;[59] and finally, but not least, deeply fractured political systems, whose splintered parliamentary structures reflected deep social and political cleavages, fostering the feeling that a strong, but 'populist', leadership was necessary to impose unity 'from above' – in the first instance by crushing those standing in the way of unity, primarily 'the marxist Left'. The different scale of the social and political conflict spheres in Italy and Germany helps explain the different level of radicalization in the two countries when beset by different, though related, comprehensive crises of the political system – directly unleashed by the War in the Italian case, unfolding, after a long period of political instability, during the world economic crisis in Germany.

It is within this perspective, rather than divorced from it in an emphasis upon Nazism as an altogether unique phenomenon, that the peculiarities of the German radical variant of fascism can be brought out by analysis of the specific features of the German political culture and its relationship to socio-economic structures. There need be no contradiction, therefore, between acceptance of Nazism as (the most extreme manifestation of) fascism and recognition of its own unique characteristics within this category, which can only properly be comprehended within the framework of German national development.

Such an argument would not, however, satisfy Bracher, Hildebrand, Hillgruber, and others, who would argue that Nazism was not only in form but in essence a uniquely German phenomenon, and that this essence or uniqueness was located in the person and ideology of Adolf Hitler. This personalization of the essence of Nazism is, in fact, at the crux of the debate over the historical place and characterization of Nazism. The major differences do not lie in explaining Nazism's origins and the circumstances of its rise to power. Bracher has tended to emphasize the specific features of German–Austrian ideological development in order to lay full weight on the racial–*völkisch* dimension of Nazi ideology; Hillgruber and Hildebrand have stressed the particular constellation of German power-politics and the overwhelming continuities between 1871 and 1933 (only to be broken thereafter) intrinsic to the Prussian–German State.[60] These are important strands of an overall explanation of Nazism and, despite differences of emphasis, are generally compatible with those works – for example, by Wehler, Kocka, Puhle, and Winkler[61] – which look rather to Germany's specific

---

[59] The importance of this simultaneous three-fold transition is stressed by Schieder, in *Total. und Fasch.*, pp. 45–9.

[60] See Bracher, 'The Role of Hitler', in Laqueur, pp. 209–10, fully developed in Karl Dietrich Bracher, *The German Dictatorship* (Harmondsworth, 1973), esp. ch. 1; Andreas Hillgruber, 'Kontinuität und Diskontinuität in der deutschen Außenpolitik von Bismarck bis Hitler', in his *Großmachtpolitik und Militarismus im 20. Jahrhundert* (Düsseldorf, 1974), pp. 11–36, and *Endlich genug?*, pp. 48 ff.; Klaus Hildebrand, 'Hitlers Ort in der Geschichte der preußisch-deutschen Nationalstaates', *HZ* 217 (1973), pp. 584–632, and his *Foreign Policy*, (see ch. 1 note 17), esp. Introdn. and Concl.

[61] E.g., Wehler, *Kaiserreich* (see ch. 1 note 16); Jürgen Kocka, *Angestellte zwischen Faschismus und Demokratie* (Göttingen, 1977); Hans-Jürgen Puhle, *Von der Agrarkrise zum Präfaschismus* (Wiesbaden, 1972); Heinrich August Winkler, *Mittelstand, Demokratie und Nationalsozialismus* (Cologne, 1972).

socio-economic structures as the focal point of their explanations. Yet this latter group have no hesitation in accepting Nazism, for all its singularities, as a form of fascism; while the former group deny this categorization and insist that it was *sui generis*. The breaking-point is clearly 'the case of Hitler': whether Nazism can be set aside from fascism in Italy and elsewhere because it was *in its essence* 'Hitlerism'. According to the latter approach, not the causes of Nazism's rise but the character of the dictatorship itself is decisive. And here, the differences between Italian fascism and Nazism, whose rule rested on the implementation of the ideas and policies of the monocratic dictator, Hitler, were fundamental.[62]

This 'Hitler-centrism' is itself an understandable over-reaction against some crude left-wing interpretations which reduced Hitler to a mere cipher. However, irreplaceable though Hitler undoubtedly was in the Nazi movement, the equation Nazism = Hitlerism unnecessarily restricts the vision and distorts the focus in explaining the origins of Nazism; deflects away from rather than orientates towards consideration of the political manifestations in other European countries which  shared (and continue to share today) important affinities and common characteristics with Nazism; and finally – as I hope to argue in later chapters – provides in itself a quite unsatisfactory explanation of the dynamic radicalization of politics within the Third Reich itself.

This evaluation of the concepts of totalitarianism and fascism in relation to Nazism's alleged uniqueness as a phenomenon has suggested the following conclusions:

*(1)* The concept of fascism is more satisfactory and applicable than that of totalitarianism in explaining the character of Nazism, the circumstances of its growth, the nature of its rule, and its place in a European context in the inter-war period. The similarities with other brands of fascism are profound, not peripheral. Nazism's features place the phenomenon squarely within the European-wide context of radical anti-socialist national–integrationist movements, which also rejected the forms though not the economic substance of bourgeois society, derived from the era of open imperialist conflict and emerged to prominence in the upheavals following the First World War.

*(2)* This is not incompatible with the retention of the concept of totalitarianism, though this latter concept is much less usable and its value is strictly limited. Nazism undoubtedly did have a 'total' (or 'totalitarian') claim, which had consequences both for its mechanics of rule and for the behaviour – acclamatory and oppositional – of its subjects. Consequences for the mechanics of rule were reflected especially in new forms of plebiscitary mass mobilization through new technologies of rule combined with an exclusive dynamic ideology and monopolistic demands on society. On the basis of these features, it is legitimate to compare the forms of rule in Germany under Hitler and the Soviet Union under Stalin, even if, for the

---

[62] See Bracher, *Zeitg. Kontrov.*, pp. 30, 88–9, 99; Hillgruber, *Endlich genug?*, pp. 40–2; and Klaus Hildebrand, 'Nationalsozialismus oder Hitlerismus?', in Michael Bosch, ed., *Persönlichkeit und Struktur in der Geschichte* (Düsseldorf, 1977), pp. 55–61, here esp. pp. 56–7.

reasons adduced earlier, this comparison is doomed from the outset to be superficial and unsatisfactory. Moreover, 'totalitarianism' according to our analysis, if to be used at all, would have to be restricted to passing phases of extreme instability reflected in the paranoid sense of insecurity of the regimes, rather than being seen as a lasting structure of rule. From a long-range perspective, the entire period of the Third Reich and the bulk of Stalin's rule could be said to fall within such a categorization. This would be a reason additional to those mentioned earlier to exclude the application of the comparative totalitarianism concept to post-Stalinist communist systems, where it rapidly approaches futility if not outright absurdity.

*(3)* The peculiar features which distinguish Nazism from other leading manifestations of fascism are only to be fully comprehended within the structures and conditions of German socio-economic and ideological–political developments in the industrial–bourgeois era. The person, ideology, and function of Hitler have to be located in and related to these structures. Without question, Hitler played personally a vital part both in the rise of Nazism and in the character of Nazi rule. But the significance of his role can only be assessed by relating his input to the conditions which produced and shaped him, and which he could not autonomously control even at the height of his power. Nazism was in many respects indeed a unique phenomenon. But its uniqueness cannot – except in a superficial sense – be solely attributed to the uniqueness of its leader.

# 3

## Politics and Economics in the Nazi State

The question of the relationship between Nazism and the dominant economic forces in Germany has remained one of the most contentious issues of debate among scholars since the theoretical deliberations of the Comintern in the 1920s and 1930s. It is a debate which shows no signs of subsiding today, and one in which preconceived theoretical (and ideological) positions are often at their most apparent. With the double development of the opening up of major archival sources and the revival of marxist scholarship in the West during the 1960s, the debates began for the first time seriously to preoccupy non-marxist historians. The enormous improvement since then in the level of empirical knowledge on the Nazi economy has been accompanied by new levels of sophistication in interpretation, though the central areas of concern and the focal points of conflicting interpretation have changed relatively little in the meantime.

One major issue revolves around the extent to which the Nazi rise to power was a product of the character of German capitalism and of the machinations and political aims of the leaders of German industry. This issue, relating to the pre-dictatorship phase, will not concern us here. It must suffice to point out that, for all the remaining scholarly divisions, a growing body of recent scholarship rejects both the crude instrumentalism of a view which sees Nazism as a movement 'reared' and controlled from the outset by capitalist interests, and the equally crass counter-argument denying any structural links between capitalism and the rise of Nazism. Such scholarship – both marxist and non-marxist – broadly accepts two structural connections between capitalism and the rise of Nazism. First, it is clear that there was an increasing readiness among powerful sectors of the industrial élite long before the Nazi political breakthrough to discard the Weimar Republic in favour of a more palatable authoritarian solution which would restore profitability in the first instance through repression of labour. Secondly, among an industrial sector in many ways split and disorientated by the economic crisis of the early 1930s, there was an increased willingness in the deepening recession even among sections of industry not especially well disposed towards the Nazis to tolerate at least a Nazi share in government in order to provide the political framework within which the capitalist system could reproduce itself.[1] Important for our concern in this chapter is the very fact

[1] For an excellent recent survey and evaluation of the literature on the relationship of capitalism and Nazism before 1933, see Dick Geary, 'The Industrial Elite and the Nazis in the Weimar Republic', in Peter D. Stachura, ed., *The Nazi Machtergreifung* (London, 1983), pp. 85–100. Despite the bitter criticism aroused by the first edition of David Abraham's *The Collapse of the Weimar Republic. Political Economy and Crisis* (Princeton, 1981), his corrected second edition

that the Nazis presented, as it were, the last hope rather than the first choice of much of industry in offering a form of State which would uphold capitalist interests. Together with the pervading and continuing divisions within the economic élites about strategies for recovery, this ruled out obvious alternatives, bound the industrial leadership even if initially only in a negative fashion to the Nazi State, and offered the new Nazi leaders some scope and potential for political initiatives.

This relates closely to the second major issue which has preoccupied scholars exploring the connections between capitalism and Nazism: the extent to which the politics of the Nazi regime between 1933 and 1945 were shaped and determined by economic considerations, notably the interests of German industry. Put in slightly different and more pointed fashion, this amounts to the question of how far the regime was able to acquire a degree of political autonomy amounting in practice to a primacy of ideological and political objectives over economic aims and interests. This question is our concern in this chapter.

## Interpretations

Even in the GDR, where economic relations had of course from the beginning been central to analyses of 'Hitler Fascism', it was only from the 1960s that more detailed archival research provided the base for a more subtle and differentiated scholarship, the prime example of which was Dietrich Eichholtz's study of the German war economy, published in 1969.[2] This brought out far more strongly than had previously been the case the contradictions and conflicts within various monopoly capitalist 'groupings' and corresponded in some of its findings with new work on the Nazi economy by western scholars. The general tenor of the gradually emerging research in the West, mainly carried out by non-marxists, was to see a far closer structural relationship between German industry and the policies of the Nazi leadership than had formerly been accepted, and to reject rather primitive notions of a highly centralized State 'command economy' which had formed part and

provides a penetrating analysis for the shifting political strategies within German industry during the deepening crisis of the Weimar Republic. (For polemics and counter-polemics in the unpleasant 'Abraham affair', which effectively terminated David Abraham's academic career, see the contributions to *CEH* 17 (1984), pp. 159–293). From an opposed perspective, rejecting theories about the structural links between capitalism and fascism, Henry A. Turner, *German Big Business and the Rise of Hitler* (Oxford, 1985), provides a meticulously researched empirical study of relations between business leaders and Nazis. The conflicting approaches of Abraham and Turner are exposed in stark relief in David Abraham, 'Big Business, Nazism, and German Politics at the End of Weimar', *European History Quarterly* 17 (1987), pp.'235–45 (a highly critical review of Turner's book). Non-polemical, and especially useful for the role of big business in the immediate prelude to Hitler's takeover of power, is Reinhard Neebe, *Großindustrie, Staat und NSDAP* (Göttingen, 1981). And for a masterly analysis of the entire economic crisis and its significance for Nazi economic policy after 1933, see Harold James, *The German Slump. Politics and Economics 1924–1936* (Oxford, 1986).

[2] Dietrich Eichholtz, *Geschichte der deutschen Kriegswirtschaft, 1933–1945* (East Berlin, 1969). The second volume appeared in 1984. For a recent survey of GDR historical writing, see Andreas Dorpalen, *German History in Marxist Perspective. The East German Approach* (Detroit, 1985). Chapter 8 examines the Nazi era.

parcel of the 'totalitarianism' model. The American scholar Arthur Schweitzer, for instance, emphasized what he regarded as a 'coalition' between the Nazi leadership and business élites in a period of 'partial fascism' down to 1936, although – anticipating, if from a different theoretical position, the debate about the 'primacy of politics' which was to take place shortly afterwards – he saw the period of 'full fascism' after 1936 as one in which business became increasingly dependent on the political and ideological goals of the Nazi leadership.[3] Dieter Petzina's analysis of the Four Year Plan demonstrated how far removed it was from a genuine 'planned economy' and how closely the political–ideological interests of the Nazi leadership coincided with the economic interests of what was emerging as the strongest sector of German big business, the great chemical combine of IG Farben.[4] And Alan Milward uncovered the underlying weaknesses of a war economy which had necessitated Blitzkrieg as the only feasible strategy and had been centralized and rationally administered only after coming under Speer's control from 1942.[5]

Scholarly debate on the character of the Nazi economy was given a sharp stimulus by the appearance in 1966 of the essay by the British marxist historian Tim Mason on the 'primacy of politics' in the Third Reich.[6] Mason's article was framed in terms of a challenge both to existing marxist–leninist orthodoxy and to the main thrust of 'liberal–bourgeois' approaches to Nazism. While the former denied the existence of an autonomous political realm in representing the political–ideological sphere as part of the superstructure of the socio-economic system, the latter had tended to treat the economy as more or less subjected along with everything else to the unquestioned political priorities and autonomy of a ruthless, ideologically-motivated dictatorship. Mason's conclusion, based on an analysis of economic relations in the Third Reich, was 'that both the domestic and foreign policy of the National Socialist government became, from 1936 onward, increasingly independent of the influence of the economic ruling classes, and even in some essential aspects ran contrary to their collective interests'. He went in fact so far as to accept that 'it became possible for the National Socialist state to assume a fully independent role, for the "primacy of politics" to assert itself'. This – from a marxist viewpoint – startling conclusion was qualified only to the extent that, in Mason's terms, this relationship in the Third Reich upturned the norm in capitalist states, and was 'unique in the history of modern bourgeois society and its governments'.[7]

Mason pointed to a number of different aspects of the economic development of Nazi Germany to support his thesis: the far-reaching exclusion of the representatives of industry from the direct decision-making processes; the extraordinarily rapid growth of the economic role of the State itself in provid-

[3] Arthur Schweitzer, *Big Business in the Third Reich* (Bloomington, Indiana, 1964).
[4] Dieter Petzina, *Autarkiepolitik im Dritten Reich. Der nationalsozialistische Vierjahresplan* (Stuttgart, 1968).
[5] Alan S. Milward, *The German Economy at War* (London, 1965).
[6] Tim Mason, 'Der Primat der Politik – Politik und Wirtschaft im Nationalsozialismus', *Das Argument* 8 (1966), pp. 473–94. All references below are to the English version, 'The Primacy of Politics – Politics and Economics in National Socialist Germany', in Henry A. Turner, ed., *Nazism and the Third Reich* (New York, 1972), pp. 175–200.
[7] Mason, 'Primacy, pp. 175–7.

ing orders for industry and thereby creating markets and acting as a determining factor in production; the transfer of capitalist competition from a struggle for markets to a struggle within an armaments-dominated economy for raw materials and labour – leading to the endangering of entire sectors of industry and extensive state intervention and regulation; the decline of economic interest groups in shaping state policy; and the inability of the leaders of the armaments economy to force through before 1942 the redistribution of the social product in terms of sharp inroads into the standard of living, which they had been demanding since the beginning of the Third Reich. In Mason's view, these features of the Nazi political economy either came into being or were massively accelerated from 1936–7, so that it is permissible to speak of 'weighty structural changes in economy and society', and consequently of a significant increase in the autonomy of the State from that date.[8]

The classical marxist–leninist counter-thrust was not long in coming. It was provided by two leading GDR scholars, Dietrich Eichholtz and Kurt Gossweiler, after Mason had parried without too much difficulty an attack by another GDR historian, Eberhard Czichon, which contained empirical weaknesses and theoretical crudity and was premised on a number of basic misunderstandings of Mason's argument.[9] Eichholtz and Gossweiler argued that Mason's interpretation removed fascism from the realms of historical explicability, reducing it to the level of an historical accident, adding that if Mason were right it would amount to 'a complete refutation of marxist social analysis' – an over-dramatized allegation which would seem to rest on a misreading of Marx and Engels. Their own approach began by attempting a justification of the Comintern definition of fascism (despite the admitted need for greater precision and refinement), followed this with a summary tribute to Lenin's theory of imperialism and its relation to fascism, and repeated the marxist–leninist theory of state monopoly capitalism. This lengthy theoretical exposition was then followed by a relatively short 'empirical' section, centring upon the changes in 1936 and aiming to show that alterations in the political course of the Third Reich were intrinsically related to developments in the dominant factions of state monopoly capitalism. It was not enough, they argued, to see finance capital simply as the beneficiary rather than the 'inspiration and initiator' of fascist policy; rather, analysis of the changing structure of state monopoly capitalism disproved Mason's thesis and demonstrated that capital was far from relinquishing its power to the State after 1936. Instead, the Nazi State provided the ground for an intensified struggle within monopoly capitalism – a struggle reaching its peak during the war, which itself was the direct product of the aims and wishes of the most reactionary, chauvinist, and imperialist sections of finance capital.[10]

---

[8] Tim Mason, 'Primat der Industrie? – Eine Erwiderung', *Das Argument* 10 (1968), p. 199. Despite its marxist intonation, Mason's argument clearly shared much common ground with the approach of 'liberal bourgeois' historians, who, not unnaturally, welcomed this advocacy of the primacy of politics over economics by a marxist writer.

[9] Eberhard Czichon, 'Der Primat der Industrie im Kartell der nationalsozialistischen Macht', *Das Argument* 10 (1968), pp. 168–92; Dietrich Eichholtz and Kurt Gossweiler, 'Noch einmal: Politik und Wirtschaft 1933–1945', *Das Argument* 10 (1968), pp. 210–27.

[10] Eichholtz and Gossweiler, 'Noch einmal', pp. 220–7.

Did then the Nazi regime follow the interests of 'big business' in pursuing policies which culminated in war and genocide, or was it 'its own boss'? The primacy of politics or economics in the Third Reich, polarized in the debate between Mason and his GDR antagonists, has remained a central area of controversy in interpreting the Nazi dictatorship. Scholarly interpretations continue to be deeply divided – on political–ideological as well as historical–philosophical grounds.

In the dominant 'liberal–bourgeois' historiography there is little doubt about the nature of the relationship. Economic issues claim little space, for instance, in Karl Dietrich Bracher's *The German Dictatorship*, and the 'primacy of politics' question was dispatched within a single paragraph:

> The very fact that a capitalist economy could be led into war in so non-economic a fashion and mobilized fully only during the war itself (after 1941–2) proves the absolute primacy of the political goals. Here, too, Hitler was anything but an instrument of the capitalists. Their cooperation followed the same pattern found in the governmental and cultural policies: the cooperating experts and economists were instruments and objects, not originators, of this policy. Economic efficiency and primacy of politics, not capitalist, middle-class, or socialist doctrines, determined the course.[11]

In similar vein, Ernst Nolte has written of the industrialists being 'completely eliminated as a major political factor'[12] and Klaus Hildebrand of 'economy in the service of politics',[13] while Andreas Hillgruber, in a brief recapitulation of differing approaches to the history of Nazism did not even regard the economy as one of his selected areas of debate.[14] Rather more cautiously, Karl Dietrich Erdmann, in a widely-read textbook, comments: 'Scholarship – apart from soviet marxist historical writing – is agreed that a determining industrial influence on the foreign and war policy decisions of Hitler cannot be proven in the sources'.[15] Finally, a most uncompromising statement of the position can be found in a recent survey of research on the Nazi economic recovery by the English historian Richard Overy, who writes: 'Over all the internal divisions within industry stood the authority and interests of the Nazi movement itself. Industry was subordinate to the requirements of the party. Control over the whole economy passed into the state's hands during the political crisis of 1936–7 and the establishment of the Four Year Plan.'[16]

Such assertive 'primacy of politics' arguments, it might be argued, posit a far clearer distinction between the sphere of politics and that of economics than in fact exists. They further imply a clarity of purpose and intent and a decisive command-role of Hitler and the Nazi leadership which might again be subject to qualification. Finally, they level the attack at an instrumentalist

---

[11] Bracher, *The German Dictatorship* (above ch. 2 note 60), p. 416.

[12] Ernst Nolte, 'Big Business and German Politics: A Comment', *AHR* 75 (1969–70), p. 76.

[13] Hildebrand, *Das Dritte Reich*, pp. 160–1.

[14] Hillgruber, *Endlich genug?*, pp. 28–32 offers only a four-page disapproving summary of marxist/bonapartist interpretations of the 'social and economic aspects of the Third Reich'.

[15] Karl Dietrich Erdmann, *Deutschland unter der Herrschaft des Nationalsozialismus 1933–1939* (Gebhardt Handbuch der Geschichte, Band 20, Munich, 1980), pp. 141–2.

[16] Richard J. Overy, *The Nazi Economic Recovery 1932–1938* (Studies in Economic and Social History, London, 1982), p. 58.

'primacy of economics' argument which would be defended by even few marxist historians today, outside the official historiography of eastern Europe.

Most western marxist approaches to the relationship of economics and politics in the Third Reich, whatever their differences of emphasis, tend to take their starting-point either from a type of 'Bonapartist' interpretation as originally advanced, for example, by August Thalheimer, or from an adaptation of Gramsci's emphasis on the state as a form of bourgeois 'hegemony'.

Mason's original 'primacy of politics' article was itself, even if not explicitly stated, closely related to Bonapartist notions of the growth of autonomy of the executive from the economic ruling class, and his position – or variants of it – has been followed by a number of leading marxist authorities on fascism. Reinhard Kühnl, for instance, accepted that 'the fascist state had to . . . possess a certain autonomy and freedom of decision as regards the economic power groups. It could not be the organ of execution of the ruling economic power groups in their entirety, for these had no common will; but it could also not be the instrument of a single economic fraction, because otherwise a stabilization of the entire system would not have been possible'. Hence there existed a 'partial independence of the political power' from the dominant economic interests. He concluded: 'That the freedom of decision of this executive is limited by the principles of the capitalist social order, remains undisputed. Even so, it seems legitimate to speak of at least a partial autonomy of the fascist executive from its allies, that is the socially dominant upper bourgeoisie'.[17] Another prominent West German marxist historian, Eike Hennig, adopted a not dissimilar position. He spoke of a 'division of labour' of 'political power' and 'economic domination' under Nazism, and commented favourably upon Mason's thesis and upon 'Bonapartist' interpretations.[18] Alfred Sohn-Rethel, who in the early years of the Third Reich was in a unique position as a marxist 'insider' at the hub of German industrial interest representation, writes of the 'subsumption' of industrial interests under 'the fascist state dictatorship of the party' and of the 'political imprisonment of the bourgeoisie in its fascist dictatorship'.[19] He makes it clear, in his analysis of the Nazi economy published decades after its initial formulation, that this is no subjection of the capitalist class or of 'big business' in the way that the 'totalitarianism' approach of 'liberal' historians would have it. Rather, the Nazi executive and the capitalist class were bound to each other inexorably by the rules of capital itself – by the need for an exceptional form of exploitation in order to revitalize capitalism and extricate it from its great crisis. The Nazi executive's monopoly of power derived from its ability to safeguard the objective interests of the bourgeoisie by maximizing its profits in these conditions of extreme crisis of capitalism. This was done by turning away from the international market economy to a more 'absolute' form of capitalist accumulation based directly upon

[17] Kühnl, *Formen* (see ch. 2 note 13), pp. 123, 141. Kühnl's points here could, of course, be argued for any capitalist state.

[18] Eike Hennig, *Thesen zur deutschen Sozial- und Wirtschaftsgeschichte 1933 bis 1938* (Frankfurt am Main, 1973), pp. 126–8, 248–9.

[19] Alfred Sohn-Rethel, *Ökonomie und Klassenstruktur des deutschen Faschismus* (Frankfurt am Main, 1973), pp. 110–11, Engl. trans. *The Economy and Class Structure of German Fascism* (2nd edn. London, 1987).

the power of the State – upon outright repression, 'plunder', and ultimately war. Once embarked on this road, there was no going back. The process was irreversible, and the economic élites were bound to it – they were 'all in the same boat' as Schacht put it. Nazi political domination was therefore anchored in the crisis position of the capitalist bourgeoisie. But at the same time, this political domination remained dependent on the dynamic of the 'absolute' form of capitalist exploitation which had been unleashed, and therefore on the continued economic dominance of big capital.[20]

A rather different marxist approach to the relationship of capitalism and the Nazi State is advanced by Nicos Poulantzas, in a theoretical work drawing for illustration upon the historical reality of fascism in Italy and Germany, and owing more to Gramsci than any other marxist thinker.[21] Central to Poulantzas's interpretation is the notion of fascism as the most extreme form of 'exceptional capitalist state' – others being military dictatorship and bonapartist regimes. The reason why fascism should be the type of 'exceptional capitalist state' to emerge was determined by the specific nature of the class struggle, relations of production, and the particular form of political crisis. Poulantzas rejected as unsatisfactory theories of fascism not only the Comintern version of fascism as the direct agent of monopoly capital, and the interpretation (which he attributes to 'social democratic circles') of fascism as 'the political dictatorship of the petty bourgeoisie', but also bonapartist conceptions based on a notion of class equilibrium. According to Poulantzas, bonapartist views rest upon a misinterpretation of Marx's formulation of the 'opposition of State and Society' and the 'independence' of the State in relation to civil society and have led marxist theoreticians 'to attribute to the fascist State a *type* and *degree* of relative autonomy which it does not in fact possess, and in the end makes them unable to define correctly the relations between fascism and big capital. . . . This relative autonomy of the State, taken to the limit, would even mean breaking the tie between the State and the hegemonic fraction; hence completely false descriptions of fascism using the war economy – openly and for a long period – against the interests of big capital and in declared opposition to it' – a misinterpretation he associates with Mason, in company with the 'élitist' theories of Schweitzer and Neumann.[22]

Though rejected by Poulantzas in connection with bonapartist approaches, the notion of 'relative autonomy' is in fact central to his own interpretation. Fascism – i.e. the fascist party and the fascist state – has in his view a 'relative autonomy' both from the unstable power bloc of the politically dominant classes and from 'the fraction of big monopoly capital' whose dominance within the power bloc fascism has (re-)established. Fascism's relative autonomy derives on the one hand from the internal contradictions within the power alliance and on the other from the contradictions between the dominant and dominated classes. Fascism's 'complex relationship' with the 'dominated classes' is in fact 'precisely what makes fascism indispensable to mediate a re-establishment of political domination and

[20] Sohn-Rethel, pp. 90 ff., 173 ff. The quotation from Schacht is cited on p. 174.
[21] Poulantzas (see ch. 2 note 17). Jane Caplan, 'Theories of Fascism: Nicos Poulantzas as Historian', *HWJ* 3 (1977), pp. 83–100, offers an excellent, penetrating critique.
[22] Poulantzas, pp. 84–5 and note 17.

hegemony'. In other words, whereas in bonapartist theory the State derives from an equilibrium between the two main social forces, without thereby becoming a neutral mediator in the class struggle, the fascist state according to Poulantzas 'never ceases to organize political domination', possesses a far smaller 'margin for manoeuvre', and serves the objective function not of increasing its own independence from capital and the creation of a primacy of politics over economics, but of re-establishing the domination of the ruling fraction of monopoly capital. In Poulantzas's writings (not just on fascism), the political sphere – state power – always enjoys a relative auton-omy from the economic sphere – capital – and this relative autonomy is extended to an exceptional degree under fascism. But it lasts in this excep-tional degree only for a short period before the dominance of big monopoly capital is re-established.[23]

Common to all the variant marxist theories summarized here is an accep-tance of some degree of autonomy of the Nazi State from the power of even the most dominant capitalist forces. The level of autonomy posited is at its maximum in the Mason approach, where it amounts to a *primacy* of politics over economics; it is at its minimum in Poulantzas's interpretation, where it lasts only for a very short time in order to reassert the dominant position of monopoly capital. These differing marxist views are at least in agreement, therefore, that the suggestion of an *identity* between Nazism and capitalism in which the Nazi State apparatus functions as the executive instrument of the ruling class of the most extreme sections of monopoly capital is simplistic and mistaken. In fact, even GDR historians have softened the earlier rigid instrumentalist line, though there is no retreat from the notion that 'in the last instance' the economic base – the interests of the monopoly bourgeoisie – determines the political course of action.

The question, therefore, which each of these marxist interpretations poses is: what weight can be attached to the concept of 'relative autonomy' as an explanatory factor in understanding the unfolding of Nazi policy and the relationship of Nazism and capitalism? Subsumed within this are a number of other problems posed by marxist analyses, some of a more empirical nature. Do marxist interpretations, for instance, accord sufficient impor-tance to Nazi ideological aims? Are they in danger, even granting the 'rela-tive autonomy' of the State, of grossly underestimating the 'Hitler factor' – not only Hitler's actual executive role (however it is defined) but also his functional position as integrating element and charismatic focus of mass plebiscitary support? Given the latter, do marxist analyses tend to exaggerate the undoubted importance of the big capital bloc and underrate correspondingly other power blocs – in particular the army leadership, the party with its mass base, and the rapidly developing power-centre in the SS-police apparatus? Do they pay sufficient attention to the changing chro-nology of relations between Nazism and the industrial élite, and to the complexities of decision-making processes in the Third Reich? (Poulantzas's historical treatment of the dictatorship period in Germany contains, for example, some serious empirical flaws which vitiate his periodization and gravely endanger his theoretical conclusions.[24]) As regards decision-making

---

[23] Poulantzas, pp. 85–6; and see Caplan, pp. 86–8.
[24] See Caplan, pp. 87 ff.

processes, do marxist analyses clearly separate direction, influence, and execution – an important distinction, not least in economic policy-making – and do they tend to assume that partial identity of aim equals influence? Finally, even accepting that exceptional forms of capitalism (Sohn-Rethel) existed under an exceptional form of capitalist state (Poulantzas), do marxist theories underrate or ignore the extent to which Nazism was prompting the growth of economic organization which had little to do with classical capitalism and, in the eyes of some authorities,[25] was moving in the direction of post-capitalist economics?

The evaluation and interpretation which follows attempts to take account of some of these critical questions alongside the problems posed by 'liberal' approaches to the 'primacy of politics'.

## Evaluation

A starting-point of analysis is to question whether the polarization into 'primacy of politics' or 'primacy of economics' does not amount to an extreme oversimplification of a complex structural interrelationship between the policies of the Nazi State and the interests of German capital. The reduction to alternatives of 'politics' and 'economics' both impermissibly narrows the concept of 'politics' and operates on a crude and misleading dichotomy between 'state' and 'society'. The tenor of recent work on the Nazi economy has been to suggest instead that the closely interwoven aims and interests of the Nazi leadership and of German capital influenced and affected each other, making it difficult to separate a specifically 'political' and specifically 'economic' sphere, and therefore to distinguish a clear 'primacy'. In William Carr's words, 'ideological, strategic, and economic factors are too closely intermeshed in a country's foreign policy to permit of a clinical separation',[26] while Hans-Erich Volkmann outrightly rejects the question of 'primacy' as now a redundant one.[27] Volkmann prefers to speak of 'a far-reaching congruity of interest' between the State and major industry, of a (partial) 'identity of interest of the economy and National Socialism', of such a close interlinkage of politics and economics in the Nazi State that one can describe it as a 'coercive identity'. He refers further to the 'interweaving' of the political–economic substructure, and to a 'mutual dependence of political leadership and industry' also during the War itself. Nor, in his view, did the 'common cause' which Germany's economic élites entered into with the Nazis from the turn of the year 1932–3 onwards develop into a 'primacy of politics' after 1936.[28] Rather, the State and the leading sectors of industry merged even more

[25] E.g. Winkler, *Revolution* (see ch. 2 note 13), pp. 100, 154 note 90; Saage, *Faschismustheorien* (see ch. 2 note 33), pp. 72-3; Gert Schäfer, 'Ökonomische Bedingungen des Faschismus', *Blätter für deutsche und internationale Politik* 15 (1970), pp. 1260 ff.: Alan S. Milward, 'Fascism and the Economy', in Laqueur (see ch. 2 note 12), pp. 435, 443-4.
[26] William Carr, *Arms, Autarky, and Aggression* (2nd edn, London, 1979), p. 65.
[27] Hans-Erich Volkmann, 'Politik, Wirtschaft und Aufrüstung unter dem Nationalsozialismus', in Manfred Funke, ed., *Hitler, Deutschland und die Mächte* (Düsseldorf, 1978), pp. 279, 289.
[28] Volkmann, 'Politik, Wirtschaft und Aufrüstung', pp. 273, 279-80, 289.

closely than before, so that before and especially during the war initiative, responsibility, and administrative control over the functioning of the economy – and with this extensive influence over political and military decisions inextricably bound up with the economy – passed to private industry. There developed, therefore, according to this interpretation, an increasing blurring of the boundaries between state economic administration and the sphere of the private economy. Volkmann argues, in distinction to the line of GDR historians, that the Nazi regime was not put into power by German capital in order to extend Germany's economy through territorial expansion at the behest of German industry. But, nevertheless, once in power the Nazis had no need to subject the economy also to its political demands. Rather, 'the leading German economic circles placed themselves in the service of the power political intentions of the German fascist government in order in this way to attain a closed economic area, largely independent of world economic vicissitudes, in which a high measure of autarky could be effected'.[29]

Such an argument is plausible and carries conviction. Nevertheless, as Volkmann's hint of the economy functioning 'at the service' of the political intentions of the regime appears tacitly to admit, the acceptance of interdependence and affinity of interest still leaves open the explanation for the peculiar thrust, dynamic, and character of Nazi policy. Unquestionably, the alliance between the Nazi leadership and the industrial–military complex, cemented by the rearmament and expansionist programme, lasted into the final phase of the Third Reich as each of the partners found itself increasingly bound to the logic of the development they had set in train. But it might still be claimed that the weighting within this 'alliance' tipped gradually but inexorably towards the Nazi leadership, so that at the crucial junctures of development in the Third Reich the political and ideological demands of the Nazi leaders came to play an increasingly dominant role in determining policy. In fact, the ultimately self-destructive irrational momentum of the Nazi regime seems only explicable on this premiss: the faster the regime careered madly out of control and towards the abyss, the greater was the scope for political–ideological initiatives out of sequence with and in the end directly negating the potential of the socio-economic system to reproduce itself.

In order to understand this process, the position and role of 'big business' has to be located with the context of the complex and changing multidimensional ('polycratic') power-structures in the Third Reich. Fundamental to this is the need to break away both from the 'totalitarianism' model of a centralized command economy and monolithic state in the hands of Hitler and a clique of Nazi leaders, and from the alternative, almost equally monolithic, model of the Nazi State as the direct representative and most aggressive form of rule of finance capital. Far more illuminating as an interpretative concept is the notion, first formulated by Franz Neumann and more recently expanded and developed by Peter Hüttenberger, of the Nazi

[29] Volkmann, 'Politik, Wirtschaft und Aufrüstung', pp. 290–1; Hans-Erich Volkmann, 'Zum Verhältnis von Großwirtschaft und NS-Regime im Zweiten Weltkrieg', in Karl Dietrich Bracher *et al.*, eds., *Nationalsozialistische Diktatur 1933–1945. Eine Bilanz* (Bonn, 1983), pp. 480–508.

regime as an unwritten 'pact' (or 'alliance') between different but inter-dependent blocs in a 'power-cartel'.[30] This cartel was initially a triad composed of the Nazi bloc (comprising the various component parts of the Nazi movement), 'big business' (including large landowners), and the army. From around 1936 it could be said to have acquired a fourth grouping as the Nazi bloc itself fell into two main subdivisions around the party organization proper and the increasingly powerful SS–Police–SD complex.[31] Though the blocs in the 'power-cartel' remained intact – and their interdependence sustained – until the end of the Third Reich, their relationship to each other and weighting within the 'cartel' altered during the course of the dictatorship. Broadly speaking, the change took place in the direction of an extension of the power of the Nazi bloc, and in particular of the SS–Police–SD complex, with a corresponding weakening – though never to the point of insignificance or complete submission – of the relative positions within the 'cartel' of 'big business' and the armed forces leadership.

The 'pact' of 1933 was based upon the mutual interests but not complete identity of the Nazi bloc, 'big business', and the army. The bond of alliance between Nazism and the army provided for a free hand for the new Nazi rulers in radically reorganizing Germany's internal political order in return for an acknowledgement of the Reichswehr as 'the most important institution in the State' together with the pledging of a comprehensive programme of rearmament which met goals held dear by the army throughout Weimar.[32] Massive rearmament came to be the main catalyst which assured the dynamic fusion of interests of army, industry, and Nazi leadership.[33] Initially, German 'big business', divided in itself and with partially contradictory economic aims, was far from uniformly or wholly enthusiastic about giving total priority to rearmament.[34] However, the crushing of the Left, the free hand accorded to industry, the reordering of industrial relations, and in general the new political climate, formed the basis of a positive relationship between the Nazi government and 'big business' – a relationship which became cemented by the stimulus to the economy through the work creation programme and then in growing measure by the massive profits to be derived from the armaments boom.

Though forming the most dynamic element within the 'power cartel', the Nazi bloc – possessing direct control neither over economic production nor over military power – was in a relatively weak position during the early years of the dictatorship. The strength of Nazism's 'partners' was reflected in the pressures prompting the destruction in June 1934 of the threat posed by the SA to the established order. Furthermore, the serious economic difficulties which confronted the regime in mid 1934, aggravated by economic repercussions abroad caused by the anti-Jewish measures, and coupled with a still precarious diplo-

---

[30] Neumann (see ch. 2 note 5); Peter Hüttenberger, 'Nationalsozialistische Polykratie', *GG* 2 (1976), pp. 417–42.

[31] Huttenberger, pp. 423 ff., 432 ff.

[32] See Wilhelm Deist, *The Wehrmacht and German Rearmament* (London, 1981), pp. 21 ff.

[33] See Dieter Petzina, 'Hauptprobleme der deutschen Wirtschaftspolitik', *VfZ* 15 (1967), p. 50, and the contribution by Hans-Erich Volkmann to Wilhelm Deist *et al.*, *Das Deutsche Reich und der Zweite Weltkrieg*, vol.1 (Stuttgart, 1979), pp. 208 ff.

[34] See Michael Geyer, 'Etudes in Political History: Reichswehr, NSDAP, and the Seizure of Power', in Stachura (see note 1), p. 114.

matic position, meant that the regime's room for manoeuvre in this period was closely circumscribed by economic as well as strictly political factors.

In these conditions, the relative strength of the 'bargaining position' of 'big business' within the 'power cartel' was assured. It was reflected in the position of Hjalmar Schacht, President of the Reichsbank and from 1934 as Economics Minister one of the most powerful men in the Nazi State. However, Schacht's key position in controlling foreign trade and exchange – and therefore the raw material imports so essential for the armaments industries – was an obvious source of potentially serious conflict, since it meant intervention in an area – armaments policy – which was absolutely central to the interests not only of Hitler and the Nazi leadership but also of the armed forces and important and influential sectors of industry (in particular the electro-chemicals lobby centred upon IG-Farben).[35] Schacht was gradually coming, therefore, to represent only one – and as it transpired not the most powerful – wing of industry concerned with improving Germany's international trading position, and losing at the same time the support of the increasingly strong industrial grouping which backed and stood most to gain from autarkic policies. At first imperceptibly, but inexorably, Schacht's power was on the wane. And by the time the immanent tension in the Nazi economy between the demands of rearmament and the demands of consumption broke into full crisis in the spring and summer of 1936, the power relations within the original 'cartel' had already therefore begun to alter shape. The clash within 'big business' between those supporting the Schacht line and those pushing for accelerated autarkic policies – with obvious corollaries for both domestic and especially foreign policy – can be said to have weakened (at least temporarily) the position of industry as a whole. Meanwhile, the position of the Nazi leadership, and of Hitler in particular, was immeasurably stronger than it had been in 1933, and a successful mastering of the crisis contained the potential for a further strengthening of the Nazi bloc within the overall power constellation in the Third Reich.[36]

The resolution of the immediate crisis – though it stored up future massive economic problems for the regime – was the introduction of the Four Year Plan, announced at the party rally in September 1936 and setting Germany on an accelerated rearmament and autarkic policy as preparation for war. It was a decision in which politics and economics, ideology and material interest, were inextricably intermeshed.

Hitler's secret memorandum justifying the Plan – which was significantly given only to Göring, Blomberg, and (much later) Speer but not to Schacht – reads like the clearest demonstration of a 'primacy of politics', emphasizing that 'the nation does not live for the economy', but rather that 'the economy, economic leaders, and theories . . . all owe unqualified service in this struggle for the self-assertion of our nation'.[37] However, it has been rightly noted that Hitler's intervention 'should not be seen primarily as

[35] See Hüttenberger, p. 433. On IG-Farben, see now Peter Hayes, *Industry and Ideology: IG Farben in the Nazi Era* (Cambridge, 1987).

[36] Hüttenberger, pp. 433-5.

[37] Jeremy Noakes and Geoffrey Pridham, eds., *Nazism 1919-1945. A Documentary Reader*, 3 vols. (Exeter, 1983-8), vol. 2, p. 283.

a capricious meedling in economic matters by a restless dictator'.[38] Rather, Hitler's memorandum came at the end of a process in which the dominant economic position had been grasped by the chemicals giant IG-Farben, which had forged an axis in particular with the Air Ministry and with the party through the key figure of Göring. IG-Farben had provided the technical details for the Four Year Plan, and their top management came to be completely merged with State officials in the running of the Plan. It would also be mistaken to imagine that industry was irredeemably split as a result of the introduction of the Plan. Heavy industry suffered more a temporary setback than the permanent defeat which Mason posited.[39] The threat posed by the setting up in 1937 of the state-owned steel corporation, the Reichswerke-Hermann-Göring, in the teeth of opposition from Germany's steel barons, can be exaggerated. The high production costs of the state concern in fact held steel prices high; and far from indicating an onslaught on private ownership, it coincided with a major 're-privatization' wave, including the return to private hands of the mammoth United Steelworks. Finally, the blockage in iron production which the state concern had been established to by-pass was over before its production had got under way.[40]

Research has done much, therefore, to qualify the notion that the Four Year Plan marked a sharp divide in the influence of industry and the breakthrough to a decisive 'primacy of politics'. At the same time, it is still significant that the economic reorientation in 1936 was carried out initially against the wishes of important sectors of the once mighty heavy industry, and that as a result of the Four Year Plan and the replacement of Schacht by Göring as the dominant figure in the economy, the constraints of what might be regarded as the previous 'economic establishment' on the Nazi leadership diminished sharply. Moreover, the foundation of the Reichswerke-Hermann-Göring in 1937, if marking no long-term threat to private industry, did register the fact, as Petzina pointed out, 'that private industrial interests were not automatically identical with the interests of the regime, and that in a case of conflict the regime would not shy away from effecting its aims against the resistance of sections of heavy industry'.[41] As Milward put it, 'nothing could have more clearly demonstrated that, however sympathetic to the business world and however dependent on it, the Nazi government had its own interests which it was prepared to pursue'.[42]

With the successful mastery of the crisis of 1936, the Nazi leadership gained an enhanced position of strength within the 'power cartel' which

---

[38] Carr, *Arms, Autarky, and Aggression*, p. vi.

[39] Mason, 'Primacy', p. 185. Hüttenberger (p. 434) rightly points out that the autarky conflict did not result in a split in the political position of 'big business'.

[40] George W. F. Hallgarten and Joachim Radkau, *Deutsche Industrie und Politik von Bismarck bis in die Gegenwart* (Reinbek bei Hamburg, 1981), pp. 255–8; see also Petzina, *Autarkiepolitik*, pp. 104 ff.

[41] Petzina, *Autarkiepolitik*, p. 105. For the economic development of the Reichswerke-Hermann-Göring, see Richard J. Overy, 'Göring's "Multi-National Empire" ', in Alice Teichova and P.L. Cottrell, eds., *International Business and Central Europe, 1918–1939* (Leicester, 1983), pp. 269–98. And for the circumstances of their foundation, see Overy's more recent article, 'Heavy Industry and the State in Nazi Germany: The Reichswerke Crisis', *European History Quarterly* 15 (1985), pp. 313–40.

[42] Milward, 'Fascism and the Economy', p. 434.

brought with it an increased priority to and scope for ideological considerations in the formulation of policy. This was particularly the case in the
spheres of foreign policy, where the traditional authority of the Foreign
Office had diminished, and strategic–military planning, where the *Wehrmacht*'s influence had also waned. By early 1938, in fact, the SS–Police–SD
bloc was powerful enough to weaken the *Wehrmacht*'s position still further
by instigating the Blomberg–Fritsch affair, a symbolic turning-point in the
army's transition from a power to a mere functional élite.[43] Certainly, the
influence of leading business circles on German foreign policy in the later
1930s, as indeed earlier, has often been underestimated.[44] Clearly, too,
German expansion into Austria and Czechoslovakia was both a logical and
necessary step economically as well as strategically. German firms profited
hugely from this expansion, as did some major concerns from the 'aryanization' of the economy in 1938. Ideological, strategic, and economic interests
still went hand in hand. But the impetus was increasingly shifting towards a
high-risk policy in which the inbuilt and unstoppable momentum of the arms
race harnessed to the ideological expansionism of the Nazi leadership shaped
the contours within which economic interest operated.

In the wake of the forced rearmament policy from 1936 onwards, Germany's economic problems – chronic shortages of foreign exchange, raw
materials, and labour, strains, blockages, over-heating, balance of payments
difficulties, inflationary tendencies – mounted alarmingly. Expansionism
as the only solution to Germany's otherwise gloomy economic prospects was
a central theme of Hitler's monologue to the leaders of the armed forces in
November 1937.[45] Hitler repeated his remarks on the threatening economic
pressures in a speech to the armed forces' commanders in August 1939, days
before the attack on Poland, when he stated that for Germany it was easy to
make decisions: 'We have nothing to lose; we have everything to gain'.
Because of our restrictions, our economic situation is such that we can only
hold out for a few more years. Göring can confirm this. We have no other
choice, we must act'.[46] The dire prognoses of Germany's economic future
without expansion were coming from all sides of industry, agriculture, and
from the *Wehrmacht*'s Economic Inspectorate. Strong though the evidence
is for this mounting economic crisis, it is weak in suggesting that economic
pressures played the decisive role in affecting either the timing or the reasons
for the outbreak of war. Strategic considerations took first rank, while the
increasingly critical economic situation, itself deriving in no small measure
from the political–ideological premises of the regime, appears to have played
chiefly the role of confirming Hitler in the view that his original diagnosis of

[43] See Hüttenberger, p. 435; and Klaus-Jürgen Müller, *Armee, Politik und Gesellschaft in
Deutschland 1933–1945* (Paderborn, 1970), pp. 39–47, Engl. trans. *Army, Politics, and Society
in Germany, 1933–1945* (Manchester, 1984).
[44] See Hallgarten and Radkau, Part II, chs. 3–4.
[45] Noakes and Pridham, vol. 3, pp. 680–7. On the 'Hossbach memorandum', see now
Jonathan Wright and Paul Stafford, 'Hitler, Britain and the Hoßbach Memorandum',
MGM 42 (1987), pp. 77–123 (abbreviated version in *History Today* (March 1988), pp. 11–17).
[46] Noakes and Pridham, vol. 3, p. 740.

Germany's plight was correct, and that time was running out.[47] Certainly, the most aggressive, expansionist noises were emanating from 'big business' circles at this time – prominent, though by no means isolated, the imperialist demands of IG-Farben boss Karl Krauch. And obviously, expansion fed expansion in economic as well as political–military terms. But compared with Austria and Czechoslovakia, as Radkau points out, the attack on Poland 'had relatively little to do with the main lines of interest of the concerns' and 'generally the east was for capital much less attractive than, say, the south-east'.[48] This did not of course hinder in any way German firms from profiting massively from the ruthless exploitation of conquered Poland.

Economic determinants continued during the war itself to be inseparably interlocked with ideological and military–strategic factors in shaping the character and pattern of German aggression. And the chronic problems of availability and allocation of raw materials and labour meant a voice for the leaders of the dominant war industries which could not be ignored in the shaping of policy decisions. Given the particular development of German capitalism during the Third Reich, especially since 1936, the imperialist war of plunder was a logical necessity – increasingly the only option available;[49] German industry was structurally implicated in the policy decisions which culminated in destruction and inhumanity on a scale unprecedented in Europe.

It is necessary, however, to distinguish between the economy as a structural determinant in helping to frame the course and character of aggression, and the specific needs and perceived interests of particular groups within the economy. Much emphasis on 'the primacy of politics' concentrates rather simplistically and misleadingly on merely the question of whether decisions in the Third Reich were taken directly in the interests of German capitalists. This line of argument remains in essence little more than a superficial attack on naïve versions of the instrumentalist 'agent theory' – of the Nazi leadership as the puppets of 'big business'. Reality was somewhat more complex, as the decision to invade the Soviet Union illustrates.

[47] Carr, *Arms, Autarky, and Aggression*, p. 65. The evidence for the economic crisis is summarized in Timothy W. Mason, 'Innere Krise und Angriffskrieg 1938/1939', in F. Forstmeier and H.-E. Volkmann, eds., *Wirtschaft und Rüstung am Vorabend des Zweiten Weltkrieges* (Düsseldorf, 1975), pp. 158–88. For criticism and qualification of Mason's emphasis upon the internal crisis as the decisive factor in the timing of the war, see Ludolf Herbst, 'Die Krise des nationalsozialistischen Regimes am Vorabend des Zweiten Weltkrieges und die forcierte Aufrüstung. Eine Kritik', *VfZ* 26 (1978), pp. 347–92; Heinrich August Winkler, 'Vom Mythos der Volksgemeinschaft', *AfS* 17 (1977), pp. 488–9; Jost Dülffer, 'Der Beginn des Krieges 1939: Hitler, die innere Krise und das Mächtesystem', *GG* 2 (1976), pp. 443–70; Milward, 'Fascism and the Economy', p. 437; Richard J. Overy, 'Hitler's War and the German Economy: A Reinterpretation', *EcHR* 35 (1982), pp. 272–91; and Overy's more recent article, 'Germany, "Domestic Crisis" and War in 1939', *Past and Present* 116 (1987), pp. 138–68. Tim Mason has responded to criticism of his interpretation in an, as yet, unpublished paper 'The Domestic Dynamics of Nazi Conquests: a reply to critics'. A separate reply to Richard Overy's criticism is forthcoming in *Past and Present*.
[48] Hallgarten and Radkau, pp. 302–3, 366–8.
[49] For emphasis upon the Blitzkrieg as the only possible strategy available to Germany, see Alan S. Milward, 'Der Einfluß ökonomischer und nicht-ökonomischer Faktoren auf die Strategie des Blitzkriegs', in Forstmeier and Volkmann, pp. 189–201, here esp. pp. 200–1. The conception of a 'Blitzkrieg economy' is wholly rejected by Overy, 'Hitler's War', and more fully in ' "Blitzkriegswirtschaft"?' *VfZ* 36 (1988), pp. 379–435.

In this decision, too, ideological motivation can hardly be separated as an autonomous factor from questions of military–strategic and economic necessity. It is too simple to look no further than Hitler's ideological obsession – important though this was – in explaining the reasons for the invasion of the Soviet Union in 1941. Unquestionably, the ideological hatred of 'Jewish Bolshevism' which had been pumped into Germans for years under the Nazi regime provided for the horrifically brutal character of the 'war of annihilation' in the east. But – a point to which we shall return in a later chapter – strategic considerations revolving around the unfinished war in the West and especially the prospects of combating the USA also played a crucial role in the thinking of Hitler and the Nazi and military leadership about the Soviet Union in 1940–1. Last, but certainly not least, there was the economic dimension. The German dependence upon raw materials from the Soviet Union, and the critical threat to grain and above all else to oil supplies posed by Soviet expansion in east and south-east Europe following the Nazi–Soviet Pact of 1939 meant that the entire German war effort was endangered if the Soviet Union remained unconquered. The possibility of the Soviet air-force destroying the vital Rumanian oil-fields, providing more than half of German supplies, was decisive. As Hitler told his generals in January 1941, 'in the era of air power Russia can turn the Rumanian oil fields into an expanse of smoking debris . . . and the life of the Axis depends on those oil fields'.[50]

This obvious importance of the economic dimension to decision-making on military–strategic questions is, however, not necessarily synonymous with the perceived needs of German industrialists. Joachim Radkau, a left-wing West German historian, argues on the basis of a detailed study of available sources, that contrary to expectation there is little evidence of complete identity of interest between Nazism and 'big business' in the preparation of the attack on the Soviet Union: 'Disregarding ideological anti-communism, in general no hostility towards Soviet Russia can be recognized from the practical wishes and recommendations of business – often indeed a striving for improvement in relations. Business [*die Wirtschaft*] played a much clearer role in advancing the Stalin–Hitler Pact than in preparing the attack on the Soviet Union'. Trade with Russia – not least for heavy industry – had been important in the 1920s and early 1930s; the evidence which Radkau assembles – though it does not speak wholly in unison – suggests that some prominent sections of industry were placing their hopes in a revival of economic links rather than in the ideologically motivated smashing of the Soviet Union, and that many industrialists were not enamoured with the investment risks and likely benefits to be gained in the newly-conquered 'Lebensraum'.[51] Again, however, such views did not limit in any way whatsoever the readiness to exploit in the most barbarous fashion the human as well as the material resources of the conquered territories. Furthermore, such views were out of step with the unstoppable momentum – economic as well as military – of the Nazi war. The dominant economic forces in Germany were completely at one with this war effort. The collabo-

50  Cited in Norman Rich, *Hitler's War Aims* (2 vols, London, 1973–4), vol. 1, p. 207. See also Hallgarten and Radkau, p. 309.
51  Hallgarten and Radkau, pp. 383 ff. See also Winkler, *Revolution*, pp. 99, 153–4 note 89.

ration of the rest was assured by the fact that there was no escape from the course of events which they themselves had helped initiate and had fostered: they were committed to flourish or perish with the Nazi regime.

The ace in the hand of proponents of a 'primacy of politics' approach is always taken to be the extermination of the Jews – on the face of it, the most blatant refutation of the view that the interests of 'big business' were behind Nazi policy. Indeed, the Ministry for the Occupied Eastern Territories already expressly stated in autumn 1941 that 'economic considerations are to be regarded as fundamentally irrelevant in the settlement of the [Jewish] problem'.[52] And, as Mason pointed out in his 'primacy of politics' essay, 'among the first Polish Jews who were gassed in the extermination camps were thousands of skilled metal workers from Polish armament factories'.[53]

The deployment of scarce transport facilities to ferry human cargo across Europe for instant extermination at a time when German industry was desperate for manpower – even though some Jewish labour did continue to be used almost to the end of the war – was hardly compatible with 'rational' economic interest. However, as we shall bring out more fully in a later chapter, it would be a distortion to remove the 'Final Solution' from the material as well as the ideological context of the complex development which led to Auschwitz. 'Big business' was largely indifferent to early anti-Jewish measures in the Nazi State, except where German foreign trade was adversely affected by negative responses abroad. Such criticisms on economic grounds of the anti-Jewish 'boycott movement' and of wild terror actions against Jews were voiced, for instance, by the Economics Minister Schacht in 1935.[54] Under the growing pressure of the armaments economy, however, 'big business' had a direct interest in the acquisition of Jewish capital and keenly promoted the 'aryanization' of Jewish concerns in late 1937 and 1938.[55] Moreover, the expanding power and autonomy within the overall power structure of the regime of the SS–Police–SD complex, which by the end of 1938 had gained control over the implementation of anti-Jewish policy, meant that anti-Jewish measures now acquired a rapidly increasing momentum of their own. With the massive extension of the 'Jewish Question' in the Occupied Territories and the administratively insoluble character of the 'problem', the inner dynamic of a course of development which could by now only logically end in physical extermination could not be checked. In any case, there was still at this stage no contradiction between the relative autonomy of the SS apparatus within the regime and the interests of German capital. Germany's major industrial concerns were more than willing to take advantage of the concentration of Jewish labour in the Polish ghettos, with a free hand for total exploitation at absolutely minimal cost. Whatever 'wastage' took place was bearable in the period of expansion, when abundant slave labour to satisfy the needs of the whole German economy seemed close

[52] Noakes and Pridham, vol. 3, p. 1098.
[53] Mason, 'Primacy', p. 195.
[54] Uwe Dietrich Adam, *Judenpolitik im Dritten Reich* (Düsseldorf, 1972), pp. 123–4; Karl A. Schleunes, *The Twisted Road to Auschwitz. Nazi Policy toward German Jews, 1933–1939* (Urbana/Chicago/London, 1970), pp. 153 ff.
[55] Schleunes, pp. 159 ff.; Helmut Genschel, *Die Verdrängung der Juden aus der Wirtschaft im Dritten Reich* (Göttingen, 1966), pp. 222 ff.

at hand.[56] By the time the course of the war – and with it the prospects and interests of German industry – had changed dramatically, wholesale physical extermination of the Jews, which had gradually crystallized as the solution to a growing administrative nightmare arising from the 'problem' the Nazi rulers had created for themselves, was in full swing and unstoppable.

The extermination of the Jews was, therefore, *ultimately* a 'policy' which contradicted economic rationality. But it emerged as the final stage in a process which for long was compatible with, even where not directly in the interests of, German capital. The 'Final Solution' became a possibility through the conditions of war and brutal conquest. The obsession with the 'Jewish Question' chiefly belonged to the Nazi bloc within the 'power cartel' of the Third Reich. However, the other power élites showed no hesitation in helping to implement anti-Jewish measures and to turn ideological obsession into policy decisions. Above all, *all* sections of the 'power cartel' worked to bring about the barbarous war of conquest which made genocide an attainable reality rather than a lunatic vision.

German industry's direct implication and collaboration in the Nazi plunder, exploitation, destruction, and mass murder in the Occupied Territories continued to the end. Whereas certain groups within the armed forces and the old aristocracy underwent a development from initial reserve to outright antipathy towards the Nazi regime, culminating in their involvement in the plot against Hitler on 20 July 1944, industrial leaders were notably missing from resistance circles. Yet by the last year of the war, it was becoming increasingly apparent to 'big business' that the complete abyss of destruction which was looming was the contradiction of any 'rational' economic policy. Even so, the divorce between the radical nihilism of the Nazi bloc and the material interests of German industry only became total during the last phase of the war, in the wild lashings of the regime in its death-throes. A symbolically decisive moment, as Alan Milward points out, occurred in January 1944 'when the Führer supported [Labour Plenipotentiary] Sauckel's impossible plans to deport a further million workers from France during that year against the advice of Speer and the Ministry of War Production to organize more war production in the occupied territories. From that moment the position of the Ministry of War Production and of the businessmen who ran it became increasingly weaker than that of the more radically fascist parts of the administration. The business circles which had sought to control the movement in 1933 now had their most pessimistic fears fulfilled; they had themselves become the plaything of a political revolution'.[57]

Until the last stages of the war, the benefits of the Third Reich to all those sections of industry and finance connected with armaments production were colossal. Undistributed profits of limited liability companies were four times higher in 1939 than they had been in 1928.[58] The monopoly concerns were the

---

56 Kurt Pätzold, 'Von der Vertreibung zum Genozid. Zu den Ursachen, Triebkräften und Bedingungen der antijüdischen Politik des faschistischen deutschen Imperialismus', in Eichholtz and Gossweiler, *Faschismusforschung* (see ch. 1 note 27), pp. 181–208, here pp. 206–8.

57 Milward, 'Fascism and the Economy', pp. 434–5. The growing gulf between the interests of the regime and those of a crucial industry, that of coal, are well demonstrated in John R. Gillingham. *Industry and Politics in the Third Reich* (London, 1985).

58 Dietmar Petzina, *Die deutsche Wirtschaft in der Zwischenkriegszeit* (Wiesbaden, 1977), p. 141; Milward, 'Fascism and the Economy', p. 435.

greatest single winners – and in prime place the chemicals giant IG-Farben, whose annual net profit, which had stagnated between 1933 and 1935, doubled in 1936 from 70 to 140 million RM, rocketed to 300 million RM by 1940, and doubtless reached stratospheric heights – though these are undocumented – thereafter.[59] The mammoth profits of the major concerns were no incidental by-product of Nazism, whose philosophy was closely tied in with provision of a free hand for private industry and eulogization of the entrepreneurial spirit.[60] Private industry was indispensable to the rearmament effort, and this gave its representatives a very considerable bargaining power, which they did not hesitate to use to their advantage throughout the Third Reich. However, it is important to recall the distinction between the initiation, execution, and exploitation of policy. I have argued here that while major capitalist enterprise could massively increase its profits through Nazi policy, control over the execution of policy moved unmistakably towards the specifically 'Nazi bloc' in the 'power cartel'. And as the groups in the 'Nazi bloc' gained the upper hand in policy execution, so also the initiation of policy in crucial areas with a direct bearing on the economy shifted inexorably away from 'big business', though coming only at a late stage to stand diametrically in opposition to the prime capitalist interest in its own reproduction. By then, the level of intervention by the Nazi State in both labour and capital markets, coupled with the autarkic exclusion of the new German *imperium* from world markets, had certainly promoted a capitalism quite differently structured from that analysed by Marx.[61] However, speculation about the future nature and role of capitalism in a victorious Nazi 'new order' seems vacuous. Ultimately, the madly escalating nihilistic dynamic of Nazism was incompatible with the lasting construction and reproduction of any economic order.

In the preceding analysis, I have attempted to break away from what are in my view oversimplistic alternative interpretations – the 'primacy of politics' or 'primacy of economics' – of the complex relationship of Nazism and 'big business' in the Third Reich. To insist that 'in the last instance' economic factors determine, seems indeed – to say the least – an inadequate explanation of the growing paramountcy of Nazism's radical nihilism over 'rational' economic interest. At the same time, the classic 'liberal' interpretation of the 'primacy of politics', posited implicitly or explicitly on notions of the 'totalitarian' control over an economy 'in the service' of a single-minded dictatorship, is scarcely more convincing in its simplification of the power structure of the Third Reich and its inbuilt overemphasis upon the personality and ideology of Hitler. This, however, and the contrasting interpretation offered here, based upon an understanding of the 'polycratic' character of the 'power cartel' in the Third Reich, raises a new set of questions revolving around the place and function of Hitler in the government of Nazi Germany. The next chapters focus upon this central problem of interpretation.

---

[59] Hallgarten and Radkau, p. 262.
[60] See Hallgarten and Radkau, pp. 227 ff., 269 ff.
[61] Milward goes so far as to claim ('Fascism and the Economy', p. 435) that fascist regimes did not preserve capitalism, but 'changed the rules of the game so that a new system was emerging'.

# 4

# Hitler: 'Master in the Third Reich' or 'Weak Dictator'?

Locating Hitler's role and function within the Nazi system of rule is less straightforward than initially it may seem. Indeed, it has become a central problem of interpretation in a debate between leading historians of the Third Reich – a debate which, it has been said, sometimes resembles in its complexities the theological wrangles of the Middle Ages,[1] and which certainly contains a degree of rancour extending beyond the conventional disagreements of historians. The unusually heated and sometimes bitter tone of the debate[2] reflects in some ways the three dimensions – historical–philosophical, political–ideological, and moral – of writing on Nazism (especially in West Germany) which were outlined in chapter 1. Above all, the moral issue – the feeling that the evil of the central figure of the Third Reich is not being adequately portrayed, that Hitler was underestimated by contemporaries and is now being trivialized by some historians – lies at the root of the conflict and determines the character of the debate. The moral issue is itself indissoluble from questions about historical method and philosophy – how to write the history of Nazism – which in turn are inseparable from political and ideological value-judgements also relating to present-day society.

The key issue in historical–philosophical terms is the role of the individual in shaping the course of historical development, as against the limitations on the individual's freedom of action imposed by impersonal 'structural determinants'. In the present case, this focuses upon the question of whether the terrible events of the Third Reich are chiefly to be explained through the personality, ideology, and will of Hitler, or whether the Dictator himself was not at least in part a (willing) 'prisoner' of forces, of which he was the

---

[1] John Fox, 'Adolf Hitler: The Continuing Debate', *International Affairs* 55 (1979), p. 261.

[2] See the rancorous exchanges prompted by Klaus Hildebrand, 'Nationalsozialismus ohne Hitler?', *GWU* 31 (1980), pp. 289–305: 'Externus', 'Hildebrands Lied – oder: Wie die GWU ihre Leser informiert', *Geschichtsdidaktik* 5 (1980), pp. 325–7; K.D. Erdmann, 'Antwort an einen Dunkelmann: Wie informiert GWU ihre Leser?', *GWU* 32 (1981), pp. 197–8; Klaus Hildebrand, 'Noch einmal: Zur Interpretation des Nationalsozialismus', *GWU* 32 (1981), pp. 199–204; 'Externus', 'Die GWU und ihr Frontberichterstatter: Fortsetzung eines "Gedankenaustausches" ', *Geschichtsdidaktik* 6 (1981), pp. 233–8; Wolfgang J. Mommsen, 'Die "reine Wahrheit" über das nationalsozialistische Herrschaftssystem?', *GWU* 32 (1981), pp. 738–41; and Klaus Hildebrand, 'Die verfolgende Unschuld', *GWU* 32 (1981), p. 742. The tone is upheld in Hofer's later essay (see ch. 1 note 2). Hildebrand's original piece was a one-sided report on a conference staged by the German Historical Institute, London, at Windsor in 1979, which highlighted the huge divides in interpretation of the Third Reich, especially among West German historians. The conference papers published in Hirschfeld and Kettenacker (see ch. 1 note 23), some considerably revised, scarcely convey the acrid debates which accompanied some of them during the conference.

instrument rather than the creator, and whose dynamic swept him too along in its momentum. The historiographical positions are graphically polarized in the frequently-cited comment of the American historian Norman Rich, that 'the point cannot be stressed too strongly: Hitler was master in the Third Reich',[3] and in the diametrically opposed interpretation of Hans Mommsen, of a Hitler 'unwilling to take decisions, frequently uncertain, exclusively concerned with upholding his prestige and personal authority, influenced in the strongest fashion by his current entourage, in some respects a weak dictator'.[4] Before attempting to evaluate these interpretations, it is necessary to outline the contours of the debate in the light of the recent historiography on Hitler and the structure of the Nazi State.[5]

## Personality, Structure, and 'the Hitler Factor'

Studies founded upon the centrality of Hitler's personality, ideas, and strength of will to any explanation of Nazism take as their starting-point the premise that, since the Third Reich rose and fell with Hitler and was dominated by him throughout, 'National Socialism can indeed be called Hitlerism'.[6] Behind such an interpretation is in general a philosophy which stresses the 'intentionality' of the central actors in the historical drama, according full weight to the freedom of action of the individual and the uniqueness of his action. This type of thinking obviously characterizes biographies of Hitler, as well as the more recent vogue of 'psycho-historical' studies. It also, however, underlies some outstanding non-biographical studies of Nazism.

The 1970s saw the appearance of a number of Hitler biographies – amid the outpouring of mainly worthless products of the so-called 'Hitler Wave', indicating a macabre fascination with the bizarre personality of the Nazi leader.[7] Some of the findings of the new biographies themselves seemed to add little more than antiquarian detail to existing knowledge about Hitler, though the best of them, by Joachim Fest – significantly the first full-scale biography of Hitler by a German – went a long way towards replacing Bullock's dated classic of the 1950s.[8] Even so, as perceptive critics pointed out amid the paeans of praise, Fest's stylistic study revealed some of the inbuilt

[3] Rich (ch. 3 note 50), vol. 1, p. 11.

[4] Hans Mommsen, 'Nationalsozialismus', in *Sowjetsystem und demokratische Gesellschaft* (ch. 2 note 12), vol. 4 (Freiburg, 1971), column 702. Mommsen appears to have first made this heuristic point in his *Beamtentum im Dritten Reich* (Stuttgart, 1966), p. 98 note 26, where he stated that Hitler was 'in all questions which needed the adoption of a fundamental and definitive position, a weak dictator'.

[5] For historiographical surveys, see Wolf-Rüdiger Hartmann, 'Adolf Hitler: Möglichkeiten seiner Deutung', *AfS* 15 (1975), pp. 521–35; Andreas Hillgruber, 'Tendenzen, Ergebnisse und Perspektiven der gegenwärtigen Hitler-Forschung', *HZ* 226 (1978), pp. 600–21; Wolfgang Michalka, 'Wege der Hitler-Forschung', *Quaderni di storia* 8 (1978), pp. 157–90 and 10 (1979), pp. 123–51; William Carr, 'Historians and the Hitler Phenomenon', *German Life and Letters* 34 (1981), pp. 260–72; and now, comprehensively, Schreiber (see ch. 1 note 6).

[6] Bracher, 'The Role of Hitler' (ch. 2 note 3), p. 198.

[7] For a devastating critique of 'Hitler-Wave' publications, see Eberhard Jäckel, 'Rückblick auf die sog. Hitler-Welle', *GWU* 28 (1977), pp. 695–710.

[8] Joachim C. Fest, *Hitler. Eine Biographie* (Berlin, 1973), Engl. trans. *Hitler* (London, 1974). Alan Bullock, *Hitler. A Study in Tyranny* (orig. edn., London, 1952; revised edn., Harmondsworth, 1962).

weaknesses of the biographical approach – in particular when the subject of study was such a 'non-person' as Hitler.[9] Fest's work is rather unbalanced in coverage, for instance, in devoting undue attention to Hitler's early years; it ignores or plays down socio-economic issues; it is excessively concerned with the historically futile question of whether Hitler can be attributed with qualities of 'negative greatness'; and generally, it shows a far less sure touch when relating Hitler to the broader developments of German society and politics than when dealing with his personality. The inability of the biographical approach to avoid the extreme personalization of complex issues, reducing them to questions of Hitler's personality and ideology, characterizes, too, the widely-read and highly influential piece of quality journalism by Sebastian Haffner, which treats Nazism solely in terms of Hitler's 'achievements', 'successes', 'errors', and so on.[10]

The apogée of 'Hitler-centrism' is reached in the psycho-historical approach characterizing a number of new studies in the 1970s and coming close to explaining the war and the extermination of the Jews through Hitler's neurotic psychopathy, oedipal complex, monorchism, disturbed adolescence, and psychic traumas (allegedly fitting into the collective psychology of the German people).[11] Even if the findings were less dependent on conjecture and speculation, it is difficult to see how this approach could help greatly in explaining how such a person could become ruler of Germany and how his ideological paranoia came to be implemented as government policy by non-paranoids and non-psychopaths in a sophisticated, modern bureaucratic system. Wehler's sarcasm – and he is one of the few historians to have seriously tested the applicability of psycho-analysis to historical method – seems not misplaced: 'Does our understanding of National Socialist politics really depend on whether Hitler had only one testicle? . . . Perhaps the Führer had three, which made things difficult for him – who knows? . . . Even if Hitler could be regarded irrefutably as a sadomasochist, which scientific interest does that further? . . . Does the "final solution of the Jewish question" thus become more easily understandable or the "twisted road to Auschwitz" become the one-way street of a psychopath in power?'[12]

The most important studies which take the centrality of Hitler's person and ideology as their interpretative focus are of immeasurably higher quality, and are not biographically orientated at all. Unlike most of the biographies (excluding Bullock and Fest), the wide range of works by Bracher, Hillgruber, Hildebrand, and Jäckel – to name the leading figures – has made a major contribution to an understanding of Nazism. What links their individually different approaches together is the notion that Hitler had a 'programme' (though not a crude blueprint for action), which in all essentials he held to consistently from the early 1920s down to his suicide

[9] See Hermann Graml, 'Probleme einer Hitler-Biographie. Kritische Bemerkungen zu Joachim C. Fest', *VfZ* 22 (1974), pp. 76–92. Bracher's doubts about the biographical approach are expressed in his 'The Role of Hitler', pp. 194–7.

[10] Sebastian Haffner, *Anmerkungen zu Hitler* (Munich, 1978), Engl. trans. *The Meaning of Hitler* (London, 1979).

[11] Among the leading productions are Robert Waite, *Adolf Hitler. The Psychopathic God* (New York, 1977), and Rudolf Binion, *Hitler among the Germans* (New York, 1976).

[12] Hans-Ulrich Wehler, 'Psychoanalysis and History', *Social Research* 47 (1980), p. 531.

in the Berlin bunker in 1945. His own actions were directed by his ideological obsessions; and the Third Reich was directed by Hitler; therefore the Führer's ideology became implemented as government policy. Roughly summarized, this is the basis of the 'programmatist' type of interpretation.

The conception of Hitler as a man fanatically pursuing defined objectives with relentless consistency (though with tactical flexibility) – replacing as late as the 1960s the view that he was little more than a power-grabbing, unprincipled opportunist – produced in sophisticated works such as those of Andreas Hillgruber a picture of the 'programmatist' Hitler bending German foreign policy to his determined will to accomplish long-term but clear-cut ideological goals.[13] This picture depended in turn upon a corresponding perception of Hitler's role in domestic policy as the supreme Machiavellian working, with whatever tactical adroitness, to a preordained concept and pushing in a perniciously logical and internally rational series of steps towards total power in order to implement his ideological aims as government practice. The development of this interpretation of Hitler owed most to the work of Karl Dietrich Bracher.

For Bracher, a political scientist, the key question was how liberal democracy disintegrated and made way for 'totalitarian' dictatorship.[14] His exposition of the workings of the German 'totalitarian' dictatorship, emerging in a flow of centrally important studies from the mid 1950s onwards, attributed a pivotal role to Hitler and emphasized the motivating force of Hitler's ideology.[15] In an interesting bridge to the later 'structuralist' emphasis on the 'institutional anarchy' of the Third Reich, Bracher was already writing in 1956 that 'the antagonism between rival agencies was resolved solely in the omnipotent key position of the Führer', which 'derived precisely from the complex coexistence and opposition of the power groups and from conflicting personal ties'.[16] The emphasis on the Führer's actual omnipotence, however, distinguishes Bracher's position clearly from that of the later 'structuralists'. Moreover, the title of Bracher's essay – 'stages of totalitarian *Gleichschaltung*' – reflected the stress he placed upon the essentially planned, regulated, and 'rational' progression to pre-conceived goals, an argument he consistently reformulated in his major works. By a different route, Bracher had developed an interpretation of Hitler which clearly married with the 'programmatist' approach to foreign policy, and also with the Hitler-centrism of the best biographies.

Bracher affirmed his position in an interpretative essay in the mid 1970s addressed to the problem of 'the place of the individual within the historico-political process'.[17] He argues vehemently that Hitler was fatally underestimated in his own time, and that new patterns of research which reject 'totalitarianism' as a concept and view Nazism instead as a German variant

[13] See esp. Hillgruber, *Hitlers Strategie* (cf. above ch. 1 note 17).
[14] This was the central problem tackled in Bracher, *Auflösung* (see above, ch. 1 note 32).
[15] The arguments are fully developed in two main monographs, *Machtergreifung* (see above ch. 1 note 32) and *The German Dictatorship* (ch. 2 note 60).
[16] Karl Dietrich Bracher, 'The Stages of Totalitarian Integration (*Gleichschaltung*)', in Hajo Holborn, ed., *Republic to Reich. The Making of the Nazi Revolution* (New York, 1973), p. 128. This is the Engl. trans. of 'Stufen totalitärer Machtergreifung', *VfZ* 4 (1956), pp. 30–42.
[17] Bracher, 'The Role of Hitler', pp. 193–212.

of fascism are in danger of repeating the underestimation. Hitler, in his assessment, was a uniquely German phenomenon: the most radical expression of the ideas of extreme German nationalism and a genuine revolutionary, even if the changes he ultimately wrought were the opposite of those he had intended. Nazism cannot therefore be divorced from the person of Hitler, and, consequently, it is legitimate to call it 'Hitlerism': 'It was indeed Hitler's *Weltanschauung* and nothing else that mattered in the end, as is seen from the terrible consequences of his racist anti-semitism in the planned murder of the Jews'.[18]

This interpretation is advanced in its most uncompromising form in the work of Eberhard Jäckel and Klaus Hildebrand. In Jäckel's opinion, the Nazi regime can be dubbed an '*Alleinherrschaft*' – literally 'sole rule' – which he takes as meaning 'that the essential political decisions were taken by a single individual, in this case by Hitler'.[19] And implicit, if not stated in so many words, is the notion that these decisions followed logically from Hitler's *Weltanschauung*, which Jäckel analysed in a detailed study with the sub-title (in the English version): 'A Blueprint for Power'.[20] Hildebrand, too, though accepting that Nazism cannot be reduced solely to the personality of the Führer, insists upon the absolute centrality of the 'Hitler factor' to the course of development of the Third Reich, especially in the spheres of foreign and race policy, and argues forcefully for the *monocratic* rather than polycratic nature of Nazi rule. For Hildebrand, too, Nazism is ultimately Hitlerism.[21]

The contrasting approach, variously described as 'structuralist', 'functionalist', or (more disparagingly) 'revisionist', offers a fundamentally different interpretation of the Third Reich – concentrating, as the epithets suggest, more on the 'structures' of Nazi rule, the 'functional' nature of policy decisions, and 'revising' what is taken for an unjustifiable overemphasis of the personal role of Hitler in 'orthodox' historiography. In essence, all 'structuralist' interpretations go back to the masterly analyses published by Ernst Fraenkel and Franz Neumann in the 1940s.[22] It was only during the course of the 1960s, however, that the challenge to notions of the 'monolithic' 'totalitarian' State together with the theoretical influence of the newly developing 'structural history' and, derived from political science, of systems analysis, gradually affected writing on the Third Reich.

By the end of the 1960s a number of penetrating studies had laid bare the 'leadership chaos' of Nazi Germany, and established the base of what grew into the notion of 'polycratic' rule – a multidimensional power-structure, in

---

18 Bracher, 'The Role of Hitler', p. 201.
19 Eberhard Jäckel, 'Wie kam Hitler an die Macht?', in Karl Dietrich Erdmann and Hagen Schulze, eds., *Weimar. Selbstpreisgabe einer Demokratie. Eine Bilanz heute* (Düsseldorf, 1980), p. 305. And see now Jäckel's *Hitler in History* (Hanover/London, 1987), pp. 28–30.
20 Eberhard Jäckel, *Hitlers Weltanschauung. Entwurf einer Herrschaft* (Tübingen, 1969), Engl. trans. *Hitler's Weltanschauung. A Blueprint for Power* (Middletown, Connect., 1972).
21 Of Klaus Hildebrand's numerous essays, see esp. 'Nationalsozialismus oder Hitlerismus?' (see ch. 2 note 62), and 'Monokratie oder Polykratie?' (ch. 1 note 23).
22 Ernst Fraenkel, *The Dual State* (New York, 1941); Neumann, *Behemoth* (see ch. 2 note 5). For theoretical comments on 'structuralist' approaches, see Jürgen Kocka, 'Struktur und Persönlichkeit als methodologisches Problem der Geschichtswissenschaft', in Bosch (see ch. 2 note 62), pp. 152–69.

which Hitler's own authority was only one element (if a very important one).[23] Important works on, for example, the civil service, Party–State relations, the Gauleiter and their provincial power enclaves, the Rosenberg agency, the economy, and policy-implementation at regional and local level (in a study suggestively entitled *The Limits of Hitler's Power*), all helped to revise understanding of how Nazi rule operated in practice.[24]

Unquestionably the outstanding general analysis of the internal structure of the Nazi regime was Martin Broszat's *The Hitler State*, first published in German in 1969.[25] In a strict sense the title was a misnomer, since Broszat broke away from a personality-based, Hitler-centred treatment of Nazism to explore the causal connections between the development of the internal power-structure and the progressive radicalization of the Nazi regime, culminating in European-wide destruction on an unprecedented scale and genocide. In another sense, however, the title was apt. It reflects the antagonisms of a form of absolute leadership which could not be reconciled with the normal practice and organization of government. In Broszat's view – and here he differs from Bracher and others who accept the chaotic governmental structure of the Third Reich as a consequence of Hitler's skilful deployment of a skilful 'divide and rule' strategy – the administrative chaos was not consciously devised, but nor was it pure chance. Rather, it was the inevitable result of the form of authority exerted by Hitler, of his unwillingness and inability to regulate systematically the relationship between Party and State and to create an ordered system of authoritarian government. There was an uneasy 'power-sharing' in the early years of the dictatorship between the conservative 'authoritarian' forces in State and society and the vague, largely negative 'totalitarian' forces of the Nazi mass movement, which having attained power indeed sought to take over as many spheres as possible, but otherwise had no clear ideas what to do with it – apart from attacking the Jews, the Left, and other 'enemies of the State' and minorities which did not fit into the 'national community'. This allowed Hitler's own authority to detach itself from both Party and from State and to develop a wide sphere of autonomy – expressed, however, in haphazard, piecemeal, and inconsistent fashion. The demise of collective, centralized government (the Cabinet never met again after 1938) promoted the disintegration of government into a proliferation of departments with ministries working largely independently of each other. Alongside ministries and Party offices were vital power-bases which crossed Party–State boundaries and derived their authority solely from a mandate of the Führer. The Four Year Plan and especially the SS–Police empire were the most important of these. The overall structure of government was reduced thereby to a shambles of

[23] See esp. Hüttenberger, 'Polykratie' (see ch. 3 note 30). The term seems to have been coined originally by Carl Schmitt, one of the prime legal theorists of the Third Reich, and to have been first employed in a major analysis of Nazi government structure in 1960 by Gerhard Schulz in Bracher *et al.*, *Machtergreifung*, though within the context of a 'totalitarianism' interpretation.
[24] Hans Mommsen, *Beamtentum*; Peter Diehl-Thiele, *Partei und Staat im Dritten Reich* (Munich, 1969); Peter Hüttenberger, *Die Gauleiter* (Stuttgart, 1969); Reinhard Bollmus, *Das Amt Rosenberg und seine Gegner. Studien zum Machtkampf im nationalsozialistischen Herrschaftssystem* (Stuttgart, 1970); Petzina, *Autarkiepolitik* (see ch. 3 note 4); Edward N. Peterson, *The Limits of Hitler's Power* (Princeton, 1969).
[25] See above ch. 2 note 39 for full reference.

constantly shifting power-bases and warring factions – but a shambles which unleashed immense energy and contained its own inbuilt destructive momentum. In Broszat's interpretation, the Darwinian rivalry immanent to the system and the ill-co-ordinated attempts of the fractured government machine to 'interpret' the will of the Führer – to bureaucratize charismatic authority and channel vague ideological imperatives into coded law and practices of conduct – led inexorably to an accelerating decline into aggression, lawlessness, and criminal brutality.

Hitler's ideological obsessions were by no means ignored in this analysis. But the emphasis was shifted to the functional pressures within the various, and competing, components of the governmental 'system', aligned to chiliastic but in essence of necessity destructive goals, which could be transmuted into reality through the growing decay and collapse of coherent, 'rational' governmental control and policy planning. This posed a challenge to notions of a planned, consistent, systematic pursuit of clear objectives, which had underlain 'totalitarianism' theories and 'Hitlerism' approaches.[26] Hitler is seen by Broszat as tending more to *sanction* pressures operating from different forces within the regime rather than creating policy: the symbolic Führer authority is more important than the direct governing will of the person Hitler. The fixed points of Hitler's personal *Weltanschauung* served, therefore, largely a functional role.[27] They had so little to do with divisive day-to-day social and political issues that they could be resorted to as 'directions for action' (*Aktionsrichtungen*) and advanced as ultimate, long-range goals. Furthermore, 'Hitler was all the more compelled to keep coming back to them and to keep the Movement going, as other Party ideas of a new order proved illusory'. In this sense, Hitler's fixations with anti-semitism, anti-bolshevism, and with *Lebensraum* might be said to have had, at least in the early years of the Third Reich, a largely symbolic function, serving in Broszat's phrase chiefly as 'ideological metaphors'. In this rather complex argument, Hitler is certainly accorded a vital role in shaping the course of the Third Reich, but not in so simple and straightforward a fashion as the ideological 'intentionalists' would have it.

The most uncompromising exposition of the implications of the 'structuralist' approach for a reassessment of Hitler's position in the power-constellation of the Third Reich has been consistently advanced by Hans Mommsen, in a stream of important essays from the mid 1960s to the present time.[28] Mommsen's interpretation, showing many similarities to that of Broszat though generally expressed in bolder and more combative language, has developed into the dialectical counterpoint of Hildebrand's

[26] See Broszat, *Der Staat Hitlers*, p. 9.

[27] The argument is fully expounded in Martin Broszat, 'Soziale Motivation und Führer-Bindung des Nationalsozialismus', *VfZ* 18 (1970), pp. 392–409, here esp. pp. 403–8.

[28] See e.g. Hans Mommsen, *Beamtentum*, esp. pp. 13–19; 'Nationalsozialismus' (see above, note 4), columns 695–702; 'Ausnahmezustand als Herrschaftstechnik des NS-Regimes', in Funke (see ch. 3 note 27), pp. 30–45; 'Nationalsozialismus oder Hitlerismus?', in Bosch (see ch. 2 note 62), pp. 62–7; 'National Socialism: Continuity and Change', in Laqueur (see ch. 2 note 12), pp. 151–92; 'Hitlers Stellung im nationalsozialistischen Herrschaftssystem', in Hirschfeld and Kettenacker (see ch. 1 note 23), pp. 43–72; and his short text for the Deutsches Institut für Fernstudien an der Universität Tübingen, *Adolf Hitler als 'Führer' der Nation* (Tübingen, 1984).

'monocratic' 'Hitlerist' line of argument.[29] In a direct clash with Hildebrand in 1976,[30] Mommsen rejected 'personalistic' interpretations of Nazism as raising more questions than they answer and offering a retrospective over-rationalization of Hitler's 'policy'. Rather than operating on the basis of the concrete political calculations and compromise which are the essence of 'normal politics', Hitler's limited number of fanatically held but vague ideological fixations were (in Mommsen's view) incapable of offering a platform for rational decision-making. Hitler remained first and foremost a propagandist, with an eye to the *presentation* of an image and the exploitation of the opportune moment. His ideological statements ought therefore to be seen more as propaganda than as 'firm statements of intent'. Domestic policy is impossible to deduce from Hitler's ideological premises. Such a deduction would be hazardous, too, in the sphere of racial policy, where the 'Final Solution' cannot simply be reduced to the implementation of Hitler's intentions and has to be seen as the product of the complex structure of decision-making processes and the cumulative radicalization of the Third Reich. Even in foreign policy, which Mommsen elsewhere incorporated in his model,[31] there was little or no consistent planning to be seen. Rather than being based upon rational calculation, foreign policy was largely an outward projection of domestic policy – a spiralling radicalization in which the regime lurched from crisis to crisis, burning its boats in a series of *ad hoc* responses to recurrent emergencies, and creating a diminishing sense of reality in the pursuit of extravagant objectives.

Two issues lie at the forefront of Mommsen's concern: the absence of clear planning and consistent direction from Hitler; and the complicity of the German élites in Nazi policy. Both are directly related to the collapse of ordered government into self-destructive, self-generating disintegratory impulses. In a recent, particularly clear statement of his interpretation, Mommsen summed up: 'Hitler's role as a driving force, which with the same inner compulsion drove on to self-destruction, should not be under-estimated. On the other hand, it must also be recognized that the Dictator was only the extreme exponent of a chain of antihumanitarian impulses set free by the lapse of all institutional, legal, and moral barriers, and, once set in motion, regenerating themselves in magnified form'. Moreover, since Hitler was by no means always the protagonist of the most radical solution – for example, in Church or economic policy where there was a danger of provoking unrest – it is far too easy 'to emphasize as the final cause of the criminal climax and terroristic hubris of National Socialist policy the determining influence of Hitler'. And if the most horrific crimes cannot be explained solely or even largely with reference to Hitler's personality, ideology, and will, then the role and complicity of the dominant élites that helped Hitler into power and sustained him when there, co-operating in and benefiting in good measure from the Nazi 'restoration of social order', must

---

[29] Compare their contributions in Hirschfeld and Kettenacker.

[30] In Bosch, pp. 62–71, following Hildebrand's contribution, pp. 55–61.

[31] See Hans Mommsen, 'Hitlers Stellung', pp. 57–61, 69–70; 'Ausnahmezustand', p. 45; 'National Socialism: Continuity and Change', pp. 177–9; his review of Hans-Adolf Jacobsen, *Nationalsozialistische Außenpolitik* (Frankfurt am Main/Berlin, 1968), *MGM* (1970), Heft 1, pp. 180–5; and now *Adolf Hitler*, pp. 91–109.

be the subject of special concern. Historical assessment of the Third Reich cannot, therefore, be reduced to the uniqueness of 'the Hitler phenomenon', but must instead tackle the more difficult but still relevant problems of the conditions and structures which allowed such barbarity to emerge and expand in a civilized and sophisticated industrial society.[32] The implications for wider interpretations and their attendant historical philosphies, and their underlying political standpoints, are clear.

What has come to be labelled the 'intentionalist' approach – i.e. deducing the development of the Third Reich from Hitler's ideological intentions – has an immediate and obvious appeal. Seldom has a politician stuck with such fanatical consistency to an ideological fixation as Hitler appears to have done in the period extending from his entry into politics to his suicide in the bunker. That the quest for *Lebensraum* and the extermination of the Jews, far from remaining the wild ravings of a lunatic-fringe beer-hall rabble-rouser, became horrific reality and were implemented as government policy by a regime led by Hitler, seems to point conclusively to the validity of the 'intentionalist' argument. However, for all its superficial attractiveness, such an argument contains a number of potentially serious flaws, as Tim Mason has pointed out. Methodologically, argued Mason, a concentration on Hitler's intentions short-circuits all fundamental questions of the character of social, economic, and political agencies of change. Underlying the approach is the dubious assumption that historical development can be explained by recourse to intuitive understanding of the motives and intentions of leading actors in the drama. Subsequent events are then rationalized in necessarily teleological fashion by their relation to such intentions, which function, therefore, both as cause and as sufficient explanation. In addition, there are major problems – simply in terms of the availability and quality of the sources – in attempting to reconstruct Hitler's reasons for decisions and the processes which led to decisions being made. The evidence is not always plain and consistent, and can be read in different ways. The 'Hitlerist' case has to be demonstrated, not merely asserted. Even its moral implications are not altogether clear. Since Hitler was by definition unique and unrepeatable, and his actions and intentions both a premise and a conclusion, whatever moral warning might be drawn from a study of Nazism is limited in its application.[33]

The 'structuralist' argument seems inherently more difficult to express, as the convoluted language sometimes employed by its exponents appears to betray. Notions of Hitler as weak and indecisive, of antisemitism and *Lebensraum* as 'ideological metaphors', of Nazism being bent on upholding rather than revolutionizing the social order, and of foreign policy as a device of domestic policy, do not carry instant conviction. There appears to be some strength in the argument that the 'structuralists' might have a point in the realm of domestic policy, where Hitler showed little active interest, but that in anti-Jewish and foreign policy it is a different story. And that, rather

---

[32] Hans Mommsen, 'Hitlers Stellung', pp. 66–7, 71.
[33] Mason, 'Intention and Explanation' (see ch. 1 note 25), pp. 29–35.

than collapsing under the weight of its own internal contradictions, administrative chaos, and self-destructive dynamic, Nazi Germany was only defeated by the assembled might of the Allies, also seems to speak against the 'structuralist' argument. Finally, the counter-factual rhetorical question of what the course of the German government might have been without Hitler in charge appears to clinch the case for stressing rather than de-emphasizing Hitler's importance.

The 'structuralists' do not, however, ignore or play down Hitler's importance. They merely seek to locate this importance within the framework of numerous additional pressures built into the governmental system. They start from the premise that the processes of cumulative and progressive radicalization in the Third Reich were so complex in themselves that it would be imposssible to explain them without widening the focus away from Hitler's personality and ideology, and without considering the Führer less in personality terms than in his functional role within a multi-dimensional (polycratic) system of rule. The 'structuralist' argument is less easily disposed of than the 'intentionalists' often claim. A full assessment of these polarized interpretations must, however, extend over three inter-related but separate areas: the character of Hitler's rule and the internal power structure of the Nazi State; the implementation of anti-Jewish policy, in particular the process of decision-making which initiated the 'Final Solution'; and the regime's foreign policy and expansionist ambitions. Central to all three areas is the question of how decisions were reached in the Third Reich. The last two areas, lying at the heart of Hitler's *Weltanschauung*, are dealt with in subsequent chapters. The first area forms the subject of the evaluation which follows.

## Hitler's Power: an Evaluation

An examination of Hitler's power, whether he is to be seen as 'master in the Third Reich' or 'a weak dictator', must begin with some conception of what, potentially, might comprise his 'strength' and 'weakness' within the overall power constellation in the Third Reich. At least three categories of possible weakness appear to be distinguishable:

*(i)* It might be argued that Hitler was 'weak' in the sense that he regularly shirked making decisions, and was compelled to do so in order to protect his own image and prestige, dependent upon the Führer remaining outside factional politics and unassociated with mistaken or unpopular decisions. This would mean that the chaotic centrifugal tendencies in the Third Reich were 'structurally' conditioned and not simply or mainly a consequence of Hitler's ideological or personal predilections, or of a machiavellian 'divide and rule' strategy.

*(ii)* Hitler could be regarded as 'weak' if it could be shown that his decisions were ignored, watered-down, or otherwise not properly implemented by his subordinates.

*(iii)* It might be claimed that Hitler was 'weak' in that his scope for action, his manoeuvrability, was preconditioned and limited by factors outside his control but immanent to the 'system', such as the demands of the economy or fear of social unrest.

The following analysis attempts to relate these categories to an assessment of Hitler's rule and the internal power structure of the Third Reich.

Historians are in no fundamental disagreement over the fact that the government of Nazi Germany was chaotic in structure. It is, of course, easy to exaggerate the 'ordered' character of any modern governmental system. However, it seems clear that the fragmentation and lack of co-ordination in the internal administration of the Third Reich existed to such an extreme degree that the overlapping, conflicting, and sometimes outrightly contradictory spheres of authority can be aptly depicted as 'chaotic'. The question is, what significance should be attached to this 'chaos'?

The 'intentionalist' type of approach sees in the confused lines of authority in the Third Reich a reflection of a calculated policy of 'divide and rule', testimony therefore of Hitler's pivotal role, his real power, and his preconceived planning of the take-over, consolidation, and wielding of total power with a view to carrying out his long-term objectives.[34] The opposed 'structuralist' line of interpretation regards the fragmented machinery of government rather as the inevitable product of Hitler's 'charismatic' form of leadership. This preconditioned rejection of the institutional and bureaucratic norms necessary for the 'rational' government of a modern state in favour of dependence on personal loyalty as the basis of authority – a transmission of the ethos of the Nazi Party since its early days to the task of running a sophisticated, modern government machine.[35] 'Charismatic' leadership also predetermined an essentially propagandistic preoccupation with avoiding any harmful inroads into the prestige and image of the Führer, hence the need to refrain from interference in internal conflicts and to remain aloof from day-to-day decision-making and association with possibly unpopular policy options.[36] In contrast to conceptions of a 'monocratic' dictatorship relentlessly pursuing its fixed goals with remorseless zeal and energy, this interpretation emphasizes the lack of efficiency, fragmentation of decision-making, absence of clear, rational 'middle-range' policies, and diminishing sense of reality – all promoting the immanent instability of the political system, the inevitable selection of negative goals, and cumulative radicalization.[37] Hitler's personal scope for action was limited, moreover, by the continued existence of other, real – if fluctuating – centres of power.[38]

[34] See e.g. Bracher, 'Stages', and Diehl-Thiele, p. ix (where he speaks of a 'permanent improvisation within the framework of a principled divide-and-rule tactic').
[35] For the impact on the NSDAP of Hitler's 'charismatic' leadership, see Joseph Nyomarkay, *Charisma and Factionalism within the Nazi Party* (Minneapolis, 1967), and Wolfgang Horn, *Führerideologie und Parteiorganisation in der NSDAP (1919–1933)* (Düsseldorf, 1972).
[36] I try to tackle the making and impact of Hitler's popular image in my study *The Hitler Myth'. Image and Reality in the Third Reich* (Oxford, 1987), and more briefly in 'The Führer Image and Political Integration: The Popular Conception of Hitler in Bavaria during the Third Reich', in Hirschfeld and Kettenacker, pp. 133–63.
[37] See Hans Mommsen, 'National Socialism: Continuity and Change', pp. 176–8; Broszat, 'Soziale Motivation'; and the valuable essay of Jane Caplan, 'Bureaucracy, Politics, and the National Socialist State', in Peter D. Stachura, ed., *The Shaping of the Nazi State* (London, 1978), pp. 234–56.
[38] See Hüttenberger, 'Polykratie', and above ch. 3, for shifts within the 'power-constellation' of the Third Reich.

Evidence of a machiavellian 'divide and rule' strategy – a claim which Hitler's former press chief Otto Dietrich made in his post-war memoirs[39] – is usually found in the deliberate blurring of lines of command and creation of a duplication or triplication of office. An example is the way in which Hitler broke up the unified control over the Party's organization which Gregor Strasser had built up. Following Strasser's resignation in December 1932, Hitler himself took over the formal leadership of the Party's 'Political Organization', strengthened the position of the Gauleiter at the expense of the Reich Leadership, and divided power at the centre between Robert Ley, who eventually adopted Strasser's old title as 'Reich Organization Leader' but with diminished power, and Rudolf Heß, given the title of 'Deputy Führer' in April 1933, with the right to decide in Hitler's name in all questions relating to the Party leadership.[40]

Another example is the refusal of Hitler to back the attempts of Wilhelm Frick, Reich Minister of the Interior, to instigate a rational system of centralized state control through far-reaching plans for 'Reich Reform'. In the early years of the Third Reich, Frick struggled to establish authority over the Reich Governors, most of whom were at the same time Gauleiter of the Party. The Reich Governors had been put in as Reich delegates in the Länder in April 1933, bearing a loose mandate to ensure the execution of the Reich Chancellor's policy through the Länder governments.[41] By January 1934 it looked as if Frick was on the way to success. The 'Law for the Reconstruction of the Reich', signed by Hitler, placed the Reich Governors under the administrative supervision of the Reich Minister of the Interior. (In abolishing Länder sovereignty, the law technically did away with the logic of having Reich Governors at all, but, typically, they remained in existence.) Following massive protests by the Reich Governors about their right of appeal to the Führer, Frick had to be content with a gloss by Hitler which in practice completely undermined Frick's authority. It was now stated that, although generally subordinated to Frick, 'an exception must be made for those cases which are concerned with questions of special political importance. In the view of the Reich Chancellor, such a regulation is consistent with his position of leadership'.[42] Frick's patiently devised schemes for Reich reform, aimed at introducing a centralized and rational system of authority, based on a Reich Constitution instead of the Enabling Act, went much the same way and were finally abandoned in the middle of the war, as were plans to introduce a senate to assist the Führer and to elect his successor.[43]

Whether one can read into these and other examples a systematic 'divide and rule' strategy is debatable. Hitler, in fact, promoted the construction of some huge power-bases. In the example mentioned above, Robert Ley was given control over the mammoth Labour Front to add to his authority over

[39] Otto Dietrich, *Zwölf Jahre mit Hitler* (Cologne/Munich, 1955), pp. 129 ff. See Noakes and Pridham, vol. 2, p. 205.
[40] Diehl-Thiele, pp. 204–6.
[41] Noakes and Pridham (see ch. 3 note 37), vol. 2, p. 247; and see Diehl-Thiele, pp. 37–60. The relevant document is printed in the first edition of Noakes and Pridham, *Documents on Nazism* (London, 1974), pp. 239–40.
[42] Noakes and Pridham, vol. 2, p. 252; see Diehl-Thiele, pp. 61–73.
[43] See Peterson, pp. 102–25; Broszat, *Hitler State*, pp. 286–8; and Hans Mommsen, 'National Socialism: Continuity and Change', p. 169.

questions of party organization. But even this mini-empire was insignificant compared with the massive accretions of power which came to Göring and Himmler, with Hitler's active support. Nor was there much sign of anxiety on Hitler's part about Martin Bormann's accumulation of power in the war years. And the greatest threat to Hitler in the early phase of the Dictatorship, Ernst Röhm and the SA leadership, was eliminated only after Hitler had bowed to intense pressure from the army and had been pushed into it by Göring and Himmler.

What does seem clear is that Hitler was hypersensitive towards any attempt to impose the slightest institutional or legal restriction upon his authority, which had to be completely untrammelled, theoretically absolute, and contained within his own person. 'Constitutional Law in the Third Reich', stated Hans Frank, head of the Nazi Lawyers Association, in 1938, 'is the legal formulation of the historic will of the Führer, but the historic will of the Führer is not the fulfilment of legal preconditions for his activity'.[44] Hitler was correspondingly distrustful of all forms of institutional loyalty and authority – of army officers, civil servants, lawyers and judges, of Church leaders, and of cabinet ministers (whom he was unwilling to see even gathering informally between the increasingly infrequent cabinet sessions).[45]

The corollary of Hitler's extreme distrust of institutional bonds was his reliance on personal loyalty as the principle of government and administration. He appears to have had no consuming distrust of power-bases deriving from his own Führer-authority and held by his own chosen paladins – hence, his ultimate despair in the bunker at the final stab-in-the-back by Himmler, his 'loyal Heinrich'.[46] The appeal to personal loyalty had been Hitler's hallmark, especially in moments of crisis, since the early years of the Party.[47] The loyalty principle, a feature of *Party* management before 1933 in binding leaders as well as ordinary members to the person of the Führer, was carried over after 1933 into the practice of governing the Reich. In this sense, Robert Koehl's depiction of the Third Reich as less a totalitarian state than a neo-feudal empire has some meaning as an analogy.[48] In fact, however, the bonds of personal loyalty – a pure element of 'charismatic' rule – did not replace but were rather superimposed upon complex bureaucratic structures. The result was not complete destruction as much as parasitic corrosion. The avoidance of institutional restraints and the free rein given to the power ambitions of loyal paladins offered clear potential for the unfolding of dynamic, but unchannelled, energies – energies, moreover, which were inevitably destructive of rational government order.

As numerous studies have shown, the bonds of loyalty between Hitler and the Gauleiter, his trusted regional chieftains, vitiated any semblance of

---

44  Noakes and Pridham, vol. 2, p. 200.
45  Lothar Gruchmann, 'Die "Reichsregierung" im Führerstaat. Stellung und Funktion des Kabinetts im nationalsozialistischen Herrschaftssystem', in G. Doecker and W. Steffani, *Klassenjustiz und Pluralismus. Festschrift für Ernst Fraenkel zum 75. Geburtstag* (Hannover, 1973), p. 202. For Hitler's attitude towards the 'establishment' élites, see Michael Kater, 'Hitler in a Social Context', *CEH* 14 (1981), pp. 251 ff.
46  H.R. Trevor-Roper, *The Last Days of Hitler* (Pan Books, London, 1972 edn.), p. 202.
47  See Nyomarkay, Horn (see above note 35) and Dietrich Orlow, *The History of the Nazi Party. Vol. 1: 1919–1933* (Newton Abbot, 1971).
48  Robert Koehl, 'Feudal Aspects of National Socialism', in Turner, *Nazism and the Third Reich* (see ch. 3 note 6), pp. 151–74.

ordered government in the provinces.[49] Hitler invariably sided with his Gauleiter (or, rather, with the strongest Gauleiter) in any dispute with central authority or government ministries, protecting their interests and at the same time securing himself a powerful body of support, loyal to him and to no one else. In Rauschning's judgement Hitler 'never ran counter to the opinion of his Gauleiter. . . . Each one of these men was in his power, but together they held him in theirs. . . . They resisted with robust unanimity every attempt to set limits to their rights of sovereignty. Hitler was at all times dependent on them – and not on them alone'.[50] As we saw, Frick's attempts to gain control over the Reich Governors foundered on Hitler's support for the objections of the Gauleiter. The mighty Himmler encountered the same problem in his dealings with the Gauleiter after he had been made Reich Minister of the Interior in 1943.[51]

At the level of central government, too, Hitler's ideological predisposition to let rivals fight it out and then side with the winner – an instinctive application of social darwinistic precepts – together with his ready recourse in a crisis to the establishment of new agencies, bypassing or cutting through existing institutions, with plenipotentiary powers directly commissioned by the Führer and dependent on his authority alone, militated strongly against the setting of rational policy priorities. The consequence was the inevitable disintegration of central government – reflected by the increasing infrequency of cabinet meetings down to their complete cessation in early 1938 – and the dissolution of government into a multiplicity of competing and non-co-ordinated ministries, party offices, and hybrid agencies all claiming to interpret the Führer's will. Hand in hand with this development went the growing autonomy of the Führer-authority itself, detaching itself and isolating itself from any framework of corporate government and correspondingly subject to increasing delusions of grandeur and diminishing sense of reality.[52]

The chaotic nature of government in the Third Reich was also markedly enhanced by Hitler's non-bureaucratic and idiosyncratic style of rule. His eccentric 'working' hours, his aversion to putting anything down on paper, his lengthy absences from Berlin, his inaccessibility even for important ministers, his impatience with the complexities of intricate problems, and his tendency to seize impulsively upon random strands of information or halfbaked judgements from cronies and court favourites – all meant that ordered government in any conventional understanding of the term was a complete impossibility. 'Ministerial skill', it was pointed out after the war, 'consisted in making the most of a favourable hour or minute when Hitler

[49] E.g. Diehl-Thiele; Hüttenberger, *Gauleiter*; Peterson; Jochen Klenner, *Verhältnis von Partei und Staat 1933–1945. Dargestellt am Beispiel Bayerns* (Munich, 1974); and Jeremy Noakes, 'Oberbürgermeister and Gauleiter. City Government between Party and State', in Hirschfeld and Kettenacker, pp. 194–227, esp. pp. 207 ff.
[50] Cited in Peterson, p. 7, and see also pp. 14–15, 18–19. Rauschning was, however, spoiling a good point by exaggerating when he added that the secret of Hitler's leadership 'lay in knowing in advance what course the majority of his Gauleiter would decide upon and in being the first to declare for that course': Hermann Rauschning, *Hitler Speaks* (London, 1939), pp. 214–15.
[51] Diehl-Thiele, pp. 197–200 (and note 70).
[52] See Broszat, *Hitler State*, chs. 8–9.

made a decision, this often taking the form of a remark thrown out casually, which then went its way as an "Order of the Führer" '.[53]

It would be misleading to conclude from this comment that, however eccentrically arrived at, a steady stream of decisions flowed downwards from Hitler's lofty pinnacle. Rather, he was frequently reluctant to decide in domestic affairs and generally unwilling to resolve disputes by coming down on one side or the other, much preferring parties to a dispute to sort it out themselves.[54] It would be too simple to attribute this, and the governmental disorder in the Third Reich in general, solely to Hitler's personal quirks and eccentric style. Certainly, he was languid, lethargic, and uninterested in what he regarded as trivial matters of administrative detail beneath his level of concern. But it does seem clear that the protection of his own position and prestige was an important factor in predetermining his unwillingness to intervene in problem areas and to let things ride as long as possible – by which time a solution almost invariably suggested itself, and the contours of support had been clarified, the opposition (if any) already isolated. Thus, cabinet meetings in the early years of the Dictatorship were in no sense a forum for genuine debate preceding a policy decision. Hitler hated chairing the meetings in which he might potentially be forced into retreat on a given issue. Consequently, he 'reserved the right to decide when a difference of opinion could be brought before the cabinet. This way it came less and less to discussion. Each minister presented his draft, on which agreement had already been reached and Lammers [the head of the Reich Chancellory] recorded that all were agreed'.[55] Even so, the cabinet meetings were allowed to atrophy into non-existence. As regards legislation, this remained the usual procedure: draft laws were circulated to all ministers concerned, difficulties and disputes ironed out, and Hitler's sanction given only after all parties concerned had already resolved their differences. In 1943 Bormann reiterated the procedure that 'all orders and decrees must be given to all involved before their declaration; the Führer is to be approached only after *all* involved have taken a clear position'.[56] Effectively, it was the transfer to the complex business of state administration of the Party's basic 'principle of letting things develop until the strongest has won' – hardly a foundation for 'rational' decision-making. In any case, already by the mid 1930s influence on important affairs of state had passed to the shifting personnel of Hitler's most trusted cronies and government ministers were left to read in the press about what had taken place.[57]

Distant rather than immediate leadership in everyday affairs, and hesitancy about deciding before the situation had all but resolved itself were

---

[53] Noakes and Pridham, vol. 2, p. 197. See also Fritz Wiedemann, *Der Mann, der Feldherr werden wollte* (Velbert, 1964), pp. 68 ff.

[54] See Peterson, pp. 4 ff.

[55] Lutz Graf Schwerin von Krosigk, *Es geschah in Deutschland* (Tübingen/Stuttgart, 1951), p. 203. See also Peterson, p. 31.

[56] Cited in Peterson, p. 39.

[57] Krosigk, p. 203; Gruchmann, pp. 193–4. The quotation is from a memorandum from the office of the Gauleiter of Weser-Ems in 1942 (Noakes and Pridham, first edition, *Documents on Nazism*, p. 261). For the likely authorship, date, and content of this interesting document, see Dietrich Orlow, *History of the Nazi Party. Vol. 2: 1933–1945* (Newton Abbot, 1973), pp. 352 ff.

not simply a reflection of Hitler's style of rule, but were necessary components of his 'charismatic' Führer-authority, helping to maintain both in the ruling circle and among the people themselves the myth of Hitler's unerringly correct judgement and his independence from factional disputes – from 'normal politics'. The soaring popularity of Hitler, contrasted with the massive unpopularity of the Party and of so many aspects of the daily experience of Nazism, can only be attributed to the image of a Führer who seemed to stand aloof from political infighting and the grey daily reality of the Third Reich.[58] To an extent, Hitler had to live up to his image. This, too, conditioned a leadership style of aloofness, non-interference, 'moderation' in sensitive areas (such as the 'Church struggle'), and tendency always to side with 'the big battalions'.[59] The need to produce ever greater feats of achievement to bind the masses closer to him and to prevent a sagging of the regime's 'vitality' into stagnation, disenchantment, and likely collapse was one further weighty factor which militated against the establishment of a 'state of normalcy' in the Third Reich, promoting instead the radical but essentially negative dynamism which had formed the basis of the social integration of the Nazi movement, but which could hardly end but in destruction.

The governmental chaos of the Third Reich seems better explained if the notion of a systematic strategy of 'divide and rule' is left aside – even though Hitler's conscious protection of his authority against any potential attempt to limit it institutionally is evident. Though the chaotic structure of government was for the most part not a deliberate creation, it would seem unsatisfactory evidence for the view that Hitler was 'in some respects a weak dictator'.[60] Indeed, the notion of 'weakness' seems misplaced in this case. If Hitler had *wanted* a different governmental structure, but been prevented from attaining it; or if he had *intended* to make decisions, but found himself unable to do so, then there would have been some conflict between 'intention' and 'structure' and it might have been possible to conclude that Hitler was 'weak'. Since there is no evidence for either point, but rather every indication that Hitler was content, indeed wanted, to keep out of wrangles among his subordinates, had little interest in participating in the legislative process – especially in areas of peripheral concern – and actively furthered rather than tried to hinder the government chaos on occasion, then one would have to accept that was no incompatibility in this area between 'intention' and 'structure', and thus reject the conclusion that, because of the 'structural' restrictions imposed on his dictatorship, Hitler was 'weak'.

Our second criterion of weakness was whether Hitler made decisions which were then ignored, by-passed, or inadequately implemented by subordinates.

Certainly, Hitler's inclination towards often impulsive, verbal agreement to proposals casually presented to him at opportune moments by his underlings, who thereafter interpreted his spontaneous remarks as sufficient sanction and an 'unalterable decision', did lead to occasional embarrassment. One

[58] I attempt to argue this in my essay 'Alltägliches und Außeralltägliches: ihre Bedeutung für die Volksmeinung', in Detlev Peukert and Jürgen Reulecke, eds., *Die Reihen fast geschlossen Beiträge zur Geschichte des Alltags unterm Nationalsozialismus* (Wuppertal, 1981), pp. 273–92, esp. pp. 285 ff.
[59] Peterson, p. 7.
[60] See above note 4.

such instance occurred in October 1934, when Labour Front boss Robert Ley persuaded Hitler to sign a decree enhancing the authority of the Labour Front at the expense of both employers and the Trustees of Labour. Ley had not taken his proposal to either the Ministry of Labour or the Ministry of Economics, and both, together with Hess on behalf of the Party, protested so vehemently that Hitler – unwilling to antagonize Schacht and the industrial leadership – was obliged to yield to the pressure. Characteristically, the decree was not revoked – which would have been a slight on the Führer's prestige – but remained a dead letter, simply ignored by all with Hitler's tacit approval, even though Ley continued to refer to it in an attempt to extend his own power.[61] Difficulties were also caused in early 1935 by Hitler's agreement to a proposal by Labour Minister Seldte to a unified wage structure for building workers (replacing the regionally weighted system in operation). The objections of the Gauleiter – most prominently of Gauleiter Kaufmann of Hamburg – about the effects of the necessary reduction of wages in certain areas on worker morale, carried weight with Hitler, however, and he typically ordered a further indefinite period of deliberation before the proposed wage revision should come into force – meaning that the matter was shelved and forgotten.[62] Examples can also be found, especially in the early years of Nazi rule, where Hitler had to bow to economic pressure, and where unpalatable decisions were forced upon him – such as in 1933, when he had to accept the provision of financial support for ailing Jewish department stores in order to prevent staff redundancies adding to the total unemployed.[63] On the other hand, in one of the few divisive issues to come before the Reich Cabinet, and one on which he himself felt strongly, Hitler pushed through the Sterilization Law of July 1933 despite the voiced objections of Vice Chancellor Von Papen (who on this occasion was articulating the views of the Catholic lobby).[64]

It would be rash to claim, on the evidence for the implementation of Führer directives, that Hitler was a 'weak dictator'. The 'limits of Hitler's power' which Peterson advanced are arguably 'limits' only when juxtaposed with a wholly idealistic notion of 'total power'. Moreover, Peterson provided no convincing example of a directive held by Hitler to be of central importance that was ignored or blocked by his subordinates or others. More important for the workings of Nazi government than whether Hitler can be regarded as a 'strong' or 'weak' dictator, is the fact that he produced so *few* directives in the sphere of domestic politics. It becomes difficult, therefore, to establish precisely what his aims were in the domestic sphere, other than the elimination of 'enemies of the State' and the psychological as well as material mobilization for the war which he felt was inevitable within a very short time.[65] This aim was compatible with social developments diametrically opposite to those which had been preached by Nazi ideologues.[66]

[61] Noakes and Pridham, vol. 2, pp. 343–5.
[62] BAK, R43II/541, fos. 36–95 and R43II/552, fos. 25–50. See also Timothy W. Mason, *Sozialpolitik im Dritten Reich* (Opladen, 1977), pp. 158–9.
[63] Peterson, p. 48.
[64] Gruchmann, p. 191.
[65] See Peterson, p. 432.
[66] See Schoenbaum (see ch. 2 note 26), p. 285.

It is nevertheless in the area of mobilization of the German people for war, the central task of domestic policy, that it has been claimed that Hitler's real 'weakness' was to be found.

Tim Mason, above all, has argued that Hitler's scope for action – especially in the central period of the Third Reich between 1936 and 1941 – was seriously restricted by tensions built into the Nazi economy and not subject to control by the Führer's 'will' or 'intention'.[67] The key determinant, in his view, of the Nazi leadership's thought and action in the domestic sphere was the lesson drawn from the Revolution of 1918 of the dangers of working-class unrest. Hitler in particular was extraordinarily sensitive towards discontent among workers, aware that psychological motivation alone was extremely short-lived, and consequently that material sacrifices must be kept to a minimum. Hence, according to Mason, the Third Reich amounted to a huge social imperialist gamble, in which the material satisfaction of the masses could only be brought about through successful foreign expansion, but where the accomplishment of that expansion was significantly impaired by the unwillingness of the regime to impose even short-term reductions in living standards necessary for the effective functioning of an armaments-led economy. As a consequence, the regime developed no consistent social policy and was in essentially a weak position when faced with the logic of the economic class struggle and the need to square the circle of paying for armaments without drastic reductions in consumer spending. Hitler's own role was one of increasing helpless apathy and inactivity, a product of 'anxious insecurity' and growing pessimism. Strength of will alone, argues Mason, could not suffice to combat the class antagonism. The industrial opposition of German workers, exploiting their bargaining position in a time of acute labour shortage even without the help of trade unions, assisted in promoting a major economic crisis, which developed into a general crisis for the regime and necessarily affected the timing of war, determining that on economic grounds – and to preserve the social peace and protect the regime's own threatened position – war had to come sooner rather than later. Moreover, the war itself had to be conducted without major sacrifices of a material kind by the German people. Hence, mobilization of the population was half-hearted and incomplete (compared, for example, with Britain), and production for the war economy was hampered.[68] The weakness of the regime, therefore, went to the very heart of its ethos – war – and limited its potential to such an extent that it could be argued that the regime's destruction was not simply a matter of external defeat, but was implicit in its essence – was 'structurally determined' by its internal contradictions.

---

[67] Timothy W. Mason, 'The Legacy of 1918 for National Socialism', in Anthony Nicholls and Erich Matthias, eds., *German Democracy and the Triumph of Hitler* (London, 1971), pp. 215–39; *Sozialpolitik*, esp. chs. 1 and 6; 'Innere Krise und Angriffskrieg' (see ch. 3 note 47); and 'Labour in the Third Reich', *Past and Present* 33 (1966), pp. 112–41.

[68] See Timothy W. Mason, *Arbeiterklasse und Volksgemeinschaft* (Opladen, 1975), esp. ch. 21, and also Milward, *German Economy at War* (above ch. 3 note 5). The counter-position is that of Overy (refs. in ch. 3 notes 47 and 49). For labour and the war economy see now the rather different interpretations of Wolfgang Werner, *'Bleib übrig!' Deutsche Arbeiter in der nationalsozialistischen Kriegswirtschaft* (Düsseldorf, 1983), and Stephen Salter, *The Mobilization of German Labour* (unpubl. D. Phil. thesis, Oxford, 1983).

There is no shortage of evidence to illustrate Hitler's acute sensitivity towards any sign of threat to 'social peace'. Speer recorded in his memoirs Hitler's private admissions of anxiety about loss of popularity giving rise to domestic crises.[69] Worries about the social unrest which might ensue from rapidly rising prices in 1934 prompted Hitler to restore the office of Reich Commissar for Price Surveillance and to maintain it purely for propaganda purposes long after its head, Carl Goerdeler, had requested its dissolution on the grounds that there was nothing effective for it to do.[70] During mounting consumer problems and worrying reports of growing tension in industrial areas in 1935–6, Hitler was even prepared – temporarily – to forego imports for armament production in order to prevent the socially undesirable consequences of food rationing.[71] In 1938, despite desperate pleas from the Ministry of Food and Agriculture, Hitler categorically refused to raise food prices because of the damaging effect on living standards and worker morale.[72] In the first months of the war, the regime retreated on its plans for labour mobilization in the wake of worker protest at the impact on wages, working conditions, and living standards.[73] And the unwillingness of the regime to push through the comprehensive mobilization of women for the war effort probably has to be located not simply in Hitler's views on the role of women but in Nazi fears of the possible repercussions on morale and work discipline.[74]

The far-reaching conclusions which Mason draws from such evidence about the 'weakness' of Hitler and the regime have, however, been subjected to searching criticism from quite different directions, and Mason's overall thesis has found little general acceptance. It has been argued, for instance, that, whatever objective problems existed in the economy in 1938–9, the Nazi leadership – and in particular Hitler – exhibited no *consciousness* of a general political crisis of the system forcing a need for imminent war as the only way out.[75] In addition, it might be claimed that Mason has exaggerated the political significance and even the scale of industrial unrest, labelling as worker opposition to the system what was not specific to Nazism, but a feature (as in England during the war) of capitalist economies in periods of full employment.[76] The interpretation of a political crisis of the Nazi system in 1938–9 provoked by industrial opposition is, on these grounds, therefore highly dubious. As regards the timing of the war, it has been forcefully argued that, important though the domestic situation was, the decisive factor was the international balance of power and in particular the comparative armaments position of Germany's rival powers. The compulsion to act was not, therefore, conditioned by fear of internal unrest, but by

69 Albert Speer, *Erinnerungen* (Frankfurt am Main, 1969), p. 229.
70 See BAK, R43II/315a, esp. fols. 188–240.
71 BAK, Zsg 101/28, fol. 331 ('Vertrauliche Informationen' for the press, 7 Nov. 1935).
72 BAK, R43II/194, fol. 103.
73 Mason, *Arbeiterklasse*, ch. 21; *Sozialpolitik*, pp. 295 ff.
74 See Dörte Winkler, *Frauenarbeit im Dritten Reich* (Hamburg, 1977); Tim Mason, 'Women in Nazi Germany', *HWJ* 1 (spring, 1976), pp. 74–113 and esp. *HWJ* 2 (autumn, 1976), pp. 5–32; and Salter, *Mobilization*.
75 See Herbst (see ch. 3 note 47).
76 See Winkler, 'Vom Mythos der Volksgemeinschaft' (see ch. 3 note 47).

the state of the arms race which Germany had unleashed.[77] While West German critics maintain that Mason underrates Hitler's 'politically autonomous aims', and that Hitler's 'decisions for war arose from political motives alone',[78] GDR historians claim that in underestimating the aggressive imperialist aims, intentions, and policies of monopoly capital, Mason elevates Hitler to the level of 'the only decisive acting force'.[79] Both sets of critics share, therefore, from wholly opposed perspectives, the unease that Mason's attribution of weakness to Hitler and the Nazi regime leads to an interpretation in which the *intentions* of the regime are underplayed and it is mistakenly seen as stumbling into war from a position of weakness and without clear direction.[80]

These are weighty criticisms, even if at times they appear somewhat to distort the claims of Mason, who, for example, stresses that the primary *cause* of the war must be sought in the racial and anti-communist aims of the Nazi leadership and the economic imperialism of German industry, not in the crisis of the Nazi system.[81] They point, however, to the need to look for a synthesis of 'intention' and 'structure', rather than seeing them as polarized opposites. It seems, indeed, clear that Hitler's intentions and the socio-economic 'structural determinants' of Nazi rule were not antagonistic poles, pushing in opposite directions, but acted in a dialectical relationship which pushed in the same direction. Consequently, it is as good as impossible to separate as a causal factor 'intention' from the impersonal conditions which shape the framework within which intentions can become 'operational'. At the same time, it seems important to recognize that an 'intention' is not an autonomous force, but is affected in its implementation by circumstances which it may itself have been instrumental in creating, but which have developed a momentum of their own. In the present case, Hitler and the Nazi leadership (actively supported by prominent sections of the economic and military élites) unquestionably intended to wage the war which, in their view, would solve Germany's problems. But the war only gradually adopted concrete shape and form, and then by no means wholly in the way Hitler had envisaged it. As late as autumn 1935, Hitler's directive to ministers and army leaders, according to Goebbels's report, was as vague as: 're-arm and get ready. Europe is on the move again. If we're clever, we'll be the winners'.[82] The absolute priority accorded to rearmament, a *political* decision made at the very outset of the Third Reich, was at the root of the unresolvable tension in the economy between provision for armaments production and consumption. From 1936 onwards the die was cast and there could be no retreat if the regime were to survive. The course was set, and, despite preparations for a long war expected to commence around the mid 1940s, in practice for the only

[77] See Dülffer, 'Der Beginn des Krieges' (see ch. 3 note 47).
[78] Hilderand, *Das Dritte Reich*, p. 159.
[79] Lotte Zumpe, review of Mason, *Arbeiterklasse*, in *Jahrbuch für Wirtschaftsgeschichte* (1979), Heft 4, p. 175.
[80] From the GDR side, the point is forcefully made by Kurt Gossweiler in a review of Mason, *Arbeiterklasse*, in *Deutsche Literaturzeitung* 99 (1978), Heft 7/8, p. 538.
[81] Mason, 'Innere Krise', p. 186. Rather, in his view, the crisis explains and determined the sort of war which Germany could conduct. See above ch. 3 note 47 for references to Mason's replies to his critics.
[82] Elke Fröhlich (ed.), *Die Tagebücher von Joseph Goebbels. Sämtliche Fragmente* (4 vols., Munich/New York/London/Paris, 1987), vol. 2, p. 529 , entry of 19 Oct. 1935.

possible sort of war Germany could fight – a Blitzkrieg – in the nearer rather than more distant future. The economic problems intensified rapidly and enormously in 1937–9. Hitler could do little about them, though the impression to be gleaned from the sources is that he had little interest in doing anything, and fatalistically regarded the situation as only soluble after final victory in the war which he had always forecast as inevitable. By this date, Hitler was in any case more preoccupied with strategic questions and foreign affairs. The rapidly accelerating momentum of the worsening international situation confirmed Hitler's fears that time was running against Germany, that the only hope of success lay in gaining the advantage through an early strike. Diplomatic, strategic, and economic factors were by this time so intermeshed that it is impossible to single out one or the other as the sole determinant.[83] Together, they meant that by 1939 Hitler got the war which he had intended – but, from his 'programmatic' standpoint against the 'wrong' enemy (Britain) and at the best available but by no means ideal juncture for Germany. Once in the war, a string of Blitzkrieg successes concealed for a while the underlying weaknesses of the German war economy which the Nazis were unable fully to mobilize and which only began to operate to some extent efficiently when the nation had its back to the wall.

Hitler's 'intentions' are indispensable to explaining the course of development in the Third Reich. But they are by no means an adequate explanation in themselves. The conditions in which Hitler's 'will' could be implemented as government 'policy' were only in small measure fashioned by Hitler himself, and, moreover, made the ultimate failure of his aims and the destruction of the Third Reich almost inevitable. The fact that little of what happened in domestic politics before at least the middle of the war can be said to have run counter to or contradicted Hitler's 'will' and 'intention' makes it difficult to conceive of him as a 'weak dictator' – however useful the concept might have proved heuristically. On the other hand, the implementation of Hitler's 'will' is not such a straightforward matter and foregone conclusion as the 'intentionalists' want to have it. If not a 'weak dictator', Hitler was not 'master in the Third Reich' in the implied meaning of omnipotence.

'Intention' and 'structure' are both essential elements of an explanation of the Third Reich, and need synthesis rather than to be set in opposition to each other. Hitler's 'intentions' seem above all important in shaping a climate in which the unleashed dynamic turned them into a self-fulfilling prophecy. The Third Reich provides a classic demonstration of Marx's dictum, cited by Mason: 'Men do make their own history, but they do not make it as they please, not under conditions of their own choosing, but rather under circumstances which they find before them, under given and imposed conditions'.[84]

In the two following chapters we need to ask what relevance such conclusions have for anti-Jewish and foreign policy – areas in which Hitler's own ideological obsessions were more obvious than in the domestic arena.

---

[83] See Carr, *Arms, Autarky, and Aggression* (see ch. 3 note 26), p. 65.
[84] Cited in Mason, 'Intention and Explanation', p. 37. See Karl Marx, The *Eighteenth Brumaire of Louis Bonaparte* (Progress Publishers, Moscow, 1954 edn), p. 10.

# 5

## Hitler and the Holocaust

Explaining the Holocaust stretches the historian to the limits in his central task of providing rational explanation of complex historical developments. Simply to pose the question of how a highly cultured and economically advanced modern state could 'carry out the systematic murder of a whole people for no reason other than that they were Jews' suggests a scale of irrationality scarcely susceptible to historical understanding.[1] The very name 'the Holocaust', which acquired its specific application to the extermination of the Jews only in the late 1950s and early 1960s, when it came to be adopted (initially by Jewish writers) in preference to the accurately descriptive term 'genocide', has been taken to imply an almost sacred uniqueness of terrible events exemplifying absolute evil, a specifically Jewish fate standing in effect outside the normal historical process – 'a mysterious event, an upside-down miracle, so to speak, an event of religious significance in the sense that it is not man-made as that term is normally understood'.[2]

The 'mystification' and religious–cultural eschatology which has come for some writers to be incorporated in the term 'the Holocaust' has not made the task of Jewish historians an easy one in a subject understandably and justifiably 'charged with passion and moral judgement'.[3] Given the highly emotive nature of the problem, non-Jewish historians face arguably even greater difficulties in attempting to find the language sensitive and appropriate to the horror of Auschwitz. The sensitivity of the problem is such that over-heated reaction and counter-reaction easily spring from a misplaced or misunderstood word or sentence.

The perspective of non-Jewish historians is, however, inevitably different from that of Jewish historians. And if we are to 'learn' from the Holocaust, then – with all recognition of its 'historical' uniqueness in the sense that close parallels have not *so far* existed – it seems essential to accept that parallels *could* potentially occur in the future, and among peoples other than Germans and Jews. The wider problem alters in essence, therefore, from an attempt to 'explain' the Holocaust specifically through Jewish history or even German–Jewish relations, to the pathology of the modern state and an

[1] Lucy Dawidowicz, *The War against the Jews 1933–45* (Harmondsworth, 1977), p. 17. For the following remarks, see Geoff Eley, 'Holocaust History' (see above ch. 1 note 43).
[2] Yehuda Bauer, *The Holocaust in Historical Perspective* (London, 1978), p. 31. The chapter from which the quotation is taken is an attack on the 'mystification' (as Bauer put it) of the Holocaust. Bauer himself distinguished (pp. 31–5) between genocide – 'forcible, even murderous denationalization' – and the 'uniquely unique' Holocaust – 'total murder of every one of the members of the community'. I have to confess that I do not find the definitions or distinction very convincing or analytically helpful.
[3] Dawidowicz, *War*, p. 17.

attempt to understand the thin veneer of 'civilization' in advanced industrial societies. Specifically applied to the Nazi Dictatorship, this demands an examination of complex processes of rule, and a readiness to locate the persecution of the Jews in a broader context of escalating racial discrimination and genocidal tendencies directed against various minority groups. This is not to forget the very special place which the Jews occupied in the Nazi doctrine, but to argue that the problem of explaining the Holocaust is part of the wider problem of how the Nazi regime functioned, in particular of how decisions were arrived at and implemented in the Nazi State.

The central issue remains, therefore, how Nazi hatred of the Jews became translated into the practice of government, and what precise role Hitler played in this process. Deceptively simple as this question sounds, it is the focal point of current controversy on 'the Holocaust' and forms the basis of the following enquiry, which attempts to survey and then evaluate recent research and interpretation.

## Interpretations

Historians in both parts of Germany after the war came only slowly to concern themselves with anti-semitism and the persecution of the Jews. It was only in the wake of the Eichmann trial in Israel and the revelations of concentration camp trials in the Federal Republic that serious historical work on the Holocaust advanced in West Germany. Even then, historical scholarship and public 'enlightenment' on the fate of the Jews found only a muted echo in the German population, and popular consciousness was reached only through the showing of the American filmed 'soap-opera' dramatization of the Holocaust on West German television in 1979.[4] In the GDR, too, scholarly work on the persecution of the Jews effectively dates from the 1960s, though the subsuming, in the marxist–leninist conception of history, of race hatred within the nature of the class struggle and imperialism has meant that to the present day few important works specifically on the Holocaust have appeared.[5] The recent publications of Kurt Pätzold, while remaining firmly anchored within the marxist–leninist framework, have marked a significant advance in GDR scholarship in this field.[6]

The major impulses to research and to scholarly debate have, therefore, been initiated outside Germany – in the first instance by Jewish scholars in

[4] See the excellent historiographical survey by Konrad Kwiet, 'Zur historiographischen Behandlung der Judenverfolgung im Dritten Reich', *MGM* (1980), Heft 1, pp. 149–92, here esp. pp. 149–53; and the valuable study by Otto Dov Kulka, 'Major Trends and Tendencies of German Historiography on National Socialism and the "Jewish Question" (1924–1984)', *Yearbook of the Leo Baeck Institute* 30 (1985), pp. 215–42. For recent, thorough analyses of the, by now, massive extent of research on most aspects of the Holocaust, see the essays by: Saul Friedländer, 'From Anti-Semitism to Extermination. A Historiographical Study of Nazi Policies towards the Jews and an essay in Interpretation', *Yad Vashem Studies* 16 (1984), pp. 1–50; and Michael Marrus, 'The History of the Holocaust. A Survey of Recent Literature', *JMH* 59 (1987), pp. 114–60.
[5] See Konrad Kwiet, 'Historians of the German Democratic Republic on Antisemitism and Persecution', *Yearbook of the Leo Baeck Institute* 21 (1976), pp. 173–98.
[6] See Kurt Pätzold, *Faschismus, Rassenwahn, Judenverfolgung* (East Berlin, 1975), and 'Vertreibung' (see ch. 3 note 56).

Israel and other countries, and secondarily from non-Jewish historians out-side Germany. However, even where the initial stimulant to debate emanated from non-German writers – and the controversies stirred up by Hannah Arendt's publications on the Eichmann trial[7] and more recently David Irving's attempt to whitewash Hitler's knowledge of the 'Final Solution'[8] provide merely the most spectacular examples – ensuing discussion in the Federal Republic has been strongly influenced by the intellectual climate of German historical writing on Nazism which we have already examined. Hence, the contours of the debate about Hitler and the implementation of the 'Final Solution' – the subject of this chapter – are again peculiarly West German, even where valuable contributions have been made by foreign scholars.

The interpretational divide on this issue brings us back to the dichotomy of 'intention' and 'structure' which we have already encountered. The conven-tional and dominant 'Hitlerist' approach proceeds from the assumption that Hitler himself, from a very early date seriously contemplated, pursued as a main aim, and strived unshakeably to accomplish the physical annihilation of the Jews. According to such an interpretation, the various stages of the persecution of the Jews are to be directly derived from the inflexible continuity of Hitler's aims and intentions; and the 'Final Solution' is to be seen as the central goal of the Dictator from the very beginning of his political career, and the result of a more or less consistent policy (subject only to 'tactical' deviation), 'programmed' by Hitler and ultimately imple-mented according to the Führer's orders. In contrast, the 'structuralist' type of approach lays emphasis upon the unsystematic and improvised shaping of Nazi 'policies' towards the Jews, seeing them as a series of *ad hoc* responses of a splintered and disorderly government machinery. Although, it is argued, this produced an inevitable spiral of radicalization, the actual physical extermination of the Jews was not planned in advance, could at no time before 1941 be in any realistic sense envisaged or predicted, and emerged itself as an *ad hoc* 'solution' to massive, and self-induced, administrative problems of the regime.

The interpretation of the destruction of European Jewry as the 'pro-grammatic' execution of Hitler's unchangeable will has an immediate (though actually superficial) attractiveness and plausibility. It marries well with the views of those historians who incline to explanations of the Third Reich through the development of a specifically German ideology, where a great deal of weight is attached, as a causal factor in Nazism's success, to the spread of anti-semitic ideas and an ideological climate in which Hitler's own radical anti-semitism could find appeal.[9] There is, of course, no difficulty in demonstrating the basic continuity and inner consistency of Hitler's violent

---

[7] See Hannah Arendt, *Eichmann in Jerusalem. A Report on the Banality of Evil* (London, 1963).

[8] David Irving, *Hitler's War* (London, 1977). See the devastating critique by Martin Broszat, 'Hitler und die Genesis der "Endlösung". Aus Anlaß der Thesen von David Irving', *VfZ* 25 (1977), pp. 737–75, esp. pp. 759 ff. Engl. transl., 'Hitler and the Genesis of the "Final Solu-tion": An Assessment of David Irving's Theses' in H. W. Koch, ed., *Aspects of the Third Reich* (London, 1985), pp. 390–429.

[9] E.g. George L. Mosse, *The Crisis of German Ideology* (London, 1964).

hatred of the Jews – ranging from his entry into politics in 1919 to the composition of his Political Testament in the bunker at the end of April 1945 – voiced throughout in the most extreme language conceivable. The interpretation corresponds, too, to the 'totalitarianism' model where state and society were 'co-ordinated' to the level of executors of the wishes of Hitler, the unchallenged 'master in the Third Reich', who determined policy from above, at least in those spheres – like the 'Jewish Question' – where he had a paramount interest. Seen in this light, the logic of the course of anti-Jewish policy from the boycott and legislation of spring 1933 down to the gas chambers of Treblinka and Auschwitz seems clear. In crude terms, the reason why the Jews of Europe were murdered in their millions was because Hitler, the dictator of Germany, wanted it – and had done since he entered politics over two decades earlier.[10] It is in short an explanation of the Holocaust which rests heavily upon an acceptance of the motive force and autonomy of individual will as the determinant of the course of history.

Numerous influential works on the destruction of the Jews have advanced this or similar types of 'Hitlerist' approach. Lucy Dawidowicz, in her widely acclaimed *The War against the Jews*, for instance, declares that Hitler's idea for the 'Final Solution' went back to his experience in the Pasewalk hospital in 1918, and that by the time he wrote the second volume of *Mein Kampf* in 1925 he 'openly espoused his programme of annihilation' in words which 'were to become the blueprint for his policies when he came to power'. She writes of 'the grand design' in Hitler's head, the 'long-range plans to realize his ideological goals' with the destruction of the Jews at their centre, and that the implementation of his plan was subject only to opportunism and expediency. She concludes: 'Through a maze of time, Hitler's decision of November 1918 led to Operation Barbarossa. There never had been any ideological deviation or wavering determination. In the end only the question of opportunity mattered'.[11]

A similar inclination to a personalized explanation of 'the Holocaust' can be found, not unnaturally, in leading biographies of Hitler. Toland has Hitler advocating, as early as 1919, the physical liquidation of Jewry and transforming his hatred of the Jews into a 'positive political programme'.[12] Haffner, too, speaks of a 'cherished wish to exterminate the Jews of the whole of Europe' as being Hitler's aim 'from the beginning on'.[13] Fest relates the first gassing of Jews near Chelmno in Poland in 1941 to Hitler's own experience in the First World War and the notorious lesson he drew from it, as recorded in *Mein Kampf*, that perhaps a million German lives would have been saved if 12,000–15,000 Jews had been put under poison gas at the start of or during the war.[14] And Binion's 'psycho-historical' study argues that Hitler's mission 'to remove Germany's Jewish cancer and to poison out Germany's Jewish poison' emanated from his hallucination while recovering

10  Mason, 'Intention and Explanation' (see ch. 1 note 25), p. 32.
11  Dawidowicz, *War*, pp. 193–208.
12  John Toland, *Adolf Hitler* (New York, 1976), pp. 88–9.
13  Haffner (see ch. 4 note 10), pp. 178–9.
14  Fest (see ch. 4 note 8), vol. 2, p. 930 (Ullstein edn., Frankfurt am Main/Berlin, Vienna, 1976); Adolf Hitler, *Mein Kampf* (Munich, 1943 edn.), p. 772.

from mustard-gas poisoning at Pasewalk, when he allegedly traumatized his mother's death while under treatment from a Jewish doctor and brought this in hysterical association with his trauma at Germany's defeat in 1918. Hitler 'emerged from his trance resolved on entering politics in order to kill the Jews by way of discharging his mission to undo, and reverse, Germany's defeat'. This was his 'main line political track' which ran from Pasewalk to Auschwitz.[15]

The same basic premise of the early formulation and unshakeable retention of Hitler's will to exterminate the Jews as sufficient explanation of 'the Holocaust' underlies Gerald Fleming's recent study, which seeks to document as fully as possible Hitler's personal responsibility for the 'Final Solution'. Though concentrating almost exclusively on the period of extermination itself, the introductory chapters deal with the growth of Hitler's anti-semitism. There, the claim is repeatedly made that 'a straight path' led from Hitler's personal anti-semitism and the development of his original hatred of the Jews to his personal liquidation orders during the war – 'a straight path from Hitler's anti-semitism as shaped in Linz in the period 1904–1907 to the first mass shootings of German Jews in Fort IX in Kowno on 25 and 29 November 1941'. Physical extermination, in Fleming's view, was the aim maintained continually by Hitler from his experience of the November Revolution in 1918 down to his end in the bunker, and at the beginning of the 1920s 'Hitler developed . . . a strategic plan for the realization of his political aim'.[16]

Unwavering continuity of aim, a dominance in shaping anti-Jewish policy from first to last, and the decisive role in the initiation and implementation of the 'Final Solution' are also attributed to Hitler in the most influential works of leading West German experts on the Third Reich. Though prepared to accord 'the historical situation a comparatively high rank in the implementation of National Socialist "Jewish Policy" ',[17] the 'programmatist' line (as it has been styled) sees Nazi anti-Jewish aims and measures as integrally linked to foreign policy, framed along with foreign policy in terms of long-range 'final goals', and advancing 'with inner logic, consistency, and in stages'.[18] Klaus Hildebrand summarizes the position clearly and concisely: 'Fundamental to National Socialist genocide was Hitler's race dogma. . . . Hitler's programmatic ideas about the destruction of the Jews and racial domination have still to be rated as primary and causative, as motive and aim, as intention and goal (*Vorsatz and Fluchtpunkt*) of the "Jewish Policy" of the Third Reich'.[19] For the Swiss historian Walter Hofer, 'it is simply incomprehensible how the claim can be made that the National Socialist race policy was not the realization of Hitler's *Weltanschauung*'.[20]

Hofer's remarks were part of a particularly aggressive critique of the

---

[15] Binion (see ch. 4 note 11), p. 85 and chs. 1, 4; Toland, p. 934.
[16] Gerald Fleming, *Hitler und die Endlösung. 'Es ist des Führers Wunsch'* (Wiesbaden/ Munich, 1982), pp. 13–27 (where Hitler's 'straight path' is mentioned at least four times). An English translation is now available: *Hitler and the Final Solution* (Oxford, 1986).
[17] Hildebrand, *Das Dritte Reich*, p. 178.
[18] Hillgruber, *Endlich genug?*, pp. 64–6 and p. 52 note 88.
[19] Hildebrand, *Das Dritte Reich*, p. 178.
[20] Hofer (see ch. 1 note 2), p. 14.

'structuralist' approach of 'revisionist' historians. The particular target of attack in this instance was Hans Mommsen, who is accused of not seeing because he does not want to see the obvious connection between the announcement of Hitler's programme (in *Mein Kampf* and elsewhere) and its later realization.[21] Mommsen himself has argued forcefully in a number of essays that the implementation of the 'Final Solution' can by no means be attributed to Hitler alone, nor to purely ideological factors in the German political culture.[22] Rather, the explanation has to be sought in the peculiarly fragmented decision-making processes in the Third Reich, which made for improvised bureaucratic initiatives with their own inbuilt momentum, promoting a dynamic process of cumulative radicalization. In his view, the assumption that the 'Final Solution' had to stem from a 'Führer Order' is mistaken. Though unquestionably Hitler knew of and approved of what was taking place, such an assumption, argues Mommsen, flies in the face of his known tendency to let things take their own course and to put off decisions wherever possible. Moreover, it is not compatible with his conscious attempts to conceal his own personal responsibility, with his more subconscious suppression of actual reality even to himself – for all the violence of his propagandistic statements, he never spoke in concrete terms about the 'Final Solution' even in his intimate circle – nor with maintaining the fiction of 'labour deployment' and 'natural wastage' through work. Accordingly, concludes Mommsen, there could have been no formal 'Führer Order' – written or verbal – for the 'Final Solution' of the 'European Jewish Question'. References in the sources to an 'order' or 'commission' as opposed to a vague 'wish of the Führer' relate invariably to the '*Kommissarbefehl*' complex of orders of spring 1941. Though the mass shootings of Russian Jews derived from the '*Kommissarbefehl*' group of directives, they must be distinguished from the 'Final Solution' proper – the systematic extermination of European Jewry. And that the latter was based on a Hitler order is, in Mommsen's view, neither supported by the evidence, nor inherently likely. Rather, although Hitler was the 'ideological and political originator' of the 'Final Solution', a 'utopian objective' could be translated into hard reality 'only in the uncertain light of the Dictator's fanatical propaganda utterances, eagerly seized upon as orders for action by men wishing to prove their diligence, the efficiency of their machinery, and their political indispensability'.

An essentially similar interpretation was advanced by Martin Broszat in his penetrating analysis of the genesis of the 'Final Solution'.[23] Broszat argued that 'there had been no comprehensive general extermination order at all', but that 'the "programme" of extermination of the Jews gradually developed institutionally and in practice out of individual actions down to early 1942 and gained

[21] Hofer, p. 14.
[22] See Hans Mommsen, 'Nationalsozialismus oder Hitlerismus?', pp. 66–70; 'National Socialism: Continuity and Change', p. 179; 'Hitlers Stellung', pp. 61 ff. (full references above ch. 4 note 28), and esp. his outstanding essay 'Die Realisiering des Utopischen: Die "Endlösung der Judenfrage" im "Dritten Reich" ', *GG* 9 (1983), pp. 381–420, here esp. pp. 394–5 and notes 48–9, 399, 416–18. An extended version of last last essay is now published in English translation, 'The Realization of the Unthinkable: the "Final Solution of the Jewish Question" in the Third Reich', in Gerhard Hirschfeld, ed., *The Policies of Genocide* (London, 1986), pp. 97–144.
[23] Broszat, 'Genesis' (above note 8), pp. 753–7.

determinative character after the erection of the extermination camps in Poland (between December 1941 and July 1942)'. In Broszat's view, deportation of the Jews was still the aim until autumn 1941, and it was only in the light of the unexpected failure of the Blitzkrieg invasion of the Soviet Union that problems in the deportation plans and the inability of Gauleiter, police chiefs, SS bosses, and other Nazi leaders in the Occupied Territories to cope with the vast numbers of Jews transported to and concentrated in their domains that led to a growing number of 'local initiatives' being taken to liquidate Jews, which then gained retrospective sanction 'from above'. Following this interpretation, therefore, 'the destruction of the Jews arose, so it seems, not only out of a previously existent will to exterminate, but also as the "way out" of a cul-de-sac in which [the regime] had manoeuvred itself. Once begun and institutionalized, the practice of liquidation nevertheless gained dominant weight and led finally *de facto* to a comprehensive "programme" '.

Broszat went out of his way in this essay (as had Mommsen in his writings) to emphasize that his interpretation could in no sense be seen in moral terms as removing the responsibility and guilt for the 'Final Solution' from Hitler, who approved, sanctioned, and empowered the liquidation actions 'whoever suggested them'. However, it does mean that in terms of actual practice of the implementation of the 'Final Solution', Hitler's personal role can only be indirectly deduced.[24] And morally, this clearly extends the responsibility and culpability to groups and agencies in the Nazi State beyond the Führer himself.

The role of Hitler is reduced still further in the analysis of the GDR historian Kurt Pätzold, who also demonstrates clearly the gradual and late emergence of an extermination 'policy' arising from unco-ordinated but increasingly barbarous attempts to drive Jews out of Germany and German-ruled territory.[25] While his description of the process which led from the aim of expulsion to genocide matches 'structuralist' explanations of western historians, Pätzold relates this to a sense of dynamic 'purpose' and direction of the Nazi regime which sometimes appears to be missing from 'structuralist' accounts. Despite a ritualistic overemphasis upon the functional purpose of anti-Jewish measures in serving the interests of monopoly capital, Pätzold's treatment has the merit, it seems to me, of locating the destruction of the Jews as an element within the overall context of the ruthless and dehumanizing expansionist drive of the Nazi State. This is to turn round the 'Hitlerist' interpretation, where the purposeful direction of Nazism is attributed as good as exclusively to the ideology of the Führer, and where Nazi *Lebensraum* ambitions are regarded as subsumed within and ultimately subordinate to Hitler's manic determination to destroy the Jews.

The lack of a long-range extermination programme has also come to be accepted by leading Israeli experts on 'the Holocaust'. Yehuda Bauer, for instance, writes that 'Nazi policy towards the Jews developed in stages, but that does not mean that at any given turning point there were not other options open to the Nazis that were considered seriously; there developed in Nazi Germany only one clear idea regarding Jews that was accepted by all

[24] Broszat, 'Genesis', pp. 756–7.
[25] Pätzold, 'Vertreibung' (see above ch. 3 note 56).

policy makers, namely the idea that ultimately the Jews had no place in Germany'.[26] Such a position is a recognition of the findings of detailed historical research on the course of anti-Jewish policy during the 1930s, where thorough analysis has suggested that the 'road to Auschwitz', was a 'twisted' one, and not at all the 'straight path' which Fleming and others have seen.[27] Karl Schleunes's conclusion was, in fact, that 'the figure of Adolf Hitler during these years of search is a shadowy one. His hand appears only rarely in the actual making of Jewish policy between 1933 and 1938. One can only conclude from this that he occupied his time with more important concerns. In part the vagaries and inconsistencies of Jewish policy during the first five years of Nazi rule stem from his failure to offer guidance'.[28] Absence of clear objectives led to varying and rival 'policies', all of which ran into difficulties. But there was no turning back on the 'Jewish Question', and it was in this fashion that Hitler's known ideological obsession with the Jews had the objective function – without Hitler having to lift a finger – of pushing a failure in one direction (boycott, legislation, 'Aryanization', or emigration) into a renewed effort to 'solve the problem'.[29] Once again, there is no doubting Hitler's moral responsibility, nor the role his intentions – real or *presumed* – played. But of a consistent implementation of ideological prerogatives, there is little or nothing to be seen: 'The Final Solution as it emerged in 1941 and 1942 was not the product of a grand design'.[30]

[26] Bauer, p. 11.

[27] See particularly the works of Schleunes and Adam (see above ch. 3 note 54).

[28] Schleunes, p. 258. This interpretation has been directly called into question in a well-researched article by David Bankier, 'Hitler and the Policy-Making Process in the Jewish Question', *Holocaust and Genocide Studies* 3 (1988), pp. 1–20, which has just appeared. Bankier succeeds in demonstrating that Hitler did intervene in the 'Jewish Question' more often than has been thought, and that he showed from time to time interest even in the minutiae of anti-Jewish policy. Even so, Bankier takes the thrust of his findings too far in claiming that Hitler 'conceived, initiated, and directed the entire process' (p. 17), and his argument appears to be based in part on a misunderstanding (or exaggeration) of the structuralist (or functionalist) case he is attacking. No one, for example, doubts Hitler's pragmatism and opportunism in the 'Jewish Question', which Bankier is rightly keen to emphasize (pp. 5–8). Bankier's attack on the view (attributed to me among others) that Hitler was 'a moderate' in antisemitic policy rests on a misunderstanding. Even the most ardent 'structuralist' would regard Hitler as the most radical of the radicals in sentiment and any 'moderation' – a term, incidentally, which Bankier himself uses on one occasion (p. 16) – as merely deployed for tactical purposes, a point I myself sought to emphasize in The 'Hitler Myth', (see above ch. 4 note 36) e.g. pp. 236, 239, 250–1. Nor has it ever been in dispute that Hitler's 'profound interest in all matters concerning Jews served as a guideline for state policy in the Jewish Question' (p. 11), or that 'Hitler's ideology was an undeniably powerful factor in the shaping of Nazi antisemitic policy' (p. 16). Within this framework, on which there can be little disagreement, the evidence cited by Bankier interestingly reveals instances of contradictions (p. 13) in Hitler's stance, as well as 'non-decisions' (pp. 10–11). Cases which Bankier cites of Hitler's intervention more often than not arise from points of contention where he is asked to settle a problem, and the generalization that 'it was in fact Hitler and not others who initiated radical measures' (p. 7) is overdrawn. Hitler's own words on 25 August 1941, which Bankier cites (p. 7, from H. R. Trevor-Roper, ed., *Hitler's Table Talk* (London, 1953), p. 90), that 'even with regard to the Jews, I have found myself remaining inactive' – for tactical reasons, let it again be stressed – are themselves an indication that radicalization in the 'Jewish Question' could occur in the absence of his close involvement in the direction of policy.

[29] See Schleunes, p. 259.

[30] Schleunes, Introduction, p. 2.

The exploration of Uwe Dietrich Adam, which had the added advantage of continuing the investigation into the wartime period down to the implementation of the 'Final Solution' itself, arrived at similar conclusions: 'The empirical facts confirm first of all that there can be no talk of a planned and directed policy in this field, that a comprehensive plan for the method, content, and extent of the persecution of the Jews never existed, and that the mass killing and extermination, too, was most probably not striven after *a priori* by Hitler as a political aim'. Unlike Broszat, Adam attributes the commencement of the 'Final Solution' to a personal order of Hitler in autumn 1941. However, in his view this has to be placed in the context of 'an inner development, which bound Hitler too in no small part'.[31]

At the root of the divergence in historical explanations of 'the Holocaust' summarized here lies the basic dichotomy between 'intention' and 'structure'. Was the systematic extermination of European Jewry the direct realization of Hitler's ideologically motivated 'design for destruction', which, after various stages in an exorable process of development, he set into operation through a written or, more likely, verbal 'Führer Order' sometime in 1941? Or did the 'Final Solution' emerge piecemeal, and without any command of Hitler, as 'an imperative result of the system of cumulative radicalization'[32] in the Third Reich? We turn now to a brief evaluation of these positions and an appraisal of some of the available evidence on which an interpretation must be based.

## Evaluation

It seems important to re-emphasize at the outset that, despite claims sometimes made by those adopting a 'Hitlerist' interpretation, Hitler's continuous personal hatred of the Jews, his unique and central importance to the Nazi system in general and to the unfolding of its anti-Jewish policy in particular, and his moral responsibility for what took place are not at stake in the debate.

Historians favouring a 'structuralist' approach readily accept the overwhelming evidence that Hitler maintained a personal, pathologically violent hatred of Jews (whatever its derivation) throughout his political 'career', and recognize, too, the importance of that paranoid obsession *in determining the climate* within which the escalating radicalization of anti-Jewish policies took place. To put the counter-factual point at its crudest: without Hitler as head of the German State between 1933 and 1945, and without his fanaticism on the 'Jewish Question' as impulse and sanction, touchstone and legitimation, of escalating discrimination and persecution, it seems hardly conceivable that the 'Final Solution' would have occurred. This thought itself is sufficient to posit a fundamental link between Hitler and genocide. Moreover, the moral allegation against 'structuralist' historians – that they are 'trivializing' the wickedness of Hitler – is also misplaced. The 'structuralist' approach in no sense denies Hitler's personal, political, and moral responsibility for 'the

---

[31] Adam, *Judenpolitik*, pp. 313, 357–60. See also Uwe Dietrich Adam, 'An Overall Plan for Anti-Jewish Legislation in the Third Reich?', *Yad Vashem Studies* 11 (1976), pp. 33–55, here pp. 34–5.

[32] Mommsen, 'Realisierung', p. 399 note 65.

Holocaust'. But it does broaden that culpability to implicate directly and as active and willing agents large sections of the German non-Nazi élites in the army, industry, and bureaucracy alongside the Nazi leadership and Party organizations. In fact, if anything it is the apparent need to find a supreme culprit which comes close to trivializing *in terms of historical explanation* by diverting attention from the active forces in German society which did not have to be given a 'Führer Order' to turn the screw of Jewish persecution one thread further until extermination became the logical (and only available) 'solution'. The question of allocating guilt thus distracts from the real question the *historian* has to answer: precisely *how* genocide could happen, how an unbalanced, paranoid hatred and chiliastic vision became reality and implemented as horrific government practice.

Rather, the central areas of debate among historians are: whether evidence of Hitler's continued and consistent personal hatred is sufficient explanation in itself of the Holocaust (given a background of widespread racial anti-semitism and ideological hatred of Jews, and a corresponding readiness to carry out 'Führer Orders'); whether physical extermination was Hitler's aim from a very early date or emerged as a realistic idea only as late as 1941 or so – the last remaining option in 'solving the Jewish Question'; and finally, whether it was necessary for Hitler to do more than establish the underlying objective of 'getting rid of Jews' from German territory, and then sanction the unco-ordinated but increasingly radical steps of the various groups in the State who were seeking, often for their own reasons and by no means primarily motivated by anti-semitic ideology, to turn this distant objective into practical reality. These are open questions, not foregone conclusions or matters for dogmatic assertion.

A problem with the 'intentionalist' position – in particular with its extreme 'grand design' variant – is an implicit teleology which takes Auschwitz as a starting-point and looks backwards to the violent expression of Hitler's early speeches and writing, treating these as a 'serious declaration of intent'.[33] Because Hitler frequently spoke about destroying the Jews, and the destruction of the Jews actually took place, the logically false conclusion is drawn that Hitler's expressed 'intention' must have *caused* the destruction. In the light of hindsight, it is easy to attribute a concrete and specific meaning to the barbarous, but vague and fairly commonplace, generalities about 'getting rid' (*Entfernung*) or even 'extermination' (*Vernichtung*) of Jews, which were part and parcel of Hitler's language (and that of others on the *völkisch* Right) from the early 1920s onwards. Coupled with this is the problem of establishing empirically Hitler's initiation or direct instigation of shifts in policy towards fulfilment of his aims – a problem accentuated by Hitler's obvious desire not to be publicly associated with inhumane and brutal measures, and the secrecy and euphemistic language which camouflage the 'Final Solution' itself. If 'programme', 'plan', or 'design' in the context of Nazi anti-Jewish policy are to have real meaning, then they ought to imply something more than the mere conviction, however fanatically held, that somehow the Jews would be 'got rid of' from German territory and from Europe as a whole, and the 'Jewish Question' solved. Before 1941,

33 Mommsen, 'Nationalsozialismus oder Hitlerismus?', p. 67.

the evidence that Hitler had more than such vague and imprecise convictions is slender. Finally, the moral 'lesson' to be drawn from the 'Hitlerist' position – apart from the 'alibi' it provides for non-Nazi institutions in the Third Reich – is by no means obvious. Fleming's rather jejune moral conclusion based upon his 'intentionalist' account of the 'Final Solution' is that hatred feeds the animal instinct for destruction of human life which resides in us all.[34]

More important than such bland moralization is the question posed by 'structuralist' approaches, of how and why a political system in all its complexity and sophistication can within the space of less than a decade become so corrupted that it regards the implementation of genocide as one of its supreme tasks. The central issue here revolves around the nature of 'charismatic' politics – how Hitler's vaguely expressed 'intent' was interpreted and turned into reality by government and bureaucratic agencies which developed their own momentum and impetus. The 'structuralist' type of interpretation also has some weaknesses. The empirical data are seldom good enough to allow detailed reconstruction of the processes of decision-making, on which much of the argument resides. And the emphasis upon contingency, lack of planning, absence of co-ordination, governmental chaos, and the *ad hoc* 'emergence' of policy out of administrative disorder seems at times potentially in danger of neglecting the motive force of intention (however vaguely expressed) and distorting the focus of the regime's ideologically rooted thrust and dynamic drive. However, the 'structuralist' approach does provide the opportunity of *locating* Hitler's 'intentions' within a governmental framework which allowed the bureaucratic implementation of a loose ideological imperative, turning a slogan of 'get rid of the Jews' into a programme of annihilation. And concentration on the historical question of how 'the Holocaust' happened rather than, implicitly or explicitly, seeking to allocate guilt makes the issue of whether Hitler took the initiative at every turn, or whether a particular decision was his alone, seem less relevant and important.

During the pre-war years, as the evidence assembled and analysed by Schleunes and Adam convincingly demonstrates, it seems clear that Hitler took no specific initiative in the 'Jewish Question' and *responded* to rather than instigated the confused and often conflicting lines of 'policy' which emerged. The main impulses derived from the pressure 'from below' of Party activists, the internal organizational and bureaucratic dynamism of the SS–Gestapo–SD apparatus, the personal and institutional rivalries which found an outlet in the 'Jewish Question', and, not least, from economic interest in eliminating Jewish competition and expropriating Jewish capital.

The national boycott of Jewish businesses which took place on 1 April 1933 was organized chiefly as a response to the pressure of Party radicals, especially within the SA, during the wave of violence and brutality unleashed

---

[34] Fleming, p. 206. See also p. 204 for his conclusion that those implementing Hitler's orders acted out of opportunism, servility, lack of character, and 'the petty-bourgeois zeal of a following whose idealism was abused'.

by the 'seizure of power'. The only 'plans' of the NSDAP for tackling the 'Jewish Question' which had been formulated before Hitler became Chancellor related to measures for legal discrimination and deprivation of civil rights.[35] Such vague and undetailed administrative 'plans' hardly accorded with the wild and dangerous mood of Party activists in the post- 'seizure of power' euphoria of spring 1933. In these weeks, in fact, no directives at all on 'the Jewish Question' came either from the Reich Chancellory or from the Nazi Party headquarters.[36] Meanwhile, the SA, whose 'enthusiasm' could hardly now be checked, had started its own anti-Jewish campaign of boycotts and violence. When Gestapo chief Rudolf Diels complained about the excesses of the Berlin SA, he was informed that 'for very human reasons, certain activity must be found which will satisfy the feelings of our comrades'.[37] Under pressure, Hitler reacted towards the end of March with the call for a general boycott against Jewish businesses and professions, starting on 1 April and to be organized by a 14-man steering committee under the direction of Julius Streicher. As is well known, the boycott was a notable failure, and in the light of the negative echo abroad, the lack of enthusiasm among important sectors of the conservative power-élite (including President Hindenburg), and the cool indifference of the German people, it was called off after a single day and a co-ordinated national boycott was never again attempted. The shameful discriminatory legislation of the first months of the Dictatorship, aimed at Jews in the civil service and the professions, arose in the same climate and under the same pressures. Hitler's own direct role was a limited one dictated by the need he felt, despite his obvious approval of the boycott, to avoid association with the worst 'excesses' of the Party radicals. But the pace was forced by the momentum of the violence and illegalities, which produced their own compulsion to provide *post facto* legitimation and sanction – a process which was to repeat itself in later stages of the persecution of the Jews.[38]

Following a relatively quiet period between the summer of 1933 and the beginning of 1935, a new anti-semitic wave began and lasted until the autumn of 1935. Again, the agitation was set in motion and sustained 'from below' through the pressure at Gau level and from activists in the Party and in Hitler Youth and SA units in the localities. One Gauleiter noted in his report that stirring up the 'Jewish Question' had been useful in revamping the sagging morale of the lower middle class.[39] The agitation was, of course, backed by propaganda from the Party and from the State. But other than that, there was remarkably little intervention from either the Party's headquarters or from the Reich government before mid August, when the boycotts and violence were becoming recognizably counter-productive, both in the repercussions for the German economy and on account of the unpopularity of the frequent breaches of the peace. Hitler himself was hardly involved in any direct sense. Despite his radical instincts, he was

---

35 Schleunes, p. 70; Adam, *Judenpolitik*, pp. 28 ff.
36 Schleunes, p. 71.
37 Cited in Schleunes, p. 74.
38 Schleunes, pp. 92–102; Adam, *Judenpolitik*, pp. 64 ff., esp. p. 68.
39 Marlis G. Steinert, *Hitlers Krieg und die Deutschen* (Düsseldorf/Vienna, 1970), p. 57.

effectively compelled in this phase – in the interests of 'order', of the economy, and of diplomatic relations – to recognize the necessity of bringing the
damaging campaign to a close.[40] This had to be balanced against the need not
to lose face with Party activists and the pressure to comply with Party
demands for 'action' – particularly for legislation in line with the demands
of the Party programme – in the 'Jewish Question'. The resulting 'compromise' was effectively the promulgation of the notorious 'Nuremberg Laws'
in September 1935 – at one and the same time according with demands for
clear guidance and 'regulation' of the 'Jewish Question', and a further turn
of the discriminatory screw.

The creation of the Nuremberg Laws demonstrates clearly how Hitler and
the Nazi leadership responded to the considerable pressures from below in
their formulation of anti-Jewish policy at this date.

The agitation and violence of the spring and summer 1935 rekindled
expectations within the Party of incisive anti-Jewish legislation.[41] Hints and
half-promises of measures were made by Reich Minister of the Interior Frick
and others, bureaucrats hurried to regulate discrimination which was
already taking place, and bans on various Jewish activities introduced independently by the Gestapo also forced retrospective sanctions by the
administrators. One area of discontent among Party agitators was the failure
to introduce the long-awaited exclusion of Jews from German citizenship.
Despite indications from the Reich Ministry of the Interior, where preparations were underway, the summer brought nothing to satisfy the hotheads.
The other major issue whipped up by propaganda and agitation was that of
mixed marriages and sexual relations between 'Aryans' and Jews. Again,
illegal but sanctioned terroristic actions in cases of 'racial defilement' forced
the pace and shaped the atmosphere. The urgent need for legislation was
accepted by the regime's leaders at an important ministerial meeting chaired
by Schacht on 20 August. Only the timing remained undecided. There were
in fact already rumours in the foreign press in late August that the official
proclamation might come at the Nuremberg Party Rally in September.
Though such rumours turned out to be accurate, it is possible that they were
at the time no more than intelligent speculation since it still appears that the
decision to promulgate the laws at a special meeting of the Reichstag
summoned to Nuremberg was taken only after the Rally had actually
started – probably under renewed pressure from 'Reich Doctors' Leader'
Gerhard Wagner who, apparently after talks with Hitler, announced on 12
September the intention of promulgating a 'Law for the Protection of
German Blood'. From this point, as is well known, things moved fast.
'Experts' on the 'Jewish Question' were suddenly summoned to Nuremberg
on 13 September and told to prepare a law regulating marriage between

[40] Adam, *Judenpolitik*, p. 121.
[41] This account of the genesis of the Nuremberg Laws is primarily based upon Adam,
*Judenpolitik*, pp. 118–22, 126; Schleunes, pp. 120–1; and, especially, upon the new analyses of
Lothar Gruchmann, ' "Blutschutzgesetz" und Justiz. Zur Entstehung und Auswirkung des
Nürnberger Gesetzes vom 15. September 1935', *VfZ* 31 (1983), pp. 418–42, here esp.
pp. 428–33, and Otto Dov Kulka, 'Die Nürnberger Rassengesetze und die deutsche
Bevölkerung im Lichte geheimer NS-Lage- und Stimmungsberichte', *VfZ* 32 (1984), pp. 582–
624, here esp. pp. 614–20.

'Aryans' and Jews. The sudden decision to promulgate anti-Jewish laws during the Rally seems to have been predominantly determined by questions of propaganda, presentation, and image. The Reichstag had been summoned to Nuremberg, where Hitler originally intended, in the presence of the Diplomatic Corps, to make an important statement on foreign policy, exploiting the Abyssinian conflict to articulate German revisionist demands. On the advice of Foreign Minister von Neurath, this plan was dropped on 13 September. A suitable replacement programme for the Reichstag and for Party consumption had rapidly to be found.[42] The rather undramatic 'Flag Law' hardly matched the demands of the occasion. Hence, the 'Blood Law', now being frantically drafted, and a Reich Citizenship Law, drafted in an hour on 14 September, were brought in as a substantial offering to the Reichstag and the assembled Party faithful. Hitler himself, who chose the mildest of the four drafts of the 'Blood Law' presented to him, apparently preferred to remain in the background during the drafting, pushing the Racial Political Office to the forefront. His role was a characteristically vague and elusive one in the question of how to define 'a Jew', when a conference for this purpose met at Munich at the end of the month. Hitler confined himself to a long monologue on the Jews, announced that the definitional problem would be sorted out between the Reich Ministry of the Interior and the Party, and adjourned the conference. It was mid November before State officials and representatives of the Party could iron out a compromise solution – after Hitler had cancelled a further planned meeting in early November at which he had been expected to resolve the matter.[43]

Hitler continued to take no initiative in the 'Jewish Question' during the relatively quiet years of 1936–7, in which the rivalries mounted between the various agencies with an interest in Jewish affairs – the Ministry of the Interior, the Economics Ministry, the Foreign Ministry, the Four Year Plan Administration, the Rosenberg Agency, and, not least, the SS and Gestapo apparatus. A clear line of policy was as distant as ever. To go from Goebbels's informative diary record of these years, Hitler appears to have spoken directly about the Jews only infrequently, and then in general terms, as in November 1937, when, in a long discussion with Goebbels about the 'Jewish Question', he allegedly said: 'The Jew must get out of Germany, yes out of the whole of Europe. That will take some time yet, but will and must happen'. According to Goebbels, the Führer was 'firmly decided' on it.[44]

These comments followed only a few weeks after Hitler had made his first public attack on the Jews for some time in a rhetorical propaganda tirade against 'the Jewish–Bolshevik World Enemy' during the Party Rally in September 1937.[45] This was enough to set the tone for a renewal of anti-semitic

---

[42] Mommsen, 'Realisierung', p. 387 and note 20. See also, for this section, Adam, *Judenpolitik*, pp. 125 ff., and Schleunes, pp. 121 ff.

[43] Adam, *Judenpolitik*, pp. 135–40; Schleunes, p. 128. Bankier (p. 14) points out that the first implementation ordinances to the Nuremberg Laws, legally defining a Jew, were reshaped to conform with Hitler's view. But Hitler's uncertainty, then anxiety to reach a compromise solution, are confirmed by Goebbels's diary notes, – *Die Tagebücher von Joseph Goebbels* (see p. 80 note 82), vol. 2, pp. 520–1, 536–7, 540–1, entries of 1 Oct., 7 and 15 Nov. 1935.

[44] *Die Tagebücher von Joseph Goebbels*, vol. 3, p. 351, entry of 30 Nov. 1937.

[45] Adam, *Judenpolitik*, p. 173.

activity on a large scale. However, Hitler himself needed to do no more in order to stimulate the process of 'aryanization' of Jewish concerns in the interests of 'big business', which set in at the end of 1937 and where Göring was the chief driving-force, nor to direct the escalating wave of violence which followed the *Anschluß* and became magnified during the Sudeten crisis of the summer. The agitation and terror of the Party rank-and-file in the summer and autumn of 1938, together with the expulsion in October of some 17,000 Polish Jews living in Germany – a move itself prompted by actions of the Polish government to deny them re-entry into Poland – shaped the ugly atmosphere which exploded in the so-called 'Crystal Night' pogrom of 9–10 November. And, as is generally known, the initiator here was Goebbels, who sought to exploit the situation in an attempt to re-establish his waned favour and influence with Hitler. Other than apparently giving Goebbels the green light verbally, Hitler himself took care to remain in the background, and to accept no responsibility for actions which were both unpopular with the public and castigated (though of course not from humane motives) by Nazi leaders.[46]

'Crystal Night', concludes Schleunes, 'was a product of the lack of co-ordination which marked Nazi planning on Jewish policy and the result of a last-ditch effort by the radicals to wrest control over this policy'.[47] In propaganda terms, it was a failure. But, as usual, Nazi leaders, differing in their proposals for tackling the problem, concurred in the view that radical measures were needed. Jews were now excluded from the economy, and responsibility for 'the solution of the Jewish Question', though formally entrusted to Göring, was effectively placed in the hands of the SS. Emigration, which had significantly increased in the panic after the pogrom, remained the main aim, and was to be channelled through a central office set up in January 1939. The start of the war did not alter this aim. But it did alter the possibilities of its implementation.

The war itself and the rapid conquest of Poland brought about a transformation in the 'Jewish Question'. Forced emigration was no longer an option, and plans, for instance, to try to 'sell' Jews for foreign currency were not now feasible. After working on the idea of making German territory 'free of Jews', the Nazis now of course had an additional three million Polish Jews to cope with. On the other hand, there was now little need for consideration of foreign reactions, so that treatment of Polish Jews – as 'eastern Jews' particularly despised and dehumanized, the lowest form of existence in a conquered enemy itself held in contempt – reached levels of barbarity far in excess of what had taken place in Germany or Austria. Moreover, the more or less free hand given to Party and police, untrammelled by legal restraints or worries about 'public opinion', provided wide scope for autonomous individual 'initiatives' in the 'Jewish Question'.

Before considering the debate about whether the 'Final Solution' was instigated by a single, comprehensive 'Führer Order', and when such an

---

[46] See Adam, *Judenpolitik*, pp. 206–7; Schleunes, ch. 7 (esp. pp. 240 ff.); and, in general, for the pogrom and its aftermath, Rita Thalmann and Emmanuel Feinermann, *Crystal Night: 9–10 November 1938* (London, 1974).
[47] Schleunes, p. 236.

order might have been given, it seems important to glance briefly at the process of radicalization as it gathered momentum between 1939 and 1941.

An administrative decree of 21 September 1939, in which Heydrich laid down the general lines of Jewish persecution in Poland, distinguished between a long-term 'final aim' or 'planned overall measures' – not further elucidated and to remain strictly secret – and short-term 'preliminary measures' with the intention of concentrating the Jews in larger cities around railway junctions.[48] It would be mistaken to draw the conclusion that the vaguely indicated 'final aim' meant the programmed annihilation of the actual 'Final Solution' which later evolved. Clearly, however, the operative part of the decree related to the provisional concentration of Jews for further transportation. On Himmler's order a few weeks later, on 30 October, all Jews in the north-western part of Poland, now called the Warthegau and annexed to the Reich, were to be deported into the so-called *General-gouvernement* – the rest of German-occupied Poland under the governorship of Hans Frank – in order to make housing and jobs available for the Germans to be settled there. Hans Frank had accordingly to be prepared to receive several hundred thousand deported Jews and Poles from the Warthegau.[49] The policy of forced expulsion led unavoidably to the establishment of ghettos – the first of which was erected at Łódź (Litzmannstadt) in December 1939. Almost at the same time, compulsory labour was introduced for all Jews in the *Generalgouvernement*. The twin steps of ghettoization and forced labour provided part of the momentum which was later to culminate in the 'Final Solution'.[50] For the present, it was presumed that the deportations from the annexed areas would bring about the rapid end of the 'Jewish Question' there, and that in the *General-gouvernement* those Jews (including women and children) incapable of work should be confined to ghettos, and Jews available for hard labour should be assigned to forced labour camps. This decision, taken at a meeting of top SS leaders in January 1940, and accepting the inevitable deaths of thousands through exhaustion, hunger, and disease, marks a point at which 'the murderous anti-semitic idea, previously existing in a general, abstract form, began to take the shape of a concrete project. The decision to murder millions had at this point still not been taken. But in thought and practice a step in that direction had been taken'.[51]

In early 1940 there were still substantial differences of opinion on finding a 'solution to the Jewish Question', and there was no sign of any clear or comprehensive programme. Obviously not anticipating an early 'solution', Hans Frank indicated in a speech in March that the Reich could not be rendered 'free of Jews' during the war.[52] A few months later, Frank was faced with a demand to receive quarter of a million inhabitants of the Łódź ghetto, whom Gauleiter Greiser of the Warthegau wanted to be rid of from his domains. Frank refused, at which one of Greiser's team declared

48   Pätzold, 'Vertreibung', p. 193. Doc. in Noakes and Pridham, vol. 3, p. 1051.
49   Pätzold, 'Vertreibung', p. 194.
50   Pätzold, 'Vertreibung', pp. 196–7; Mommsen, 'Realisierung', p. 406.
51   Pätzold, 'Vertreibung', p. 196.
52   Pätzold, 'Vertreibung', p. 198.

ominously that the 'Jewish Question would have to be solved in some sort of way'.[53]

'Jewish policy' in mid 1940 – by which time West European Jews had also fallen into German hands and the real possibility of an overall European 'solution' had arisen – was still in a state of confusion. Eichmann still nurtured ideas of a comprehensive programme of emigration to Palestine.[54] Attempts to further the emigration of Jews from Germany itself (mainly via Spain and Portugal) continued to be promoted well into 1941.[55] However, arbitrary deportation of Jews from eastern areas of the Reich into the *Generalgouvernement* was banned by Göring in March 1940, after Hans Frank had refused to accept any further deportees.[56] And for the 'eastern Jews' – by far the majority under German rule – emigration was in any case not an option. In June 1940 Heydrich informed Foreign Minister Ribbentrop that the 'overall problem' of the approximately three and a quarter million Jews in German-ruled territory could 'no longer be solved through emigration' and that 'a territorial solution' was therefore necessary.[57] Jewish representatives were told that a reservation in an as yet undefined colonial territory was what the government had in mind.[58] A few days earlier Franz Rademacher, head of the Jewish desk of the Foreign Office, had presented plans to create the reservation in Madagaskar – a suggestion apparently approved by Himmler, mentioned by Hitler in talks with Mussolini and Ciano that same month, and finally laid to rest only at the start of 1942.[59] The reservation plans were certainly taken seriously for a while, and in the light of recent research cannot be regarded as simply a camouflage for the early stages of the 'Final Solution' itself – though undoubtedly any reservation plan would have led to physical extermination.[60]

Towards the end of 1940 there was no end of the Jewish ghettos in Poland apparent in the foreseeable future. At the same time, the condition of the inhabitants was worsening daily, and coming to resemble the appalling caricature of Jewish existence portrayed in the nauseating propaganda film of 1940, *The Eternal Jew*.[61] From the point of view of the Nazi overlords, the acute problems of hygiene, food provisioning, accommodation, and administration attached to the ghettos called out for 'a relief from the burden and a solution'. Possible ways out were already being mooted: in March 1941 Victor Brack, a leading official in the Führer Chancellory who had been in charge of the so-called 'Euthanasia Action' which had liquidated

53 Pätzold, 'Vertreibung', p. 197.
54 Mommsen, 'Realisierung', p. 407.
55 Pätzold, 'Vertreibung', pp. 199–200; Christopher Browning, *The Final Solution and the German Foreign Office* (New York, 1978), pp. 44; Helmut Krausnick *et al., The Anatomy of the SS State* (London, 1968), p. 67.
56 Browning, *Final Solution*, p. 46; Mommsen, 'Realisierung', p. 407. Doc. in Noakes and Pridham, vol. 3, p. 1058.
57 Pätzold, 'Vertreibung', p. 201.
58 Mommsen, 'Realisierung', p. 407.
59 Browning, *Final Solution*, pp. 38, 79.
60 Mommsen, 'Realisierung', pp. 395 note 52, 408; Pätzold, 'Vertreibung', p. 206.
61 See David Welch, *Propaganda and the German Cinema 1933–1945* (Oxford, 1983), pp. 292 ff.

over 70,000 mental patients and others in Germany between 1939 and 1941, proposed methods for sterilizing between 3,000 and 4,000 Jews a day.[62]

By this time, spring 1941, the Nazi and military leadership were fully engaged in the preparations for the invasion (and expected rapid Blitzkrieg victory) of the Soviet Union. In these preparations, the 'Jewish problem' entered a new dimension – the last phase before the actual 'Final Solution'. The instructions to the SS-*Einsatzgruppen* to shoot Russian Jews marked a radicalization of anti-Jewish policy, which Christopher Browning justifiably labelled 'a quantum jump'.[63] This brings us back to our central concern of Hitler's personal role in the genesis of the 'Final Solution'.


The inadequacy of the sources, reflecting in good measure the secrecy of the killing operations and the deliberate unclarity of the language employed to refer to them, has led to historians drawing widely varying conclusions from the same evidence about the timing and the nature of the decision or decisions to exterminate the Jews. Eberhard Jäckel hints that a Hitler order for the extermination of the European Jews might have been given as early as summer 1940 – on the basis of a source, which he himself admits is not a good one (the memoirs of Himmler's masseur and *confidant* Felix Kersten). However, he adjudges spring 1941 to be the period when the key decisions were taken, in the context of preparations for the Russian campaign.[64] Krausnick writes of a 'secret decree . . . that the Jews should be eliminated' being issued by Hitler not later than March 1941, in the context of the directives to shoot the political commissars of the Red Army.[65] Hillgruber points to a verbal order of Hitler to either Himmler or Heydrich by at latest May 1941 for the systematic liquidation of Russian Jews, and implies the issuing of an order extending this to all European Jews before the end of July 1941, when Heydrich received from Göring the commission to undertake preparations for 'a total solution of the Jewish Question' in the German sphere of influence and to submit an overall plan of measures necessary 'for the accomplishment of the final solution of the Jewish question which we desire'.[66] Most leading accounts (for instance of Reitlinger, Hilberg,

[62] Pätzold, 'Vertreibung', p. 204.

[63] Browning, *Final Solution*, p. 8.

[64] Eberhard Jäckel, 'Hitler und der Mord an den europäischen Juden', in Peter Märthesheimer and Ivo Frenzel, eds., *Im Kreuzfeuer: Der Fernsehfilm 'Holocaust'. Eine Nation ist betroffen* (Frankfurt am Main, 1979), pp. 151–62, here p. 156. See now Jäckel, *Hitler in History*, pp. 51 ff; Eberhard Jäckel, *Hitlers Herrschaft* (Stuttgart, 1986), pp. 99 ff; and Eberhard Jäckel and Jürgen Rohwer, *Der Mord an den Juden im Zweiten Weltkrieg* (Stuttgart, 1985), pp. 9–17, 190–1.

[65] Krausnick, *Anatomy*, p. 60 (and see also p. 68).

[66] Andreas Hillgruber, 'Die ideologisch-dogmatische Grundlage der nationalsozialistischen Politik der Ausrottung der Juden in den besetzten Gebieten der Sowjetunion und ihre Durchführung 1941–44', *German Studies Review* 2 (1979), pp. 264–96, here p. 273, and also pp. 277–8; Andreas Hillgruber, 'Die "Endlösung" und das deutsche Ostimperium als Kernstück des rassenideologischen Programms des Nationalsozialismus', in Funke (see ch. 3 note 27), pp. 94–114, here pp. 103–5. The text of Göring's order is in Noakes and Pridham (see ch. 3 note 37), vol. 3, p. 1104 and Gerald Reitlinger, *The Final Solution* (Sphere Books edn, London, 1971), p. 85.

Dawidowicz, and now Fleming) concur in indicating a decision by Hitler to implement the 'Final Solution' during the spring or more likely the summer of 1941, and seeing this incorporated in the Göring mandate of 31 July.[67] Christopher Browning, too, emphasizes the centrality of Göring's order as reflecting a decision which Hitler had taken in the summer to extend the killing to all European Jews. However, he relativizes Hitler's decision by seeing it more in the shape of a prompting initiative rather than a clear directive, which the Führer approved and sanctioned in October or November.[68] Adam argues for a decision by Hitler in the autumn rather than the summer, at a time when the German advance in Russia had halted and vague ideas of a 'territorial solution' east of the Urals had obviously become totally illusory.[69] A more radical position is adopted by Broszat, Mommsen, and Streit, who reject altogether the existence of a single, specific, and comprehensive 'Führer Order' – written or verbal – and place the emphasis upon the cumulative 'sanctioning' of '*de facto*' exterminations, initiated by other agencies and wildly escalating, between the summer of 1941 and early 1942, out of which the 'Final Solution' proper – the systematic gassing in the extermination camps – 'evolved'.[70] A similar interpretation seems implicitly offered by Hans-Heinrich Wilhelm at the end of a recent exhaustive study of the *Einsatzgruppen*, when he writes of a Hitler decision in the summer of 1941, but only relating to 'eastern Jews', with gradual later extension and radicalization, though not without Hitler's express agreement.[71]

As these varied interpretations of leading experts demonstrate, the evidence for the precise nature of a decision to implement the 'Final Solution', for its timing, and even for the very existence of such a decision is circumstantial. Though second-rank SS leaders repeatedly referred in post-war trials to a 'Führer Order' or 'Commission', no direct witness of such an order survived the war. And for all the brutality of his own statements, there is no record of Hitler speaking categorically even in his close circle of a decision he had taken to kill the Jews – though his remarks leave not the

[67] Reitlinger, pp. 82–6; Raul Hilberg, *The Destruction of the European Jews* (New Viewpoints edn, New York, 1973), pp. 177, 257, 262; Dawidowicz, *War*, p. 169; Fleming, p. 59.

[68] Browning, *Final Solution*, p. 8, and Christopher Browning, 'Zur Genesis der "Endlösung". Eine Antwort an Martin Broszat', *VfZ* 29 (1981), pp. 97–109, here pp. 98, 108 (also now in Engl. trans.: 'A Reply to Martin Broszat regarding the Origins of the Final Solution', *Simon Wiesenthal Center Annual* 1 (1984), pp. 113–32). For Browning's position, see now above all his *Fateful Months* (New York, 1985), ch. 1, 'The Decision concerning the Final Solution'.

[69] Adam, *Judenpolitik*, pp. 312–13. A similar date is favoured in a recent article by Shlomo Aronson, 'Die dreifache Falle. Hitlers Judenpolitik, die Alliierten und die Juden', *VfZ* 32 (1984), pp. 51–2.

[70] Broszat, 'Genesis', pp. 753 note 26, 763 ff.; Mommsen, 'Realisierung', pp. 416 and note 148, 417; Christian Streit, review of Helmut Krausnick and Hans-Heinrich Wilhelm, *Die Truppe des Weltanschauungskrieges. Die Einsatzgruppen der Sicherheitspolizei und des SD 1938–1942* (Stuttgart, 1981) in *Bulletin of the German Historical Institute, London* 10 (1982), p. 17. In his earlier book, *Keine Kameraden. Die Wehrmacht und die sowjetischen Kriegsgefangenen 1941–1945* (Stuttgart, 1978), pp. 126 and p. 355 note 274, Streit appears to favour Adam's argument, though he found Broszat's then recent 'Genesis' article also 'convincing'.

[71] Krausnick and Wilhelm, pp. 634–5. The decision-making process in the 'Final Solution' has recently been the subject of a major international conference, at which all interpretations were discussed. See Jäckel and Ruhwer (ref. in note 64 above).

slightest doubt of his approval, broad knowledge, and acceptance of the 'glory' for what was being done in his name.[72] Interpretation rests, therefore, on the 'balance of probabilities.'[73] We need briefly to consider the evidence in this light.

Hitler did not need to issue directives or take clear initiatives in order to promote the process of radicalization in the 'Jewish Question' between 1939 and 1941. Rather, as we have seen, the momentum was largely stimulated by a combination of bureaucratic measures emanating from the Reich Security Head Office (whose administrative consequences were not clearly envisaged), and *ad hoc* initiatives taken 'on the ground' by individuals and agencies responsible for coping with an increasingly unmanageable task. Typical of Hitler's stance was his wish, expressed towards the end of 1940, that his Gauleiter in the East should be accorded the 'necessary freedom of movement' to accomplish their difficult task, that he would demand from his Gauleiter *after 10 years* only the single announcement that their territories were purely German, and would not enquire about the methods used to bring this about.[74] His own direct role was largely confined to the propaganda arena – to public tirades of hatred and dire but vague prognostications about the fate of the Jews. The most notorious of these is his Reichstag speech of 30 January 1939, when he 'prophesied' that the war would bring about the 'annihilation [*Vernichtung*] of the Jewish race in Europe' – a prophecy to which he made frequent reference in the years to come, and which he significantly post-dated to 1 September 1939, the day of the outbreak of war.[75] This itself reflected Hitler's mental merger of the war and his 'mission' to destroy the Jews, which reached its fateful point of convergence in the conception of the 'war of annihilation' against the Soviet Union.[76]

The orders to the *Einsatzgruppen* to exterminate Russian Jews formed part of the complex of barbarous preparations for the attack on the Soviet Union which implicated the *Wehrmacht*, too, in the series of criminal directives associated with the '*Kommissarbefehl*' – the ordered shooting of political commissars in the Soviet army. Like the *Kommissarbefehl*, the instructions to the SS death-squads, conveyed to them by Heydrich during their 'training' and briefing sessions in the weeks before the invasion, were almost certainly grounded in a verbal blanket empowering directive from Hitler, as *Einsatzgruppen* leaders themselves repeatedly claimed after the war.[77] The *Einsatzgruppen* made a major contribution to the murder of in all

[72] See Mommsen, 'Realisierung', pp. 391 ff. It is uncertain whether and how far Hitler was directly informed about the actual details of the killings in the East (see p. 409 and note 117), even though directives had been given to keep him in the picture regarding the 'progress' of the *Einsatzgruppen* (see Fleming, p. 123; Krausnick and Wilhelm, p. 335). For Hitler's public references to the 'Final Solution', see Kershaw, *The 'Hitler Myth'*, pp. 243–4.

[73] Broszat, 'Genesis', p. 753; Browning, 'Zur Genesis', pp. 98, 105, 109.

[74] Cited in Krausnick and Wilhelm, pp. 626–7. Doc. in Noakes and Pridham, vol. 3, p. 1081.

[75] Hillgruber, 'Die ideologisch-dogmatische Grundlage', pp. 271, 285 ff.; Jäckel, 'Hitler und der Mord', pp. 160–2.

[76] See esp. Hillgruber's essays on this point, references above note 66.

[77] Krausnick, *Anatomy*, pp. 60–4; Krausnick and Wilhelm, pp. 150 ff., 634; Hillgruber, 'Die ideologisch-dogmatische Grundlage', p. 243; Heinz Höhne, *The Order of the Death's Head* (Pan Books edn, London, 1972), pp. 329–30. For controversy about the nature of the orders given to the *Einsatzgruppen*, see Browning, *Fateful Months*, pp. 17–20.

over two million Russian Jews; *Einsatzgruppe* A alone reported the 'execution' of 229,052 Jews by the beginning of January 1942.[78] Their detailed
monthly 'reports of events' belong to the most horrific surviving relics of the
Third Reich. The vast numbers of Russian Jews massacred speaks plainly in
favour of a general commission from above, rather than local initiatives on the
part of trigger-happy units of the *Einsatzgruppen*.[79] At the same time, the difference in practice among the various units implies that their instructions had
not been stated in unequivocal, unambiguous terms. Morever, it is certain that
this was not *the* order for the 'Final Solution'. It was 'confined' to 'eastern
Jews' and was in all probability extended only after a month or two (possibly
on Himmler's initiative) to include women and children.[80] It seems likely, as
Wilhelm has argued,[81] that during the various briefings of the *Einsatzgruppen*
there was talk not only of exterminating Jews in the Russian territories, to
which they were about to be sent, but of the annihilation of all Jews in the
German-occupied parts of Europe. But at that stage, clearly, nothing concrete
had been decided upon. Indeed, there was evidently a lack of clarity among the
heads of the *Einsatzgruppen* and other leaders of SS, Party, and police in the
eastern occupied territory both about the precise scope of their task and about
the nature of any long-term solution to the 'Jewish problem'. Wilhelm has
pointed out that the sharp differences of opinion and varying interpretations
show that 'the "Führer Order" to exterminate the Jews was for those commissioned with its implementation just as little sacrosanct as many an other
"Führer Order". Its interpretation and expedient modifications could be
and were pondered over'.[82] Even Hitler himself spoke, to the uncertainty of
those involved, in his inner circle at this time in ambivalent and contradictory
terms about the future course of anti-Jewish actions.[83]

A hint that the possibility was being mooted, even before the
*Einsatzgruppen* had begun their massacres of Russian Jews, of a 'solution'
involving all European Jews is given in Eichmann's circular of 20 May 1941,
advising of Göring's ban on Jewish emigration from France and Belgium (in
order not to block any further possible emigration of German Jews) and men-
tioning the imminent proximity of the 'final solution of the Jewish problem'
which was 'doubtless to come'.[84] It was, however, over two months later, after
the death-squads had been rampaging in the Soviet Union for almost six
weeks, that Heydrich received the order from Göring to prepare for 'a total
solution of the Jewish question'.[85] As we noted earlier, this authorization,
initiated and drafted by Heydrich for Göring's signature in the context of the
expected imminent victory over the Soviet Union,[86] has frequently been

---

[78] Krausnick, *Anatomy*, p. 64; Krausnick and Wilhelm, p. 619. Wilhelm's conservative estimate of the total number of murdered Russian Jews, on the basis of the most exhaustive analysis
possible of incomplete evidence, is 2.2 million (Krausnick and Wilhelm, pp. 618–22). The large
proportion of these killed specifically by the *Einsatzgruppen* cannot be precisely determined.
[79] Krausnick and Wilhelm, p. 634.
[80] Krausnick and Wilhelm, pp. 164–5; Streit, review (see above note 70), p. 18.
[81] Krausnick and Wilhelm, p. 627.
[82] Krausnick and Wilhelm, p. 630.
[83] Krausnick and Wilhelm, pp. 630–1.
[84] Krausnick, *Anatomy*, p. 67; Reitlinger, p. 84; Fleming, p. 57. Doc. in Noakes and Pridham,
vol. 3, pp. 1084–5
[85] Reitlinger, p. 85. Doc. in Noakes and Pridham, vol. 3, p. 1104.
[86] See Jäckel and Ruhwer, p. 15.

interpreted as giving voice to a Hitler directive marking *the* order for the 'Final Solution'. This interpretation seems open to question. Whether Göring (who of course denied it at Nuremberg), Heydrich, or Himmler received a firm directive or precise verbal orders from Hitler himself at or around this time cannot be proven and may be intrinsically doubted. Perhaps, as Browning suggests, Hitler gave a 'nod of the head' which, given the nature of decision-making and policy implementation in the Third Reich, was all that was necessary to approve a suggestion that the time had come to contemplate a 'total solution' of the 'problem'.[87] If discussed at all with Hitler at this time, the language used on both sides was probably draconian but extremely vague and open-ended. The direct initiative may well have come from the Reich Security Head Office, and not from Hitler himself.

Certainly, the summer and autumn of 1941 were characterized by a high degree of confusion and contradictory interpretations of the aims of anti-Jewish policy by the Nazi authorities (and even, as we saw, by Hitler himself). It was a period of experimentation and resort to 'self-help' and 'local initiatives' in liquidating Jews, particularly once the transportations from the Reich and from the west of Europe had (in this case clearly on Hitler's orders) started rolling eastwards in autumn 1941, persuading Nazi bosses in Poland and Russia to adopt radical *ad hoc* measures – liquidation – to cope with the countless numbers of Jews from the west pouring into their domains and randomly deposited on their doorsteps.[88] Meanwhile the killing process was escalating rapidly – and not just in the 'Jewish Question'. Christian Streit has demonstrated how the *Wehrmacht* willingly collaborated in the multiplying barbarity of the 'war of annihilation' through its close co-operation with the *Einsatzgruppen* and by its direct involvement in the liquidation of almost two-thirds of the Soviet prisoners-of-war to fall into German hands.[89] It was initially to house Soviet captives that the then small concentration camp at Auschwitz was expanded, and the first experiments with the gas chambers there had as their victims not Jews but Soviet war prisoners.

The confusion, contradictions, and improvisations of the summer and autumn 1941 are, however, by no means incompatible with the view that the Reich Security Head Office had interpreted the Göring commission as a brief to plan for the physical extermination of all Jews in Europe and was working towards that end.[90] Rudolf Höss (the Commandant of Auschwitz) and Adolf Eichmann both stated in post-war testimony that they had received the order for the physical liquidation of the Jews in summer 1941, and, though not conclusive evidence in itself, this testimony is supported by the circumstantial evidence of the timing of the extermination developments in the autumn.[91]

On 23 October 1941 the Gestapo circulated Himmler's order banning all further Jewish emigration.[92] In the same month permission was granted to the

---

87   Browning, 'Zur Genesis', p. 105; *Fateful Months*, p. 22. See also Mommsen's comments on the Göring order, 'Realisierung', pp. 409 and 417 note 149.

88   Brozat, 'Genesis', pp. 750 ff.; see also Mommsen, 'Realisierung', pp. 410–12.

89   Streit, *Keine Kameraden* (see above note 70); see the review of Streit's book by Hans Mommsen, *Bulletin of the German Historical Institute, London* 1 (1979), pp. 17–23. On the behaviour of the German troops on the eastern fronts, see now Omer Bartov, *The Eastern Front, 1941–45, German Troops and the Barbarisation of Warfare* (London, 1985).

90   See Browning, 'Zur Genesis', p. 103.

91   Browning, 'Zur Genesis', pp. 100–1.

92   Krausnick, pp. 68–9.

Reich Commissar for the *Ostland* (Baltic), Hinrich Lohse, to liquidate Jews incapable of work – also those deported from Germany itself – by carbon-monoxide gassing in extermination vans devised by Viktor Brack of the Chancellory of the Führer, who had developed the gassing techniques while head of the 'euthanasia action'.[93] By this date, it is clear that not only the SS leadership, but also the Foreign Office, the Ministry for the Occupied Eastern Territories, and the Chancellory of the Führer were in the picture.[94] Construction of the extermination camp at Belzec and the extermination complex at Auschwitz-Birkenau began in all probability around November or December 1941. At the end of November the first German Jews were shot at Riga, and at the beginning of the following month the first gassings in the extermination vehicles attached to the camp at Chelmno in Poland took place. Himmler reportedly told his masseur, Kersten, in mid November that the extermination of the Jews was imminent, and at the end of the month Heydrich sent out the invitations for the Wannsee Conference, initially planned for 9 December, then postponed until 20 January 1942, whose purpose was to regulate and co-ordinate an extermination policy already underway.[95] Though some questions of method, technique, and organization had to be clarified at the conference, there could by December 1941 be little lingering doubt about the aim of anti-Jewish policy. Hans Frank told Nazi leaders in the *Generalgouvernement* that month that since Jews could not be deported from their area they had better see to their liquidation themselves.[96] And in reply to a request as to whether all Jews in the east irrespective of age, sex, and economic requirements should be liquidated, Lohse, head of the Baltic region, was told: 'The Jewish question has probably been clarified by now through verbal discussions. Economic considerations are to be regarded as fundamentally irrelevant in the settlement of the problem'.[97]

The conclusion which Browning plausibly draws from this confused evidence is that Hitler approved in late October or November 'the extermination plan he had solicited the previous summer'.[98] This interpretation reconciles the undoubted lack of clarity and *ad hoc* actions in Jewish policy in summer and autumn 1941 with the existence of an, admittedly chaotic, process of development within the context of a vaguely expressed proposal for a 'total solution' – implying but not categorically stating annihilation – approved by Hitler in the summer and sanctioned when at a more concrete stage in the autumn. This accords with the testimony – inconclusive in itself – of two of the main actors involved, Höss and Eichmann, and better matches the timing of the preparations for extermination than Adam's late date of autumn 1941 for Hitler's decision. The only doubt is whether any

[93] Krausnick, *Anatomy*, pp. 96–8; Browning; 'Zur Genesis', pp. 101–2; Fleming, pp. 81–4. Doc. in Noakes and Pridham, vol. 3, p. 1144.
[94] Browning, 'Zur Genesis', p. 102. The Foreign Ministry's 'Jewish experts' apparently still imagined that 'a basic solution of the Jewish Question' would be brought about after the war (whose end was at that date presumed to be imminent): see Browning, *Final Solution*, p. 66.
[95] This chronology follows Browning, 'Zur Genesis', pp. 106–7.
[96] Browning, 'Zur Genesis', p. 107.
[97] Noakes and Pridham, vol. 3, p. 1098.
[98] Browning, 'Zur Genesis', p. 107 ('A Reply', p. 126). See also the balanced assessment of Wolfgang Scheffler, 'Zur Entstehungsgeschichte der "Endlösung" ', *APZ* (30 Oct. 1982), pp. 3–10.

autumn approval by Hitler was at all necessary. His blanket sanctioning earlier in the summer would surely have sufficed. The rest could have been left to Himmler, Heydrich, and their minions.

Though Hitler's precise role remains hidden in the shadows, the findings of recent research have allowed a relatively high level of consensus to emerge from the earlier scholarly disagreement on the complex process of decision-making which led to the full emergence of the 'Final Solution' by the spring of 1942. Summarizing the above evaluation, it is now widely accepted: that the orders given to the *Einsatzgruppen* in the spring of 1941 marked a decisive and irreversible step into outright genocidal policy, even if full clarification of the evidently loosely-framed instructions only took place in mid-summer; that central direction was plainly visible from the start, though much scope was left to local initiatives to force the pace; that the whole development was unthinkable without some sort of order by Hitler, though this may have been no more than a signal to Himmler and Heydrich rather than a specific and unequivocal command; that the decision to extend the extermination programme to the whole of European, not just Russian, Jewry must have been taken by the end of July at the latest; and that, despite overlapping and confused developments between mid-1941 and spring 1942, the basic contours of the annihilation programme were already taking clear shape by October 1941.

Relating this discussion of the genesis of the 'Final Solution' to the polarized 'Hitlerist' and 'structuralist' interpretations – the one emphasizing a Hitler order as the culmination of a planned long-term programme directed towards extermination, the other stressing a process of permanent improvisation as a way out of self-made administrative difficulties – one would have to conclude that neither model offers a wholly satisfactory explanation, and that some room for compromise is obvious.

For all the unparalleled barbarity of his language, Hitler's direct actions are difficult to locate. Though his hatred of the Jews was undoubtedly a constant, the relationship of this hatred to actual policy changed considerably over time as the policy options themselves narrowed. Hitler himself took relatively little part in the overt formulation of that policy, either during the 1930s or even the genesis of the 'Final Solution' itself. His major role consisted of setting the vicious tone within which the persecution took place and providing the sanction and legitimation of initiatives which came mainly from others. More was not for the most part necessary. The vagaries of anti-Jewish policy both before the war and in the period 1939–41, out of which the 'Final Solution' evolved, belie any notion of 'plan' or 'programme'. The radicalization could occur without any decisive steerage by Hitler. His influence was, however, all-pervasive, and his direct intervention in anti-Jewish policy was on occasion crucial. Above all, his dogmatic, unwavering assertion of the ideological imperative – 'getting rid of the Jews' from Germany, then finding a 'final solution to the Jewish question' – which had to be translated into bureaucratic and executive action, was the indispensable prerequisite for the escalating barbarity and the gradual transition into full-scale genocide.

Without Hitler's fanatical will to destroy Jewry, which crystallized only by 1941 into a realizable aim to exterminate physically the Jews of Europe, the

Holocaust would almost certainly not have come about. But it would also not have become reality, as Streit has emphasized,[99] without the active collaboration of the *Wehrmacht* – the one force still capable of checking the Nazi regime; or, for that matter, without the consent ranging to active complicity of the civil service bureaucracy, which strived to meet the requirements of spiralling discrimination, or the leaders of Germany's industries, who manufactured the death machinery and set up their factories at the concentration camps.[100] And within the SS–SD–Gestapo organizational complex, it was less the outright racial fanatics so much as the ambitious organizers and competent administrators like Eichmann and ice-cold executioners like Höss who turned to hellish vision into hell on earth.[101]

The lengthy but gradual process of depersonalization and dehumanization of Jews, together with the organizational chaos in the eastern territories arising from the lack of clear central direction and concept, the hording together in the most inhumane circumstances of increasing masses of 'non-persons', provided the context in which mass killing, once it had been instigated in the Russian campaign, was applied *ad hoc* and extended until it developed into full-scale annihilation. At the same time, the 'Final Solution' did not simply emerge from a myriad of 'local initiatives': however falteringly at first, decisive steps were taken at the centre to co-ordinate measures for total extermination. Such central direction appears for the most part to have come from the Reich Security Head Office, though undoubtedly the most important steps had Hitler's approval and sanction.

Hitler's 'intention' was certainly a fundamental factor in the process of radicalization in anti-Jewish policy which culminated in extermination. But even more important to an explanation of the Holocaust is the nature of 'charismatic' rule in the Third Reich and the way it functioned in sustaining the momentum of escalating radicalization around 'heroic', chimeric goals while corroding and fragmenting the structure of government. This was the essential framework within which Hitler's racial lunacy could be turned into practical politics.

This examination of the complex development of racial policy, lying at the very heart of Hitler's *Weltanschauung*, has shown that, while it would be meaningless to speak to him as a 'weak dictator', it is also misleading to regard the Third Reich as a dictatorship with a single command structure providing for the regulated and centrally directed consistent implementation of Hitler's will. It remains to turn our attention to the area where Hitler's directing hand seems most evident: foreign policy.

[99]  Streit, *Keine Kameraden*, esp. chs. 3, 6, 13.
[100]  See above ch. 3 for a brief discussion of the economic context in which the 'Final Solution' came about.
[101]  Hannah Arendt's controversial report of the Eichmann trial ended: 'The trouble with Eichmann was precisely that so many were like him, and that the many were neither perverted nor sadistic, that they were, and still are, terribly and terrifyingly normal' (Arendt, *Eichmann* (see above note 7), p. 253; see also pp. 18–31. According to their editor, Höss's autobiographical recollections reveal him as a 'petty-bourgeois, normal person' rather than a sadistic brute: Martin Broszat, ed., *Kommandant in Auschwitz. Autobiographische Aufzeichungen des Rudolf Höß* (dtv- edn, Munich, 1978), p. 15. Ideological anti-semitism seems at best to have provided a secondary motive in these cases, as it does in the career of Franz Stangl, Commandant at Treblinka death-camp: see Gitta Sereny, *Into that Darkness* (London, 1974). However, it has to be added that there is no intrinsic contradiction between ideological conviction and managerial talent.

# 6

## Nazi Foreign Policy: Hitler's 'Programme' or 'Expansion without Object'?

Several important aspects of German foreign policy in the Third Reich are still unresolved issues of scholarly debate. In this sphere too, however, interpretations – especially among West German scholars – have come to be divided in recent years around the polarized concepts of 'intention' and 'structure', which we have encountered in other contexts. Research in the GDR has shown no interest in this division of interpretation, and has proceeded on the basis of predictably different premises, concentrating on documenting and analysing the expansionist aims of Germany's industrial giants – a task which has been accomplished with no small degree of success. Nevertheless, with all recognition of the imperialist aspirations of German capitalism, explanations which limit the role of Hitler and other leading Nazis to little more than that of executants of big business aims have never carried much conviction among western scholars. Conventional orthodoxy in the West, resting in good measure upon West German scholarship, has in fact, as we saw in an earlier chapter, tended to turn such explanations on their heads in advocating an uncompromising 'primacy of politics' in the Third Reich. And whatever the nuances of interpretation, Hitler's own steerage of the course of German aggression in accordance with the 'programme' he had outlined (for those with eyes to see) in *Mein Kampf* and the *Second Book* is generally and strongly emphasized. Parallel to explanations of the Holocaust, outright primacy is accorded to Hitler's ideological goals in shaping a consistent foreign policy whose broad outlines and objectives were 'programmed' long in advance.

Such an interpretation has in recent years been subjected to challenge by historians seeking to apply a 'structuralist' approach to foreign policy as to other aspects of Nazi rule – even if the 'structuralist' argument appears in this area to be on its least firm ground. Exponents of a 'structuralist' approach reject the notion of a foreign policy which has clear contours unfolding in line with a Hitlerian ideological 'programme' in favour of an emphasis upon expansion whose format and aims were unclear and unspecific, and which took shape in no small measure as a result of the uncontrollable dynamism and radicalizing momentum of the Nazi movement and governmental system. In this gradual and somewhat confused process of development – as in the 'Jewish Question' – terms such as '*Lebensraum*' served for long as propaganda slogans and 'ideological metaphors' before appearing as attainable and concrete goals. Again, the *function* of Hitler's foreign-policy image and ideological fixations rather than his direct personal intervention and initiative is stressed. And rather than picturing Hitler as a man of unshakeable will and crystal-clear vision, moulding events to his liking in accordance with his ideological aims, he is portrayed as 'a man of improvization, of experiment, and the spur-of-the-moment bright idea'.[1] Any 'logic' or inner 'rationality' of the course of German foreign policy gains its appearance, it is argued, only teleologically – by looking at the end results and interpreting these in the light of Hitler's apparently prophetic statements of the 1920s.

Before attempting a brief evaluation of Hitler's role in the making of foreign policy decisions, the part played by his ideological fixations in determining the development of foreign policy, and the extent of Nazi expansionist ambitions, we need to examine in rather greater detail the main trends in historiography and the arguments of leading exponents of the interpretations just indicated.

## Interpretations

Exactly what objectives Hitler was pursuing has long been a matter of debate among experts on German foreign policy. Two long-standing areas of controversy – whether Hitler was an ideological visionary with a 'programme' for aggression or merely a supremely 'unprincipled opportunist', and whether his foreign policy aims were novel and revolutionary or in essence a continuation of traditional German expansionism – can be seen in embryonic fashion in the antagonistic positions taken up long ago by the British historians Trevor-Roper and Taylor. While Taylor argued (somewhat capriciously as usual) that 'in international affairs there was nothing wrong with Hitler except that he was a German',[2] Trevor-Roper was among the first historians to deduce – what now seems fairly commonplace – a fundamental and unmoveable consistency in Hitler's ideas and in fact to take Hitler seriously as a genuine man of ideas which, however repulsive, were novel and broke through traditional boundaries of political thinking.[3] In a way, both views were traceable to different readings of (among other texts) the sometimes ambivalent comments of Hermann Rauschning, the former President of the Danzig Senate.[4] It was, of course, soon pointed out that there was no necessary contradiction between the interpretations as they stood: Hitler could be seen both as a fixated ideologue, and as a man with a particular talent for exploiting the needs of opportunities which were presented to him in foreign affairs.[5]

Once advanced, however, the conception of Hitler as a fanatical visionary pursuing his defined objectives with relentless consistency rapidly established itself. Major studies, especially those exploring German foreign

---

[1] Hans Mommsen, review of Jacobsen (see above ch. 4 note 31), p. 183.

[2] A.J.P. Taylor, *The Origins of the Second World War* (Harmondsworth, 1971), p. 27.

[3] H.R. Trevor-Roper, 'Hitlers Kriegsziele', *VfZ* 8 (1960), pp. 121–33.

[4] See Hermann Rauschning, *Hitler Speaks* (London, 1939) and *The Revolution of Nihilism* (New York, 1939). Indispensable to an evaluation of Rauschning's evidence is Theodor Schieder, *Hermann Rauschnings 'Gespräche mit Hitler' als Geschichtsquelle* (Opladen, 1972). See now, however, Wolfgang Hänel, *Hermann Rauschnings 'Gespräche mit Hitler' – Eine Geschichtsfälschung* (Ingolstadt, 1984), which casts doubt on the authenticity of Rauschning's evidence.

[5] See Alan Bullock, 'Hitler and the Origins of the Second World War', in Esmonde M. Robertson, ed., *The Origins of the Second World War* (London, 1971), pp. 189–224, here esp., pp. 192–3.

policy, were now erected on the premise that Hitler's expansionist ideology had to be regarded with deadly seriousness, and that the underestimation of Hitler within and outside Germany had been one fatal key to his success. The emphasis which Trevor-Roper had laid upon the seriousness of Hitler's *Lebensraum* plans for eastern Europe was now extended by Günter Moltmann who, for the first time, advanced the argument that Hitler's aims were not confined to Europe but were quite literally directed at world mastery for Germany.[6] This claim was soon more systematically worked out in Hillgruber's analysis of Hitler's war strategy, published in 1963, in which the concept of a three-stage plan (*Stufenplan*) for establishing German hegemony first over the whole of Europe, then over the Middle East and other British colonial territory, and finally – at a distant future date – over the USA and with that the entire world, was advanced as the basis of Nazi foreign policy.[7] The heuristic device of the 'stage by stage plan' set the tone for most later influential work on foreign policy, prominent among which was Klaus Hildebrand's massive study of German colonial policy.[8] More recently, the 'world domination' thesis has been further supported in analyses of German naval plans, grandiose architectural projects, and policies towards Britain's Middle-Eastern possessions.[9]

A 'sub-debate' rumbles on between the 'continentalists' (such as Trevor-Roper, Jäckel, and Kuhn), who see Hitler's 'final aims' as comprising the conquest of *Lebensraum* in eastern Europe, and the 'globalists' (Moltmann, Hillgruber, Hildebrand, Dülffer, Thies, Hauner, and others), whose interpretation – the dominant one – accepts nothing short of total world mastery as the extent of Hitler's foreign ambitions. Common to both positions, however, is the emphasis upon the intrinsically related components of conquest of *Lebensraum* and racial domination as programmatic elements of Hitler's own *Weltanschauung* and as the essence of his politics. Concepts such as that of the 'stage by stage plan' (*Stufenplan*) or 'programme' are, it is emphasized, not intended to denote a 'timetable' for world domination, but rather to encapsulate 'the essential driving forces and central aims of Hitler's unshakeable foreign policy (conquest of *Lebensraum*, racial domination, world power status), without mistaking the "improvization" of the Dictator and the high measure of his tactical flexibility'.[10] Whether 'continentalist' or 'globalist', German foreign policy, in the interpretations summarized so far, was Hitler's foreign policy. One historian, for instance, advancing a representative view of Hitler's personal role in determining Nazi foreign policy, sees him 'within the framework of the totalitarian state' as 'not only the final

[6] Günter Moltmann, 'Weltherrschaftsideen Hitlers', in O. Bruner and D. Gerhard, eds., *Europa und Übersee. Festschrift für Egmont Zechlin* (Hamburg, 1961), pp. 197–240.

[7] Hillgruber, *Hitlers Strategie* (see above ch. 1 note 17).

[8] Hildebrand, *Vom Reich zum Weltreich* (see above ch. 1 note 17).

[9] Jost Dülffer, *Weimar, Hitler und die Marine. Reichspolitik und Flottenbau 1920–1939* (Düsseldorf, 1973); Jochen Thies, *Architekt der Weltherrschaft. Die 'Endziele' Hitlers* (Düsseldorf, 1976); Milan Hauner, *India in Axis Strategy: Germany, Japan, and Indian Nationalists in the Second World War* (Publications of the German Historical Institute, London, Stuttgart, 1981).

[10] Klaus Hildebrand, 'Die Geschichte der deutschen Außenpolitik (1933–1945) im Urteil der neueren Forschung: Ergebnisse, Kontroversen, Perspektiven', ('Nachwort' to the fourth edition of his *Deutsche Außenpolitik 1933–1945. Kalkül oder Dogma?* (Stuttgart etc., 1980), pp. 188–9. Hildebrand has consistently advanced this view in many publications.

arbiter but also its chief animator'.[11] So important was the Führer to the development of German foreign policy that the same historian, Milan Hauner, in another essay expounding the aim of world dominion, felt it necessary to 'warn the reader that in this survey the name "Hitler" will be frequently used in place of "Germany" ' – the apogee of the 'Hitlerist' interpretation; for such, in his view, 'was the charismatic appeal of this man and the totalitarian character of his power, that Hitler can justifiably be seen as the personification of Germany's will-power from the moment he assumed full control over her foreign and military affairs'.[12] Hauner ends by repeating Norman Rich's epithet of Hitler as 'master in the Third Reich'. Equally uncompromising is the statement of Gerhard Weinberg, one of the foremost authorities of Nazi foreign policy, at the end of his exhaustive diplomatic history of the pre-war years: 'The power of Germany was directed by Adolf Hitler. Careful analyses by scholars have revealed internal divisions, organizational confusions, jurisdictional battles, institutional rivalries, and local deviations behind the façade of monolithic unity that the Third Reich liked to present to its citizens and to the world in word and picture. The fact remains, however, that the broad lines of policy were determined in all cases by Hitler himself. Where others agreed, or at least did not object strenuously, they were allowed the choice of going along or retreating into silence, but on major issues of policy the Führer went his own way'.[13]

Serious attempts to challenge this dominant orthodoxy which emphasizes the autonomy of Hitler's programmatic aims in determining foreign policy have come from a number of different directions. They might conveniently be fitted into three interlocking categories:

*(i)* Rejection of any notion of a 'programme' or 'plan in stages', denial of concrete and specific long-range foreign policy aims, and portrayal of Hitler as a man of spontaneous response to circumstances – not far removed from the image of the 'unprincipled opportunist' – with a central concern in propaganda exploitation and the protection of his own prestige.

*(ii)* The claim that Hitler was not a 'free agent' in determining foreign policy, but was subjected to pressures from significant élite groups (*Wehrmacht* leadership, industry etc.), from a variety of agencies involved in making foreign policy, from the demands of the Party faithful for action consonant with his wild promises and propaganda statements (with the corresponding need to act to maintain his Führer image), from the international constellation of forces, and from mounting economic crisis.

*(iii)* The view that foreign policy has to be seen as a form of 'social imperialism' an outward conveyance of domestic problems, a release from or compensation for internal discontent with the function of preserving the domestic order.

[11] Milan Hauner, 'The Professionals and the Amateurs in National Socialist Foreign Policy: Revolution and Subversion in the Islamic and Indian World', in Hirschfeld and Kettenacker (above ch. 1 note 23), pp. 305–28, here p. 325.
[12] Milan Hauner, 'Did Hitler want a World Dominion?', *JCH* 13 (1978), p. 15.
[13] Gerhard Weinberg, *The Foreign Policy of Hitler's Germany. Starting World War II* (Chicago/London, 1980), p. 657.

The most radical 'structuralist' approach, that of Hans Mommsen, returns in part, in its emphasis on Hitler's improvised, spontaneous responses to developments which he did little directly to shape, to the early view of the German Dictator as little more than a gifted opportunist. In Mommsen's view, 'it is questionable, too, whether National Socialist foreign policy can be considered as an unchanging pursuit of established priorities. Hitler's foreign policy aims, purely dynamic in nature, knew no bounds; Joseph Schumpeter's reference to "expansion without object" is entirely justified. For this very reason, to interpret their implementation as in any way consistent or logical is highly problematic. . . In reality, the regime's foreign policy ambitions were many and varied, without clear aims, and only linked by the ultimate goal: hindsight alone gives them some air of consistency' – a danger implicit in such concepts as 'programme' or 'stage-by-stage plan'.[14] According to Mommsen, Hitler's behaviour in foreign as in domestic and anti-Jewish policy was shaped largely – apart, that is, from the demands of the international situation – by considerations of prestige and propaganda. Seen in this light, then, Nazi foreign policy was 'in its form domestic policy projected outwards, which was able to conceal (*überspielen*) the increasing loss of reality only by maintaining political dynamism through incessant action. As such it became ever more distant from the chance of political stabilization'.[15]

A not dissimilar interpretation is advanced by Martin Broszat, who also sees little evidence of a design or plan behind Hitler's foreign policy.[16] Rather, the pursuit of *Lebensraum* in the East – parallel to the case of anti-semitism – has to be regarded as reflecting Hitler's fanatical adherence to the need to sustain the dynamic momentum he had helped unleash. In foreign policy this meant above all breaking all shackles of restraint, formal bonds, pacts or alliances, and the attainment of complete freedom of action, unrestricted by international law or treaty, in German power-political considerations. The image of unlimited land in the East, according with traditional mythology of German colonization, with utopian ideals of economic autarky, re-agrarianization, and the creation of a master-race, meant that *Lebensraum* (matching as it did also expansionist aims of the First World War) was perfectly placed to serve as a metaphor and touchstone for German power-politics in which, as in the 'Jewish Question' and by equally circuitous route, the distant symbolic vision gradually emerged as imminent and attainable reality. The absence of any clear thinking by Hitler before 1939 on the position of Poland, despite the fact that its geographical situation ought to have made it a central component of any concrete notions of an attack on the Soviet Union, is seen by Broszat as one example of the nebulous, unspecific, and essentially 'utopian' nature of Hitler's foreign policy goals. He reaches the conclusion, therefore, that 'the aim of winning *Lebensraum* in the east had until 1939 largely the function of an ideological metaphor, a symbol to account for ever new foreign political activity'. Ultimately, for Broszat, the

---

[14] Mommsen, 'National Socialism: Continuity and Change', p. 177; see also his 'Ausnahmezustand', p. 45 and *Adolf Hitler*, pp. 97, 102 (full references above, ch. 4 note 28).
[15] Mommsen, 'Ausnahmezustand', pp. 43–5.
[16] See Broszat, 'Soziale Motivation' (see ch. 4 note 27), esp. pp. 407–9.

plebiscitary social dynamic of the 'Movement', which in the sphere of foreign policy pushed Hitler and the regime inexorably in the direction of turning the *Lebensraum* metaphor into reality, was, in its demand for ceaseless action, the only guarantee of any form of integration and diversion of 'the antagonistic forces' in the Third Reich. As a consequence, it was bound to veer further and further from rational control, and to end in 'self-destructive madness'. And though Hitler remains indispensable to the explanation of developments, he ought not to be envisaged as an autonomous personality, whose arbitrary whim and ideological fixations operated independently of the social motivation and political pressures of his mass following.

Tim Mason's interpretation, which we already encountered in chapter 4, can be regarded as a third variant of 'structural' approaches to Nazi foreign policy. In Mason's view, the domestic–economic crisis of the later 1930s greatly restricted Hitler's room for manoeuvre in foreign affairs and war preparation, and an inability to come to terms with the growing economic crisis forced him back on the one area where he could take 'clear, world-historical decisions': foreign policy.[17] More recently, Mason has again argued that the later 1930s bore more the hallmarks of confusion than of a programmatic line of development in Hitler's foreign policy.[18] Mason's own emphasis on the 'legacy of 1918' and the compulsion this brought to bear on German foreign as well as domestic policy meant that for him – as in somewhat different ways for Mommsen and Broszat – Nazi foreign policy and the war itself could be seen under the rubric of the 'primacy of domestic politics', as a barbarous variant of social imperialism.[19]

Other historians have in recent years also attempted to diffuse what they regard as an unduly Hitler-centric treatment of German foreign policy by applying 'polycratic' or 'pluralist' models to the decision-making processes in foreign affairs. Wolfgang Schieder, for instance, took as a case-study the circumstances of Germany's decision in July 1936 to intervene in the Spanish Civil War, arguing that the crucial factor in determining intervention was Göring's interest in acquiring Spanish raw materials. The initial pressure for participation – against German foreign ministry advice – came from representatives of the Party's *Auslandsorganisation*, who engineered an audience with Hitler between opera performances at the Bayreuth Festival. Hitler himself took no initiative before deciding to intervene after deliberations (which excluded the foreign ministry) with Göring, Blomberg, and Canaris. Schieder's conclusion was that Nazi policy on the Spanish Civil War, 'while not an arbitrary product of chance decisions', was 'also not the calculated result of long-term planning', but rather a combination of both, as, he suspected, was Nazi foreign policy in general. In his opinion, any notion of a 'programmatic' Hitlerist foreign policy had to see it on two levels: ideologized global aims, in which Hitler showed 'unusually fanatical consistency'; and relatively definable objectives, where Hitler was extremely flexible and where concrete decisions followed. In this sense, Hitler's foreign

---

17 Mason, *Sozialpolitik* (see ch. 4 note 62), p. 40.
18 Mason, 'Intention and Explanation' (see ch. 1 note 25), pp. 32–3.
19 Mason, *Sozialpolitik*, p. 30, and 'The Legacy of 1918' (ch. 4 note 67), p. 218.

policy could be interpreted neither as the putting into operation of a long-term programme, nor simply as the product of an 'objectless nihilism'. Rather, it consisted of 'a frequently contradictory mixture of dogmatic rigidity in fundamentals and extreme flexibility in concrete matters', between which, however, there was no necessary connection.[20] The trouble with Schieder's case-study, as he himself realized, was that since Spain did not play a primary role in Hitler's ideological constructs and whatever long-term strategic thinking he might have had, a convincing *general* case could hardly be drawn from this example. Furthermore, Hitler's own considerations in this issue, as opposed to those of Göring, do appear to have been primarily ideological – the 'fight against Bolshevism' – which on the whole tends to confirm rather than contradict any argument about consistency in his thought, motivation, and policy-making. And whatever the influence of Göring (and War Minister Blomberg), the decision to involve Germany in the Spanish arena appears to have been taken by Hitler alone.

Other approaches to what has been somewhat misleadingly dubbed 'pluralistic' foreign policy formulation also seem compatible with the 'intentionalist' interpretation. Hans-Adolf Jacobsen, for example, and more recently Milan Hauner, have analyzed the many agencies involved in foreign policy, with their different functions and policy emphases. Jacobsen was prepared to accept that centrifugal forces influenced 'the structure of the totalitarian system' far more than pure will and directives to ideological unity, and saw the presence of 'lack of system' and 'administrative chaos' also in the sphere of foreign policy. Nevertheless, it is mistaken in his view to attribute the development of foreign policy to absence of planning or pure opportunism. Rather, there was a consistent basic line in foreign policy common to all individuals or groups involved in the formulation of foreign policy, where here – as in other branches of policy – they were striving to put into concrete form what they presumed to be Hitler's intentions (which Jacobsen interprets as the striving for a racially new formation of Europe, a revolutionary goal consistently held by Hitler since the 1920s).[21] Milan Hauner reached similar conclusions. Conflict between the Foreign Office professionals and other agencies with a finger in the foreign policy pie was not about different conceptions of foreign policy, but was merely a part

[20] Wolfgang Schieder, 'Spanischer Bürgerkrieg und Vierjahresplan. Zur Struktur national-sozialistischer Außenpolitik', in Wolfgang Michalka, ed., *Nationalsozialistische Außenpolitik* (Darmstadt, 1978), pp. 325–59; see also, William Carr, *Hitler. A Study in Personality and Politics* (London, 1978), p. 52; Gerhard Weinberg, *The Foreign Policy of Hitler's Germany. Diplomatic Revolution in Europe 1933–36* (Chicago/London, 1970), pp. 288–9; and Hans-Henning Abendroth, 'Deutschlands Rolle im Spanischen Bürgerkrieg', in Funke (see above ch. 3 note 27), pp. 471–88, here pp. 473–7, where Hitler's ideological interest is advanced as the main cause of Germany's entry, with Göring initially opposed. Unduly sharp in his criticism of Schieder is Hofer (see ch. 1 note 2), pp. 12–13. Conflicting interpretations of Göring's role and motivation in the decision to support Franco can be found in the recent biographies of Göring: Stefan Martens, *Hermann Göring* (Paderborn, 1985), pp. 65–7; and Alfred Kube, *Pour le mérite und Hakenkreuz* (Munich, 1986), pp. 163–6.

[21] Hans-Adolf Jacobsen, 'Zur Struktur der NS-Außenpolitik 1933–1945', in Funke (ch. 3 note 27), pp. 137–85, here esp, pp. 169–75. Hitler's consistent 'striving towards a goal' (*Zielstrebigkeit*) is emphasized even more sharply in Jacobsen's massive monograph on Nazi foreign policy – a point strongly criticized by Hans Mommsen in his review of this work (see above ch. 4 note 31 for references).

of the tug-of-war for power and influence which was endemic to the Nazi system. Once more, there was no contradiction between such institutional or personal rivalries together with the conflicting interests and influences which ensued, and the developments of a central line of policy-making in which Hitler's personal role was the decisive element.[22]

The notion of 'concept pluralism' – a rather grandiose term to imply that there were a number of different views among the leaders of the Third Reich about the foreign policy Germany should pursue – has recently been taken a step further by Wolfgang Michalka in his analysis of Ribbentrop's own foreign-policy ideas and influence upon Hitler. Michalka argues that from the mid 1930s onwards an anti-English rather than essentially anti-Russian policy provided the main thrust of Ribbentrop's own conception of foreign policy – one which was more pragmatically power-political than directly aligned to Hitler's fixation in race ideology. He demonstrates how, in the later 1930s, Hitler's increasing recognition of the failure to win over England allowed Ribbentrop a considerable scope for exerting influence, culminating in the signing of the Non-Aggression Pact with the Soviet Union in 1939. This temporary and opportunistic use of Ribbentrop's 'conception' between 1939 and 1941 was in Michalka's view, however, bound to founder ultimately on the primacy of Hitler's racial 'programme' directed at the Soviet Union. Ultimately, therefore, Michalka comes down on the side of a very 'intentionalist' position, if one moderated by looking to important influences upon the Dictator.[23]

None of the 'structural–functionalist', 'concept pluralist', or 'polycratic' approaches to foreign policy which we have rapidly summarized here has shaken the conviction of the 'intentionalists' (or 'programmatists') that the character and consistency of Hitler's ideology was the crucial and determining element in the equation. Indeed, as we have just seen, the latest studies of the varying centres of influence in the formation of foreign policy all come down ultimately to similar or compatible conclusions. Klaus Hildebrand, articulating as ever the 'programmatist' line in its clearest and most forthright form, rejects 'revisionist' interpretations on four grounds: *(1)* They ignore the relatively high degree of autonomy of Hitler's programme, whose aims were formulated by the Dictator himself as intentions which were then put into effect. *(2)* Anti-semitism and anti-bolshevism were not in the first instance functional in character, but ought to be regarded as primary and autonomous, 'real' political aims. *(3)* The 'revisionists' stand in

---

[22] Hauner, 'Professionals', p. 325.
[23] See Wolfgang Michalka, 'Die nationalsozialistische Außenpolitik im Zeichen eines "Konzeptionen-Pluralismus" – Fragestellungen und Forschungsaufgaben', in Funke, pp. 46–62; 'Vom Antikominternpakt zum Euro-Asiatischen Kontinentalblock. Ribbentrops Alternativkonzeptionen zu Hitlers außenpolitischem "Programm" ', in Michalka, ed., *Nationalsozialistische Außenpolitik*, pp. 471–92; and his major work, *Ribbentrop und die deutsche Weltpolitik 1933–1940. Außenpolitische Konzeptionen und Entscheidungsprozesse im Dritten Reich* (Munich, 1980). See also summaries of his position in English: 'Conflicts within the German Leadership on the Objectives and Tactics of German Foreign Policy, 1933–9', in Wolfgang J. Mommsen and Lothar Kettenacker, eds., *The Fascist Challenge and the Policy of Appeasement* (London, 1983), pp. 48–60; and 'From the Anti-Comintern Pact to the Euro-Asiatic Bloc: Ribbentrop's Alternative Concept of Hitler's Foreign Policy Programme', in Koch, *Aspects of the Third Reich*, pp. 267–84.

danger in this respect of mistaking the consequences of Hitler's policies for their motives. *(4)* The dynamic of the system, which, Hildebrand accepts, Hitler could control only with increasing difficulty, never posed the Dictator with unacceptable fundamental alternatives, but rather pushed him 'programmatically' in the direction of the 'final aims' which he had set, even if affecting the realization of these goals.[24]

Though each of these assertions is, of course, open to debate, the important fourth point suggests that – as in the case of domestic and race policy – interpretations are less far apart than they appear to be at first sight, and that therefore some degree of synthesis seems possible. An evaluation of the debate on the aims and execution of German foreign policy in the Third Reich might focus on three central issues: *(1)* Were the key decisions in the sphere of foreign policy taken by Hitler himself? Did they simply voice a consensus which had already been reached, or were they taken in the face of weighty advice offering alternative policy? And to what extent was Hitler curtailed in his freedom of action in taking foreign policy decisions? *(2)* How far is it possible to see in the course of German foreign policy an inner consistency (subject to tactical 'deflections') determined by Hitler's ideological obsessions, without imposing this consistency in teleological fashion? *(3)* Was the extent of Hitler's foreign policy ambition European or literally world domination? The following pages provide an attempt to assess the arguments and evidence for answering these questions.

## Evaluation

### I

These seems little disagreement among historians that Hitler did personally take the 'big' decisions in foreign policy after 1933. Even the most forceful 'structuralist' analyses accept that Hitler's 'leadership monopoly' was far more in evidence in the foreign-policy decision-making process than in the realm of domestic policy.[25] There is less agreement, however, about the extent to which Hitler stamped a peculiarly personal mark on the development of German foreign affairs and whether 1933 can be seen to indicate a break in German foreign policy deriving from Hitler's own ideological pre-possessions and 'programme'.[26] The question of the continuity or discontinuity of German foreign policy after 1933 lies, therefore, at the centre of the first part of our enquiry.

Whatever the differences in interpretation, there has been a general readiness since the publication of Fritz Fischer's work in the early 1960s to accept that Germany's expansionist aims form one of the continuous threads

---

[24] Hildebrand, 'Nachwort' (see above note 10), p. 191.
[25] Mommsen 'Ausnahmezustand', p. 43. See also the comments of Mason, *Sozialpolitik*, p. 40. Broszat's work leaves no doubt that he also sees Hitler as the actual executant of Nazi foreign policy.
[26] In addition to the works referred to above ch. 2 note 60, see on the 'continuity question' in German foreign policy, Jacobsen, *Nationalsozialistische Außenpolitik* (ch. 4 note 31) and Konrad H. Jarausch, 'From Second to Third Reich: The Problem of Continuity in German Foreign Policy', *CEH* 12 (1979), pp. 68–82. A recent monograph of direct importance and relevance is Hans-Jürgen Döscher, *Das Auswärtige Amt im Dritten Reich* (Berlin, 1987).

linking the Bismarkian and especially the Wilhelmine era with the Third Reich. The clamour for massive expansion and subjection of much of central and eastern Europe, as well as overseas territories, to German dominance was by the early years of the twentieth century not confined to a few extremists, but featured in the aspirations and propaganda of heavily supported and influential pressure groups.[27] It was reflected during the war itself in the aims of the German High Command – aims which can certainly be seen as a bridge to Nazi *Lebensraum* policy. Defeat and the loss of territory in the Versailles settlement kept alive expansionist demands on the Right, and encouraged revisionist intentions and claims, which seemed legitimate to the majority of Germans. The popular success of Hitler in the foreign policy arena after 1933 was based squarely upon this continuity of a consensus about the need for German expansion which extended from the power élite to extensive sections of society (with the general exception of the bulk of the now outcast and outlawed adherents of the left-wing parties). This is the context in which the role of Hitler in the formulation of German foreign policy after 1933 has to be assessed.

The most significant steps in German foreign policy during the first year of Nazi rule were the withdrawal from the League of Nations in October 1933, and the reversals in relations with Russia and Poland which had taken place by the beginning of 1934. Obviously, these developments were not unconnected with each other. Together they represented a break with past policy which conceivably could have taken place under a different Reich Chancellor – say Papen or Schleicher – but which, at the same time, in the manner, timing, and speed it came about owed not a little to Hitler's own direction and initiatives.

In the decision to leave the Geneva disarmament conference and the League of Nations, not much more than the timing was Hitler's. The withdrawal was inevitable given the generally accepted commitment to rearmament (which would have been high on the agenda of any nationalist-revisionist government in Germany at that time), and Hitler acted in almost total concert with leading diplomats, the army leadership, and the other dominant revisionist forces in the country.[28]

In the case of Poland, Hitler played a greater role personally – initially in the teeth of the traditional foreign ministry line, against revisionist instincts, and against the wishes of Party activists in Danzig – in steering a new course of *rapprochement*. While Foreign Minister von Neurath, representing the traditional approach, argued at a Cabinet meeting in April 1933 that 'an understanding with Poland is neither possible nor desirable',[29] Hitler was prepared to explore the possibilities of a new relationship with Poland, especially following initial feelers put out by the Polish government in April. The withdrawal from the League of Nations made a *rapprochement* more

---

[27] See esp. Geoff Eley, *Reshaping the German Right. Radical Nationalism and Political Change after Bismarck* (New Haven/London, 1980), and Roger Chickering, *We Men who feel Most German: a Cultural Study of the Pan-German League 1886–1914* (London, 1984). The imperialist tradition in Germany is thoroughly explored by Woodruff D. Smith, *The Ideological Origins of Nazi Imperialism* (Oxford, 1986).

[28] See Weinberg, *Diplomatic Revolution* (see note 20), pp. 159–67.

[29] Cited in Weinberg, *Diplomatic Revolution*, p. 62.

urgently desirable from the point of view of both sides. Again it was a Polish initiative, in November 1933, which accelerated negotiations. Agreement to end the long-standing trade war with Poland – a move which satisfied many leading German industrialists – was followed by a decision, taking up an original suggestion of Hitler himself, to embody the new relationship in a non-aggression treaty, which came to be signed on 26 January 1934. The Polish minister in Berlin wrote to his superiors in December that 'as if by orders from the top, a change of front toward us is taking place all along the line'.[30] While Hitler was by no means isolated in his new policy on Poland, and while he was able to exploit an obvious desire on Poland's part for a *rapprochement*, the indications are that he personally played a dominant role in developments and that he was not thinking *purely* opportunistically but had long-term possibilities in mind. In a mixture of admiration and scepticism, the German ambassador in Bern, von Weizsäcker, wrote shortly afterwards that 'no parliamentary minister between 1920 and 1933 could have gone so far'.[31]

The mirror image of the changing relations with Poland in 1933 were those with the Soviet Union. After the maintenance during the first few months of Nazi rule of the mutually advantageous reasonably good relations which had existed since the treaties of Rapallo (1922) and Berlin (1926) – despite some deterioration even before 1933 and the anti-communist propaganda barrage which followed the Nazi takeover – Hitler did nothing to discourage a new basis of 'natural antagonism' towards the Soviet Union from the summer of 1933 onwards.[32] This development, naturally conducive ideologically to Hitler and matching the expectations of his mass following, took place against the wishes both of the German foreign ministry and – despite growing fears and suspicions – of Soviet diplomats, too. When, however, suggestions came from the German foreign ministry in September 1933 for a renewed *rapprochement* with the Soviet Union, Hitler himself rejected it out of hand, stating categorically that 'a restoration of the German–Russian relationship would be impossible'.[33] In like fashion, and now supported by the opportunistic foreign minister von Neurath, he personally rejected new overtures by the Soviet Union in March 1934 – a move which prompted the resignation of the German ambassador to the Soviet Union.[34] In this case, too, Hitler had not acted autonomously, in isolation from the pressures within the Nazi Party and the ranks of its Nationalist partners for a strong anti-Russian line. But he had certainly been more than a cypher or a pure opportunist in shaping the major shift in German alignment, here as in relations with Poland.

More than in any other sphere of foreign policy, Hitler's hand was visible

---

[30] Cited in Weinberg, *Diplomatic Revolution*, p. 73.
[31] Cited in Jost Dülffer, 'Zum "decision-making process" in der deutschen Außenpolitik 1933–1939', in Funke, pp. 186–204, here p. 190 note 12. See also Carr, *Hitler*, pp. 48–9; Weinberg, *Diplomatic Revolution*, pp. 57–74.
[32] See Carr, *Hitler*, p. 50.
[33] Cited in Weinberg, *Diplomatic Revolution*, p. 81. See also William Carr, *Der Weg zum Krieg* (Nationalsozialismus im Unterricht, Studieneinheit 9, Deutsches Institut für Fernstudien an der Universität Tübingen, Tübingen, 1983), pp. 17–18.
[34] Weinberg, *Diplomatic Revolution*, pp. 180–3; Carr, *Der Weg zum Krieg*, pp. 18–19.

in shaping the new approach towards Britain. As is well known, this was also the area of the most unmitigated failure of German foreign policy during the 1930s. The first major (and successful) initiative led to the bilateral naval treaty with Britain concluded in 1935. Hitler's personal role was decisive both in the formation of the idea for the treaty, and in its execution. Von Neurath thought the idea 'dilettante' and correspondingly found himself excluded from all negotiations and not even in receipt of the minutes. Hitler's insistence also carried the day on the nature of German demands, which were lower than those desired by the German navy. In the light of criticism to be heard in the foreign ministry and in the navy, signs of growing coolness towards the idea in Britain, and the absence of any notable influence from economic interest groups, an armaments lobby, or the *Wehrmacht*, Hitler's own part – and to a lesser extent that of Ribbentrop – was the critical factor.[35] Hitler himself, of course, attached great importance to the treaty as a step on the way towards the British alliance he was so keen to establish.

The remilitarization of the Rhineland – and with it the breaking of the provisions of Versailles and Locarno – was again an issue which would have been on the agenda of any revisionist German government. The question was already under abstract discussion between the army and foreign ministry by late 1934, and before that Hitler had played with the idea of introducing a demand for the abolition of the demilitarized zone into the disarmament negotiations that year. The issue was revived by the foreign ministry following the ratification of the French–Soviet pact in May 1935, and Hitler mentioned it as a future German demand to the English and French ambassadors towards the end of the year. A solution through negotiation was by no means without prospect of success, and corresponded to the traditional revisionist expectations of Germany's conservative élites. Hitler's main contribution in this case was timing – he claimed he had been originally thinking in terms of a reoccupation in early 1937 – and a decision for the theatrical coup of immediate military reoccupation rather than a lengthier and less dramatic process of negotiation. The opportunistic exploitation of the diplomatic upheaval – which Hitler feared would be shortlived – arising from Mussolini's Abyssinian adventure was coupled with internal considerations: the need to lift popular morale, revitalize the sinking élan of the Party, and to reconsolidate the support for the regime which various indicators suggested had seriously waned by early 1936.[36] Though a surprisingly large body of diplomatic and military 'advisers', along with leading Nazis, shared the secret planning for the reoccupation, the decision was Hitler's alone, and was taken after much worried deliberation and again in the face of coolness from the foreign ministry and nervousness on the part of the military. Jost Dülffer's conclusion, that 'Hitler was the actual driving force' in the affair, seems undeniable.[37]

[35] This section is based largely on Dülffer's analysis, 'Zum "decision-making process" ' (see note 31), pp. 191–3.
[36] See Dülffer, 'Zum "decision-making process" ', p. 196; Manfred Funke, '7. März 1936. Fallstudie zum außenpolitischen Führungsstil Hitlers', in Michalka, *Nationalsozialistische Außenpolitik*, pp. 277–324, here pp. 278–9; Orlow, *Nazi Party*, vol. 2 (ch. 4 note 57), pp. 174–6.
[37] See Dülffer, 'Zum "decision-making process" ', pp. 194–7, and in general Weinberg, *Diplomatic Revolution*, pp. 239–63.

In the case of Austria, which along with Czechoslovakia had an intrinsic economic and military–strategic significance according with Nazi ideological expansionist ideas, early Nazi policy of supporting the undermining of the State from within was shown to be a disastrous failure, and was promptly ended, following the assassination of the Austrian Chancellor Dollfuss in July 1934. The Austrian question thereafter took a subordinate place to the improvement of relations with Italy in foreign policy thinking until the latter part of 1937. In the actual *Anschluß* crisis which unfolded in March 1938, it was Göring rather than Hitler who pushed the pace along – probably because of his interest in seizing Austrian economic assets and avoiding the flight of capital which a prolonged crisis would have provoked.[38] Before the events of February and March 1938, the indications are that Hitler was thinking in terms of subordination rather than the outright annexation of Austria. In fact, he appears to have taken the decision for annexation only *after* the military invasion had occurred – characteristically, under the impact of the delirious reception he had encountered in his home town of Linz.[39] While this points to Hitler's spontaneous, *reactive* decisions even in vitally important matters, and though the chain of developments in the crisis weeks again shows his opportunistic and *ad hoc* exploitation of favourable circumstances, it would be insufficient to leave it at that. The evidence suggests that Göring and Wilhelm Keppler, whom Hitler had placed in charge of Party affairs in Austria in 1937, both believed that Hitler was determined to move on the Austrian question in spring or summer 1938.[40] Goebbel's diary entries also record Hitler speaking about imposing a solution by force 'sometime' on a number of occasions in August and September 1937,[41] and of course Austria formed an important part of Hitler's thinking in November 1937, according to the notes which Colonel Hossbach made of the meeting with top military leaders.[42] In this case too, therefore, Hitler had played a prominent personal role in determining the contours for action, even if his part in the actual events – which could not have been exactly planned or foreseen – was opportunistic, even impulsive.

The remaining events of 1938 and 1939 are sufficiently well known to be summarized briefly. The Sudeten crisis of summer 1938 again illustrates Hitler's direct influence on the course of events. Although traditional power politics and military–strategic considerations would have made the neutralization of Czechslovakia a high priority for any revisionist government of Germany, it was Hitler's personal determination that he would 'smash Czechoslovakia by military action'[43] – thereby embarking on a high-risk policy in which everything indicates he was not bluffing – that, because of the speed and danger rather than the intrinsic nature of the enterprise, seriously alienated sections of the regime's conservative support, not least in the army. Only the

[38] Weinberg, *Starting World War II* (see note 13), p. 299 note 170.
[39] Carr, *Hitler*, p. 55.
[40] Weinberg, *Starting World War II*, pp. 287–9.
[41] *Die Tagebücher von Joseph Goebbels*, vol. 3, pp. 223, 263, 266, entries of 3 Aug., 12 Sept., 14 Sept. 1937. The 'overrunning' of Czechoslovakia was also mentioned in the entry of 3 Aug. 1937 and the forceful solution of the Czech question on a number of occasions in these months before the Hossbach meeting.
[42] Noakes and Pridham (see ch. 3 note 37), vol. 3, pp. 680–7.
[43] Noakes and Pridham, vol. 3, p. 712.

pressure put on Hitler at the Munich Conference deflected him from what can justifiably be regarded as *his* policy to wage war *then* against Czechoslovakia. As is well known, it was Hitler – learning the lessons of Munich – who rejected any alternative to war in 1939, whereas Göring, the second man in the Reich, attempted belatedly to defer any outbreak of hostilities.

Our first set of questions about Hitler's influence on the making of decisions in foreign policy has met with a fairly clear response – and one which would be further bolstered if we were to continue the survey to embrace foreign, strategic, and military affairs during the war years. Whereas in domestic matters Hitler was uninterested in making decisions, and in anti-Jewish policy, which was ideologically highly conducive to him, felt unwilling for prestige reasons to become openly involved, he showed no reluctance to unfold new initiatives or to take vital decisions in the field of foreign policy. In some important areas, as we have seen, he not only set the tone for policy, but pushed through a new or an unorthodox line despite suspicion and objections, particularly of the foreign ministry. There is no sign of any foreign-policy initiative from any of the numerous agencies with an interest in foreign affairs which could not be reconciled with – let alone flatly opposed – Hitler's own thinking and intentions. Evidence of a 'weak dictator' is, therefore, difficult to come by in Hitler's actions in the foreign-policy arena.

Any 'weakness' would have to be located in the presumption that Hitler was the captive of forces limiting his ability to take decisions. Certainly there were forces at work, both within and outside Germany, conditioning the framework of Hitler's actions, which, naturally, did not take place in a vacuum as a free expression of autonomous will. The pressures of foreign policy revisionism and rearmament, for instance, which would have preoccupied any German government in the 1930s and demanded adjustments to the international order, developed in the years after 1933 a momentum which substantially restricted Germany's options and ran increasingly out of control. The arms race and diplomatic upheaval which Germany had instigated, gradually imposed, therefore, their own laws on the situation, reflected in Hitler's growing feeling and expression that time was running against Germany. Built into Germany's accelerated armaments production were additional economic pressures for German action, confirming the prognosis that war would have to come about sooner rather than later. The nature of his 'charismatic' authority and the need not to disappoint the expectations aroused in his mass following also constrained Hitler's potential scope for action. Finally, of course, and most self-evidently of all, the relative strength and actions of other powers, and strategic–diplomatic considerations imposed their own restrictions on Hitler's manoeuvrability – though these restrictions diminished sharply in the immediate pre-war years.

Hitler's foreign policy was, therefore, in no way independent of 'structural determinants' of different kinds. These, however, pushed him if anything still faster on the path he was in any case determined to tread. When all due consideration is given to the actions – and grave mistakes – of other governments in the diplomatic turmoil of the 1930s, the crucial and pivotal role of Germany as the active catalyst in the upheaval is undeniable. Many of the developments which took place were in certain respects likely if not inevitable as the unfinished business of the First World War and the post-war settlement. The continuities in German foreign policy after 1933 are manifest, and formed part of the basis of the far-reaching identity of interest – certainly until 1937–8 – of the conservative élites with the Nazi leadership, rooted in the pursuit of a traditional German power policy aimed at attaining hegemony in central Europe. At the same time, important strands of discontinuity and an unquestionable new dynamism were also unmistakable hallmarks of German foreign policy after 1933 – such that one can speak with justification of a 'diplomatic revolution'[44] in Europe by 1936. Hitler's own decisions and actions, as we have seen, were central to this development.

In the framework of foreign policy decision-making, Jost Dülffer's conclusions seem apposite:[45] *(1)* The influence of the old leadership élites waned in correspondence with the growing influence of the 'new' Nazi forces. *(2)* Though not undertaken autonomously and in a social vacuum, the major initiatives in German foreign policy in the 1930s can be traced to Hitler himself. *(3)* Economic factors contributed to the framework within which decisions had to be made, but did not play a *dominant* role in Hitler's decisions. *(4)* Hitler cannot be seen as simply a machiavellian opportunist, but rather advanced a consistent anti-Soviet policy (until 1939), necessitating a realignment of Germany's relations with Poland and Britain.

This suggestion of an inner consistency directed at war against the Soviet Union brings us to the second question of our enquiry.

## II

We have established that Hitler actively intervened and personally played a central role in shaping German foreign policy during the 1930s. The interpretation that the course of German foreign policy had an inner consistency determined more than any other factor by Hitler's ideology remains, however, open to dispute. Historians have put forward three (in some ways interlinked) alternative explanations.

The first is that Hitler's ideological motivation, while basically unchanging, was not the decisive factor. Rather, Hitler articulated and represented the expansionist–imperialist demands of the German ruling class and made possible the imperialist war sought after by monopoly capital. Hitler had a certain functional role, therefore, but a similar course of action would have unfolded even without him. There can be no doubting, of course, the expansionist aims of influential sectors of the German military, economic, and bureaucratic élites. However, as we saw in considering foreign-policy decision-making earlier in this chapter, it would be short-circuiting the evidence to give the impression that the course of foreign policy was a foregone conclusion after 1933, that it followed closely and at all points the perceived wishes and interests of the traditional élites, that genuine policy options even with the context of revisionism were not available at crucial junctures, and that Hitler himself did not take a prominent part in deciding policy options. Certainly Hitler was never out of step with the

---

[44] The sub-title of the first of Weinberg's two-volume study of Nazi foreign policy (see note 20).
[45] Dülffer, 'Zum "decision-making process" ', pp. 200–3.

*dominant* sectors within the élites. But that does not mean he was their captive. The dominance of particular factions within the élites was itself related to the speed with which they could attune to policy initiatives and make them their own, as well as to their ability to influence the formulation of policy in the first place. The evidence suggests, therefore, that German expansionism in the 1930s was an inevitability, but that its precise direction and dynamic was not independent of Hitler's personal role.

A second approach lays the weight of explanation on the 'primacy of domestic politics', accepting an underlying consistency in foreign affairs, but seeing this less in the implementation of Hitler's ideology than in the need to preserve and uphold the domestic social order. This, too, seems inadequate as a general interpretation. Again, we have accepted in earlier chapters that domestic pressures undoubtedly contributed to the character and the timing of some foreign-policy initiatives, especially in the earlier years of the regime. Domestic, as well as diplomatic, considerations seem to have played a part, for instance, in the decision to reoccupy the Rhineland in March 1936. But there was no such pressure dictating other major developments or shifts in policy, such as the Non-Aggression Treaty with Poland in 1934 or the Naval Treaty with Britain the following year. And by the later 1930s the mounting economic problems appear to have corroborated, not caused, the direction of foreign policy, and, indeed, to have been in no small part a product of it. The evidence is suggestive, therefore, of a total inter-dependence of domestic and foreign policy, in which domestic consider-ations helped shape the parameters of foreign-policy action – though to a diminishing extent; and, vice versa, in which foreign policy objectives heavily determined the nature and aims of domestic policy.[46] Ideologically, and practically, foreign and domestic policy were so fused that it seems quite misplaced to speak of a primacy of one over the other: there was no contra-diction between the imperialist and social imperialist aims of the regime, and there is no means analytically of separating them. Nor does it appear satis-factory to perceive Nazi aims as lying in the preservation of the *existing* social order, however unclear and nebulous the social ambitions of any 'new order' might have been.

A final alternative explanation argues that German foreign policy had no single, clear direction, that it simultaneously pursued a variety of basically unconnected objectives, and that it was characterized by Hitler's own dilettante opportunism which, in the context of a fragmented political system, produced a diminishing sense of reality and an accelerating nihilistic momentum. Even among historians favouring a 'structuralist' inter-pretation of foreign policy, Hans Mommsen, it has to be said, seems alone in advancing such an argument so emphatically.[47] Martin Broszat, the other foremost exponent of the 'structuralist' approach, appears, as we saw earlier, to accept the existence of a more or less consistent 'directional force'

[46] See on this esp. Erhard Fordran, 'Zur Theorie der internationalen Beziehungen – Das Verhältnis von Innen-, Außen- und internationaler Politik und die historischen Beispiele der 30 er Jahre', in Erhard Fordran *et al.*, eds., *Innen- und Außenpolitik unter nationalsozialistischer Bedrohung* (Opladen, 1977), pp. 315–61, here esp. pp. 353–4.

[47] See Mommsen, 'National Socialism: Continuity and Change', p. 177 and *Adolf Hitler*, esp. p. 93.

aimed at expansion in the east, though in his view this served only the function of an 'ideological metaphor'.[48] This raises the question of whether, in fact, the debate about the existence and consistency of foreign-policy objectives has not been falsely polarized by the vagueness of some of the key terms employed by historians. While, for example, 'intentionalists' naturally reject categorically the view that Hitler was simply an opportunist and improviser without basic orientation or goal, their own frequent usage of concepts such as 'programme' (sometimes begun with a capital letter and with the inverted commas omitted), 'basic plan' (*Grund-Plan*), or 'stage by stage plan' (*Stufenplan*), is not without problems.[49] These terms, it is often emphasized, do not imply detailed blueprints for action. Rather, they are, it seems, meant to suggest only that Hitler had fixed ideas in the sphere of foreign policy (especially *Lebensraum*), to which he clung obsessively from the 1920s; that as Führer he directed foreign policy in accordance with these ideas; and that, although having a clear target in mind (above all conquest of the Soviet Union) and a basic strategy for reaching that target (the alliance with Britain), he had no concrete design worked out. The gap between this view and Broszat's suggestion that *Lebensraum* in the East was so vacuous a notion that it served merely as a directional guide to action (*Aktionsrichtung*)[50] certainly exists, but is perhaps less wide than at first sight. The gap seems unbridgeable only if *exclusive* weight is attached to *either* intention *or* function as a factor determining the course of foreign policy. While it could indeed be argued that *Lebensraum* served the function of an ideological metaphor in providing the Movement with a directional focus for action, it seems inadequate to view this function as the sole or even main *raison d'être* of foreign policy, to deny that there was indeed a genuine reality to Nazi foreign policy aims, a reality which was at least in part shaped by Hitler's ideological aims and intentions.[51] However vague the notion, *Lebensraum* did mean something concrete – even if the way there was uncharted: war against the Soviet Union. Hitler's words and actions in the period 1933–41 are consistent with the interpretation that he was convinced that such a war would come about, that although he did not know how or when, it would be sooner rather than later, that he was steering German foreign policy towards that goal, and that he was attempting to shape German society for participation in that war.

As we saw earlier, the basic orientation of German foreign policy was shifted as early as 1933, when Hitler determined that 'natural antagonism' should shape relations with the Soviet Union. In autumn 1935, according to Alfred Sohn-Rethel's account, talk at the 'fireside discussions' with leaders of the army and economy of stifling rearmament expenditure was invariably countered by Göring's reminder to Hitler about his coming war against the Soviet Union.[52] The beginning of the Spanish Civil War must have

---

[48] Broszat, 'Soziale Motivation', pp. 406–9.

[49] The rather contorted passage of Klaus Hildebrand, 'Hitlers "Programm" und seine Realisierung 1939–1942', in Funke, pp. 63–93, here p. 65, suggests some of the difficulties of formulating a clear definition of Hitler's 'programme'.

[50] Broszat, 'Soziale Motivation', p. 403.

[51] This is clearly accepted by Broszat, 'Soziale Motivation', p. 403.

[52] Sohn-Rethel (see ch. 3 note 19), pp. 139–41.

contributed to Hitler's growing preoccupation with this idea in 1936. His secret memorandum on the Four Year Plan, compiled in the summer, rested on the basic premise that 'the showdown with Russia is inevitable',[53] and the recently published Goebbels diaries reveal how much the coming clash with Russia was on Hitler's mind in the years 1936 and 1937. In June, according to Goebbel's diary notes, Hitler spoke of a coming conflict between Japan and Russia, after which 'this colossus will start to totter [*ins Wanken kommen*]. And then our great hour will have arrived. Then we must supply ourselves with land for 100 years'. 'Let's hope we're ready then' (added Goebbels) 'and that the Führer is still alive. So that action will be taken'.[54] In November the same year, Goebbels recorded: 'After dinner I talk thoroughly with the Führer alone. He is very content with the situation. Rearmament is proceeding. We're sticking in fabulous sums. In 1938 we'll be completely ready. The show-down with Bolshevism is coming. Then we want to be prepared'.[55] Less than a month later, set in the context of the Spanish Civil War, Hitler portrayed the danger of Bolshevism to his cabinet in a three-hour meeting, arguing (according to Goebbel's account): 'Europe is already divided into two camps. We can't go back any longer. . . . Germany can only wish that the danger be deferred till we're ready. When it comes, seize the opportunity [*zugreifen*]. Get into the paternoster lift at the right time. But also get out again at the right time. Re-arm, money can play no role'.[56] According to his reported comments in February 1937, Hitler expected 'a great world showdown' in five or six years' time.[57] In July Goebbels reported Hitler's puzzlement over the purges in the Soviet Union and his view that Stalin must be mad. Hitler's alleged comments ended: 'But Russia knows nothing other than Bolshevism. That is the danger which we will have to knock down sometime'.[58] In December Hitler repeated the same sentiments about Stalin and his supporters, concluding: 'Must be exterminated [*Muß ausgerottet werden*]'.[59] Finally, there is the well-known comment by Hitler to the Swiss Commissioner to the League of Nations, Carl Burckhardt, in 1939: 'Everything that I undertake is directed against Russia. If those in the West are too stupid and too blind to understand this, then I shall be forced to come to an understanding with the Russians to beat the West, and then, after its defeat, turn with all my concerted force against the Soviet Union'.[60] That Hitler was saying this in the knowledge that the message would be relayed to the West does not detract from its basic reality.

The cosmic struggle with Bolshevism gradually became imminent reality, just as the vision of destroying the Jews had emerged as a realizable goal. In

---

[53] Noakes and Pridham, vol. 2, p. 288, and see also pp. 281–2.

[54] *Die Tagebücher von Joseph Goebbels*, vol. 2, p. 622, entry of 9 June 1936.

[55] *Die Tagebücher von Joseph Goebbels*, vol. 2, p. 726, entry of 15 Nov. 1936.

[56] *Die Tagebücher von Joseph Goebbels*, vol. 2, p. 743, entry of 2 Dec. 1936.

[57] *Die Tagebücher von Joseph Goebbels*, vol. 3, p. 55, entry of 23 Feb. 1937. See also the entries of 28 Jan. 1937, where Hitler reportedly hoped to have six years, but would act before then if an advantageous situation arose, and 16 Feb. 1937, where he expected 'the great world struggle' in 'several years' ' time (pp. 26, 45).

[58] *Die Tagebücher von Joseph Goebbels*, vol. 3, p. 198, entry of 10 July 1937.

[59] *Die Tagebücher von Joseph Goebbels*, vol. 3, p. 378, entry of 22 Dec. 1937.

[60] Cited in Hildebrand, *Foreign Policy* (see ch. 1 note 17), p. 88; Carl J. Burckhardt, *Meine Danziger Mission 1937–1939* (dtv-edition, Munich, 1962), p. 272.

neither case do Hitler's 'intentions' come near providing a full or satisfactory explanation. But the chances of either coming about without those 'intentions' would have been diminished – greatly so in the case of the extermination of the Jews, to a much lesser extent in the case of the war against the Soviet Union. The 'twisted road' to this ideological 'war of annihilation' needs no emphasis. The only strategy was the alliance with Britain. By the mid 1930s that had failed irretrievably, and any 'policy', 'programme', or 'basic plan' worth the name was in tatters – resulting in fact by 1939 in forced, if temporary, alliance with the arch-enemy and a state of war with the would-be 'friend' which had spurned him. Only in these conditions, the reverse of what had been hoped for, could the war against the Soviet Union, from summer 1940 onwards, be planned, not merely 'targeted'. And despite German supremacy in western Europe, the unresolved problem of the United States was by then looming ever larger in the background.

## III

The debate about the extent of Hitler's long-term ambitions whether he wanted world dominion or whether his final goal was 'merely' the conquest of *Lebensraum* in the East – has a rather artificial ring about it. As we noted earlier, the view has generally prevailed since the publications of Moltmann and especially Hillgruber in the 1960s that Hitler's intentions stopped at nothing short of German mastery of the entire globe, a goal to be achieved in stages and perhaps not accomplished until long after his death. Some leading historians have, however, doggedly held to the view that Hitler's final aim was that which he had expressed consistently throughout practically his whole career: the attainment of *Lebensraum* at the expense of Russia. One might question at the outset whether this difference of interpretation reflects much more than the weighting historians have attached to the *relative* clarity and consistency of the focus on the East in Hitler's thinking as compared with his more nebulous and sporadic musings on the long-term possibilities (and inevitability) of further expansion following the expected German victory over Bolshevism. There are indeed few ground for doubting that Hitler did at times entertain 'world domination' thoughts. It is less clear, however, what significance such notions had for formulating practical policy. We suggested earlier that, while the term *Lebensraum* indeed possessed a metaphorical quality, and that neither Hitler nor anyone else had a clearly worked-out conception of what precisely it would amount to, it also did have a concrete meaning in denoting war against the Soviet Union and the need to prepare as much as possible for such a struggle. Thoughts of this war, however unclear the path to it might have seemed, were never far from the minds of Hitler and the top Nazi and army leadership, and practical military, strategic, and diplomatic consequences ensued. Whether vague megalomaniac meanderings about future global domination can be seen in the same light might be intrinsically doubted; even more so, whether such notions ought to be elevated to the status of a 'programme', let alone 'grand strategy'.[61]

---

[61] The latter term is used by Hauner, 'World Dominion' (see note 12), p. 23.

In its most forthright formulation, the 'world mastery' thesis claims that 'at no time between 1920 and 1945 did [Hitler], as his statements prove, lose sight of the aim of world domination'[62] – an aim which, another historian adds, he wanted to achieve 'in a series of blitz campaigns, extending stage by stage over the entire globe'.[63] The main supporting evidence comprises Hitler's early writings (especially his *Second Book* of 1928), Rauschning's version of Hitler's monologues in 1932–4, the *Table Talk*, audiences with foreign diplomats, aspects of military planning during the years 1940–1, and – as has been more recently emphasized – the deductions to be drawn from Hitler's monumental architectural plans, and long-term naval planning. We need briefly to consider the strength of this evidence.

Hitler's *Second Book* raises the spectre of a contest for hegemony at some point in the distant future between the United States of America and Europe. His view was that the USA could only be defeated by a racially pure European state, and that it was the task of the Nazi movement to prepare 'its own fatherland' for the task.[64] Before this time, the United States had attracted little of Hitler's attention. His early speeches and writings (including *Mein Kampf*) contain few references to America going beyond conventional and general denunciation for its part in the First World War and the peace settlement.[65] By the late 1920s views of a long-term threat from America to Germany were fairly commonplace, and it was in this climate that Hitler expressed his vague notions about the great conflict between the German-dominated Eurasian empire and the USA in the distant future.[66] Hitler's image of America, vague as it was, did not in fact remain constant. By the early 1930s, under the impact of the Depression, America was taken to be a weak, racially mongrel state which would be incapable of engaging again in a European war, and whose only hope of salvation lay in German-Americans rejuvenated by Nazism.[67] By the later 1930s American distaste for Nazi racial and religious policy had confirmed Hitler's assessment of the USA's debility. He did not at this stage regard the United States as an actual or potentially strong military power to be feared by Germany; his vision remained primarily continental, and he paid little attention in concrete terms to areas outside Europe.[68] If the vague idea of a future conflict with the USA remained, it had no practical importance in policy formulation.

Evidence of Hitler's 'programme' for global mastery for the period between the *Second Book* and the later 1930s is dependent on references to 'world domination', or to Germany being the 'greatest power in the world',

[62] Thies, *Architekt* (see note 9), p. 189. See also his essays: 'Hitler's European Building Programme', *JCH* 13 (1978), pp. 413–31; 'Hitlers "Endziele": Zielloser Aktionismus, Kontinentalimperium oder Weltherrschaft?', in Michalka, *Nationalsozialistische Außenpolitik*, pp. 70–91; and 'Nazi Architecture – A Blueprint for World Domination: The Last Aims of Adolf Hitler', in David Welch, ed., *Nazi Propaganda. The Power and the Limitations* (London, 1983), pp. 45–64.

[63] Hauner, 'World Dominion', p. 23.

[64] Telford Taylor, ed., *Hitler's Secret Book* (New York, 1961), p. 106.

[65] Weinberg, *Diplomatic Revolution*, p. 21.

[66] Dietrich Aigner, 'Hitler und die Weltherrschaft', in Michalka, *Nationalsozialistische Außenpolitik*, pp. 49–69, here p. 62.

[67] Weinberg, *Diplomatic Revolution*, pp. 21–2; Rauschning, *Hitler Speaks*, pp. 75–7.

[68] Weinberg, *Starting World War II*, pp. 252–3; *Diplomatic Revolution*, p. 20.

in a few public speeches – in which presumably the propaganda effect was the greatest consideration – and in private conversations subsequently recapitulated by participants (and which cannot, in their printed form, be regarded as accurate *verbatim* records of what transpired).[69] Of the latter category, Hermann Rauschning's *Hitler Speaks*, published in 1939 (at a timely date for western propaganda purposes), is the most important. Though it cannot be taken as accurate to the last word as a record of what Hitler actually said there is nothing in it which is not consonant with what is otherwise known of Hitler's character and opinions.[70] There are, indeed, passages in Rauschning in which Hitler pontificates, for instance, about the future German domination of Latin America and the exploitation of the treasures of Mexican soil by Germany. As Rauschning himself pointed out, however, Hitler was on such occasions invariably repeating, on the basis of no detailed information, banal popular images of these countries. He added that Hitler had always been a *poseur*, so that it was difficult to know how serious he was about any comments he made.[71] German relations with Latin America in the 1930s turned out, not surprisingly, to have nothing to do with Hitler's wild visions and megalomaniac mouthings.[72] Again these cannot be seen as falling within the framework of any 'plan' or 'strategy'.

Jochen Thies has recently argued that evidence for the consistency of Hitler's 'world domination' aim between 1920 and 1945 can best be found in his plans for the erection of representative buildings on a monumental scale, as images of German strength which would last for up to 10,000 years.[73] Clearly, they were intended as symbols of Germany's lasting world-power status and are testimony to Hitler's grandiose vision of German potential. But it seems to be stretching the argument to see the building plans themselves as an unambiguous reflection of a consistent 'programme' leading to 'world domination'.

Rather more convincing is the view that the growing proximity of war and the inability to cement the intended alliance with Britain, at the same time, however, the growing confidence derived from a series of diplomatic coups, led in the later 1930s to Hitler giving greater strategic consideration to a range of possibilities which could emerge from armed conflict, in which Germany's struggle might take on a global character. He hinted at this on a number of occasions to his generals from 1937 onwards.[74] From this time, too, he began to show more interest in naval strategy, culminating in the Z-Plan of January 1939, in which Hitler's insistence on the building of a huge battle-fleet by 1944 (as opposed to the navy's preference for U-Boats, which made a better offensive weapon against Britain, and in detriment to steel allocations for the army and *Luftwaffe*) has been taken to point beyond a war with Britain to a future German mastery of the oceans and the

---

[69] Thies, 'Hitlers "Endziele" ', p. 78 note 45 and see also pp. 72–3; and Aigner, pp. 53–4.
[70] This is the general tenor of Theodor Schieder's conclusion: see above note 4, also for the reference to Hänel's more recent analysis, which attacks the authenticity of Rauschning's book.
[71] Rauschning, *Hitler Speaks*, pp. 69–75, 138.
[72] See Weinberg, *Starting World War II*, pp. 255–60.
[73] Thies, *Architekt*, and 'Hitlers "Endziele" ', esp. pp. 83–4.
[74] Thies, 'Hitlers "Endziele" ', pp. 86–8.

inevitability of global conflict.[75] At the same time, the inconsistency and ambiguity of Hitler's 'global' thinking is shown by his lack of interest in inciting revolution in the Islamic world and actively supporting nationalist undermining of British rule in India.[76]

More specific evidence of Hitler's strategic global thinking is largely confined to the war period, especially to the years 1940–1. By this time, however, Hitler was largely *reacting* (not wholly consistently) to circumstances which he had indeed done much to bring about, but which were now rapidly going beyond any measure of his control. It is difficult, therefore, to relate strategic considerations at this date directly to the earlier vague utterances about 'world domination'.[77] As Hillgruber has argued, planning for the war against the Soviet Union (much though Hitler wanted the war ideologically), and the urgent need of a speedy victory, was conditioned strategically by the necessity of bringing Britain to the peace table, keeping America out of the war, and ending the war in the only way possible to Germany's advantage.[78] Convinced that America (whose image in Hitler's eyes had again shifted from one of weakness back to one of strength) would enter the war by 1942 at the latest, the overriding need was to have done with the eastern war in order to be in a position to fend off the United States. At the height of his powers, Hitler thought for a short while of 'destroying' America in tandem with Japan, and of stationing long-range bombers in the Azores in autumn 1941 in order to attack the USA. But with the imminent entry of America into the war, and the German offensive stuck in the Russian mud, he reverted to the vague notion of a showdown with the USA 'in the next generation', declared war on the USA in a gesture of resignation, and told the Japanese ambassador two months later that he still did not know how to conquer the United States.[79] Further musings during the remainder of the war about 'world domination' after a hundred years of struggle, of a later ruler of Germany being 'master of the world', and of an 'unshakeable conviction' that German world mastery would ultimately be attained,[80] were pipe-dreams not evidence of a *Stufenplan*. As the Third Reich was collapsing in ruins and the Red Army stood at the gates of Berlin, Hitler returned to more modest targets: the destruction of Bolshevism, the conquest of 'wide spaces in the East', and a continental *Lebensraum* policy as opposed to the acquisition of overseas colonies. His last message to the army, a day before his suicide, was equally utopian: it should fight to 'win territory for the German people in the East'.[81]

It seems necessary to draw a distinction between strategic aims and vague

---

[75] Jost Dülffer, 'Der Einfluß des Auslandes auf die nationalsozialistische Politik', in Fordran *et al.* (above note 46), pp. 295–313, here p. 302; Hauner, 'World Dominion', p. 27; Carr, *Hitler*, p. 131. For a sceptical view of the weight attached to the Z-Plan, see Aigner, pp. 60–1.

[76] Hauner, 'Professionals' (above note 11) and his *India in Axis Strategy* (note 9).

[77] Andreas Hillgruber, 'Der Faktor Amerika in Hitlers Strategie 1938–1941', *APZ* (11 May 1966), p. 4.

[78] Hillgruber, 'Amerika', p. 13.

[79] Hillgruber, 'Amerika', pp. 14–21. See also Jäckel, *Hitler in History*, ch 4, and William Carr, *Poland to Pearl Harbor. The Making of the Second World War* (London, 1985), esp. pp. 167–9.

[80] See Meir Michaelis, 'World Power Status or World Dominion?', *The Historical Journal* 15 (1972), pp. 331–60, here p. 351.

[81] Cited in Michaelis, pp. 351, 357.

and visionary orientations for action. The evidence for Hitler's strategic global thinking is concentrated in the years immediately prior to the war, when his underlying concept of the alliance with Britain had collapsed, and in the first years of the war, when faced with the increasingly certain entry of the United States into the conflict. Before those years, there are only grey visions of a cosmic struggle at some dim and distant time in the future. After those years, there are again glimmers of a far-off utopia, now presumably compensating for the reality of inevitable and crushing defeat. To label this a 'programme' for world mastery seems inappropriate. As Rauschning saw, however, Nazism could not have ceased its 'perpetual motion';[82] its internal and external dynamism could never have brought stability or subsided into stagnation; not least, Hitler's own social darwinist interpretation of exist- ence itself as struggle, transmuted into the titanic struggles of nations in which there was no half-way between total victory and complete destruction, added a decisive component which was wholly compatible with short-term opportunistic exploitation but quite irreconcilable with long-term rational calculation and planning. In this respect, perhaps, 'expansion without object' (following the presumed victory over the Soviet Union) fits the ethos of Nazism and corresponds to Hitler's utopian dreams far better than does the concept of a 'programme' for world domination.

Our survey of differing interpretations of Hitler's contribution to shaping domestic, anti-Jewish, and foreign policy in the Third Reich is now com- pleted. In each case, we have argued, Hitler's 'intentions' *and* impersonal 'structures' are both indispensable components of any interpretation of the course of German politics in the Nazi State. And there is no mathematical formula for deciding what weighting to attach to each factor. We have seen that Hitler shaped initiatives and personally took the major decisions in foreign policy, though this was seldom the case in domestic affairs or even in anti-Jewish policy. In domestic matters he seldom intervened; in the 'Jewish Question' his main contribution consisted of setting the distant target, shaping the climate, and sanctioning the actions of others; in foreign policy he *both* symbolized the 'great cause' which motivated others *and* played a central role personally in the course of aggression. Hitler's ideological aims were one important factor in deciding the contours of German foreign policy. But they fused for the most part in the formulation of policy so inseparably with strategic power-political considerations, and frequently, too, with economic interest that it is usually impossible to distinguish them analytically. And alongside Hitler's personality, the *function* of his Führer role was also vital to the framing of foreign policy and determining the road to war in its legitimation of the struggle towards the ends it was presumed he wanted. It legitimized the self-interest of an army leadership only too willing to profit from unlimited rearmament, over-ready to engage in expansionist plans, and hopeful of a central role for itself in the State. It legitimized the ambitions of a foreign office only too anxious to prepare the ground diplo- matically for upturning the European order, and the various 'amateur' agencies dabbling in foreign affairs with even more aggressive intentions.[83]

[82] See Michaelis, p. 359.
[83] See Hauner, 'Professionals'. For an example of 'local initiatives' of 'amateurs' making the running in the Balkans, see Weinberg, *Diplomatic Revolution*, p. 23 note 81.

And it legitimized the greed and ruthlessness of industrialists only too eager to offer plans for the economic plunder of much of Europe. Finally, it provided the touchstone for the wildest chauvinist and imperialist clamour from the mass of the Party faithful for the restoration of Germany's might and glory. Each of these elements – from the élites and from the masses – bound in turn Hitler and the Nazi leadership to the course of action, gathering in pace and escalating in danger, which they had been partly instrumental in creating. The complex radicalization, also in the sphere of foreign policy, which turned Hitler's ideological dreams into living nightmares for millions can, thus, only inadequately be explained by heavy concentration on Hitler's intentions divorced from the conditions and forces – inside and outside Germany – which structured the implementation of those intentions.

# 7

## The Third Reich: 'Social Reaction' or 'Social Revolution'?

Assessing the nature and extent of Nazism's impact on German society is one of the most complex – and most important – tasks facing historians of the Third Reich. And, clearly, the social impact of an ideologically doctrinaire and ruthlessly repressive authoritarian state has potential implications extending far beyond the geographical and chronological confines of Germany under Nazism.

A differentiated understanding of German society in the Third Reich has become possible since the 1960s, when serious scholarly research in this field was first carried out. The major advances, however, came as late as the 1970s, when the source base was massively extended, and continue to the present time. The huge expansion and attractiveness of *Alltagsgeschichte* ('history of everyday life') or *Geschichte von unten* ('history from below') in West Germany during the past decade or so has provided a plethora of detailed empirical studies – of greatly varying quality – of the experience of different social groups, frequently in a local or regional context, during the Nazi Dictatorship. A good deal of material is, therefore, now available for examining the social impact of Nazism. That there are often major difficulties of interpretation built into the sources emanating from such a political system goes without saying. As in other issues we have considered, however, the problems and perspectives of interpretation are far more closely related to different theoretical startingpoints and unbridgeable ideological divisions among historians. The debate is characterized by fundamental disagreements about the very nature of Nazism, its social aims and intentions; about the criteria and methods needed to evaluate change under Nazism; and about the terms used to define that social change.

Part of the problem rests in the eclectic nature and internal contradictions of the Nazi Party itself, its ideology and its social composition. There are considerable difficulties involved even in attempting to define clearly what its social goals and objectives were, and in distinguishing these ends from the means necessary to attain them, which in practice often seem to have produced the diametrically opposite result. Hence, Nazism has been interpreted by some leading historians as genuinely revolutionary in content, and branded by others as quintessentially counter-revolutionary; some have regarded it as a modernizing force despite archaic, reactionary aspects of its ideology; others as violently anti-modernist, or – paradoxically – 'revolutionary reaction'; while still others have found no cause to see in Nazism any other than plain social reaction.[1] In any event there is a genuine question mark over the extent to which

---

[1] A number of the contradictory positions are summarized in Francis L. Carsten, 'Interpretations of Fascism', in Laqueur (ch. 2 note 3), pp. 457–87, here esp. pp. 474 ff.

Nazi 'social ideology' ought to be regarded as a serious declaration of intent as opposed to mere manipulative propaganda.

A second part of the problem derives from the complexity of attempting to construct some type of 'balance-sheet' of social change in Germany under Nazism. While some aspects of 'social change', such as rate of social mobility, can be measured with difficulty, changes in attitudes, mentality, and value systems can only be qualitatively assessed on the basis of evidence which is far from ideal for the purposes. Moreover, the time scale is extremely short. The Third Reich lasted only 12 out of its scheduled 1,000 years, and six of those were war years. Since war, especially on the scale of the Second World War, contains its own momentum for rapid social change promoted by massive destruction, displaced populations, mobilization and demobilization, and post-war expectations, there is an obvious problem involved in extrapolating such change from that which was intended by the Nazi system (even accepting that the war itself was a product of Nazism). It is necessary, therefore, to try to distinguish between change which the Nazi regime brought about directly, and that which indirectly and even unintentionally stemmed from Nazism. A further difficulty is how to relate such change to long-term secular changes in society which were taking place in Germany as elsewhere in the industrial era. It has even been suggested that in order to assess social change under Nazism it would be necessary to build a counter-factual model to estimate what change would have come about by 1945 had Nazism never existed.[2] This raises the further question: are we trying to assess whatever social change did take place under Nazism against our understanding of what we presume Nazism was setting out to accomplish, against what might have happened without Nazism, against the rate and nature of change in other industrial societies at the same time, or against some notional 'ideal type' of development?

The third part of the problem is definitional. As is frequently the case in the social, political, and historical sciences, the terms and concepts used are often imprecise, capable of more than a single interpretation, or ideologically 'loaded'. To use the term 'revolution', it has been said, 'is to enter a semantic minefield',[3] and one furthermore in which personal predilections for what might be taken to constitute a 'revolution' – in particular a 'social revolution' – evidently play a determining role. While it may be reasonable to object that 'revolution' need not be something 'positive', 'progressive', or 'morally commendable', nor confined to marxist terms of fundamental alteration to the economic substance of a society,[4] this negative point brings us little closer to defining precisely what *would* constitute a 'social revolution'. It goes almost without saying that 'reaction' and 'counter-revolution' are hardly 'cleaner' as intellectual concepts.

Certainly, terms like 'social change' or 'social development' are more neutral, though they are so vague in themselves that they only become operable when attached to some theory or concept of change over time. Only

[2] Matzerath and Volkmann (see ch. 2 note 53), p. 109 (comment of T. Sarrazin).
[3] Jeremy Noakes, 'Nazism and Revolution', in Noel O'Sullivan, ed., *Revolutionary Theory and Political Reality* (London, 1983), pp. 73–100.
[4] See Karl Dietrich Bracher, 'Tradition und Revolution im Nationalsozialismus', in his *Zeitgeschichtliche Kontroversen* (above ch. 1 note 40), pp. 62–78, here esp., pp. 66–70.

marxist theories and modernization theories suggest themselves as possible explanatory models.

Marxist theorists tend to restrict their analyses of 'social change' primarily to alterations in the structure of the mode of production – that is, in modern times, in the structure of capitalism – and to the state of the 'class struggle', with a corresponding tendency to underplay change in social forms or culture unless the economic substance of society has also been transformed. Notions of 'social change' locked into a marxist approach quickly, therefore, lose their tones of vagueness, but also their tones of intellectual neutrality.

Alternative explanations of 'social change', which have commended themselves in varying degrees to non-marxist or 'liberal' historians, are linked to 'modernization' approaches. The concept of 'modernization' – a product of American social science – attempts to embrace the various elements of cultural, political, and socio-economic development which gained their major impulse with the industrial and French revolutions in western Europe, transforming the 'traditional' societies of the West and gradually of large sections of the globe into 'modern societies'. This transformation includes a huge growth in the quantity and availability of goods and services; increasing access to these goods and services; growth in social differentiation, more complex division of labour, and increased specialization in function; and a heightened capacity for the institutional regulation of social and political conflict.[5] Although modernization approaches have become greatly refined since their early rather unsophisticated usage, they remain eclectic, imprecise, and open to widely differing subjective weightings attached to some of the fundamental premises and concepts used. The implicit or explicit linkage of modernization approaches to 'ideal types' suggested by western liberal democracies, the relative neglect of class conflict, and the relegation of economic structures to only one – if very important – component of 'social change' add to the highly debatable nature of the 'modernization' concept in its conventional usages, and makes it generally unacceptable to marxist scholars.

Any attempt to evaluate Nazism's impact on German society must grapple with the difficulties we have raised. Before attempting our own evaluation, we need to survey the main divisions in interpretation among historians who have tackled the problem.

## Interpretations

Resting on the basic premise that Hitler-Fascism was the dictatorship of the most reactionary elements of the German ruling class, it is hardly surprising

---

[5] See Werner Abelshauser and Anselm Faust, *Wirtschafts- und Sozialpolitik. Eine national-sozialistische Sozialrevolution?* (Nationalsozialismus im Unterricht, Studieneinheit 4, Deutsches Institut für Fernstudien an der Universität Tübingen, Tübingen, 1983), p. 4; Matzerath and Volkmann, p. 95. For an evaluation of modernization theories and applicability in historical writing, Hans-Ulrich Wehler, *Modernisierungstheorie und Geschichte* (Göttingen, 1975) is invaluable. Helmut Kaelble *et al., Probleme der Modernisierung in Deutschland. Sozialhistorische Studien zum 19. und 20. Jahrhundert* (Opladen, 1978), apply modernization models explicitly to German social development.

that GDR historiography has accorded short shrift to notions that the Third Reich brought about change in German society amounting to a 'social revolution'. While a heavy concentration upon organized communist resistance groups has imposed a straitjacket on research into wider aspects of the social history of the Third Reich, the possibility of long-term, 'modernizing' consequences of Nazism for German society is, of course, a 'non-question' for GDR historians. Modernization theories are regarded as merely a bourgeois pseudo-doctrine of industrial society, so lacking in definition as to be purely subjective in application, anti-marxist by intent and implication, euphemizing fascism in regarding it as (even unwittingly) a 'push into modernity', and, in so far as Nazism is taken to have been instrumental in promoting a 'social revolution', arbitrarily distorting and misusing the concept of revolution for a phenomenon which was blatantly counter-revolutionary.[6] Conceptions built into modernization theories over 'progress' within capitalist society – and not in the direction of marxist–leninist socialism – are clearly irreconcilable with the emphasis placed upon the continuities of imperialist monopoly capitalism outliving the Third Reich and ensuring the reactionary character of the Federal Republic. From this starting-point, it is obvious that questions of any lasting or long-term impact of the Third Reich on the development of German society are irrelevant for GDR historiography. Genuine social revolution can, they would argue, come about only under the aegis of marxism–leninism. In the case of Germany, this took place through the agency of the Red Army and the Socialist Unity Party (SED), while the reaction continued in new guise under a different political system of bourgeois domination in the Federal Republic.

Without sharing this fundamentalist position, western marxist and marxist-influenced historical writing – which has contributed to some of the most important work on the social history of the Third Reich during the past decade or so – is equally impatient with suggestions of a 'social revolution' under Nazism. The historical balance, it is argued, is clear: Nazism destroyed working-class organizations, reshaped class relations by greatly strengthening the position of employers, who were backed with all the weight of a repressive police state, and kept down living standards while providing for soaring profits.[7] Clear though this balance may be, however, it arguably marks the beginning, not the end, of the enquiry. The Nazi regime unquestionably enjoyed until well into the war a degree of popularity and active support which cannot adequately be explained by the manipulative power of propaganda or the heavy repression of a police state. It has to be accepted that Nazism made real – if partial – inroads into wide sectors of German society, not excluding the working class, and that a considerable degree of material as well as affective integration into the Nazi State was attained, even though Catholic, communist, and socialist subcultures proved relatively resistant and impenetrable barriers. Recognition of considerable

[6] See Gerhard Lozek and Rolf Richter, 'Zur Auseinandersetzung mit vorherrschenden bürgerlichen Faschismustheorien', in Gossweiler and Eichholtz, *Faschismusforschung* (ch. 1 note 27), pp. 417–51, here pp. 427–9; and Gerhard Lozek *et al.*, eds., *Unbewältigte Vergangenheit. Kritik der bürgerlichen Geschichtsschreibung in der BRD* (East Berlin, 1977), pp. 340–1.
[7] See e.g. the comments of Ernest Mandel, in Trotsky, *Struggle* (ch. 2 note 16), p. 13.

and extensive Nazi penetration, which in itself is, of course, perfectly compatible with marxist approaches, requires explanation which does not block any notion of Nazism's impetus for social change (even if only of a negative kind through its massive destructive drive) on the grounds that Nazism equalled social reaction. Recent research on the social bases of Nazi support before 1933 has, in fact, completely undermined earlier generalizations about the backward-looking, reactionary (in a literal sense) nature of Nazism's mass backing, and has emphasized the strong, dynamic motivation for radical social change and undeniable 'modern' tendencies and aspirations among the socially heterogeneous support for the NSDAP.[8] Nazi support was no mere search for a return to yesteryear, whatever restorative tendencies were undoubtedly *also* present. The pressures in the Movement for social change, even if inchoate and pressing in different directions, could not have been totally ignored or repressed after 1933, even if that had been the intention of the Nazi leadership. Moreover, even on the most cursory common-sense ground, the Germany – even taking the nascent Federal Republic alone – of the later 1940s or early 1950s was, with all recognition of the numerous and inevitable continuities, a very different place and a very different society from the Germany of 1933. Whatever the complexities of the enquiry, the question of whether Nazism marked a caesura in Germany's social development, or left a lasting legacy in its impact on social and political values and attitudes, is, therefore, a legitimate one to pose.

Two works by non-marxist 'liberal' scholars, the German sociologist Ralf Dahrendorf and the American historian David Schoenbaum, appeared at roughly the same time in the mid 1960s and attempted to answer the question, by quite different routes, by arguing that the Third Reich did indeed produce a 'social revolution', the main feature of which was 'the break with tradition and thus a strong push toward modernity'.[9]

For Dahrendorf, Nazism completed the social revolution in Germany that had been 'lost in the faultings of Imperial Germany and again held up by the contradictions of the Weimar Republic'.[10] The substance of the revolution was 'modernity', by which he understood in essence the structures and values of western liberal–democratic society. Such a revolution had, he argued, naturally not been intended by the Nazis, whose social ideology rested on a recovery of past values. But in practice, their *Gleichschaltung* ('co-ordination') of German society had destroyed German 'tribal loyalties', breaking traditional anti-liberal religious, regional, family, and corporative bonds, had reduced élites to a 'monopolistic clique', and had levelled down social strata to the equalizing status of the *Volksgenosse*, the 'people's comrade'. In order to retain power, in fact, Nazi 'totalitarianism' had been compelled to turn against all traces of the social order that provided the basis of conservative authoritarian rule. Through the destruction of traditional loyalties, norms, and values, concluded Dahrendorf, Nazism 'finally abolished the German past as it was embodied in Imperial Germany. What came after it was free of the mortgage that burdened the Weimar Republic at its beginning, thanks to the suspended revolution. There could be no return

---

[8]  See e.g. Broszat, 'Zur Struktur der NS-Massenbewegung' (ch. 2 note 53).
[9]  See above ch. 2 note 26 for references; quotation from Dahrendorf, p. 403.
[10]  For this paragraph, see Dahrendorf, pp. 402–18 (quotation from p. 403).

from the revolution of National Socialist times'.[11] Unwittingly, therefore, Nazism had paved the way for a liberal–democratic society in post-war West Germany.

Dahrendorf's highly influential interpretation was contained in a single chapter of his sociological analysis of modern Germany. David Schoenbaum's stylishly written study, on the other hand, was entirely directed at an examination of what he called 'Hitler's social revolution'.[12] Confining his investigation to the years 1933–9, Schoenbaum omitted from consideration any changes deriving from the wartime period, but in a complex discussion, developed an argument which, though more thoroughly researched, came close to Dahrendorf's. Schoenbaum's main thesis, in his own words, was that 'the Third Reich was a double revolution . . . of means and ends. The revolution of ends was ideological – war against bourgeois and industrial society. The revolution of means was its reciprocal. It was bourgeois and industrial since, in an industrial age, even a war against industrial society must be fought with industrial means and bourgeois are necessary to fight the bourgeoisie'.[13] This paradox runs through Schoenbaum's entire analysis, a crucial element of which is the distinction between what he termed 'objective' and 'interpreted social reality'. While 'objective social reality', he argued, 'was the very opposite of what Hitler had presumably promised and what the majority of his followers had expected him to fulfil' – with greater urbanization, industrialization, concentration of capital, inequality of income distribution, and the preservation of social divides – 'interpreted social reality' reflected 'a society united like no other in recent German history, a society of opportunities for young and old, classes and masses, a society that was New Deal and good old days at the same time'.[14] On this premise, Schoenbaum argued that 'Hitler's social revolution' amounted to the destruction of the traditional relationship between class and status: 'In the Third Reich, relative approximation of class and status came to an end', since 'in the wonderland of Hitler Germany' nobody knew 'what was up and what was down'.[15] Thus, too, workers' 'loss of *liberté* . . . was practically linked with the promotion of *égalité*', so that, though we might regard their status as one of slavery, 'it was not necessarily slavery from the point of view of a contemporary'.[16] The collapse of the status–class underpinning was, in fact, sufficient for Schoenbaum to go still further, and to argue that 'in the resultant collision of ideological and industrial revolution, traditional class structure broke down', so that one could speak of a 'classless reality of the Third Reich'.[17] As these remarks demonstrate, Schoenbaum is arguing for 'a revolution of class and a revolution of status at the same time' – amounting in class terms to unprecedented social

---

[11] Dahrendorf, p. 418.
[12] Hans Mommsen provides a good critical commentary in a 'Nachwort' to the German edition of Schoenbaum's book, *Die braune Revolution. Eine Sozialgeschichte des Dritten Reiches* (Munich, 1980, edn), pp. 352–68.
[13] Schoenbaum (ch. 2 note 26), pp. xxi–xxii.
[14] Schoenbaum, pp. 285–6.
[15] Schoenbaum, pp. 280–1.
[16] Schoenbaum, pp. 110–11.
[17] Schoenbaum, p. 283.

mobility, in status terms even to 'the triumph of egalitarianism'.[18] The contrast between such an interpretation and marxist approaches – as typified by Franz Neumann's view that 'the essence of National Socialist social policy consists in the acceptance and strengthening of the prevailing class character of German society' – could hardly be starker.[19]

Nazi 'social ideology' has generally been regarded by historians either as nothing more than a propagandistic sham, or as serious in intent but impossible to implement because of its internal contradictions. Hence, marxist writers have usually stressed the distinction between social base and social function, of a heavily lower-middle-class mass movement but a regime which consistently 'betrayed' its mass support in the interests of big capital.[20] Alternatively, Schoenbaum's argument is followed, emphasizing the paradox that anti-industrial social ends needed industrial social means. In an influential essay, Henry Turner pushed this paradox further than Schoenbaum had been prepared to take it, in accepting Nazi ideology at its word as an absolutely serious intent to do away with modern society, in which modern means would be used to bring about anti-modern conclusions through a successful war.[21] As Turner saw it, 'by reducing Germany's need for industry and thus for industrial workers, and by providing fertile soil upon which these displaced workers and others could be resettled, the acquisition of *Lebensraum* was expected to open the way to a vast new wave of German eastward colonization comparable to that of the Middle Ages, making possible a significant degree of de-urbanization and de-industrialization'.[22] Of course, the conquest of *Lebensraum* could only come about through a vast industrial war, and the Nazis, therefore 'practised modernization out of necessity in order to pursue their fundamentally anti-modern aims'. Once realized, the goal of *Lebensraum* would have rendered them largely unnecessary.[23] The Nazi solution of escape from the modern world by a 'desperate backward leap' could therefore be characterized as 'a utopian form of anti-modernism – utopian in the double sense of being a visionary panacea and being unrealizable'.[24] The last point seems the most important one: the vision was wholly unrealizable. Turner seems, in fact, in danger of attributing a rationality and cohesion to Nazi 'anti-modern aims' which is scarcely warranted in the light of the gulf between the actual reality of the 'New Order' in eastern Europe and the visionary pipe-dreams of Himmler or Darré; the character of the development of German industry and technology during the

---

[18] Schoenbaum, pp. 272–3. This view of a 'socialist side' of Nazism, which fostered the progressive breakdown of status privilege and class barriers has been very influential, particularly when assisted by the multiplier-effect of mass-circulation works such as Haffner, *Anmerkungen* (ch. 4 note 10), pp. 48–53.

[19] Neumann, *Behemoth* (ch. 2 note 5), p. 298.

[20] E.g. Kühnl, *Formen bürgerlicher Herrschaft* (ch. 2 note 13), pp. 80 ff., 118 ff.; and, more crudely, Reinhard Opitz, 'Die faschistische Massenbewegung', in Kühnl, *Texte* (ch. 2 note 13), pp. 176–90. For a summary and assessment of this type of argument, see Saage, *Faschismustheorien* (ch. 2 note 33), pp. 131 ff., and Adelheid von Saldern, *Mittelstand im Dritten Reich. Handwerker – Einzelhändler – Bauern* (Frankfurt am Main/New York, 1979), pp. 9–15, 234 ff.

[21] Turner, 'Fascism and Modernization' (ch. 2 note 52), pp. 117–39.

[22] Turner, 'Fascism and Modernization', pp. 120–2.

[23] Turner, 'Fascism and Modernization', pp. 126–7.

[24] Turner, 'Fascism and Modernization', pp. 120–1.

war; and the fact that modern armaments were going to remain an absolute necessity for the perpetual struggle to defend conquered territory and continue expansion, ingrained in Hitler's philosophy. Naturally, of course, speculation about an illusory future can say little about Nazism's *actual* impact on German society.

The most recent discussion of this problem, by Werner Abelshauser and Anselm Faust, adopts a position not far from the interpretations of Dahrendorf and Schoenbaum.[25] Again, Abelshauser and Faust are prepared to consider Nazism's effects as part of a 'social revolution' – a concept they use in the sense of long-term but incisive processes of change in social and economic life, as in 'industrial revolution', 'Keynesian revolution', and 'modernizing revolutions', and attributing to Nazism 'not more and not less than the role of a catalyst of modernization, in that it exploded with force the bonds of tradition, region, religion, and corporation which were so specially pronounced in Germany'.[26] In their interpretation, Nazi social and economic policy was in a two-fold sense a means of social revolutionary change: both in anticipating the 'Keynesian revolution' of postwar German capitalism by its policies of economic stimulus to master the slump; and in its imposed 'coordination', which destroyed the trade unions, subordinated the employers to the primacy of politics of the authoritarian state, and thus altered the life of the Germans in the shortest possible time more decisively than the Revolution of 1918–19 had been able to do.[27]

Still operating with the concept of 'modernization', but now within the framework of a consciously theoretical model, Horst Matzerath and Heinrich Volkmann arrived at conclusions differing from those of both Turner and Abelshauser and Faust, in a stimulating if contentious conference paper published in 1977.[28] They argued strongly for the value of applying the concept of modernization to Nazism by considering the degree of both quantitative and qualitative economic, social, and political change between 1933 and 1939, using indicators of modernization such as those we discussed earlier in this chapter.

Their findings suggested a picture of contradictions, featuring in all sectors of their modernization model the continuation or accentuation of earlier trends, but also anti-modern counter-developments, especially in the political sphere (such as anti-parliamentary, anti-emancipatory, and anti-participatory measures).[29] They rejected the notion of a 'social revolution' as proposed by Dahrendorf and Schoenbaum, and built instead on aspects of Talcott Parsons's hypothesis, formulated as long ago as 1942. Parsons had argued that Nazism arose out of a conflict between modern economic and social structures and traditional value systems and patterns of socialization, producing an 'anomie' which found effect not in adjustment to changing reality, but in irrational flight to a radical denial of the new and the modern through resort to an extreme version of traditional values.[30] Taking Parsons's

[25] See above note 5 for full reference.
[26] Abelshauser and Faust, p. 116.
[27] Ableshauser and Faust, p. 118.
[28] Matzerath and Volkmann (see ch. 2 note 53).
[29] Matzerath and Volkmann, pp. 95–7.
[30] See ch. 2 note 18 for references.

hypothesis a stage further, Matzerath and Volkmann argued that Nazism was structurally determined by the conditions which produced the Movement: the aggressive reaction of traditional values against modernity in the shape of 'the accelerated change of the economic, social, and political system, sharpened through an acute crisis unleashed through war, defeat, inflation, depression, and the danger of an alternative system', all primarily manifesting itself in the social anxieties and resentments featured in Nazi ideology.[31] Thus, Nazi ideology functioned as 'a suitable instrument for the mobilization of sensitive strata of the population affected by problems of modernization'. Since, however, Nazism in power was unable to produce any positive or constructive social concept, but had destroyed all alternative concepts derived from the previous system, a new basis of legitimation was necessary. This was found in the diversion of inherited conflicts on to internal and external opponents, who were used in turn to justify the central aims of the system – establishment of a totalitarian apparatus of domination and preparation of a war of brutal conquest. This meant the destruction of traditional loyalties and the distortion to the point of destruction of traditional values. Nevertheless, the 'anti-modernity' of Nazism ought not to be misunderstood as the programmatic reconstruction of pre-modern conditions (as Turner, for instance, had seen it), or as a 'conservative revolution'. Rather, according to Matzerath and Volkmann, 'National Socialism is the attempt at a special path out of the problems of modernization into the utopia of a third way, beyond the internal social crises and conflicts of the parliamentary democratic capitalist society, and beyond the concept – releasing anxiety and aggression – of a communist total alteration [of society], but essentially without giving up the capitalist and industrial economic bases of this development'.[32] Such a definition accords, in the authors' view, with the partly modern, partly anti-modern ambivalent reality of Nazism. Even so, Matzerath and Volkmann reach the conclusion that the partially modernizing effects of Nazism cannot be seen as the result of conscious modernizing policies, and in fact ought best to be described as 'pseudo-modernization'. Moreover, and an important point in the overall argument, the Nazi regime was incapable of developing any lasting structures. Through its inability to recognize social conflict and cope with it, the system was incapable of producing stability with change. Even as an 'exceptional or transitional form of social organization in a stress phase of modernization', Nazism was 'dysfunctional': 'it was not a roundabout path to modernization, but the expression of its failure, the historical cul-de-sac of a process, whose steerage problems had overtaxed the social capacities'.[33]

In their emphasis on Nazism's inbuilt failure to produce lasting social structures, Matzerath and Volkmann were returning by a circuitous route to something approaching the position which Rauschning had impressionistically – and from an entirely different vantage point – reached in the later 1930s, when he claimed that Nazism could bring about only a 'revolution of nihilism'.[34] In essence, this corresponds, too, to Winkler's argument that 'the

[31] Matzerath and Volkmann, p. 98.
[32] Matzerath and Volkmann, p. 99.
[33] Matzerath and Volkmann, p. 100.
[34] The title of his book (see ch. 6 note 4), first published in German as *Die Revolution des Nihilismus* (Zurich, 1938).

greatest social caesura which National Socialism brought about is its collapse', and that nothing of the social change which took place during the Dictatorship itself compared in its significance with the devastation of the last year of the war and total defeat, with their far-reaching consequences for the two German societies which replaced the Third Reich.[35] A similar conclusion was reached by Jeremy Noakes who, in a recent thorough examination of the whole problem, argues that whatever was revolutionary about Nazism lay in the destruction and self-destruction which were inevitable corollaries of its irrational goals: 'Arguably, therefore, the Nazi revolution was the war – not simply because the war accelerated political, economic, and social change to a degree which had not occurred in peacetime, but more profoundly because in war Nazism was in its element. In this sense, Nazism was truly 'a revolution of destruction' – of itself and of others on an unparalleled scale'.[36]

The approaches we have rapidly summarized here can be subsumed under three main categories on interpretation:

*(i)* One central interpretation, favoured especially but not only by marxist historians, is that, whatever superficial changes were made in social *forms* and institutional *appearances* in the Third Reich, the fundamental *substance* of society remained unchanged, since the position of capitalism was strengthened and the class structure enhanced, not broken down, by Nazism.

*(ii)* In contrast, an influential interpretation advanced by 'liberal' scholars suggests that the changes in the structures of society and in social values brought about directly or indirectly by Nazism were so profound that it is not going too far to regard them as a 'social revolution'.

*(iii)* A third position can be distinguished from both of these interpretations, though in practice it comes closer to the second than to the first. It is argued here, that whatever changes Nazism itself brought about were negligible and amounted in no sense to a 'social revolution'. Its social effects were, in fact, contradictory – some 'modernizing', others reactionary. Nevertheless, the Third Reich did have important consequences for post-war society, especially in the nature of its own total collapse and destruction, bringing down with it authoritarian structures which had dominated Germany since Bismarck's era, and wreaking such havoc, dislocation, and upheaval that in radically different ways new starts were necessary in the eastern and the western zones of defeated Germany.

We can now consider these interpretations in the light of recent research on the social history of the Third Reich.

## Evaluation

An evaluation of the social impact of Nazism must begin with the nature and social dynamic of the Nazi movement.

[35] Winkler, 'Vom Mythos der Volksgemeinschaft' (ch. 3 note 47), p. 490.
[36] Noakes, 'Nazism and Revolution', p. 96. See also Peukert (ch. 2 note 45), p. 294 for emphasis on the socially 'destructive forces and effects' of Nazism, out of which a more 'modern' society arose following the end of the regime and the war.

As innumerable studies have shown, it is simplistic to regard the Nazi movement as no more than the direct product and instrument of reactionary capitalist forces. It was the outgrowth of extreme socio-political unrest and disaffection, with a most heterogeneous mass following ideologically integrated only through radical negative protest (anti-marxism, anti-Weimar, anti-Semitism) coupled with a chiliastic, pseudo-religious vision of a 'national awakening' – socially expressed through the vague (and ultimately also negative) 'idea' of the 'national community' (*Volksgemeinschaft*). The appeal before 1933 of the 'national community' slogan – symbolizing the transcending of class, denominational, and political divisions through a new ethnic unity based on 'true' German values – is undeniable. Socially, it reflected not only the desire to banish the cancer of marxism, but also to overcome the rigid immobility and sterility of the old social order by offering mobility and advancement through merit and achievement, not through inherited social rank and birthright. The mood of social protest was at its most radical, as is well known, among young Germans, where the drive and élan of the Nazi movement held especial appeal.[37]

Before 1933 the one uniting aim of the dynamic but unstable and ramshackle Nazi movement was to gain power. The 'seizure of power', however, could only be attained through the collaboration of the ruling élites. The relative strength of these groups in the early period of Nazi rule, together with the regime's allocated priority to rearmament, ensured that sectional interests within the Party (such as those of small retailers or craftsmen) were inevitably sacrificed where they did not fit the needs of Germany's large-scale (especially armaments-geared) capitalist enterprises. The perceived lingering challenge to the 'social order' posed by the SA had its sting removed through the liquidation of Röhm and other SA leaders in the so-called 'Night of the Long Knives' in June 1934. But although pruned of its socially most 'dangerous' elements, the Nazi Party and ancillary organizations were hardly a source of stability. Deprived of any real governing function after 1933, the role of the amorphous Nazi movement was confined largely to providing action for activists through social control tasks, propaganda of the word and 'deed', and the whipping up of acclamation for the Führer's 'achievements'. The disappointment of many social aspirations in the Third Reich was compensated to some degree by the channelling of pent-up energies into activism levelled at helpless and disparaged minorities who formed the racial and social pariahs of the 'national

---

[37] On the sozial 'drive' of Nazism before 1933, Broszat's articles, 'Soziale Motivation' (ch. 4 note 27) and 'Zur Struktur der NS-Massenbewegung' (ch. 2 note 53) provide stimulating general interpretations. The most valuable insights on the appeal to youth – apart from works on the youth movement and on Nazi youth organizations such as Peter D. Stachura, *Nazi Youth in the Weimar Republic* (Santa Barbara/Oxford, 1975) and *The German Youth Movement 1900–1945* (London, 1981) – have emerged from recent work, differing in orientation and interpretation, on the SA: Peter H. Merkl, *The Making of a Stormtrooper* (Princeton, 1980); Conan Fischer, *Stormtroopers. A Social, Economic, and Ideological Analysis 1929–1935* (London, 1983); Richard Bessel, *Political Violence and the Rise of Nazism. The Storm Troopers in Eastern Germany 1925–1934* (New Haven/London, 1984); and Jamin (ch. 2 note 29). I have attempted briefly to evaluate some recent interpretations of the appeal of Nazism in 'Ideology, Propaganda, and the Rise of the Nazi Party', in Peter D. Stachura, *The Nazi Machtergreifung* (London, 1983), pp. 162–81.

community'. Alongside the escalating discrimination against Jews and other 'outcasts', the subordination of sectional material interests within the Party to the overriding 'national' goals of the Führer was equally inevitable. Everything had to be subsumed in the preparation for the inexorably coming struggle. But, obsessively single-minded in ends, Hitler was wholly eclectic in means. Thus, there could be no thought of destroying Germany's industry to satisfy the needs of archaic *Mittelstand* interests or romantic peasant ideal-ists in the Party.[38] The Party's ideologues and representatives of Party sec-tional interests with their own ideas about what the 'national community' should look like were invariably shunted on to sidelines sooner or later – the fate of Feder, Wagener, Darré, and Rosenberg. Unlike such Party 'theore-ticians', Hitler had no real interest in social structures as long as they were not dangerous or obstructive. Long-term, it is true, his own views were dominated by vague notions of a racial élite, rule by those who had proved themselves fit to rule, and the passing of social groups for whom he had little but contempt (such as the aristocracy, and 'captains of industry'). But in the real world of the short-term, Hitler was uninterested in tampering with the social order. Just like industry and capitalism, social groups were there to serve in their different ways the political goal of the struggle for 'national survival'. In any case, quite apart from Hitler's own predilections, the Nazi movement was such an amalgam of contradictory social forces that it was capable of producing neither theory nor practice of any realistic new social construct. It was as parasitic as it was predatory.

Where Nazism was ambitious – and extraordinarily so – was in attempting a transformation in subjective consciousness rather than in objective realities.[39] Since the Nazi diagnosis of Germany's problem was in essence one of attitudes, values, and mentalities, it was these which they were attempting to revolutionize psychologically by replacing all class, religious, and regional allegiances by massively enhanced national self-awareness to mobilize the German people psychologically for the coming struggle and to bolster their morale during the inevitable war. Not the revamping of comfortable, small-town, lower-middle-class social views, but the moulding of a people in the image of an army – disciplined, resilient, fanatically single-minded, obedient to death for the cause – was the intention. The idea of the 'national com-munity' was not a basis for changing social structures, but a symbol of trans-formed consciousness. The attempt to inculcate such values into the German people was in essence a task of propaganda more than of social policy.

These remarks on the character of the Nazi movement and its social aims suggest that notions of social change were – inevitably given its nature, composition, and dominant leadership – negative (destruction of working-class organizations, increased discrimination against minorities); confined to long-term but vacuous, utopian ambitions bearing little relation to reality, or to short-term sectional interests incompatible with war preparation and

---

[38] See Hitler's reported comments to Otto Strasser in Noakes and Pridham (ch. 3 note 37), vol. 1, p. 67; and, for Hitler's social aims, see Noakes, 'Nazism and Revolution', pp. 76 ff. A thorough analysis of Hitler's thinking on social developments is now provided by Rainer Zitelmann, *Hitler. Selbstverständnis eines Revolutionärs* (Hamburg/Leamington Spa/New York, 1987).
[39] Broszat, *Hitler State* (ch. 2 note 39), p. 18.

therefore dispensable; and, finally, rested on conceptions of a revolution of attitudes which, given the strength of previous loyalties to Church, region, or class, were again illusory as a short- or middle-range objective. The nature of the Nazi movement offers pointers towards understanding the impact of Nazism on specific social groups; the widespread disillusionment and disappointments during the Third Reich; the compensatory mechanism of the 'selection of negative stereotypes'[40] as the victims of ever more vicious discrimination; and the difficulty of regarding Nazism as capable of bringing about a 'social revolution' on its own terms.

Understanding of what Schoenbaum dubbed 'objective reality' – actual changes in the class structure and social formations in Germany during the Third Reich – has been greatly advanced by much valuable empirical research in the past few years. The findings of this research have pointed unequivocally in the direction of Winkler's conclusion, 'that there can be no question in real terms of a revolutionary transformation of German society between 1933 and 1945'.[41] The notion that the Third Reich had brought about a social revolution was, as Winkler indicates, largely attributable to an over-ready acceptance of the regime's own pseudo-egalitarian propaganda and exaggerated claims, and, partly too, to actual social changes of the post-war era which were often projected backwards into the Third Reich, though they had little to do with Nazism, even indirectly.[42]

The emphasis in recent research has, therefore, been far more heavily laid upon the essential continuities in the class structure of Nazi Germany, rather than upon incisive changes. Schoenbaum himself had accepted that the social position of the élites remained relatively unscathed down to the last phase of the war. He may, however, have rather exaggerated the extent of the fluidity in social structures and the amount of upward mobility which took place. Of course, it is true that thrusting, energetic, ruthless, and often highly efficient 'technologists of power'[43] such as Heydrich or Speer pushed their way to the top. And the war certainly accelerated changes in the high ranks of the *Wehrmacht*. But the new political élite co-existed and merged with the old élites rather than supplanting them.[44] Non-Party preserves such as big business, the civil service, and the army recruited their leadership for the most part from the same social strata as before 1933. Education remained overwhelmingly dominated by the middle and upper middle classes. The most important and powerful Party affiliation, the SS, recruited heavily from the élite sectors of society.[45] If the traditional ruling classes had to

---

40 Broszat, 'Soziale Motivation', p. 405.
41 Matzerath and Volkmann, p. 103 (comment of H.A. Winkler).
42 Matzerath and Volkmann, p. 102 (comment of H.A. Winkler). See also Winkler, 'Vom Mythos der Volksgemeinschaft', p. 490.
43 Broszat, 'Zur Struktur der NS-Massenbewegung', p. 67.
44 See Noakes, 'Nazism and Revolution', pp. 80–5, and also Hans Mommsen, 'Zur Verschränkung tranditioneller und faschistischer Führungsgruppen in Deutschland beim Übergang von der Bewegungs- zur Systemphase', in Schieder, *Faschismus als soziale Bewegung* (ch. 2 note 29), pp. 157–81.
45 See e.g. Gunnar C. Boehnert, 'The Jurists in the SS-Führerkorps 1925-1939', in Hirschfeld and Kettenacker (ch. 1 note 23), pp. 361–74, and 'The Third Reich and the Problem of "Social Revolution": German Officers and the SS', in Volker R. Berghahn and Martin Kitchen, eds., *Germany in the Age of Total War* (London, 1981), pp. 203–17; and Bernd Wegner, *Hitlers Politische Soldaten: Die Waffen-SS, 1933-1945* (Paderborn, 1982), ch. 15, esp. pp. 222–6.

make some room for social upstarts from lower ranks of society who had gained advancement through positions of power and political influence, such changes amounted to little more than a slight acceleration of changes already perceptible in the Weimar Republic.

At the other end of the social scale, the working class – deprived of a political voice, its social gains of the Weimar Republic reversed, and exposed in the shadow of mass unemployment to the brutal exploitation of employers backed by the repressive apparatus of the police state – had its living standard reduced in the first years of the Third Reich even from the lowly level of the Depression era.[46] The slight rise in real wages in the later 1930s was a by-product of the armaments boom, and was accompanied by intensified pressure – physical and mental – upon the industrial workforce. The class position of workers remained basically unchanged into the middle of the war – except that the most extreme exploitation now fell upon foreign workers. The most significant changes in the nature and composition of German labour occurred in the last phase of the war and were, in the main, the consequence of military service, losses at the Front, destruction of industries, dislocation of the workforce, evacuation and homelessness, and ultimately foreign conquest.[47] Whatever changes had taken place by 1945 were, therefore, a product of Nazism's collapse more than of its policies while in power.

Studies of middle-class groups in the Third Reich have also stressed how for all the Nazis' archaic rhetoric and anachronistic legislation – such as the Entailed Farm Law of 1933 – such change as took place was the product of industrial recovery and accelerated development in a capitalist economy.[48] Continuity rather than dramatic change was the hallmark down to the mid-war period. Before then, there was some decline in the number of small retail and craft concerns, but no fundamental threat to their position. The number of white-collar employees, the service sector, and the bureaucracy expanded, as in all contemporary capitalist societies, if at a somewhat faster rate. There was no major shift in the pattern of landholding, despite the Entailed Farm Law, and after the early promises of a new deal, peasants found themselves yet further victims of the armaments economy, their labourers drained away to the higher wages of industry and the better living conditions of the city. Again, whatever major shift took place in the social position of the *Mittelstand* and peasantry was a consequence of the extreme disruption and dislocation of the final phase of the war and – especially in the eastern zone – of the immediate post-war era.

Finally, research on the position of women and the structure of their employment has illustrated both the extent to which Nazi anti-feminism corresponded to the traditions and patterns of bourgeois anti-feminism in a capitalist society, and at the same time the contradictions within the Nazi system, where the increased need for female labour forced concessions to the point of ultimate

---

[46] See Mason, *Sozialpolitik* (ch. 4 note 62), esp. ch. 4.
[47] See the works of Salter and Werner (above ch. 4 note 68).
[48] See esp. von Saldern (above note 20) and Heinrich August Winkler, 'Der entbehrliche Stand. Zur Mittelstandspolitik im "Dritten Reich" ', *AfS* 17 (1977), pp. 1–40.

reversal of ideological prerogatives by the middle of the war.[49] Once more, the continuities in social structures under Nazism greatly outweigh the change which, far from being revolutionary, was simply that of an advanced capitalist economy, if one with an unusual degree of state intervention,[50] and one which long before the war was extraordinarily lopsided in its concentration on armaments production, and spinning rapidly out of control.

In Schoenbaum's view, it was above all 'interpreted social reality' – attitudes, values, mentality, subjective consciousness – which underwent a transformation in the Third Reich. His assertions in this area, however, were highly speculative and impressionistic. In the nature of things, evaluation of changes in subjective attitudes and consciousness is fraught with difficulties, the evidence full of pitfalls, conclusions necessarily tentative. Recent research, however, which paints an extremely complex picture of social behaviour and attitudes in the Third Reich, suggests strongly that it is easy to exaggerate the nature of changes in values and attitudes under Nazism, and that here too there can be no suggestion of Nazism having effected a social revolution.[51]

The most continuous, and usually the most dominant, influence upon the subjective perception by differing social groups of their own socio-economic position during the Third Reich was, it seems, formed by the material conditions which directly affected the everyday lives of the population. And here, the acute perception of social injustice, the class-conscious awareness of inequalities, and the persistent feelings of exploitation appear to have changed little in the period of the Dictatorship. The alienation of the working class, the ceaseless expression of sectional grievances by middle-class groups and farmers, the massive disillusionment and discontent in most sections of the population deriving from their actual daily experience under Nazism is scarcely compatible with Schoenbaum's view that 'interpreted social reality . . . reflected a society united like no other in recent German history' and a status revolution amounting to a 'triumph of egalitarianism'.[52]

In Nazi eyes, the greatest need to reshape status awareness and to replace class by national consciousness was with regard to the industrial working class. Yet here especially, for all that there *was* some penetration of Nazi values and attitudes, the regime's social propaganda made little serious dent in traditional class loyalties, particularly among older industrial workers. It

---

[49] See Dörte Winkler (ch. 4 note 74); Mason; 'Women' (ch. 4 note 74); Jill Stephenson, *Women in Nazi Society* (London, 1975); Stefan Bajohr, *Die andere Hälfte der Fabrik* (Marburg, 1979); Gisela Bock, 'Frauen und ihre Arbeit im Nationalsozialismus', in Annette Kuhn and Gerhard Schneider, eds., *Frauen in der Geschichte* (Düsseldorf, 1979), pp. 113–49; Frauengruppe Faschismusforschung, ed., *Mutterkreuz und Arbeitsbuch* (Frankfurt am Main, 1981); Dorothee Klinsiek, *Die Frau im NS-Staat* (Stuttgart, 1982).

[50] See Overy, 'Göring's "Multi-National Empire" ' (ch. 3 note 41) and – still fundamental as an analysis of the Nazi economy – Neumann, *Behemoth* (ch. 2 note 5).

[51] I have attempted to argue this case in full in my *Popular Opinion and Political Dissent* (ch. 2 note 44). See also Peukert (ch. 2 note 45), and the contributions to Peukert and Reulecke (ch. 4 note 58) for some of the best recent research in this field, of which a perceptive survey is provided by Richard Bessel, 'Living with the Nazis: Some Recent Writing on the Social History of the Third Reich', *European History Quarterly* 14 (1984), pp. 211–20.

[52] Schoenbaum, pp. 273, 286.

would appear that Dahrendorf equally overestimated the extent of the breakdown in traditional loyalties to the Christian Churches. The decline in Church membership was trivial during the 1930s, while religious observance and attendance at services increased sharply during the war years. Defence of Church traditions and institutions against piecemeal Nazi attacks was extensive, and partly successful. The hold of the Church and clergy over the population, especially in country areas, was often strengthened rather than weakened by the 'Church struggle'. And, finally, the Churches as institutions recovered enormous social power and political influence in post-war West Germany. Everything points to the conclusion that Nazi policy failed categorically to break down religious allegiances. Even in their attempt to inculcate the German people with racial, eugenic, and social darwinist values – the core of their ideology – the Nazis, it appears, had only limited success.[53] Enhancement of existing prejudice against Jews and other racial minorities and 'social outsiders' unquestionably occurred, and within the SS in particular – but also to some extent within the *Wehrmacht* – indoctrination with a new value-system was effected.[54] But the growing protest against the 'euthanasia action' and the regime's perception of the need for utmost secrecy in the 'Final Solution' are indirect testimony that exposure to Nazi race values had come nowhere near completely eradicating conventional moral standards.

Much suggests that the Nazis made their greatest impact on young Germans, and that there was a pronounced generation gap between those who had reached adulthood in the Imperial or Weimar eras and those who had experienced little else other than Nazism. The rejection of the old bourgeois world and idealistic notions of a new and more mobile and egalitarian society were the basis of the Nazis' dynamic mobilization of youth. But even here, the regime had only partial success. Hitler's own view, as it was recorded in 1945, was that it would have taken 20 years to produce an élite which would have imbibed Nazi values like its mother's milk. The illusory nature of such hopes was demonstrated by his further comment that he could not afford to wait so long: time was now as always against Germany.[55] In fact, as recent studies have demonstrated, signs of conflict, tension, and opposition within certain sections of German youth were already apparent by the later 1930s and increased in the war years, suggesting that the Nazis had been only temporarily successful in winning over, mobilizing, and integrating young Germans.[56]

---

[53] See my essay, 'The Persecution of the Jews and German Popular Opinion in the Third Reich', *Yearbook of the Leo Baeck Institute* 26 (1981), pp. 261–89; Otto Dov Kulka, ' "Public Opinion" in Nazi Germany and the "Jewish Question" ', *The Jerusalem Quarterly* 25 (1982), pp. 121–44, and ' "Public Opinion" in Nazi Germany: the Final Solution', *The Jerusalem Quarterly* 26 (1983), pp. 34–45; and Sarah Gordon, *Hitler, Germans, and the 'Jewish Question'* (Princeton, 1984).

[54] See the works of Wegner (above note 45) and Streit (ch. 5 note 70).

[55] F. Genoud, ed., *The Testament of Adolf Hitler* (London, 1961), pp. 58–9.

[56] See Lothar Gruchmann, 'Jugendopposition und Justiz im Dritten Reich', in Wolfgang Benz, ed., *Miscellanea. Festschrift für Helmut Krausnick zum 75. Geburtstag* (Stuttgart, 1980), pp. 103–30; Matthias von Hellfeld, *Edelweißpiraten in Köln* (Cologne, 1981); Arno Klönne, *Jugend im Dritten Reich. Die Hitler-Jugend und ihre Gegner* (Düsseldorf, 1982); Heinrich Muth, 'Jugendopposition im Dritten Reich', *VfZ* 30 (1982), pp. 369–417; Detlev Peukert,

Finally, though it is still an under-researched and difficult subject, there is no evidence to suggest that family structures came anywhere near breaking down under Nazism, despite the undoubted accentuation of generational conflicts between children and parents fostered by Nazi youth organizations. There were, in fact, signs in the Third Reich itself of a reaction against the release of youth from the close shackles of adult authority in the school, the parental home, and elsewhere, and the reaction had not inconsiderable success, particularly in the post-war era.

It seems clear, then, that Nazism did not come remotely near producing a 'social revolution' in Germany during the period of the Third Reich – whether one of 'objective' or of 'interpreted social reality'. As we noted earlier, the nature of the Nazi movement and the character of its social aims make it possible to go further and to argue that it was in any case incapable of bringing about a complete and permanent social revolution and was not in any rational sense aiming to do so. Nazism's intentions were directed towards a transformation of value- and belief-systems – a psychological 'revolution' rather than one of substance – and could only have been effected through the attainment of long-term goals which were themselves illusory, contradictory, and thus innately destructive and self-destructive.

Once the misleading notion that German society was radically changed during the Third Reich is removed, it seems possible to argue both that during the period of its rule Nazism substantially bolstered the existing class order of society, and that, above all through its destructive dynamism, it paved the way for a new start after 1945.

On the one hand, obvious though it is, the point deserves emphasis that Nazism was not the product of 'pre-modern' society, but emerged in an advanced industrial state whose fragile political system was, in an unprecedented crisis of capitalism, ripped apart by class conflict. The Nazi regime's initial objective function was to re-establish the socio-economic order and the threatened position of the ruling élites by ruthlessly crushing the labour movement. The fateful political intervention of Nazism in 1933 has, therefore, to be seen as a decisive step in the struggle between capital and labour in an advanced industrial economy. And, indeed, Nazism in power was the most ruthless and exploitative form of industrial class society encountered – one which from a contemporary working-class perspective made the Kaiser's Germany seem in retrospect like 'a heaven of freedom'.[57] The new ordering of class relations in 1933 reversed in violent fashion the advances made by the working class not only since 1918, but since Bismarck's era, strengthened the weakened position of capitalism, and upheld the reactionary forces in the social order.

---

'Edelweißpiraten, Meuten, Swing. Jugendsubkulturen im Dritten Reich', in Gerhard Huck, ed., *Sozialgeschichte der Freizeit* (Wuppertal, 1980), pp. 307–27, and 'Youth in the Third Reich', in Richard Bessel, ed., *Life in the Third Reich* (Oxford, 1987), pp. 25–40. By the latter half of 1943, the SD was reporting widespread negative attitudes towards the party and other aspects of Nazi rule among youth and schoolchildren: see SD-Berichte zu Inlandsfragen, 12 Aug., 22 Nov. 1943, Heinz Boberach, ed., *Meldungen aus dem Reich* (Herrsching, 1984), vol. 14, pp. 5603–7, vol. 15, pp. 6053–5.

[57] Archiv der Sozialen Demokratie, Bonn, Bestand Emigration Sopade, M32, report of the Border Secretary of Northern Bavaria, Hans Dill, of 18 Nov. 1935.

It is, however, insufficient to leave it at that, and to deny Nazism any motive force for social change of a long-term nature – even if this was in the main a 'negative' feature emanating from the destructive force of the regime. It has been suggested, for instance, that the necessary individualization of the working-class struggle within the Nazi system to gain maximum benefit from the armaments boom had lasting effects in weakening worker solidarity and paving the way for 'a new, more individualistic, performance-orientated, "sceptical" type of worker as described by sociologists in the fifties'.[58] Whether this is to project back into the Third Reich behavioural patterns which were largely a product of the post-war conditions of economic recovery and the 'economic miracle' itself is difficult to estimate. Also speculative, though inherently not unlikely, is the suggestion that Nazi atomization of society led to a 'retreat into the private sphere' which had lasting implications for 'depoliticized' popular culture – a part of the basis of the consumer and 'achievement' society of the 'economic miracle' era.[59]

The extent to which this can be linked to or explained by concepts of 'modernity' or 'modernization' seems debatable. As conventionally deployed in sociological and historical writing, 'modernization' implies long-term change spanning centuries and transforming 'traditional' society based on agricultural and artisanal production, personal relations of dependance, local loyalties, rural cultures, rigid social hierarchies, and religious world-views, into industrial class society with highly developed industrial technologies, secularized cultures, 'rational' bureaucratic impersonal socio-political orders, and political systems of mass participation. Some form of applied modernization theory seems an essential component in explaining long-term historical change. But in such a process, the Nazi era is a mere flash in time. And while 'traditional' value systems and social structures were undoubtedly in certain ways more resistant to the changes of industrialization in Germany than, for example, in Britain, their 'traditionality' can be overplayed and the emphasis on anti-modernization as the secret of Nazism's appeal can easily be greatly exaggerated. On the contrary: though Nazism contained obvious archaic and atavistic elements, they often served as propagandistic symbols or ideological cover for wholly 'modern' types of appeal offering social mobility, a society of equal chances where success came from merit and achievement, and new opportunities to thrive and prosper through letting youth and vigour have its head at the expense of the old, the sterile, the rigid, and the decayed.[60] Though vicious and extreme in its form and nature, this darwinistic appeal to the pure 'achieving society' (*Leistungsgesellschaft*) has parallels in other advanced capitalist economies. In evaluating the brief era of the Dictatorship itself, the modernization concept is unhelpful. What change took place was within the context of, for its date, an already highly advanced capitalist society. And while some Nazi

---

[58] Peukert, *Volksgenossen* (ch. 2 note 45), pp. 136, 140.
[59] Peukert, *Volksgenossen*, pp. 230, 280–8, 294. This argument is backed by the findings of a recent major oral-history project in the Ruhr: see Lutz Niethammer, ed., *'Die Jahre weiß man nicht, wo man die heute hinsetzen soll'. Faschismuserfahrungen im Ruhrgebiet* (Berlin/Bonn, 1983) and *'Hinterher merkt man, daß es richtig war, daß es schiefgegangen ist'. Nachkriegserfahrungen im Ruhrgebiet* (Berlin/Bonn, 1983).
[60] See Broszat, 'Zur Struktur der NS-Massenbewegung' (ch. 2 note 53).

measures had an archaic tinge to them, more were (in a neutral sense) 'advancing' or 'modern' – though in a fashion little different from those of other contemporary advanced capitalist states. Nor is the counterfactual question wholly misplaced: much of what is frequently dubbed Nazism's 'modernizing push' would, given the nature of the German economy, undoubtedly have taken place under any form of government.

We return, therefore, to what seems to be the crucial point in the question of Nazism's impact on social change: the intrinsic, all-consuming destructive essence of the system. In its drive to attain increasingly irrational goals, Nazism was a parasitic growth on the old social order, neither wanting nor capable of stability. Through the allocation of absolute priorities to rearmament, war, and expansion – goals actively furthered by collaboration from Germany's ruling classes – Nazism produced a maelstrom of destruction which threatened, then inevitably sucked in, the representatives of the existing social order. Hence, the destructive dynamic of the Nazi regime brought down the pillars of the old social order in its own violent end, and paved the way for a drastically revised form of capitalist state in the west and a genuine social revolution in the east. If the notion of a 'zero hour' in the defeat of 1945 marking a complete break with Germany's past – a notion very popular in West Germany after the war – is a fiction masking the many spheres of continuity in socio-economic structures, institutions, and mentalities, then it is nevertheless true that the demise of the German aristocracy, the bankruptcy of the old army leadership and its Prusso-German ideals, the unending columns of refugees from the east, the physical division of Germany, the social demands of reconstruction, and allied 're-education' policy, denoted a caesura with the past beside which the social changes of the Third Reich itself pale into insignificance.

# 8

## 'Normality' and Genocide: The Problem of 'Historicization'

At the time this book was first conceived and written, there was no knowing that within a year or so the historical–philosophical, political–ideological, and moral dimensions of the problem of historians in grappling with the phenomenon of National Socialism, dealt with in Chapter 1, would all form elements of a major debate which flared up among prominent West German historians in 1986, and has preoccupied the historical profession ever since. I will add an outsider's reflections on the '*Historikerstreit*', as it rapidly came to be labelled, in the following and final chapter. Before coming to the '*Historikerstreit*' itself, however, I want to explore an issue which, while intrinsic to the dispute and forming one significant strand of it, is separable from it, in fact preceded it, and raises distinctive theoretical and methodological problems which are best dealt with in detachment from the polemics of the '*Historikerstreit*' itself. This is the problem of the so-called 'historicization' ('*Historisierung*') of National Socialism, a term which first entered serious discussion when advanced by Martin Broszat in an important and programmatic essay published in 1985,[1] over a year before the '*Historikerstreit*' broke out. It revolves around the question of whether, more than 40 years after the collapse of the Third Reich, it is possible to treat the Nazi era in the ways that others eras of the past are treated – as 'history' – and what new perspectives such a shift in conceptualization and method would demand. In intellectual terms, the controversy which Broszat's article provoked, though more narrowly confined in terms of the number of participants and receiving (until recently) far less public attention, is much more significant and rewarding than the '*Historikerstreit*' itself. Interestingly, too, this controversy crosses the hardened battle-lines which rapidly formed in the '*Historikerstreit*'. And it involves consideration of the contribution and potential of what has, in many respects, proved a most fruitful approach in research on the Third Reich in recent years, that of '*Alltagsgeschichte*' ('the history of everyday life').

During the past 12 or so years, new and exciting avenues of research have been explored in a massive outpouring of studies ranging over most of the important aspects of the impact of Nazism on German society. Yet just as the time seems ripe – almost quarter of a century since the appearance of Schoenbaum's wide-ranging social history of the Third Reich, seen as

---

[1] Martin Broszat, 'Plädoyer für eine Historisierung des Nationalsozialismus', *Merkur* 39 (1985), pp. 373–85, reprinted in Martin Broszat, *Nach Hitler. Der schwierige Umgang mit unserer Geschichte*, Munich, 1986, pp. 159–73. All references which follow are to the latter version.

'Hitler's social revolution', and Dahrendorf's equally influential interpretation of Nazism as 'the German revolution'[2] – for a new full-scale study which would synthesize and incorporate much of this work and offer a revised interpretation of German society under Nazism, the 'historicization' controversy casts doubt upon even the theoretical possibility of constructing such a social history without losing sight of the central aspects of Nazism which provide it with its lasting world-historical significance and its moral legacy. The first part of this chapter offers an outline of this important controversy, while the second part seeks to evaluate its implications for a potential history of German society in the Third Reich.

## The 'Historicization' Approach

A major breakthrough in deepening awareness of the complexity of German society in the Third Reich, it is universally recognized, was the research undertaken and published between the mid 1970s and early 1980s within the framework of the 'Bavaria Project'. This project, run by the Munich Institute of Contemporary History and carried out under the rubric of 'Resistance and Persecution in Bavaria, 1933–1945', helped to offer an entirely new dimension to the understanding of relations between state and society in Nazi Germany. It deliberately turned away from narrow, often morally loaded definitions of 'resistance' and used instead a novel concept of '*Resistenz*',[3] – a term difficult to convey in English, but taken from the language of medicine, not politics, and suggestive of morally neutral impenetrability or immunity rather than actively motivated opposition. This approach allowed the opening up of research into the grey, overlapping areas of collaboration and opposition, political conformity and nonconformity, consent and dissent apparent in the actual reality of having to adjust to and come to terms with Nazi rule. The 'Bavaria Project' was a landmark because it examined, for the first time in any systematic fashion, popular opinion, mentalities and behaviour, and because it tried – again a breakthrough – to write the history of society in the Third Reich 'from below'.

The project, it seems clear, was an important impulse, among others, in the rapid development of the 'everyday life' approach to the Third Reich. The very concept of '*Alltagsgeschichte*' ('the history of everyday life'), and the methods deployed by its exponents, have provoked much stringent criticism – some of it well justified – particularly from the leading protagonists of the 'critical history' and 'history as social science' ('*historische Sozialwissenchaften*') approach.[4] Such criticism has, however, not been able

[2] David Schoenbaum, *Hitler's Social Revolution*, New York London, 1966; Ralf Dahrendorf, *Society and Democracy in Germany*, London, 1968, ch. 25.
[3] Martin Broszat *et. al* (ed.), *Bayern in der NS-Zeit*, 6 vols., Munich 1977–83. For the concept of '*Resistenz*', see Broszat's contribution on 'Resistenz und Widerstand', in vol.4, Munich, 1981, pp. 691–709, reprinted in *Nach Hitler*, pp. 68–91.
[4] See e.g. Hans-Ulrich Wehler, 'Königsweg zu neuen Ufern oder Irrgarten der Illusionen? Die westdeutsche Alltagsgeschichte: Geschichte "von innen" und "von unten" ', in F.J. Brüggemeier and J. Kocka (eds.), '*Geschichte von unten – Geschichte von innen*'. *Kontroversen um die Alltagsgeschichte*, Fernuniversität Hagen, 1985, pp. 17–47. And for a lively debate about the merits and disadvantages of '*Alltagsgeschichte*', see *Alltagsgeschichte der NS-Zeit. Neue Perspektive oder Trivialisierung?*, Kolloquien des Instituts für Zeitgeschichte, Munich, 1984.

to stem the continued spread of '*Alltagsgeschichte*', and some, even of the sharpest critics, have accepted that, properly conceptualized, '*Alltagsgeschichte*' can have much to offer in deepening understanding.[5] The remarkable resonance of the 'everyday life' approach, exploring subjective experiences and mentalities at the grass roots of society, presumably reflects in part, not least through the opening up of previously taboo areas of consideration, a need, particularly strong among the younger generation, to come to grips with the Third Reich not just as a political phenomenon – as a horrific regime providing a resort for political and moral lessons in a post-fascist democracy – but also as a social experience, in order to understand better the behaviour of ordinary people – like their own relatives – under Nazism. By making past behaviour and mentalities more explicable, more understandable, more 'normal' – even if to be condemned – it is arguable that '*Alltagsgeschichte*' has contributed to deepened awareness of the problems of historical identity in the Federal Republic, and of the relationship of the Third Reich not just to political continuities and discontinuities, but now also to social strands of continuity pre-dating Nazism and extending well into the post-war era. This further prompts the need to locate the Third Reich as an integral component of German history, not one which can be bracketed out and detached as if it did not really belong to it. These are some of the considerations behind Martin Broszat's well known 'plea for the historicization of National Socialism', premised upon the assertion that the history of the Nazi *era*, as opposed to that of the political system of the dictatorship, still remains to be written.[6]

Broszat's use of the term '*Historisierung*' ('historicization') relates to the problems of historians, and specifically West German historians, in dealing with the Nazi past. Even 40 years and more after the end of the Third Reich, the distance which the historian puts between himself and the subject matter of Nazism provides, in Broszat's view, a major obstacle to the possibility of approaching the scholarly study and analysis of Nazism in the same way that other periods of history are tackled – with the degree of intuitive insight which 'normal' historical writing demands. Yet, without the proper integration of Nazism into 'normal' historical writing, he sees the Third Reich remaining an 'island' in modern German history,[7] a resort for lessons of political morality in which routine moral condemnation excludes historical understanding, reducing Nazism to an 'abnormality' and serving as a compensatory alibi for a restored historicism ('*Historismus*') with regard to the more 'healthy' epochs before and after Hitler.[8] The position is summed up in the following way:

---

[5] See e.g. the thoughtful assessment of the limitations but also possibilities of '*Alltagsgeschichte*' by Jürgen Kocka in reviews in *Die Zeit* Nr.42 vom 14.Okt.1983 ('Drittes Reich: Die Reihen fast geschlossen') and *taz* vom 26. Jan. 1988 ('Geschichtswerkstätten und Historikerstreit').

[6] Broszat, *Nach Hitler*, S. 167.

[7] See Broszat, *Nach Hitler*, pp. 114–20 ('Eine Insel in der Geschichte? Der Historiker in der Spannung zwischen Verstehen und Bewerten der Hitler-Zeit').

[8] Broszat, *Nach Hitler*, p. 173. See above, pp. 5–7, for brief comments on the philosophy of traditional historicism in Germany.

A normalization of our historical consciousness and the communication of national identity through history can not be achieved by avoiding the Nazi era through its exclusion. Yet it seems to me that the greater the historical distance becomes, the more urgent it is to realize that bracketing the Hitler era out of history and historical thinking also occurs in a way when it is only dealt with from a political-moral perspective and not with the same differentiated applied historical method as other historical epochs, when treated with less carefully considered judgement and in a cruder, more general language, or when, for well-intentioned didactic reasons, we grant it a sort of methodological special treatment.[9]

A 'normalization' of methodological treatment would mean the application of the normal rigours of historical enquiry in a meticulous scholarship deploying 'mid-range' concepts subjectable to empirical investigation in place of bland moralization, whether from a liberal-conservative perspective or from sterile economistic determinant theories of a marxist-leninist or 'new Left' variety.[10] This in itself would refine moral sensitivity through the increased understanding derivable from greater differentiation, as in the relativization of 'resistance' through its 'de-heroization' and recognition of the chequered grey nature of the boundaries of opposition and conformity between the 'Other Germany' and the Nazi Regime.[11] It would allow, too, Nazism's function as the exponent of modernizing change comparable with that in other contemporary societies to be properly incorporated in an understanding of the era, and hence a deeper awareness of the social forces and motivation which the Nazi Movement could mobilize and exploit.[12]

The relevance of the 'Bavaria Project' and the emphasis upon 'Alltagsgeschichte' to this line of thought is self-evident. The underlying notion behind the whole concept of 'historicization' is that below the barbarism and the horror of the regime were patterns of social 'normality' which were, of course, affected by Nazism in various ways but which pre-dated and survived it. The role of Nazi ideology hence becomes 'relativized' in the context of a 'normality' of everyday life shaped for much of the time by non-ideological factors. Nazism can be seen to accelerate some and put the brake on other trends of social change and development which form a continuum from pre-Nazi times into the Federal Republic.[13] Beneath the barbarity, society in Nazi Germany can thus be more easily related to other eras in German history, and more easily compared with other contemporary societies. The long-term structural change and modernization of German

---

[9] Broszat, *Nach Hitler*, p. 153 (and back cover). As one who has written extensively and with great sensitivity about Nazi concentration camps, in which the term 'special treatment' ('*Sonderbehandlung*') was a euphemism for murder, Broszat's use of the same term in the present context seems a remarkable and unfortunate linguistic lapse.

[10] Broszat, *Nach Hitler*, pp. 104ff, cf.also pp. 36–41. In his exchange of letters with Saul Friedländer, Broszat speaks of a 'plea for the normalization of method, not of evaluation'. – 'Dokumentation. Ein Briefwechsel zwischen Martin Broszat und Saul Friedländer um die Historisierung des Nationalsozialismus', *VfZ*, 36 (1988), pp. 339–72, here p. 365, (henceforth cited as 'Briefwechsel'). I am extremely grateful to Prof. Friedländer for allowing me to see proofs of this exchange before publication.

[11] Broszat, *Nach Hitler*, pp. 110–71.

[12] Broszat, *Nach Hitler*, pp. 171–2.

[13] For an excellent collection of essays summarizing much recent research and locating Nazism within a context of long-term social change, see W. Conze and M.R. Lepsius, *Sozialgeschichte der Bundesrepublik Deutschland*, Stuttgart, 1983.

society becomes thereby more explicable, as does the role of Nazism –
deliberate or unwitting – in relationship to that change. This perspective
challenges – and in some ways displaces – the traditional emphasis upon the
ideological, political, and criminal terroristic aspects of Nazism. One of
Broszat's critics has, for example, suggested that the approach which he is
advocating looks to a comparison with the modernizing tendencies of other
advanced western societies at the expense of neglecting the crucial differences in the essence of their development. From such a perspective, therefore, 'the racialist aspect . . . and particularly the "Final Solution of the
Jewish Question" seem to be regarded as somehow irrelevant' since the
'unique duality' of the German modernizing experience is ignored.[14]

The suggested 'historicization' can, therefore, be summarized in the following claims: that Nazism should be subjected to the same methods of
scholarly enquiry as any other era of history; that social continuities need to
be much more fully incorporated in a far more complex picture of Nazism
and the emphasis shifted away from heavy concentration upon the political-
ideological sphere as a resort for moral lessons (since moral sensitivity can
only arise from a deeper understanding, which 'historicization' offers, of the
chequered complexities of the era); and that the Nazi era, at present almost a
dislocated unit of German history, – no longer suppressed but reduced to no
more than 'required reading' ('*Pflichtlektion*')[15] – needs to be relocated in
wider evolutionary development.[16]

## Criticism of 'Historicization'

The main critics of Broszat's 'historicization' plea are the Israeli historians
Otto Dov Kulka, Dan Diner, and, especially, Saul Friedländer. They
recognize the problem of 'historicization' as expounded by Broszat as an
important methodological and theoretical issue, as representing in some
respects a legitimate perspective, and as raising a problem which 'belongs
within the realm of a fundamental scholarly-scientific dialogue' between
historians who 'share some basic concerns as far as the attitudes towards
Nazism and its crimes are concerned'. As such, they are anxious to distinguish it from the apologetics advanced by Ernst Nolte in the
'*Historikerstreit*'.[17] Even so, it is noted in passing that the exhortation, 40
years on, to treat the Nazi era like any other period of history is also Nolte's
starting point.[18] Leaving Nolte completely to one side, there are still the
implications of Andreas Hillgruber's approach to the historical treatment of

[14] Otto Dov Kulka, 'Singularity and its Relativization. Changing views in German
Historiography on National Socialism and the "Final Solution" ', forthcoming in *Yad Vashem
Studies*, 19 (1988). I am most grateful to Prof. Kulka for a preview of this article.
[15] Broszat, *Nach Hitler*, p. 161.
[16] See Saul Friedländer, 'Some Reflections on the Historization of National Socialism', *Tel
Aviver Jahrbuch für deutsche Geschichte*, 16 (1987), pp. 310–24, here p. 313.
[17] Friedländer, 'Reflections', pp. 310–11, 318; Kulka, 'Singularity and its Relativization'. The
two contributions by Ernst Nolte, which were at the forefront of the '*Historikerstreit*' are
reproduced in '*Historikerstreit*'. *Die Dokumentation der Kontroverse um die Einzigartigkeit
der nationalsozialistischen Judenvernichtung*, Munich, 1987, pp. 13–35, 39–47.
[18] Friedländer, 'Reflections', pp. 317–18; Kulka, 'Singularity and its Relativization'.

the German army on the Eastern Front for the concept of 'historicization', to which we will return.[19]

The most direct and structured critique of Broszat's 'historicization' plea has been advanced by Saul Friedländer.[20] He sees three dilemmas in the 'historicization' notion, and a further three problems which the approach raises.

The first dilemma he points to is that of periodization and the specificity of the dictatorship years themselves, the period 1933–1945.[21] The 'historicization' approach seeks to incorporate the Third Reich into a picture of long-term social change. Broszat himself uses the example of the wartime social planning of the German Labour Front both as an episode in the development of social welfare schemes which pre-dated Nazism and extended into the modern system of the Federal Republic, and as a parallel to what was taking place under entirely different political systems, as in the British Beveridge Plan.[22] These various long-term processes of social change, in this instance in social policy, can be seen, therefore, as taking place in detachment from the specifics of Nazi ideology and the particular circumstances of the Third Reich. The emphasis shifts away from the singular characteristics of the Nazi period to a consideration of the relative and objective function of Nazism as an agent forcing (or retarding) modernization.

The question of the intended or unintended 'modernization push' of Nazism has, of course, been at issue ever since Dahrendorf and Schoenbaum wrote, as we saw in the previous chapter. Friedländer accepts that recent studies have extended knowledge on numerous aspects of this 'modernization'. However, in his view, when taken as a whole such studies reveal a shift in interest from the specificity of Nazism to the general problems of modernization, within which Nazism plays a part. The issue is, therefore, one of 'the relative relevance' of such developments in an overall history of the Nazi era.[23] And, in Friedländer's judgement, the danger – in fact, the almost inevitable result – is the relativization of the political–ideological–moral framework peculiar to the period 1933–45.[24]

19 Friedländer, 'Reflections', p. 320; Dan Diner, 'Zwischen Aporie and Apologie', in Dan Diner (ed.), *Ist der Nationalsozialismus Geschichte? Zu Historisierung und Historikerstreit*, Frankfurt am Main, 1987, pp. 62–73, here p. 66. The work referred to is the first essay ('Der Zusammenbruch im Osten 1944/45 als Problem der deutschen Nationalgeschichte und der europäischen Geschichte') of Andreas Hillgruber's, *Zweierlei Untergang. Die Zerschlagung des Deutschen Reiches und das Ende des europäischen Judentums*, Berlin, 1986.

20 Friedländer, 'Reflections'.

21 Friedländer, 'Reflections', pp. 314–16.

22 Broszat, *Nach Hitler*, pp. 171–2.

23 Friedländer, 'Reflections', p. 315.

24 Friedländer, 'Reflections', p. 314. Kulka's criticism in 'Singularity and its Relativization' runs along similar lines. Diner ('Zwischen Aporie und Apologie', p. 67) also criticizes the inevitable loss of the specifics of the period 1933–45 when, as in the '*Alltagsgeschichte*' approach, the emphasis is placed on 'normality'. With reference to the oral history project directed by Lutz Niethammer on the experiences of Ruhr workers, he points out that 'the good and bad times' in subjective memory by no means accord with the significant developments of the period 1933–45. A 'considerable trivialization of the Nazi era' is allegedly the consequence. The reference is to Ulrich Herbert, 'Die guten und die schlechten Zeiten', in Lutz Niethammer (ed.), *'Die Jahre weiß man nicht, wo man die heute hinsetzen soll.' Faschismuserfahrungen im Ruhrgebiet*, Bonn, 1986, S.67–96.

The second dilemma arises from the recommended removal of the distance, founded on moral condemnation, which the historian of Nazism places between himself and the object of his research, and which prevents him from treating it as a 'normal' period of history. This raises, says, Friedländer, inextricable problems in the construction of a global picture of the Nazi era, since if few spheres of life were themselves criminal, few were completely untouched by the regime's criminality. Separation of criminality from normalcy is, therefore, scarcely an easy task. No objective criteria can be established for distinguishing which areas might be susceptible to empathetic treatment, and which still cannot be handled without the historian's distance from his subject of enquiry.[25]

The third dilemma arises from the vagueness and open-endedness of the concept of 'historicization', which implies a method and a philosophy but gives no clear notion of what the results might be. The implications of 'historicization' are, however, by no means straightforward, but might be interpreted in radically different ways – as indeed Nolte and Hillgruber demonstrate in their controversial interpretations of the Nazi era which provoked the '*Historikerstreit*'.[26]

Friedländer is prepared to discount Nolte's writings in this context. But he uses the illustration of Hillgruber's essay on the Eastern Front to demonstrate the potential dangers of 'historicization', and links this squarely with the problems of the 'everyday history' approach itself, and with the open-ended nature of the '*Resistenz*' concept used in the 'Bavaria Project'.[27] Not only the relativization of distance from the Nazi era, he argues, but also the emphasis in '*Alltagsgeschichte*' on the ordinariness of many aspects of the Third Reich, on the non-ideological and non-criminal spheres of activity, and on ever more nuanced attitudes and behavioural patterns, creates significant problems. Friedländer accepts that 'criminality' is not necessarily excluded, and that a continuum can be constructed involving 'criminality' in everyday life and normality in the regime's 'criminal' system. However, he suggests that in an overall perspective of the Third Reich premised upon the relativization and normalization of the Nazi era advocated in the 'historicization' approach, the tendency to overweight the 'normality' end of the continuum can scarcely be avoided. Despite Broszat's disclaimers, fears Friedländer, the passage from 'historicization' to 'historicism' ('*Historisierung*' to '*Historismus*') in regard to the Third Reich is a real danger.[28] Hillgruber defended his controversial empathizing and identification with the German troops in the east by comparing his approach with that of 'everyday history', as applied to other areas of research.[29] Accepting that there is some force in this defence, Friedländer suggests that one might justifiably apply the concept of '*Resistenz*' to the behaviour of the German soldiers defending the Eastern Front in the final phase of the war. Hence, many units were relatively immune to Nazi ideology and were only doing

[25] Friedländer, 'Reflections', pp. 316–17.
[26] Friedländer, 'Reflections', pp. 317.
[27] Friedländer, 'Reflections', pp. 317–21.
[28] Friedländer, 'Reflections', p. 318.
[29] Friedländer, 'Reflections', pp. 319–21; and see Diner, 'Zwischen Aporie and Apologie', pp. 66, 69.

their job like soldiers in any army in defending the Front. On the other hand, of course, the Wehrmacht was system-supporting more than any other institution. This reveals to Friedländer not only that 'Resistenz' is 'much too amorphous a concept to be of any great use',[30] but also the vacuous nature of 'historicization', which 'implies many different things' so that 'within the present context it may encourage some interpretations rather than others'.[31]

From the dilemmas arise, in Friedländer's view, three general problems. The first is that the Nazi past is still too overwhelmingly present to deal with it in the 'normal' way that one might, for example, tackle the history of sixteenth-century France. The self-reflection of the historian necessary to any good historical writing is decisive in approaching the Nazi era. The Third Reich simply cannot be regarded in the same way or approached with the same methods as 'normal' history.[32]

The second general problem is what Friedländer calls 'differential relevance'.[33] The history of Nazism, he says, belongs to everyone. The study of everyday life in the Third Reich may indeed be relevant to Germans in terms of self-perception and national identity, and thereby be a perspective which commends itself to German historians. But for historians outside Germany, this perspective might be less relevant in comparison with the political and ideological aspects of the Third Reich, and in particular the relationship of ideology to politics.

The same point is made in slightly different fashion by other critics of 'historicization'. Otto Dov Kulka sees the emphasis upon the 'normal' aspects of the Third Reich as a reflection of the present-day situation and self-image of the Federal Republic as an affluent, modern society – an image into which Nazi ideology and the 'criminality' of the regime can scarcely be accommodated. From this present-day West German perspective, he accepts the examination of, for example, long-term trends in the development of social policy as both justified and important. But the world-historical uniqueness of Nazism, he emphasizes, resides specifically in the duality of a society where 'normal' trends of modernization were accompanied by the slave labour and extermination 'in industrially rational fashion' of those ideologically excluded from the 'national community'. And in the event of a victorious Third Reich, modern German society would have looked very different from the present democratic welfare state of the Federal Republic and of the socialist German Democratic Republic.[34]

The third – and most crucial – problem is, therefore, how to integrate Nazi crimes into the 'historicization' of the Third Reich. In Friedländer's view – and he accepts that this is a value-judgement – the specificity, or uniqueness, of Nazism resides in the fact that it 'tried "to determine who should and who should not inhabit the world" '.[35] The problem – and the

---

30 Friedländer, 'Reflections', p. 319.
31 Friedländer, 'Reflections', p. 321.
32 Friedländer, 'Reflections', pp. 321–2.
33 Friedländer, 'Reflections', p. 322.
34 Kulka, 'Singularity and its Relativization', and as cited by Herbert Freeden, 'Um die Singularität von Auschwitz', Tribüne, 26, Heft 102 (1987), pp. 123–4.
35 Friedländer, 'Reflections', p. 323. The phrase is taken from the closing lines of Hannah Arendt, Eichmann in Jerusalem, London, 1963, p. 256.

limits – of 'historicization' lie consequently in its inability to integrate into its picture of 'normal' development 'the specificity and the historical place of the annihilation policies of the Third Reich'.[36]

## Evaluation

The objections to the 'historicization of National Socialism' raised by Friedländer, Kulka, and Diner cannot lightly be dismissed. They touch upon important philosophical and methodological considerations which have a direct bearing on any attempt at writing the history of German society under Nazism.

Friedländer's concern about the omission or down-playing of the political, ideological, and moral aspects of Nazism permeates his critique. But it could at the outset be queried whether the traditional concentration on the political–ideological–moral framework could lead to further major advances in the depth of that understanding which provides the basis of enhanced moral awareness. This 'traditional' emphasis, epitomized perhaps most clearly in the work of Karl-Dietrich Bracher, produced many lasting gains.[37] A 'historicized' treatment would not need to discard them. But rigidly to confine scholarship to the traditional framework would be sterile and perhaps ultimately even counter-productive, since it would put a block on precisely the approaches which have led to much of the most original – and most morally sensitive – research in recent years. Moreover, the implications of 'historicization' might be less serious both in theory and in practice than Friedländer fears.

It seems questionable whether the first dilemma posed by Friedländer – the incompatibility of doing justice to the specific character of the Nazi era in a treatment which concentrates upon the unfolding of long-term social change – is a necessary one. It might, in fact, be countered that the specific features of the period 1933–1945 can only be highlighted by a 'longitudinal' analysis crossing those chronological barriers and placing the era in a development context of elements of social change which long preceded Nazism and continued after its demise. Friedländer's fear is that there would be an inevitable shift in focus to the problem of modernization, and that a 'relativization' of the dictatorship era by its new location in a long-term context of 'neutral' social change would be bound to lose sight of, or reduce in

---

[36] Friedländer 'Reflections', p. 323. Diner ('Zwischen Aporie und Apologie', pp. 67–8, 71–3) is even more unyielding in his criticism, emphasizing the centrality of Auschwitz as a 'universalist point of departure from which to measure the world-historical significance of National Socialism', the impossibility of 'historicizing' Auschwitz, the diametrically opposed experiences of 'perpetrators' and 'victims', and the theoretical impossibility of combining the 'normality' experiences of the former and the experiences of the later of an 'absolutely exceptional situation' in one narrative history. He adds (p. 68) that any notion of 'daily routine' ('*Alltag*') has of necessity to begin from its conceptual opposite of the 'specifically exceptional'. Apparently accepting (p. 71) that some synthesis might after all be possible, he draws the conclusion with reference to the Holocaust that 'only proceeding from this extreme case allows one to make that – in the close-up perspective of everyday history and mass murders – divided coexistence of the banality of the unreally shaped real normal situation on the one hand and its monstrous upshot on the other hand even approximately comprehensible'.
[37] Most classically in Karl-Dietrich Bracher, *The German Dictatorship*, New York, 1970.

emphasis, crucial events or policy decisions in the period of Nazi rule itself.

The fear does not appear to be borne out by recent works on social change, some of which have adopted a long-term perspective and have deliberately addressed the issue of modernization and the 'social revolution' argument. Obviously, the 'criminal' side of the Third Reich is not the dominant focus in such works. But in the stress of Nazi social policy, the significance of ideology is by no means underplayed, and the relationship of this ideology to the core racial–imperialist essence of Nazism is made abundantly plain. For instance, the wartime social programme of Robert Ley – to take the example, from Marie-Louise Recker's study of wartime social policy, which Broszat cites and Friedländer sees as an example of the dangers implicit in 'historicization' – indeed reveals a number of superficial similarities to Beveridge's social insurance provisions in Britain. But what is most striking in Recker's analysis – though, admittedly, not in Broszat's reference to her findings – is the specific and unmistakable Nazi character of the programme.[38] Not only is it legitimate (and necessary) to deploy a 'longitudinal' and also a comparative perspective in analysis of Ley's programme, but such a perspective contributes directly to a clearer definition of the peculiarly Nazi essence of social policy in the years 1933–45. The same can be said of Michael Prinz's recent admirable analysis of Nazi attempts to eradicate the status barrier between white- and blue-collar workers, in which the long-term perspective serves to depict particularly clearly both the specific features of Nazi social policy towards white-collar workers, and the anchorage of this policy in Nazi ideological precepts.[39]

Applied to other subject areas, the 'longitudinal' approach highlights precisely the political–ideological–moral framework which Friedländer suspects will be ignored or downplayed – if in ways different to, and often more challenging than, the traditional approach. An instance would be Ulrich Herbert's excellent analysis of the treatment of foreign labour in Germany since the nineteenth century, which allows both the continuities which cross the Nazi era, but also the specific barbarities of that era itself, to come more clearly into view.[40] Herbert was, of course, a leading participant in the Ruhr oral-history project which was so closely linked to perceived experiences of the 'normality' of 'everyday life'. It is all the more significant, therefore, that he was the historian to contribute an outstanding monograph on foreign workers which offers the first major analysis of one of the most barbarous aspects of the Third Reich, and that he not only brings out fully the ideologically rooted nature of the regime's policy towards foreign workers, but also the extent to which 'racism was not just a phenomenon to be found among the Party leadership and the SS, . . . but a practical reality to be experienced as an everyday occurrence in Germany during the war'.[41]

---

[38] Marie-Louise Recker, Nationalsozialistische Sozialpolitik im Zweiten Weltkrieg, Munich 1985. See Broszat, Nach Hitler, p. 171.

[39] Michael Prinz, Vom neuen Mittelstand zum Volksgenossen, Munich, 1986.

[40] Ulrich Herbert, Geschichte der Ausländerbeschäftigung in Deutschland 1880 bis 1980, Bonn, 1986.

[41] Ulrich Herbert, Fremdarbeiter. Politik and Praxis des 'Ausländer-Einsatzes' in der Kriegswirtschaft des Dritten Reiches, Berlin/Bonn, 1985, back cover. See also Herbert's essay, 'Arbeit und Vernichtung. Ökonomisches Interesse und Primat der "Weltanschauung" ', in Diner (ed.) Ist der Nationalsozialismus Geschichte?, pp. 198–236.

The moral dimension is also more than evident in recent research on professional and social groups – such as the medical, legal, and teaching professions, technicians and students.[42] And there has been little difficulty in such studies in blending together long-term patterns of development and change (into which the Nazi era has to be fitted) and specific facets in such processes peculiar to Nazism. The same is abundantly true of research on the position of women. Continuities in anti-feminism have not prevented an elaboration of the specific contours of the 1933–45 era, as in Gisela Bock's work, for example, in which a direct association is made of Nazi anti-feminism and racial policy by way of an analysis of compulsory sterilization.[43] As in this instance, most other recent publications, many of them excellent in quality, on women in the Third Reich have placed particular emphasis upon the central issue of race – precisely the issue which Friedländer fears will lose significance through a social rather than political history perspective.[44]

It is difficult to see how any scholarly attempt to construct an overall picture of society under Nazism could ignore the findings of such important research. We still face, however, Friedländer's second dilemma: the inability of the historian, having removed the previously automatic 'distance' from Nazism, taken the epoch out of its 'quarantine', and abolished the 'syndrome of "required-reading" ',[45] to apply objective criteria to separate 'criminality' from 'normalcy' in the construction of a 'global' picture of the Nazi era.

Friedländer's worry is evidently that spheres of empathetic understanding might now be found in the 'normality' of everyday life under Nazism. The previous general consensus resting upon a total and complete rejection of this era would thereby be broken. But the historian, now faced with a choice other than rejection,[46] would have no objective criteria for drawing distinctions. In the context of the philosophy of 'historicism' (*'Historismus'*), and in the realm of pure theory, the problem of 'distance' or 'empathy', which Friedländer poses, does indeed appear insoluble. But even at the theoretical level, the problem is hardly peculiar to the Third Reich, and poses itself implicitly in all historical writing. In many areas of contemporary history in particular, one might think, the problem seems hardly less acute than in the case of Nazism. Whether the historian writing on Soviet society

---

[42] Not surprisingly, moral issues are particularly close to the surface in research, which has made considerable strides forward in recent years, on the place of the Third Reich in the professionalization of medical practice. For surveys of the literature see: Michael H. Kater, 'Medizin and Mediziner im Dritten Reich. Eine Bestandsaufnahme', *Historische Zeitschrift*, 244 (1987), pp. 299–352; and Michael H. Kater, 'The Burden of the Past: Problems of a Modern Historiography of Physicians and Medicine in Nazi Germany', *German Studies Review*, 10 (1987).

[43] Gisela Bock, *Zwangssterilisation im Nationalsozialismus*, Opladen, 1986.

[44] See particularly Renate Bridenthal, Atina Grossman, and Marion Kaplan (eds.), *When Biology became Destiny. Women in Weimar and Nazi Germany*, New York, 1984; and Claudia Koonz, *Mothers in the Fatherland. Women, the Family, and Nazi Politics*, New York, 1986.

[45] Friedländer, 'Reflections', p. 316.

[46] Some 20 years ago, Wolfgang Sauer pointed out that a characteristic feature of writing on Nazism was that the historian faced no other choice than rejection. (Reference in chapter 1 note 39 above.)

under Stalin, on the society of Fascist Italy or Franco's Spain, on the Vietnam war, on South Africa, or on British imperialism faces a fundamentally different dilemma might be questioned. Objective criteria resting on the historian's 'neutrality' arguably play no part in any historical writing. Selection on the basis of subjectively determined choices and emphases is inescapable. A rigorous critical method and full recognition of subjective factors shaping the approach deployed and evaluation of the findings provide the only means of control. The historian of Nazism is in no different position to any other historian in this respect.

Broszat's writings are in places certainly less clear and unambiguous than they might be on the difference between the method he advocates and the traditional or 'restored' historicism which he contrasts with it.[47] He explicitly presents 'distance' and intuitive insight or 'empathy' (*'Einfühlen'*) as opposites, and speaks of the possibility of 'a degree of sympathetic identification' (*'ein Maß mitfühlender Identifikation'*) both with victims and with 'wrongly invested achievements and virtues' (*'fehlinvestierten Leistungen und Tugenden'*). At the same time, however, he make sufficiently plain that the counter to an uncritical, positive identification with the subject matter lies precisely in the critical historical method, applied to Nazism as to others periods of history, and ultimately promoting enhanced moral sensibility precisely through meticulous scholarship which includes empathy but does not uncritically embrace it.[48] The result is the methodological tightrope which all historians have to walk, in which the choice between empathy or moral distance is reshaped by the critical method into the position which characterizes a great deal of good historical writing – that of rejection through 'understanding'. This, the premise that 'enlightenment' (*'Aufklärung'*) comes through 'explanation' (*'Erklärung'*),[49] seems the basis of Broszat's approach in his collected papers, and certainly in his own work on the 'Bavaria Project' and elsewhere.

The best work arising from *'Alltagsgeschichte'*, in fact, clearly demonstrates that a concern with everyday behaviour and mentalities by no means implies empathetic treatment. Detlev Peukert's work, in which 'normality' is rooted in a theory of the 'pathology of modernity', provides an outstanding example.[50] The dilemma posed by Friedländer is scarcely visible here. 'Everyday normality' is not presented as a positive counterpoint to the 'negative' aspects of Nazism, but as a framework within which 'criminality', arising from a 'pathological' side of 'normality', becomes more readily

[47] See Broszat, *Nach Hitler*, pp. 120, 161, for the phrases cited in the following sentence, and pp. 100–1, 173 for comments on 'historicism' (*'Historismus'*).

[48] See, in particular, the essay: 'Grenzen der Wertneutralität in der Zeitgeschichtsforschung: Der Historiker und der Nationalsozialismus', in *Nach Hitler*, pp. 92–113.

[49] Broszat, *Nach Hitler*, p. 100. See also 'Briefwechsel', p. 340, where Broszat re-emphasizes his dependence upon a 'principle of critical, enlightening (*aufklärerischen*) historical understanding which . . . is to be clearly distinguished from the concept of understanding (*Verstehens-Begriff*) of German historicism in the nineteenth century . . .'

[50] See Detlev Peukert, *Volksgenossen und Gemeinschaftsfremde. Anpassung, Ausmerze und Aufbegehren unter dem Nationalsozialismus*, Köln, 1982 (Engl. *Inside Nazi Germany. Conformity and Opposition in Everyday Life*, London, 1987). Friedländer offers a qualified acceptance of the merits of *Alltagsgeschichte* in 'Briefwechsel' pp. 354–5, though this is far from satisfying Broszat (see 'Briefwechsel', pp. 362–3).

explicable. Nor is the concern that a continuum from 'normality' to 'criminality' inevitably means in practice that the dominant emphasis falls upon the former upheld in Peukert's work, which is all the more impressive in that he has offered so far practically the only wide-ranging attempt to synthesize research emanating from a wide variety of monographs falling within the 'history of everyday life' approach to German society in the Third Reich. And, though Peukert deliberately excluded it from his consideration in his book, there is no reason why the 'road to Auschwitz' could not be fully incorporated into an analysis premised on such an approach to 'normality'. By expressly linking 'daily life and barbarism', through association with the destructive potential built into modern society's emphasis upon advances in production and and efficiency, he has himself indicated how an 'everyday history of racism', which is still in its beginnings, could contribute to a deeper understanding of the behaviour and mentalities which made the Holocaust possible.[51] Here, too, the dilemma of empathy or distance would be premised upon a false dichotomy and would not in practice present itself.

Friedländer's third dilemma arises from the vagueness and open-endedness of the term 'historicization', which is subject to different – some unattractive – interpretations. It can be readily conceded that 'historicization' is indeed an imprecise and unclear concept.[52] In some respects it is ambiguous if not outright misleading. The proximity of the term to 'historicism', which is the opposite of what it denotes, does not help clarity. And it seems related to 'normal' in at least three different ways: to the proposed 'normalization' of 'historical consciousness'; to the application of 'normal' historical method in approaching the Third Reich; and to the 'normality' of 'everyday life'. As an ordering or analytical concept, it has no obvious value, and is purely suggestive of a method of approach. The discarding of the term would arguably be no great loss. It confuses more than it clarifies. But the approach and method signified by 'historicization' could not be dispensed with. Even so, it would be necessary to distinguish the three different uses of 'normal'. The application of 'normal' historical method, and the extension of the sphere of analysis to the 'normality' of 'everyday life' can be more easily defended than can the inclusion of the Nazi era in a supposed 'normalization of historical consciousness'. This last usage, as the '*Historikerstreit*' has demonstrated, and as Friedländer and others fear, indeed appears either to elide the Nazi era altogether, or to erase or dilute the moral dimension by shifting the spotlight to parallel (and allegedly 'more original') barbarities of other 'totalitarian' states, particularly those of Bolshevik Russia. It is in the context of such distortions that Friedländer poses his third dilemma, by pointing to the use of the same term, 'historicization', in the context of an

---

[51] Detlev Peukert, 'Alltag und Barbarei. Zur Normalität des Dritten Reiches', in Diner (ed.), *Ist der Nationalsozialismus Geschichte?*, pp. 51–61, esp. 53, 56, 59–61.

[52] See the comments of Adelheid von Saldern, which offer some support to Friedländer's objections, in her critique, 'Hillgrubers "Zweierlei Untergang" – der Untergang historischer Erfahrungsanalyse', in Heide Gerstenberger und Dorothea Schmidt (ed.). *Normalität oder Normalisierung? Geschichtswerkstätten und Faschismusanalyse*, Münster, 1987, esp. pp. 164, 167–8. Meanwhile, Broszat himself accepts ('Briefwechsel', pp. 340, 361–2) that the 'historicization' concept is 'ambiguous and misleading'.

intended 'normalization' of historical consciousness in the face of a 'past which will not not pass away', by Nolte and, implicitly, by Hillgruber.[53]

The argument that the notion of 'historicization' advanced by Broszat, with its connotations of heightened moral sensitivity towards the Nazi past, might be misused 'in the present ideological context'[54] to result in the diametrically opposed 'relativization' of the regime's criminality, as in Nolte's essays which prompted the 'Historikerstreit',[55] is certainly a serious criticism of the vagueness of the concept, but not convincing in itself as a rejection of the approach – largely based on an 'everyday history of the Nazi era' – which Broszat's concept is meant to denote.

If, however, as Friedländer himself suggests, Nolte's eccentric argumentation is left on one side, there still remains the question of Hillgruber's declared adaptation of the approach of 'Alltagsgeschichte' to the problem of the troops on the Eastern Front, with the dubious conclusions he draws.[56] Friedländer astutely points out that the empathetic approach can produce startling results, and suggests that Hillgruber's essay demonstrates how Broszat's supposed 'historicization', aimed precisely at avoiding traditional 'historicism', can lead to a return of 'historicism', now dangerously applied to the Third Reich itself.[57] But the point about Hillgruber's essay is that it is squarely rooted in a crude form of the 'historicist' tradition which presumes that 'understanding' ('Verstehen') can only come about through empathetic identification. It is precisely the claim that the historian's only valid position is one of identification with the German troops fighting on the Eastern Front which has invoked such widespread and vehement criticism of Hillgruber's essay.[58] The critical method, which in his other work – not excluding his essay on 'the historical place of the extermination of the Jews' in the same volume as the controversial treatment of the Eastern Front – makes him a formidable historian whose strength lies in the careful and measured treatment of empirical data, has entirely deserted him here and is wholly lacking in this one-sided, uncritical empathizing with the German troops. Though

---

[53] Friedländer, 'Reflections', pp. 317–21. Nolte's article, 'Vergangenheit, die nicht vergehen will', is in 'Historikerstreit', pp. 39–47. Hillgruber's work referred to is the first essay in *Zweierlei Untergang*.

[54] Friedländer, 'Reflections', p. 324.

[55] See 'Historikerstreit' pp. 13–35, 39–47. Klaus Hildebrand, for example, praised Nolte in a review for the way in which he undertook 'to incorporate in historicizing fashion (*historisierend einzuordnen*) that central element for the history of National Socialism and of the "Third Reich" of the annihilatory capacity of the ideology and of the regime, and to comprehend this totalitarian fact of the matter in the interrelated context of Russian and German history'. – *Historische Zeitschrift*, 242 (1986), p. 465.

[56] See Hillgruber's remarks in 'Historikerstreit', pp. 234–5.

[57] Friedländer, 'Reflections', pp. 320–1. See the further debate between Broszat and Friedländer on this point in 'Briefwechsel', pp. 346, 355–6, 360–1.

[58] See Diner, 'Zwischen Aporie und Apologie', pp. 69–70, and von Saldern, 'Hillgrubers "Zweierlei Untergang" ', pp. 161–2, 168 for comments on Hillgruber's argument in the context of the 'historicization' problem. The most devastating critique of Hillgruber's position can be found in Hans-Ulrich Wehler, *Entsorgung der deutschen Geschichte?*, Munich, 1988, 46ff, 154ff. See also the excellent review article by Omer Bartov (whose own book, *The Eastern Front 1941–45. German Troops and the Barbarisation of Warfare*, London, 1985, offers a necessary and an important counter-interpretation to that of Hillgruber): 'Historians on the Eastern Front. Andreas Hillgruber and Germany's Tragedy', *Tel Aviver Jahrbuch für deutsche Geschichte*, 16 (1987), pp. 325–45.

Hillgruber claimed to be applying the technique of '*Alltagsgeschichte*' and the approach advocated by Broszat and others to experience events from the point of view of those at the base of society directly affected by them, it is precisely the absence of critical reflection which provides the gulf between his depiction and the work of Broszat, Peukert and others, who indeed look to 'grassroots' experiences, but do not detach these from a critical framework of analysis.

The example of Hillgruber appears, therefore, misplaced. What, apart from the dubious value of the actual term 'historicization', it illustrates, is that, in his zeal to emphasize the need for greater empathetic understanding of 'experience', Broszat appears to have posed a false dichotomy with the 'distance' which is an important control mechanism of the historian of any period, not just of the Nazi era. In reality, Broszat's own historical writing – even his latest short book in a series founded on the necessity to 'historicize' German history – plainly does not abrogate 'distance' in the interests of uncritical empathy. Neither here, nor in Broszat's other recent writing, could it be claimed that the narrative approach ('*Erzählen*') which he misses in historical treatment of the Third Reich[59] has come to dominate or to replace critical, structured analysis and reflection. 'Distance' as well as empathetic understanding might be said to be vital to the historian of any period.

The preservation of a critical distance in the case of National Socialism is, in fact, far from being dispensable, a crucial component of the new social history of the Third Reich. But it is precisely the virtue of this new social history located in description and structured analysis of 'everyday' experience, that it breaks down the unreflected distance which has traditionally been provided by abstractions such as 'totalitarian rule' and compels a deeper comprehension through greater awareness of the complexity of social reality.[60] If I understand it correctly, this is the essence of Broszat's plea for 'historicization', and for a structured '*Alltagsgeschichte*' as the most fruitful method of approach. And the findings of the 'Bavaria Project' alone demonstrate how enriching such an approach can prove.

It seems plain that Friedländer is correct to stress that the Nazi era, from whichever perspective it is approached, can not be regarded as a 'normal' part of history in the way that even the most barbarous episodes of the more distant past can be viewed. The emotions which rightly still colour attitudes to Nazism obviously rule out the detachment with which not only sixteenth-century France (Friedländer's example) but also many more recent events and periods in German history and in the history of other nations can be analysed. In this sense, Wolfgang Benz is quite right when he claims: 'Detached concern with Nazism as an era of German history among others and work on it devoted to purely scholarly interest seems then not so easily possible. The mere distance of 40 or 50 years does not yet make the Nazi era

---

[59] See Martin Broszat, *Die Machtergreifung*, Munich, 1984 (Engl. *Hitler and the Collapse of Weimar Germany*, Leamington Spa, 1987). For Broszat's remarks on the concept behind the series *Deutsche Geschichte der neuesten Zeit*, see *Nach Hitler*, p. 152. And for his advocation of narrative (*Erzählen*) as historical method, see Broszat, *Nach Hitler*, pp. 137, 161.
[60] See Broszat, *Nach Hitler*, pp. 131–9, 'Alltagsgeschichte der NS-Zeit'.

historical.'[61] But of course this does not rule out the application of 'normal' historical method to the social, as well as to the political, history of Germany in the Nazi era. Even if a wide-ranging interpretative analysis of the Nazi era based on such methods will, as Benz adds, naturally be unable 'to do justice to the longing of the citizens of the postwar society to be released from the shadow of the past', this does not mean that it cannot be written.[62] And, while the historian's relationship to his subject of study is different in the case of Nazism than, say, in that of the French Revolution, it could be argued that, even accepting the uniqueness of the Holocaust, the problems posed by 'historicization' are little different in theory to those facing the historian of, say, Soviet society under Stalin.

Like the French and Russian Revolutions, the Third Reich embraces events of world-historical importance. Its history can certainly be approached as part of the pre-history of the Federal Republic (and of the German Democratic Republic), but, as Friedländer rightly says, 'the history of Nazism belongs to everybody'.[63] Perspectives inevitably vary. The polarization of German and Jewish collective memory of the Nazi era – epitomized in the films *Heimat* and *Shoah* – is plausibly advanced by Friedländer as an important element in the current debates about approaches to the Third Reich.[64] The differences in emphasis are unavoidable, and each has its own legitimacy. It is difficult to see how they can satisfactorily be blended together in any history which, purely or largely based upon the notion of 'experience' and constructed upon a narrative method ('*Erzählen*'), attempts a 'global' description of the Nazi era. Even if one suggests that in some ways the historian who shares neither collective memory possibly has an advantageous perspective, the attempt seems in any case bound to founder on the assumption that it is theoretically possible to write the 'total' history of an entire 'era' based upon collective 'experience'.[65] Equally impossible is the construction of a history built solely around the actions or 'experiences' of the 'historical actors' themselves and detached from the often impersonally structured conditions which in good measure shape or pre-determine those 'experiences'.[66] Only the application of constructs, concepts, and even theories which reside outside the sphere of historical experience can provide order and make sense of experience in a historical

---

[61] Wolfgang Benz, 'Die Abwehr der Vergangenheit. Ein Problem nur für Historiker und Moralisten?' in Diner (ed.), *Ist der Nationalsozialismus Geschichte?*, p. 33.
[62] Benz, p. 19. Norbert Frei's recent short book, *Der Führerstaat*, Munich, 1987, offers some pointers towards the potential of such an approach.
[63] Friedländer, 'Reflections', p. 322.
[64] Saul Friedländer, 'West Germany and the Burden of the Past: The Ongoing Debate', *Jerusalem Quarterly*, 42 (1987), pp. 16–17. And see also 'Briefwechsel', pp. 346, 366–7, on the 'dissonance between memories'.
[65] See here the pertinent remarks of Wehler, 'Königsweg', p. 35. On the potential, but also substantial problems, of 'experience analysis' (*Erfahrungsanalyse*) with reference to the Third Reich, see von Saldern, 'Hillgrubers "Zweierlei Untergang"'. Friedländer emphasizes the limits of narrative as a method in 'Briefwechsel', pp. 370–1, while Diner ('Zwischen Aporie und Apologie', p. 67) is adamant that 'experienced everyday routine and existential exception can theoretically no longer be narrated as one history'.
[66] See Wehler, *Entsorgung*, p. 54, referring to the problems involved in Hillgruber's identification with the German troops on the eastern Front.

analysis which is bound to be less than 'total' or 'global'.[67] If this appears to stand in contradiction to Broszat's 'historicization' plea, it is scarcely out of synchronization with his practice in his own writing on the history of the Nazi era.

If the assumption is abandoned that the history of the Nazi era (or any other 'era'), in the sense of any 'total' grasp of the complexity of all the contradictory and often unrelated experiences which occur in a given period of time, is theoretically and practically possible, then it becomes feasible to conceive of a history of German society under Nazism which could incorporate in a structured analysis the findings of recent social historical research, in particular that of '*Alltagsgeschichte*', but which at the same time would embed this in the political–ideological–moral framework which Friedländer is anxious not to lose. Such an approach would have to jettison notions of the 'historicization' of Nazism in terms of regarding it as any other period of history or 'relativizing' its significance. But it would find indispensable the normal methodological rigour of historical enquiry, deployed as a matter of course in dealing with other eras (and already, one might add, deployed in countless scholarly works on Nazism). Applied to the social sphere of 'daily life' as well as to the political–ideological domain, conventional critical historical method would be sufficient to eliminate the modern antiquarianism which has rightly been criticized as a feature of the poorer strains of '*Alltagsgeschichte*'. Finally, it would not only be legitimate, but essential, to proceed in such an approach by way of a critical exploration of the continuum which stretches from 'normality' to barbarism and genocide, in order better to comprehend the social as well as political context in which inhumane ideologies become implemented as practical policies of almost inconceivable inhumanity. 'Auschwitz' would, therefore, inevitably form the point of departure from which the thin ice of modern civilization and its veneer of 'normality' could be critically examined.[68]

The last, and ultimately fundamental, issue preoccupying Friedländer seems resolvable in such an approach. The integration of Nazi crimes against humanity into a 'global' interpretation of society in the Third Reich ought to become, in fact, more rather than less possible in the light of the developments made in the empirical social history of Nazism in the past decade. Peukert's synthesis has, in many respects, pointed the way towards an integration of 'normality' and 'barbarism'.[69] I have attempted in my own work explicitly to relate lack of humanitarian concern with regard to the 'Jewish Question' to spheres of dissent and protest in 'everyday' matters.[70] My working hypothesis in such research was the notion that, especially under 'extreme' conditions, 'normal' daily and private concerns consume such

---

[67] See the comments by Klaus Tenfelde and Jürgen Kocka in *Alltagsgeschichte der NS-Zeit*, pp. 36, 50–4, 63–4, and by Kocka – on the need for theory in '*Alltagsgeschichte*' – in a recent review in *taz*, 26 Jan. 1988 (see above, note 5).

[68] See Peukert, 'Alltag und Barbarei', p. 61; and Diner, 'Zwischen Aporie und Apologie', pp. 71–2.

[69] Peukert, *Volksgenossen und Gemeinschaftsfremde* (Engl. *Inside Nazi Germany*, see above note 50); see also his 'Alltag und Barbarei' (above note 51).

[70] Ian Kershaw, *Popular Opinion and Political Dissent in the Third Reich*, Oxford, 1983.

energy and attention that indifference to inhumanity, and thereby indirect support of an inhumane political system, is significantly furthered. Robert Gellately, building upon the work of the late Reinhard Mann, is extending such suggestions to the areas of social consensus and active support for 'policing' measures in racial issues.[71] To posit a clear divorce between the concerns of '*Alltagsgeschichte*' and the political–ideological–moral framework which focuses upon the genocidal criminality of the Nazi regime is to adopt a misleading perspective. Out of recent work on the social history of the Third Reich, which Broszat has done more than most to promote, emerges the realization that there can be a social context in 'civilized society' in which genocide becomes acceptable. Research on the 'grassroots' history of the Nazi era has significantly deepened awareness of the troublesome reflection that 'many features of contemporary "civilized" society encourage the easy resort to genocidal holocausts'.[72]

[71] Reinhard Mann, *Protest und Kontrolle im Dritten Reich*, Frankfurt am Main/New York, 1987; Robert Gellately, 'The Gestapo and German Society: Political Denunciation in the Gestapo Case Files', *Journal of Modern History* (forthcoming) and 'Enforcing Racial Policy in Nazi Germany', as yet unpublished paper presented to the conference 'Re-Evaluating the "Third Reich": Interpretations and Debates', University of Pennsylvania, April 1988.
[72] Leo Kuper, *Genocide* Harmondsworth, 1981, p. 137.

# 9

## Living with the Nazi Past: The *'Historikerstreit'* and After

This book began by commenting that the contemporary historian and his work are public property in West Germany, and that conflicting interpretations of Nazism are inextricably bound up with the continuing reappraisal of the political identity of the Federal Republic. At the time of writing, it was impossible to realize how emphatically these points would soon be borne out by the outbreak, in 1986, of open warfare among leading German historians conducted in the public arena of leading newspapers and focused directly on the relationship of the Nazi past to the present and future identity of West Germany. The conflict rapidly came to be dubbed the *'Historikerstreit'* ('historians' dispute').[1]

The start of hostilities can be dated quite precisely. It was 11 July 1986, when the eminent philosopher and sociologist Jürgen Habermas, a left-wing intellectual of prominence since the heady days of 1968, published a broadside in the liberal weekly *Die Zeit* against 'the apologetic tendencies in the writing of German contemporary history'[2] in which he castigated the recent works of three leading historians, Ernst Nolte, Andreas Hillgruber and Michael Stürmer. Nolte, of the Free University of Berlin and with a high international repute for his earlier analyses of fascism, in an article published in the *Frankfurter Allgemeine Zeitung* on 6 June 1986, had suggested that the time was ripe for a reconsideration of the Nazi era, and in particular of the need to relocate the Holocaust as only one of a whole pattern of twentieth-century genocides. Hillgruber, of Cologne University, and a prominent authority on German foreign policy, had just brought out a short book advocating the need to identify sympathetically with the cause of the German troops fighting on the Eastern Front at the end of the war in the despairing attempt to stave off Bolshevism and to prevent the eastern parts of the German Reich and much of central and eastern Europe from falling into Soviet hands. And Stürmer, a professor at Erlangen University, best known for his work on Imperial Germany and in the 1960s and early 1970s associated with the social-liberal leanings of the 'critical' historians but who has recently acted as historical advisor to the conservative Chancellor of the Federal Republic, Helmut Kohl, had advanced in a series of essayistic 'think pieces' the need for a more active role for historians in creating a positive

---

[1] Most of the important early contributions are assembled in two anthologies: *'Historikerstreit'. Die Dokumentation der Kontroverse um die Einzigartigkeit der national-sozialistischen Judenvernichtung*, München, 1987 (henceforth cited as 'Historikerstreit'); and Reinhard Kühnl (ed.), *Vergangenheit, die nicht vergeht*, Köln, 1987.

[2] Jürgen Habermas, 'Eine Art Schadensabwicklung. Die apologetischen Tendenzen in der deutschen Zeitgeschichtsschreibung', in *'Historikerstreit'*, pp. 62–76.

sense of identity with a German past which had been largely shaped, he claimed, through Germany's fateful position in central Europe. Only a more positive, historically rooted patriotism, in Stürmer's grave and even alarmist Cassandra-like tones, could compensate for the breakdown in the postwar consensus of values in West Germany and the dangerous social and political divisions which had ensued.

Habermas's linkage of these three quite heterogeneous contributions as strands of an attempted conservative revision of attitudes towards the Nazi past in the Federal Republic detonated the explosion of feeling which reverberated throughout the summer. He deployed Stürmer's plea for the historian to provide a sense of national identity for the present by affording a positive meaning to the German past as the framework within which to denounce the 'revisionist' claims of Hillgruber and Nolte. Stürmer was seen as laying down the agenda; Nolte and Hillgruber in their different ways as providing the substance of a conservative revision, which Habermas further linked with the plans for two new national historical museums – the German Historical Museum in Berlin, and the House of History of the Federal Republic in Bonn. Habermas attacked Stürmer's contentions as an anti-pluralistic plea for a unitary picture of history based upon a national identity rooted in a revived national consciousness amounting to a 'German-nationalist coloured Nato philosophy'.[3] Habermas's stark alternative view revealed the deep gulf in historians' interpretations of the recent German past and located the common ground in the three quite distinct 'revisionist' contributions in the divide in attitude towards the significance of Auschwitz in German history: 'The only patriotism which does not alienate us from the West is a constitutional patriotism. Unfortunately, a commitment to universalist constitutional principles rooted in conviction has only been feasible in the cultural nation of the Germans after – and through – Auschwitz. Anyone who wants to expunge the shame about this fact with an empty notion such as "guilt obsession" . . ., anyone wishing to recall the Germans to a conventional form of their national identity, destroys the only reliable basis of our bonds with the West.'[4]

As these comments plainly demonstrate, historical perspectives were from the start of the *'Historikerstreit'* completely overlain with political, ideological and above all moral colouring. As one historian has put it, the debate which Nolte and Habermas triggered off amounts to 'the latest instalment in a 25-year-long argument about the moral imperatives of general historical interpretation', adding that to address the place of Nazism in the German past 'is the very opposite of a neutral or academic process', and one 'which remains highly charged with political implications for the present'.[5]

Once unleashed, the dispute rapidly developed a momentum of its own. Practically all leading West German historians felt it necessary to stake out their own positions. The fronts rapidly rigidified along the lines of trench

3  Habermas, 'Eine Art Schadensabwicklung', pp. 73–5.
4  Habermas, 'Eine Art Schadensabwicklung', pp. 75–6.
5  Geoff Eley, 'Nazism, Politics, and Public Memory: Thoughts on the West German *Historikerstreit* 1986–87', as yet unpublished typescript (forthcoming in *Past and Present*), p. 17.

warfare. Even the leading German newspapers were aligned: the *Frankfurter Allgemeine* with the conservative 'revisionists', *Die Zeit* with the social-liberal counterattack. An array of foreign observers of the German scene – historians and journalists – also had their say, whether out of bemusement or alarm, from puzzlement or anxiety at the new 'revision' of the relationship of the Federal Republic to its Nazi pre-history. By now, the debate has gone on for almost two years. The *'Historikerstreit'* has spawned an entire industry of essays, articles, seminars, workshops, and now book-length analyses.[6] The industry shows no signs of running down.

Whether the whole affair has been rewarding and worthwhile remains, however, open to question. Certainly, the vast output of literature is out of all proportion to the specific issues of historical interpretation of the Nazi era which were raised. In fact, had the *'Historikerstreit'* been a conventional debate among specialist historians, it would have been over relatively quickly. Hardly any new evidence was brought into play. No new sources were discovered. The questions posed were not as novel as they were made to sound. Intellectually, the arguments advanced by the 'revisionists' brought no breakthrough to new forms of interpretation. The 'revisionist' claims met with extensive rejection within West Germany, and foreign reactions were almost wholly negative.[7] 'The whole debate', it has been claimed, 'ultimately has little to offer anyone with a serious scholarly interest in the German past'.[8] At any rate, the *'Historikerstreit'* has resulted in no new and lasting insights into a deeper understanding of the Third Reich.

[6] The number of articles, commentaries, reports, etc. on the *'Historikerstreit'*, within and outside Germany, runs into the hundreds. Bibliographical references to much of the important literature can be found in the notes to Hans-Ulrich Wehler, *Entsorgung der deutschen Vergangenheit? Ein polemischer Essay zum 'Historikerstreit'*, Munich, 1988, pp. 212ff. and in Geoff Eley, 'Nazism, Politics, and Public Memory' esp. notes 16–17. Wehler's is the first book-length analysis of the whole controversy. Another, *The Unmasterable Past: History, Holocaust, and German National Identity* (Cambridge, Mass., 1988) written by Charles Maier (Harvard University), is imminent, while a third book by Richard Evans (University of East Anglia), entitled *Out of the Shadow of Nazism*, is also promised for the near future.

[7] For the most important early critical contributions within West Germany (other than that of Habermas), see the articles by Jäckel, Kocka, Broszat, Hans and Wolfang Mommsen, and Winkler in *'Historikerstreit'*, pp. 155–22, 132–42, 156–88, 256–63, 300–21. Wehler, *Entsorgung*, now offers the fullest and most sustained attack. Interest outside Germany in the *'Historikerstreit'* has been considerable. The quality press in Israel, the USA, Italy, the Netherlands, and France in particular reported extensively on the debate. Reactions have, not surprisingly, been most vehement in Israel. Apart from a few instances of support in the Austrian conservative press, the dominant tone of the reportage elsewhere, too, was overwhelmingly negative. Outstanding assessments by non-Germans include: Saul Friedländer, 'West Germany and the Burden of the Past: The Ongoing Debate', *Jerusalem Quarterly*, 42 (1987), pp. 3–18; Otto Dov Kulka, 'Singularity and its Relativization', forthcoming in *Yad Vashem Studies*, 19 (1988); Charles S. Maier, 'Immoral Equivalence: Revising the Nazi Past for the Kohl Era', *The New Republic*, 1 Dec. 1986, pp. 36–41; Richard J. Evans, 'The New Nationalism and the Old History: Perspectives on the West German *Historikerstreit*, *Journal of Modern History*, 59 (1987), pp. 761–97; Geoff Eley, 'Nazism, Politics, and Public Memory' (forthcoming in *Past and Present*). For a brief overview of international reactions, see Ian Kershaw, 'Nuova inquietudine tedesca? Le reazoni internazionali', *Passato e Presente*, 16 (1988), pp. 151–64.

[8] Evans, 'The New Nationalism and the Old History', p. 785.

## The 'Revision' and the Critique

The initial article by Ernst Nolte, which sparked off the entire *'Historikerstreit'*, entitled 'past which will not pass away',[9] claimed the time was now ripe for a revised perspective on the Third Reich which would break down the crude black–white images and bring out the full complexity of that era. This was indeed necessary, he argued, since, unlike the gradual fading of most periods of history from present-day consciousness and significance, the Nazi past 'appears to become still more live and forceful, not as a model but as a bogey, as a past which establishes itself as present or which is hung over the present like an executioner's sword'.[10] The isolation of the Third Reich from its long-term context of the upheavals in European society arising from the industrial revolution and especially from its intrinsic connection with the Russian Revolution – 'its most important precondition' – [11] and its role as a type of negative myth[12] for the present-day Federal Republic must be combated by new forms of analysis.

The major obstacle to a more apt perspective on the Nazi past is for Nolte the lasting impact of the Holocaust on historical consciousness. An explanation of the murder of the Jews is, therefore, at the centre of his proposed revision. And it is this explanation, both in its alleged cause and comparability of the Holocaust, which is so controversial. Whether Nolte's revised interpretation, which he was not advancing on the first occasion in 1986, would have provoked such a furore had Habermas not linked it somewhat artificially to the quite disparate works of Hillgruber and Stürmer, alleging that they formed part of a broad conservative assault on the advances made by historical scholarship in establishing the place of Nazism in German history, might be doubted. On the other hand, it was Nolte who 'went public' in the first place, advertising an abbreviated – and thereby all the more provocative – statement of his thesis for a mass readership in a leading newspaper, couched in a language and style which was guaranteed to arouse hostile reactions.

9 Ernst Nolte, 'Vergangenheit, die nicht vergehen will,' in *'Historikerstreit'*, pp. 39–47, originally published in *Frankfurter Allgemeine Zeitung*, 6 June 1986. Some of the more contentious assertions, and a more extended version of the basic argument, were contained in Nolte's earlier essay, 'Zwischen Geschichtslegende und Revisionismus?', in *'Historikerstreit'*, pp. 13–35. This latter essay was, in fact, the basis of a lecture delivered by Nolte as far back as 1980. It was published in abbreviated form the same year in the *Frankfurter Allgemeine Zeitung* under the title 'Die negative Lebendigkeit des Dritten Reiches. Eine Frage aus dem Blickwinkel des Jahres 1980', (see *'Historikerstreit'*, p. 35) and was subsequently included in revised form (and with editorial interpolations) in English translation, entitled 'Between Myth and Revisionism? The Third Reich in the Perspective of the 1980s', in H. W. Koch (ed.), *Aspects of the Third Reich*, London, 1985, pp. 17–38. Nolte's defence of his position in *Das Vergehen der Vergangenheit. Antwort an meine Kritiker im sogenannten Historikerstreit*, Berlin, 1987, further embittered the controversy, producing allegations that he had deliberately distorted by brief and misleading paraphrasing the content of lengthy and highly critical letters received from the Israeli historian Otto Dov Kulka, with the effect of making them relatively favourable to his own position. See Otto Dov Kulka, 'Der Umgang des Historikers Ernst Nolte mit Briefen aus Israel', *Frankfurter Rundschau*, 5 Nov. 1987, and the letters to the *Frankfurter Rundschau* which followed on 17 Dec. 1987 from Wolgang Schieder, 15 Jan. 1988 from Ernst Nolte, and 19 Feb. 1988 from Otto Dov Kulka.

10 *'Historikerstreit'*, p. 39.

11 *'Historikerstreit'*, p. 33; Koch, *Aspects*, p. 36.

12 *'Historikerstreit'*, p. 17; Koch, *Aspects*, p. 21.

In the full statement of his thesis, which appeared in a voluminous tome published more than a year after the '*Historikerstreit*' has flared up,[13] but which has done nothing to assuage his critics, Nolte at least provides some context for his more startling assertions. Even here, some of the key steps in the argument are purely speculative, and the implications of his approach remain deeply disturbing. In article form, however, the method of suggestion, inference, and insinuation dominates all the more strikingly, and the implications are unmistakable. His reasoning runs along the following lines.

A leading figure in the early Nazi Party, Dr Max Erwin von Scheubner-Richter, had witnessed the Turkish genocide of the Armenians in 1915 and had, according to the biography which appeared in 1938, described this as 'Asian' in its barbarity. Hitler, Himmler and Rosenberg, suggests Nolte, would not have demurred at this description. What could, therefore, have brought such men themselves to perpetrate an even more horrific genocide? He finds a key in a cryptic remark by Hitler in 1943 that captured German officers might be expected to co-operate in Soviet anti-German propaganda because of the 'rats' cage' in Moscow. Nolte rejects the interpretation that Hitler was referring directly to the Lubjanka prison. Instead, he sees the remark as a reference to a peculiar method of torture, allegedly favoured by the 'Chinese Cheka', in which prisoners had 'confessions' forced out of them by having their faces exposed to a hunger-crazed rat, similar to the well-known scene in George Orwell's *1984*. On the basis of references to such torture in obscure anti-Bolshevik literature of the civil war period, Nolte advances a speculative hypothesis that Hitler was deeply influenced by such horror stories, and that the Holocaust therefore had its origins and derivation in the obsessive lingering fear of Bolshevik terror in Hitler's mind.[14] Hence, Auschwitz – differing only in the technical methods of gassing from other genocides in the twentieth century.[15] – was in essence a reaction to a presumed threat from the east, a form of 'preventive murder', and amounted to a 'reaction born out of the anxiety of the annihilation occurrences of the Russian Revolution'.[16]

Nolte's hypothesis culminates in a list of suggestive rhetorical questions: '. . . Did the National Socialists, did Hitler, only commit an "asiatic" deed perhaps because they and those like them thought of themselves as potential or real victims of an "asiatic" deed? Was not the Gulag Archipelago more original (*ursprünglicher*) than Auschwitz? Was not the "class murder" of the Bolsheviks the logical and practical predecessor (*Prius*) of the "race murder" of the National Socialists? Are not Hitler's most secret actions to be explained also directly by the fact that he had not forgotten the "rats' cage"?'[17]

The conclusion is that while one mass murder cannot justify another, it is mistaken to ignore the connections between them, 'although a causal nexus

[13] Ernst Nolte, *Der europäische Bürgerkrieg 1917–1945. Nationalsozialismus und Bolschewismus*, Berlin, 1987.
[14] '*Historikerstreit*', pp. 43–5.
[15] '*Historikerstreit*', p. 45.
[16] '*Historikerstreit*', p. 32; Koch, *Aspects*, p. 36.
[17] '*Historikerstreit*', p. 45.

is probable'.[18] Nolte concedes that the extermination of the European Jews – together with many Slavs, mentally sick, and gypsies – is 'without precedent in its motivation and execution'.[19] But in his view this 'does not alter the fact that the so-called [*sic*!] annihilation of the Jews during the Third Reich was a reaction or a distorted copy and not a first act or an original'.[20]

In this revised perspective, Nazi genocide, while undeniable and deplorable, was only one of an array of comparable genocides which have characterized the twentieth century. Moreover, it would not have occurred at all without the class-motivated genocide of the Bolsheviks (the founders of a political system which, unlike that of Nazism, is still in existence today). The 'Final Solution', in this perspective, is therefore reduced to the status of a 'preventive murder', whose originality lies only in the specific technical methods of extermination deployed. Its cause is seen as the perceived need to prevent Bolshevik class genocide from sweeping over Germany by the destruction of those responsible for that terror – the Jews.

Apart from some support from Klaus Hildebrand and Joachim Fest,[21] and from the German conservative press, Nolte's position (which he has tenaciously upheld) has met with extensive rejection from scholars in Germany and almost universal condemnation abroad. So isolated has Nolte become that it has recently even been suggested that the 'historians' dispute' might be developing into a 'dispute between Nolte and the historians'.[22]

Nolte's hypothesis has been attacked on numerous grounds. In the first instance, on a relatively banal level, his use of evidence and the significance he attaches to the 'rats' cage' example have been called into question.[23] He realized himself that his rejection of the interpretation that Hitler was referring to the Lubjanka prison in Moscow, in the reference to the 'rats' cage' during a military briefing on 1 February 1943, could not be sustained. Hitler himself twice in adjacent comments in the text of the briefing refers specifically by name to the Lubjanka.[24] Nolte qualified his original argument, therefore, by stating that he had meant 'a practice in the Lubjanka', adding, fairly enough, that it is not important whether such a torture took place in reality, but only whether Hitler believed it did.[25] The passage originally quoted by Nolte, referring to the position of a captured German officer, apparently Field Marshall Paulus, who surrendered at Stalingrad, runs: 'You must imagine: he comes into Moscow, and imagine the "rats' cage"!

18 *'Historikerstreit'*, p. 46.
19 *'Historikerstreit'*, p. 15; Koch, *Aspects*, p. 19.
20 *'Historikerstreit'*, p. 33; Koch, *Aspects*, p. 36.
21 Klaus Hildebrand, review in *Historische Zeitschrift*, 242 (1986) pp. 465ff, of Koch, *Aspects of the Third Reich*, commenting favourably on Nolte's essay 'Between Myth and Revisionism?'; and Hildebrand, 'Zeitalter der Tyrannen', in *'Historikerstreit'*, pp. 84–92, esp. pp. 89ff. Joachim Fest, 'Die geschuldete Erinnerung', in *'Historikerstreit'*, pp. 100–12. See Wehler, *Entsorgung*, pp. 92–9, 126–37.
22 Wolfgang Schieder, letter to *Frankfurter Rundschau*, 'Freie Aussprache', 17 Dec. 1987.
23 See Eberhard Jäckel, 'Die elende Praxis der Untersteller', in *'Historikerstreit'*, pp. 115–22, esp. pp. 120–1; Wehler, *Entsorgung*, pp. 147–54.
24 Helmut Heiber (ed.), *Lagebesprechungen im Führerhauptquartier*, Berlin/Darmstadt/Vienna, 1962, pp. 75, 79–80.
25 *'Historikerstreit'*, pp. 224–5.

He signs everything there. He'll make confessions, make appeals.'[26] The two specific mentions of the Lubjanka which follow do not rule out a belief in a peculiar form of torture involving rats, but nor are they precise enough to confirm such a belief. Hitler commented further, with reference to the captured German generals Seydlitz, Schmidt and Paulus, who he claimed would be speaking on Soviet radio within eight days: 'They'll come now into the Lubljanka [*sic*], and they'll be eaten up by rats there', and 'you must be clear about it: (they'll come) to Moscow into the Lubljanka [*sic*] and will be "dealt with" there'.[27]

Whether these are allusions to a particular torture through exposure to rats is unclear, though the possibility cannot be discounted. Though it has been suggested that Nolte's version owes more to George Orwell's fictional story of 1949 than to Russian emigré sources, Nolte was able to point to the publication of the 'rats' cage' story in the main Nazi newspaper, the *Völkischer Beobachter*, in 1920.[28] In any case, in the book-length treatment, the 'rats' cage' episode is accorded less significance. It is seen as an example of anti-bolshevik horror stories which must have been familiar to Hitler in the early 1920s. Nolte speculates that such propaganda was the decisive influence in converting this existent anti-semitism into a genocidal ideology, and later returns to the 'rats' cage' story (in the Lubjanka reference) to suggest that Hitler's strongest emotions remained unchanged to the end.[29] Even so, Nolte's argument amounts to little more than a number of speculative leaps of the imagination – from the presumed widespread knowledge of a rat torture, to an obsessive belief in such a torture by Hitler, to the underlying motivation which this, as symbolizing Bolshevik horror, allegedly provided for the decision to murder the Jews.

Whatever the truth amounts to about the existence of such a torture, or Hitler's belief in it, a more important criticism of Nolte's hypothesis is that compelling reconstructions of the complex decision-making process in the spring and summer of 1941 leading up to the 'Final Solution' offer no indications that the motivation suggested by his speculation played any role whatsoever.[30] Even concentrating on Hitler's motivation alone – and we saw in chapter 5 that this can provide only a limited explanation of the 'twisted road to Auschwitz' – there are as few grounds for locating this in the need for a 'preventive murder' arising from fear of Bolshevik terror as there are in swallowing the Nazi propaganda fable that the invasion of the Soviet Union in 1941 had to be undertaken as a 'preventive measure'.[31] Though Hitler was only too ready propagandistically to exploit fear of Bolshevism and to justify anti-Soviet action in those terms, these public statements cannot simply be equated with his genuine, private motivation. The construction of Hitler's thought has been well researched. It was plainly rooted in the traditions of the *völkisch* Right, where the emergence of potentially genocidal attitudes

[26] Heiber, *Lagebesprechungen*, p. 75.
[27] Heiber, *Lagebesprechungen*, pp. 79–80.
[28] Wehler, *Entsorgung*, pp. 147–54; Nolte, *Bürgerkrieg*, pp. 115, 564 n.24.
[29] Nolte, *Bürgerkrieg*, pp. 114–23, 528–9, and see also p. 596 n.36.
[30] See Christopher Browning, *Fateful Months*, New York, 1985, pp. 8–38; Eberhard Jäckel and Jürgen Rohwer (ed.), *Der Mord an den Juden im Zweiten Weltkrieg*, Stuttgart, 1985.
[31] See Jäckel, in '*Historikerstreit*', p. 121.

towards Jews long pre-dated any Bolshevik threat. Hitler's earliest public statements on the Jews, replete with the most violent and venomous sentiment, made no reference to Bolshevism and were made almost a year before he revealed any interest in post-revolutionary conditions in Russia.[32] That Hitler was strongly influenced by Baltic emigrés like Scheubner-Richter and Rosenberg has long been accepted. But that his genocidal anti-semitic ideology can be directly traced to their depiction of Bolshevik class murders, leaving an indelible, paranoid fear in Hitler's mind, cannot be proved. Moreover, traces of the need for a 'preventive murder' are hard to locate in Hitler's thinking. From *Mein Kampf* onwards, his image of the Soviet Union was not one of strength, but of weakness. He regarded it as a 'Jew-ridden' regime, ripe for collapse.[33] This view prevailed in the summer of 1941, when the 'Final Solution of the Jewish Question' was implemented against a backcloth of presumed imminent victory over Bolshevism, rather than out of fear of Bolshevik terror.

The notion that the annihilation of the Jews could be postulated 'as punishment and preventive measure' in the face of an earlier 'class annihilation' of the Bolsheviks[34] has, therefore, found little acceptance. Nolte seems at the very least to have succumbed to the danger of taking at face value Nazi self-justificatory claims to be destroying the Jews because of their 'banditry' and partisan activities. Hence, although he states that the *Einsatzgruppen* shootings went way beyond any levels of mere retaliation, he seems to accept that retaliation was both a genuine and in some ways justifiable motive. Thus he sees the mass shootings of the *Einsatzgruppen* – in which up to 2.2 million Jews (including vast numbers of women, children and old people) were murdered – as motivated in good measure by revenge for partisan actions.[35] This leads to the remarkable assessment that 'the actions of the *Einsatzgruppen* are the most radical and comprehensive example of a preventive combating of enemies going way beyond all concrete demands of the direct conduct of war'.[36]

The implied suggestion that the victims of Nazi genocide actually provoked

[32] Eberhard Jäckel and Axel Kuhn (ed.), *Hitler. Sämtliche Aufzeichnungen 1905–1924* Stuttgart, 1980. The first mention of the 'Jewish Question' appears to be in a speech on capitalism on 25 Aug. 1919 (Doc.60). Thereafter, vitriolic attacks occur regularly (e.g. Docs. 61, 65, 66a, 69, 71, 83, 86, 87, 89, 91, 92, 93–5), mainly in the context of attacks on Jewish war profiteers, Jewish exploitation, Jewish finance capital, and Jews as responsible for Germany's current plight. The first reference to Bolshevism seems to be in the notes for a speech on 9 Feb. 1920 (Doc.80), but there is no indication of any mention of Jews either here, or in the next speech in which Bolshevism figures, on 29 Mar. 1920 (Doc.90). Hitler refers on 17 Apr. 1920 (Doc.93) to Russia's 'asiatic policy of conquest', and speaks ten days later of 'the Jewish scourge' in Russia (Doc.96). From July 1920 onwards, references to conditions in Soviet Russia, and now frequently in connection with it being run by Jews, begin to proliferate (see Docs.118, 121, 123–4, 126, 128, 136). In a speech on 21 July (Doc.121), apparently for the first time, Hitler explicitly combines the images of Bolshevism, Marxism, and Soviet Russia in the picture of the brutal rule of the Jews, for which Social Democracy was said to be preparing the ground in Germany.
[33] Adolf Hitler, *Mein Kampf*, Munich, 1930, pp. 742–3; Jäckel, in 'Historikerstreit', p. 121; Eberhard Jäckel, *Hitlers Weltanschauung. Entwurf einer Herrschaft*, Tübingen, 1969, pp. 45–6.
[34] Nolte, *Bürgerkrieg*, pp. 501–2.
[35] Nolte, *Bürgerkrieg*, pp. 511–13.
[36] Nolte, *Bürgerkrieg*, p. 513, and see Kulka, 'Singularity and its Relativization'.

the genocide, that the Jews in certain ways were responsible for their own fate, is the most appalling of the implications of Nolte's 'revision', and the one which, not surprisingly, has caused greatest offence. That the inference is a deliberate one, and not merely a linguistic lapse or misunderstanding, is plain from a number of other extraordinary passages of Nolte's writings. Such an inference is visible not least in the astonishing suggestion that blame for their wartime treatment attached to the Jews themselves, on the grounds that Chaim Weizmann's declaration at the Zionist World Congress of 1939 that Jews would fight on the side of Britain in the war justified their internment by the Germans as prisoners-of-war.[37] Nolte also makes use, in the same context, of an anti-German pamphlet published in 1940 by an obscure American Jewish writer, Theodore Kaufman, which Goebbels made great play of at the time.[38] He refers, too, to the 'far more passionate appeal' than that of Weizmann by a 'gathering of prominent Soviet Jews' in August 1941 to the Jews of all the world to support the justified struggle of the Soviet Union and its allies.[39] Finally, he also cites – completely out of context, since it appeared in a pacifist article – a satirical remark of Tucholsky (himself, of course, also Jewish) on a future gas war and the fate of the Germans. The origins of the distortion of the Tucholsky denunciation of future wars lie in the neo-Nazi Holocaust denial literature, from which, in this instance, Nolte does nothing to distance himself.[40]

The insinuation of Nolte's writing is not merely that the Jews themselves provoked Nazi 'retaliation', but that the victims of Nazi genocide have ultimately triumphed by constructing the negative myth which holds present-day Germany in thrall. Though Nolte does explicitly state in one place that 'he who takes Hitler seriously can not deny the extermination actions of Auschwitz and Treblinka and also the gas chambers',[41] he notes that a high proportion of the Holocaust literature stems from Jewish authors and, as in the Tucholsky instance just cited, is prepared on a number of occasions to take seriously the radical Right Holocaust denial literature and to flirt with the possibility that there may be something in it.[42] He remarks, for example, in comment on this literature – which, he emphasizes, is by no means merely a product of Germans and neo-fascists – that even if in view of such arguments one were to withhold judgement [!], 'there remains the fact of the death of many hundreds of thousands, and the further fact that a notably large proportion of these dead were Jews'.[43] His 'experimental' example of the way historical myth is built up is that of an imaginary destruction of the Zionist state of Israel by the Palestine Liberation Organization and the corresponding establishment of a new 'official' state-supportive, wholly distorting anti-Zionist history.[44] The implication, once more, is that the

[37] *'Historikerstreit'*, pp. 24–5; Koch, *Aspects*, pp. 27–8.
[38] See Kulka, 'Singularity and its Relativization', esp. note 10.
[39] See Kulka, 'Singularity and its Relativization', and Nolte, *Bürgerkrieg*, p. 509.
[40] See Kulka, 'Singularity and its Relativization', esp. note 11; and Kulka's article in the *Frankfurter Rundschau* of 5 Nov. 1987 (full ref. above n.9).
[41] Nolte, *Bürgerkrieg*, p. 515.
[42] Nolte, *Bürgerkrieg*, pp. 513, 592–4 notes 26–9.
[43] Nolte, *Bürgerkrieg*, p. 513, and see Kulka, 'Singularity and its Relativization'.
[44] *'Historikerstreit'*, p. 17; Koch, *Aspects*, p. 21; and see Kulka, 'Singularity and its Relativization'.

historiography of the Third Reich has been imposed on present-day Germany by the victorious enemy – the Nazis' Jewish victims.

Had the views which are represented in Nolte's writings been expressed by exponents of the extreme Right, they would scarcely have been noticed. That they were advanced by one of Germany's leading historians – thereby giving solace and sustenance to the neo-Nazi Right – meant that they could not be ignored.

It is in the context, described above, of Nolte's approach to the causation of the Holocaust, that his reduction of it to a secondary product of Bolshevik genocide has also provoked such vehement reactions and widespread rejection. While there can be no *a priori* denial of the validity of comparing forms of genocide, Nolte's hypothesis has seemed to many to attempt a 'relativization' of Nazi atrocities by shifting the focus to the common evils of illiberal twentieth-century regimes, and the evils of Soviet Communism in particular.[45] The extension of guilt for genocide and reduction of the singularity of the Holocaust largely to techniques of gassing has been perceived as an attempt to water down the crimes of the Nazis and exculpate the Germans. There may be an element of over-reaction in this, for, in a number of places, Nolte explicitly accepts the singularity of the 'Final Solution', though remaining adamant that it was not original, but a copy: 'As in tendency the complete annihilation of a world people (*Welt-Volk*), it [the 'Final Solution'] differs essentially from all other genocides and is the exact counter-image of the complete annihilation, in tendency, of a world class [*Welt-Klasse*] through Bolshevism, and, as such, is the biologically recoined copy of the social original.'[46]

Supporters of Nolte disingenuously claimed that a 'ban on questions' was restricting important and original new interpretations, particularly on discussion of the comparable crimes of the Bolsheviks.[47] Surprise was registered not that the peculiarity of Nazi crimes had been questioned, but 'that this has in serious fashion previously not happened' claiming that thereby 'the millions of dead of this century' – apart that is from the victims of the Nazis – 'have dropped from the memory of the world'.[48] In reality, of course, there is a vast literature on the Stalinist terror, while Leo Kuper's excellent comparative analysis of genocide – which covers known cases in the twentieth century including the Armenians, Nazism, Stalinism, and Pol Pot among many other examples – has a bibliography running to 15 pages.[49]

As Kuper's book amply demonstrates, a comparative study of genocide is not only valid, but is necessary in order to bring out the specific features of any single case. Only comparative method enables such a clear definition of the uniqueness of the Nazi murder of the Jews as that stated by Eberhard Jäckel at an early stage in the '*Historikerstreit*': 'never before had a state with the authority of its responsible leader determined and proclaimed its

---

45 See Jürgen Kocka, 'Hitler sollte nicht durch Stalin und Pol Pot verdrängt werden', in '*Historikerstreit*', pp. 132–42; Heinrich August Winkler, 'Auf ewig in Hitlers Schatten?', in '*Historikerstreit*' pp. 256–63. See also Wehler, *Entsorgung*, pp. 108–10.
46 Nolte, *Bürgerkrieg*, pp. 504, 506; '*Historikerstreit*', p. 15; Koch, *Aspects*, p. 19.
47 '*Historikerstreit*', p. 89.
48 '*Historikerstreit*', p. 108.
49 Leo Kuper, *Genocide*, Harmondsworth, 1981.

intention to kill, as completely as possible, a specific group of people inclusive of the old, women, children, and babies, and to implement this decision with all the power at the state's command'.[50] There can be no objection in principle to the attempt to compare the Holocaust with other instances of genocide by modern dictatorships. Nor is anything in moral terms lost by such a comparison. The fact that other peoples have also been guilty of genocide offers neither excuse nor consolation for what the German people did to the Jews, or to the gypsies.

The rejection of Nolte's argument was not because of the comparative dimension in itself, but because the comparison contains such strongly apologetic implications. In addition, it has rightly been pointed out that the value of any comparison depends upon the cases compared, what the comparison is intended to demonstrate, and what significance is attached to the singular features which emerge.[51] A crude comparison of genocide and crimes against humanity carried out in societies with wholly different political and social structures, economic systems, and levels of cultural advancement can only lead, based on such incongruous data, to simplistic and misleading conclusions. At best this will result in a revamped 'totalitarianism' theory, the weaknesses of which we considered in chapter 2. At worst, it will lead to a watering down of the responsibility for Nazi crimes through the extension of genocide to twentieth-century illiberalism in all its manifestations – the conclusion which has been drawn from Nolte's approach.

It was necessary to combat in the most forceful fashion the 'revisionist' interpretation of the causes and comparability of the 'Final Solution' offered by such an eminent historian as Nolte, even if the massive attention paid to his work has not been rewarded by scholarly advances and intellectual gain. But to regard Nolte as the vanguard of a conservative 'revisionist' assault which also embraces Hillgruber and Stürmer is a dubious proposition. Nolte has always been something of an individualistic outsider in German historical circles. And his approach has little in common with that of the other two leading figures in the '*Historikerstreit*', which, in reality, has been more of a 'Nolte affair', a 'Hillgruber affair', and a 'Stürmer affair' than a unitary dispute. It is time now to consider, rather more briefly than in the case of Nolte, the controversial assertions of the other two 'revisionists'.

The case of Hillgruber, which Habermas seized upon, is very different from that of Nolte. Though Hillgruber has never made any secret of his political conservatism, his historical work, before the '*Historikerstreit*', always stood in the mainstream of scholarship in Germany and was held in high esteem even by those who disagreed with his interpretations. And whereas Nolte's recent provocative writings follow from a distinctive path which he had been treading for many years, so that a clear pattern of development can be traced in his work,[52] the contribution of Hillgruber which has

[50] '*Historikerstreit*', p. 118.

[51] Jürgen Kocka has reiterated these points in an excellent brief summary of the '*Historikerstreit*', 'The Weight of the Past in Germany's Future'. *German Politics and Society* (Center for European Studies, Harvard University), 13 (1988), pp. 22–9, here p. 24.

[52] See Kulka, 'Singularity and its Relativization'; Wehler, *Entsorgung*, pp. 13–20; and Nolte, *Das Vergehen der Vergangenheit*, pp. 11–12.

caused such a storm appears as a type of 'rogue' article among his massive list of publications.

Controversy has centred upon Hillgruber's slim volume, entitled 'Two Forms of Downfall: The Smashing of the German Reich and the End of European Jewry'. This book, which resembles a production of separate parts thrown together on a publisher's initiative, comprised extended versions of two already published and quite disparate essays of unequal length which had begun life as lectures.[53] The second and shorter essay, 'The Historical Place of the Extermination of the Jews', had originally been a keynote lecture at a major international conference in 1984 on 'The Murder of the European Jews'. It provided a balanced and judicious treatment, consonant with serious historical scholarship on the subject. It is a valuable and significant study. The first, considerably longer, essay on 'The Collapse of the East in 1944–45 as a Problem of German National History and of European History' is a different matter altogether. Couched in far more emotive language, it is a justification of the despairing struggle of the Wehrmacht against the advance of the Red Army on the grounds that escape was made possible for much of the population of the eastern territories, that the 'threatening orgy of revenge'[54] against the civilian population of the Reich was thereby prevented, and that the whole of central Europe did not fall into Soviet hands. As we saw in the previous chapter, in Hillgruber's view empathy with the German troops is the only position tenable to the historian[55] – even in recognition of the fact that as long as the borders of the Reich were defended, the gas chambers could continue to function.

Here, then, we have one link between the 'smashing' of the Reich and the 'end' of Jewry, uneven terms whose juxtaposition in the book's title has itself been strongly criticized. Hillgruber's introduction to the volume and the dustjacket blurb – appearing presumably with his approval – outline the connection which the book is seeking to establish between the 'two kinds of downfall'. Hillgruber sees them as interlinked 'catastrophes', amounting cumulatively to a catastrophe for the whole of Europe.[56] While the extermination of the Jews can be put down to the radical racism of Hitler's Germany, the destruction of the Reich and the expulsion of the Germans from the eastern territories, he argues, cannot simply be seen as the consequences of Nazi barbarism, but have chiefly to be attributed to the war-aims of the Allies. Hillgruber – so the dustjacket explains – rejects the commonly-held notion that the destruction of the Reich was an answer to the ill deeds of the Nazi regime, and 'proves' that the 'amputation of the Reich in favour of a Greater Poland was the war aim of the Allies long before Auschwitz'. Hence, the German 'tragedy'[57] was not simply a product of Nazi expansionist policy, but also of the equally ruthless war plans of the Allies. Britain looked to destroy Prussian militarism once and for all; the Soviet

[53] Andreas Hillgruber, 'Der Zusammenbruch im Osten 1944–45 als Problem der deutschen Nationalgeschichte und der europäischen Geschichte', in his *Zweierlei Untergang. Die Zerschlagung des Deutschen Reiches und das Ende des europäischen Judentums*, Berlin, 1986.
[54] Hillgruber, 'Zusammenbruch im Osten', p. 21.
[55] Hillgruber, 'Zusammenbruch im Osten', pp. 24–5.
[56] Hillgruber, 'Zusammenbruch im Osten', pp. 9–10.
[57] Hillgruber, 'Zusammenbruch im Osten', p. 64.

Union was anxious to extend its own territorial hold in central Europe; the United States, along with Britain, and 'in complete departure from their humanitarian traditions',[58] were willing to go along with the uprooting and expulsion of entire peoples of central Europe and the permanent loss of the German eastern territories. Hillgruber concludes that the smashing of the Reich through short-sighted Allied policy amounted to a defeat for the whole of Europe, making central Europe a terrain of conflict between the super-powers, and leaving open the question of whether 'the history of the Germans as that of the nation formed by the foundation of the Reich is dying out or still has a future'.[59]

The thrust of this interpretation has encountered widespread – and out-side Germany almost universal – rejection. We have referred already in the previous chapter to the fatal flaws in Hillgruber's method of empathetic identification with the German troops. No rules of historical research or method indicate the need for such an identification. In fact, everything speaks against it.[60] Moreover, in practice his empathy does not entail a careful examination of the perspective of the troops, but rather provides a vehicle for the transmission of his personal opinion, backed by some selec-tive pieces of evidence.[61] The most charitable reading would suggest that the emotion of the native East Prussian has in this instance triumphed over the cool and rational assessment of the professional historian. Whatever the motivation, which, as in the case of Nolte, cannot be elicited with any certainty, the result is – in contrast to his accompanying essay on the 'Final Solution' – a poor and objectively apologetic piece of historical writing.

Hillgruber's interpretation in the essay on the eastern front has been inca-pable of withstanding the withering criticism to which it has been sub-jected.[62] The infelicitous empathetical method was itself grounded in the subjective belief that the fight to save the eastern parts of the Reich (and with them the whole of central Europe) from being overrun by the 'Red Army', was worth any sacrifice – and even the continued operation of the death camps. The distorted perspective, which has been criticized for its 'undocumented speculations and astonishing simplifications of the international political situation before and during World War II',[63] amounts to shifting the responsibility from Germany to the war plans, aiming at the destruction of Germany's control of central Europe, of the Soviet Union and also Britain. The proximity of Hillgruber's language to that of Nazi propa-ganda has frequently been pointed out,[64] as has the sharp difference from the cooler, more dispassionate tone of his analysis of the 'Final Solution'.

It has pained many to see Hillgruber, whose earlier solid writing on diplo-matic history continues to be held in high regard, attacked so vehemently. However, it has to be said that, even if the claim that anyone holding the

[58] Hillgruber, 'Zusammenbruch im Osten', p. 67.
[59] Hillgruber, 'Zusammenbruch im Osten', pp. 72–4.
[60] See Wehler, *Entsorgung*, pp. 46ff (esp. pp. 53–8) and pp. 154ff.
[61] See Omer Bartov, 'Historians on the Eastern Front. Andreas Hillgruber and Germany's Tragedy' *Tel Aviver Jahrubuch für deutsche Geschichte*, 16(1987), pp. 336–7.
[62] For the weakness of Hillgruber's retort to his critics, see Wehler, *Entsorgung*, pp. 154ff.
[63] Bartov, 'Historians on the Eastern Front', p. 333.
[64] Bartov, 'Historians on the Eastern Front'. pp. 327, 331, 336, 338–43.

views expressed on the dustjacket of his book deserves to be labelled a 'constitutional Nazi'[65] can be regarded as an intemperate and unworthy attack, Hillgruber's essay on the eastern front, insensitive in tone and apologetic in implication, fully warranted the sharp criticism which it provoked.

The third strand in the neo-conservative 'revision' which Habermas depicted is formed by the writings of Michael Stürmer. These differ from those of Nolte and Hillgruber in that they are not directly concerned with the Third Reich at all.[66] Nor, for that matter, are they concerned with the reinterpretation of precise events in the past. Rather, Stürmer, whose early work on Imperial Germany had, from a 'critical history' standpoint, exposed Bismarck's failures in his attempt 'to deploy the national question as a means of upholding the internal status quo',[67] has, by way of a remarkable metamorphosis, come to see himself as the spearhead of a revised approach to the past aimed at revitalizing a weakened sense of national identity in order to head off an otherwise looming disintegration of a divided society.

Stürmer speaks of Germany as a 'land without memory', a type of historical no-man's land in which 'everything is possible'. And in the 'search for the lost memory',[68] it is the historian's task to provide that positive sense of the past which is allegedly so lacking in Germany, adding in almost Orwellian tones that 'in a land without history, he wins the future who provides the memory, forms the concepts, and interprets the past'.[69] Citing Helmut Schmidt's dictum that no people can exist in the long run without a historical identity,[70] he sees the need for the historian to create that meaning from the past (*Sinnstiftung*) which will consolidate the present and ensure the future through building the national identity which had fallen apart through the pronounced 'cultural dissonances'[71] resounding since the 1960s in a society self-destructively preoccupied with its own guilt and with a past overshadowed by the ill deeds of the Nazi era. Pluralism of values and interests

---

65 Implied by Rudolf Augstein, 'Die neue Auschwitz-Lüge', in '*Historikerstreit*', pp. 196–203, here p. 198. See also Wehler, *Entsorgung*, p. 68.

66 For his recent writings, see esp. Michael Stürmer, *Das ruhelose Reich. Deutschland 1866–1918*, Berlin, 1983; 'Kein Eigentum der Deutschen: die deutsche Frage', in Werner Weidenfeld (ed.), *Die Identität der Deutschen*, Munich/Vienna, 1983, pp. 83–101; *Dissonanzen des Fortschritts. Essays über Geschichte und Politik in Deutschland*, Munich, 1986; 'Geschichte in geschichtslosem Land', in '*Historikerstreit*', pp. 36–9; 'Was Geschichte wiegt', in '*Historikerstreit*', pp. 293–5; 'Weder verdrängen noch bewältigen: Geschichte und Gegenwartsbewußtsein der Deutschen' *Schweizer Monatshefte*, 66 (1986), pp. 689–94; 'Suche nach der verlorenen Erinnerung', in *Das Parlament*, 36 (1986), nr.20/21, 17–24 May 1986. On Stürmer's metamorphosis from former adherent of the 'critical history' school to publicist of German conservatism, see Volker R. Berghahn, 'Geschichtswissenschaft und Große Politik', *Aus Politik und Zeitgeschichte*, B11/87, 14 Mar. 1987, pp. 25–37; Hans-Jürgen Puhle, 'Die neue Ruhelosigkeit: Michael Stürmers nationalpolitischer Revisionismus', *Geschichte und Gesellschaft*, 13 (1987), pp. 382–99; and Wehler, *Entsorgung*, pp. 28–36.

67 Berghahn, 'Geschichtswissenschaft und Große Politik', p. 35.

68 In *Das Parlament*, 17–24 May 1986.

69 '*Historikerstreit*', p. 36. In George Orwell's vision of the future, Winston Smith is forced to repeat the Party slogan: 'Who controls the past controls the future: who controls the present controls the past'. – George Orwell, *Nineteen Eighty-Four*, Harmondsworth 1954 (1975), p. 199.

70 '*Historikerstreit*', p. 295.

71 '*Historikerstreit*', p. 294.

without common ground, he comments darkly, unless defused through growth, leads sooner or later to 'social civil war' as at the end of the Weimar Republic.[72] The historian's role is not, therefore, one of abstract educational aspirations. It is 'morally legitimate and politically necessary', both with regard to the 'inner continuity of the German Republic and its foreign policy reliability'.[73]

Stürmer singles out Braudel's book on 'the identity of France', and its author's passionate avowal of uncritical patriotism as something to which, because of their chequered history, Germans cannot aspire.[74] Braudel is for Stürmer doubly significant, both because of his historical approach to French identity and because his work concerns itself with the question of the geographical determinants of France's development as a nation-state. Stürmer sees geography as no less significant in the case of Germany.

As his key factor in the search for a German identity, Stürmer turns to Germany's fateful 'middle position' in Europe. The 'restlessness' of the German Reich[75] could, in this view, be put down in good measure to the geopolitically determined necessity of protecting its legitimate interests at the centre of the European states system, causing, therefore, an inevitable embroilment in major international conflict. It was, in other words, Germany's fate – its 'temptation' but also its 'curse' – to suffer through the political consequences of its geographical location.[76]

Moreover, apart from the fate of geography offering an explanation for the actions of the past, the dangers of the central European role have a present-day relevance. The influence of the Greens, confrontations about the stationing of nuclear weapons on German soil, and the calling into question of the basis of West Germany's role in Nato are plainly matters of deep concern to Stürmer. He sees the legacy of Adenauer – the overcoming of the 'German special path of the moral and political separation from the West' by the construction of the Federal Republic as the 'cornerstone of the European defence arch of the Atlantic system'[77] – threatened, as ecological and pacifist concerns are allegedly in danger of encouraging forgetfulness of the gulf between democracy and dictatorship and promoting neutralist notions of 'middle Europe'.[78]

What Stürmer is seeking, then, is a positive identification with the German past – an identification with national history blocked above all by the shadow of the Third Reich. And in this aim he has friends in high places. The late Bavarian premier Franz Josef Strauß (to whose *Festschrift* Stürmer was a contributor) publically deployed 'Stürmer-esque' ideas in exhorting Germans to come out of 'the shadows of the Third Reich' and be proud to be Germans again.[79] The 'national question', concludes Stürmer rather

[72] 'Kein Eigentum der Deutschen', in Weidenfeld (ed.), *Die Identität der Deutschen*, p. 84.
[73] In *Das Parlament*, 17–24 May 1986.
[74] '*Historikerstreit*', p. 294; and see 'Kein Eigentum der Deutschen' p. 86.
[75] 'The Restless Empire' (*Das ruhelose Reich*) is the title of Stürmer's recent book (see above, note 66).
[76] See Wehler, *Entsorgung*, pp. 33–4, 76–8.
[77] '*Historikerstreit*', pp. 37–8.
[78] '*Historikerstreit*', p. 294; and see 'Kein Eigentum der Deutschen', p. 99.
[79] James M. Markham, 'Whither Strauss – Bavaria or Bonn? Premier Campaigns for "Emergence From Third Reich" ', *International Herald Tribune*, 15 Jan. 1987.

cryptically, is still a live issue: 'in the reality of a divided Germany, the Germans must find their identity, which can no longer be founded in a nation state, but also not without the nation'.[80]

The implicit apologia which can be read into the vague claim that the German Reich's fate was determined by its geographical *'Mittellage'* (central location) in Europe has been unable to avoid association with other attempts to remould attitudes towards the recent past.[81] It was Stürmer's insistence upon a pivotal function for the historian in the historical remoulding job which gave him the position of a catalyst, in Habermas's article, in uniting the disparate 'neo-conservative' positions in the *'Historikerstreit'* by appearing to offer a programme linking the historical revision with the task of political education.[82] Doubtless, the relatively high political profile of Stürmer (which he actively sought), was no small contributory factor to the massive attention which it was felt necessary to devote to his nebulous writings.

As with Nolte and Hillgruber, however, the credibility of Stürmer's position has in intellectual terms been severely undermined by his critics. He has scarcely even attempted to provide adequate replies to fundamental points of criticism about the weakness of his *'Mittellage'* argument, which is much closer to the 'geopolitical' arguments of the interwar era than he would care to admit and which elevates Germany's geographical position in central Europe to a historical determinant of such force that other factors inevitably fall into its shadows.[83] The objections to Stürmer's arguments lead, it has been said, to the rapid recognition, 'that the geopolitical interpretation at best possesses a fatally amputated power of explanation. "Fate" it is certainly not, even if a supranatural providence has to be brought into play. The plasticity and multi-dimensional character of historical processes, the capability of action on the part of individual's and groups, politicians, and military leaders, noble families and parties is grandiosly underestimated by this poverty-stricken dogma.'[84]

Stürmer has no one but himself to blame that his plethora of somewhat pompous programmatic statements about the task of the historian in supplying the meaning of the missing past to help shape the nation's identity has drawn such savage criticism. It is not at all surprising that in Germany above all sharp antennae are alert to any hints of an attack on pluralistic interpretations of the past. But in the heat of the polemics – and the internal antagonisms of the German historical profession are such that the fires are constantly being restoked – the danger which Stürmer appears to represent has arguably been greatly exaggerated. There are no signs that the existing

80 'Kein Eigentum der Deutschen', p. 98.
81 See Wehler, *Entsorgung*, pp. 69ff, 138ff, 174ff; Kocka, in *'Historikerstreit'*, pp. 138–41; Hans Mommsen, in *'Historikerstreit'*, pp. 156–73; Broszat, in *'Historikerstreit'*, pp. 193–4.
82 See e.g. Stürmer, 'Kein Eigentum der Deutschen', esp. pp. 84, 86, 99 and in *'Historikerstreit'*, pp. 36, 38, 293, 295; Jürgen Habermas, 'Eine Art Schadensabwicklung', in *'Historikerstreit'*, pp. 62–76, here esp. pp. 62–3, 73, 75; Wolfgang Mommsen, 'Weder Leugnen noch Vergessen befreit von der Vergangenheit. Die Harmonisierung des Geschichtsbildes gefährdet die Freiheit', in *'Historikerstreit'*, pp. 300–21.
83 See Wehler, *Entsorgung*, pp. 138, 177–9.
84 Wehler, *Entsorgung*, p. 183.

pluralism of interpretations of the past is in the slightest way likely to succumb to vague expectations of a unified search for the 'lost memory', whether in historical writing or even in the planned national museums, however justified is the scepticism and reserve which has been shown towards these projects by some of Germany's leading historians.[85] And certainly, in so far as there is any substantive component at all in Stürmer's revision, it seems unlikely that the somewhat hackneyed concept of the 'middle position' is the one to stir the imagination and provide 'meaning' to past and future.

## Reflections

It was necessary to combat the unattractive alternative perspectives of the Nazi era which the 'revisionists', in quite different ways, advanced, not so much because they posed a genuine challenge to scholarship, but because of their moral and political implications. It was in this sense that the '*Historikerstreit*' took on such significance, and why it raised such high emotions. The three dimensions of the dispute have seemed to raise common issues, but in some ways have remained separate. In the case of Nolte, controversy has centred upon the causes and comparability of the Holocaust. Outside Germany, Nolte's 'revision' has not unnaturally stirred up especially strong feelings in the Jewish community, where less attention has been paid to Hillgruber and very little to Stürmer. In Hillgruber's case, the Holocaust has figured only indirectly, not least since the contentious book in question contains an unobjectionable essay directly on the 'Final Solution'. Here, the question of the present-day identification with the former territories in the eastern part of the German Reich dominates, together with the issue of the justification of Germany's war effort. Finally, in the case of Stürmer the '*Historikerstreit*' becomes almost solely an internal West German affair, since there is here little or no content of specific historical debate but merely a somewhat vacuous dispute about the nature of Germany's historical national identity.

The '*Historikerstreit*', in so far as there is a common theme to it, has been in essence a political discourse – conducted through the medium of an interchange among leading historians – about the way the society of the highly developed, prosperous, and stable Federal Republic can cope with living with its Nazi past. This is an unending debate in which the expertise of historians offers no great advantage or special privilege. Rather the discourse is shaped to a considerable extent by divided political leanings, subjective moral judgement, and deep emotion. It is about the current and future sense of identity of the society of the Federal Republic, and the type of historical consciousness which is most appropriate to shaping that identity. Since the Third Reich, and everything which the name 'Auschwitz' symbolizes, lies like a great shadow across any attempt on the part of West Germans to develop any 'normal' or 'positive' sense of identity with their past, it was perhaps inevitable that at some point there would be a major debate about what forms of historical consciousness the Federal Republic would choose.

[85] See Hans Mommsen's comments in '*Historikerstreit*', pp. 169–73, and Broszat, *Nach Hitler*, pp. 304–9.

In itself, such a debate – if not very fruitful – is not unhealthy. The fact that such a painful period of recent history is able to be so thoroughly and openly discussed can be seen in a positive light. It certainly compares favourably with the absence of any genuine soul-searching about the Nazi past in the case of Austria, while the strait-jacket of marxism-leninism has prevented open debate in the German Democratic Republic. And we have already argued in the previous chapter that with the growing passage of time, new perspectives on the location of National Socialism in German history and assessments of its significance in the context of longitudinal social developments which preceded and postdate it, are justifiable as long as the specific nature of the Third Reich is not lost or ignored in the attempt. If undertaken with due sensitivity, this type of approach has the potential to offer new perspectives which will deepen and enrich a sense of historical consciousness. The problem with the 'neo-conservative' challenge offered in the '*Historikerstreit*' is that it lacked any such sensitivity. Taken cumulatively as well as individually, it could only be seen as an apologia.

Even if the neo-conservative challenge has been defeated on intellectual terms, the question still remains as to whether politically the need for a new form of historical consciousness and national identity, as advocated by the 'revisionists', exists in reality, and what, if any, the historian's role in the creation of such a consciousness might be. These questions are not matters of historical research and interpretation, but of present-day political judgement. Opinions will inevitably vary in accordance with ideological, moral and political standpoints.

It might be conceded that some form of positive identification of citizens with their state is the basis of political viability and stability. But there seem no grounds to doubt that the overwhelming majority of the population of the Federal Republic shares such a positive identification with the West German state.[86] The various forms of sub-identity – with religion or region, for instance – which exist there as elsewhere show no signs of incompatibility with loyalty towards the West German state and its institutions. A crisis of identity does not, on the face of it, exist. Nor have the deep splits which have arisen in recent years, particularly over nuclear and environmental issues, come near to a fatal undermining of the legitimacy of the political system.[87] The Federal Republic certainly does not give the impression that it is a state with a fragile base of stability which can only be shored up by the inoculation of a revised sense of the past.

How far a sense of political identity has to be rooted in a historical consciousness is, in any case, debatable, and is hardly a question which historians can answer. Arguably, a historical consciousness which transcends

---

[86] See Wehler, *Entsorgung*, pp. 171–4; and Evans, 'The New Nationalism and the Old History', pp. 796–7.

[87] To speak of 'the creeping legitimacy crisis of the parliamentary system' (Hans Mommsen, 'Aufarbeitung und Verdrängung. Das Dritte Reich im westdeutschen Geschichtsbewußtsein', in Dan Diner (ed.), *Ist der Nationalsozialismus Geschichte? Zu Historisierung und Historikerstreit*, Frankfurt am Main, 1987, pp. 74–88, here p. 82) seems to me exaggerated. See the balanced comments on the stability of the Federal Republic of Kocka, 'Weight of the Past', p. 27. His concluding comment is a pertinent reply to Stürmer: 'Those who feel alarmed by the ambiguities, the heterogeneity, and the lack of national uniformity in present-day Germany may be wrong; they should re-examine the standards by which they measure'.

banal, crude, and often quite mistaken generalization, scarcely exists, except at the level of a small sector of the 'intelligentsia', even in societies whose stability and sense of identity is never called into question. And even if a 'positive' or 'constructive' sense of a society's history is a necessary part of identity, it is far from obvious that this should be rooted in the power politics of a nation state. 'Germany', during the overwhelming proportion of its history, has been a politically divided entity. Why the identity which is to be stimulated has to be derived from that of the disastrous but mercifully short-lived German Reich is by no means clear. In any case, the 'state sup-portive' historian, who sees it as his task to create such an identity where none exists, is wholly dispensable. Such a task has nothing to do with the critical demands of historical scholarship. Pluralist forms of historical con-sciousness are not merely inevitable in any genuinely pluralist society but, as long as they remain historically legitimate and not purely mythological inter-pretations, are politically healthy. Far from an obsession with the guilt of the Nazi past providing a handicap for the Federal Republic, for which there is little evidence, the open approach to the recent past, especially in the past 15 or 20 years, has arguably been a source of strength. Avoiding idealistic or rosy-coloured evaluations, the Federal Republic could be said, even in com-parison with other European countries, to represent some values which, from a humanistic perspective, one could be proud of, and which derive in no small measure from a reaction to the experience of National Socialism. The relative absence of chauvinistic nationalism is only one of these attri-butes. 'The legacy of the Third Reich and its crimes for present-day Ger-many', it has rightly been said, 'has been far from wholly negative.'[88]

That the '*Historikerstreit*' came about when it did can probably be put down to a number of conjunctural factors. The reconsideration of the Nazi past in the context of the fortieth anniversary of the end of the war (and of the Hitler regime), the distasteful circumstances of 'Bitburg',[89] a number of indelicate and provocative formulations by leading West German politicians about the need for a less cowed attitude to the recent past,[90] the extent to which the Third Reich was in the news, also with relation to events outside Germany such as the Waldheim affair, all provided the setting. The staging of the prestigious Frankfurt '*Römerberggespräche*' - an annual series of debates on important cultural issues - on the theme of the historical responses to the Nazi past - and thereby opening up deep bitterness which had long been brewing within the historical profession - added to the cli-mate in which only Nolte's original article and Habermas's broadside in reply were needed to set the light to the fuse.[91] These conjunctural circum-

[88] Evans, 'The New Nationalism and the Old History', p. 796.

[89] See Geoffrey Hartman (ed.) *Bitburg in Moral and Political Perspective*, Bloomington, 1986; Hans Mommsen, in '*Historikerstreit*', p. 163; Winkler, in '*Historikerstreit*', pp. 256ff; and Geoff Eley's forthcoming article (in *Past and Present*), 'Nazism Politics, and Public Memory', which comments extensively on the political context.

[90] See Hans Mommsen, 'Aufarbeitung und Verdrängung', pp. 83-4, 87; Winkler, in '*Historikerstreit*', pp. 257-9; Robert Leicht, 'Nur das Hinsehen macht uns frei', in '*Historikerstreit*', pp. 361-6, here p. 362. Evans, 'The New Nationalism and the Old History', pp. 787-8; Eley, 'Nazism, Politics, and the Public Memory' (forthcoming).

[91] See Hilmar Hoffmann, *Kultur in der Bundesrepublik aus Anlaß der Frankfurter Römerberggespräche 1986*, Frankfurt am Main, 1987.

stances arose within the context of a cumulative challenge in West Germany (dubbed there the '*Tendenzwende*') to the dominant political, social, and historical values of the previous couple of decades, the growing preoccupation with historical themes – a trend also visible in the German Democratic Republic – as witnessed by the Staufen, Prussian, and Frederick the Great exhibitions, and the latent sense of irritation caused by the place of the Third Reich within this historical tradition. Taken together, the timing of the '*Historikerstreit*' can largely be explained by these circumstances. But such a dispute was probably inevitable and long overdue.

From an outside perspective, the '*Historikerstreit*' has often seemed an inbred and introverted debate.[92] Nevertheless, it is on balance good that it has taken place. It has cleared the air to some extent. And, above all, it has demonstrated the political as well as historical alertness which has combated and triumphed over the variants of neo-conservative revisionism. But it is time to move on. Continued expenditure of time and energy on pursuing the themes of the '*Historikerstreit*' is unlikely to be productive. The conflict seems destined to rumble on for some considerable time yet, but will probably shed more heat than light. New scholarly inslights seems unlikely. A return from the heady excitement of political polemics to the less glamourous but more productive realms of historical scholarship seems desirable.

At least, however, the way might now be cleared for less tendentious and more rewarding new ways of looking at the recent German past. The previous chapter suggested what some of these might look like. Political and ideological divides, so bitter in the '*Historikerstreit*' and inevitable in assessing the historical significance of the Third Reich, ensure – quite apart from differences in historical philosophy and method, problems of sources, difficulties of definition, and scholarly temperament – that the search for a general interpretation will continue to stir up heated controversy. In any case, the divisions in tackling the 'big' questions of interpretation of Nazism, as we have seen, frequently have long roots stretching back to the writings of the earliest analysts of the phenomenon in the 1920s and 1930s. At the same time, the earlier chapters of this book have suggested that substantial levels of synthesis are possible, and that the scholarly divides are not always the enormous gaping chasms that historians themselves often claim them to be.

Compared with the 1950s, for example, there is a widespread (if nowhere near unanimous) acceptance of the limitations and deficiencies of the totalitarianism concept and – whatever the problems of definition and usage – of the need for a generic 'ideal type' concept of fascism (though there are signs in the current political climate of a reversal of this interpretational advance). Regarding the Nazi economy, too, there has been growing recognition, predicated on a deepened research base, of the crudeness of the old alternatives of 'primacy' of politics or economics, and of the extent to which economic, ideological and strategic power-political considerations were fused almost indivisibly in the policies of the Nazi regime. Nor, in the controversy, which has dominated in recent years, about the position and role of Hitler and 'who determined the policy of the Third Reich', do extensive areas of agreement seem out of reach if the almost artificially hardened extreme positions are somewhat modified. This applies not least to the central and highly sensitive issue of the extermination of the Jews, where, thanks to the depth of research and the openness of scholarly debate in the past two decades, far less is open to dispute than sometimes appears to be the case – as, for example, in the controversies stirred up by well publicized but essentially 'maverick' works such as that of David Irving.[93] Finally, there has been a growing readiness among historians to reject the notion of a 'social revolution' as applied to Nazism, while accepting that in certain ways the Third Reich did objectively further the modernization of social and economic structures and, above all, through the circumstances of its total defeat, opened up the potential for a new and more firmly established democratic state and society than had been possible under the Weimar Republic.

This relates to a debate in German historiography which has been implicitly present in the earlier chapters of this book, but which has not been treated explicitly as a separate problem: the location of Nazism in the continuities of German history. While at the time of the Fischer controversy in the early 1960s this was a bitterly contentious issue, the heat has by now largely died down.[94] Few historians would now deny that Nazism arose from – and indeed temporarily bound together – a number of pronounced structural continuities in German society and politics linking Bismarck's and the Kaiser's Reich with Hitler's; or that, despite certain unmistakable chains of continuity stretching across the 1945 divide, these structures were irredeemably shattered in the Third Reich's own nemesis.

In the nature of things, wider problems of research on the Third Reich will rightly and necessarily continue to pose 'open questions' for historians, and to provoke valuable and stimulating differences of perspective and interpretation as well as the less endearing and less productive positions and polemics adopted in the '*Historikerstreit*'.[95] But the basis seems laid for full-scale works of synthesis aiming at embracing, but not artificially harmonizing, the disparate strands of research findings in a broad framework of enquiry.[96] One central focus of such a synthesis ought to be a

---

[93] See ch.5 note 8.

[94] There is still, however, vigorous disagreement over the precise nature and location of the 'continuity', and also about whether earlier periods of German history can be regarded as in some way 'flawed' – as anticipating and building up problems which had their denouement in the Third Reich. See the literature referred to in ch.2 notes 2 and 60–1, ch.6 note 26, and also Thomas Nipperdey, '1933 und Kontinuität der deutschen Geschichte', *Historische Zeitschrift*, 227 (1978), pp. 86–111 (Engl. version, '1933 and the Continuity of German History' in Koch, Aspects, pp. 489–508) and Ian Kershaw, '1933: Continuity or Break in German History?', *History Today*, Jan. 1983, pp. 13–18. Roger Fletcher puts Fritz Fischer's work in an historiographical context in the introduction to the English translation of Fischers's *Bündnis der Eliten*, Düsseldorf, 1979 (*From Kaiserreich to Third Reich. Elements of Continuity in German History, 1871–1945*, London, 1986).

[95] See 'Podiumsdiskussion: Offene Fragen in der Erforschung des Nationalsozialismus', *Bericht über die 33ste Versammlung Deutscher Historiker in Würzburg, 25–30. März 1980 (Beiheft zur GWU, 1982)*, pp. 159–71; and Tim Mason, 'Open Questions on Nazism', in Raphael Samuel (ed.), *People's History and Socialist Theory*, London, 1981, pp. 205–10.

[96] Two new attempts at broad synthesis are: Hans-Ulrich Thamer, *Verführung und Gewalt. Deutschland 1933–1945*, Berlin, 1986, which is, however, stronger on political and ideological than social developments; and Norbert Frei, *Der Führerstaat. Nationalsozialistische Herrschaft*

systematic analysis, building upon Max Weber's theoretical conceptualization, of the growth, character, and function of charismatic leadership, the conditions of its emergence, and its pivotal role in the government and society of the Third Reich – the latter a consideration, indeed, which is visible in most of the chapters of this book.[97] The nature of Hitler's charismatic leadership and rule could profitably by embedded in another construct drawn from sociological writing – 'the pathology of modern civilization' – in an attempt to grasp the social and political conditions in which anti-humanitarian and anti-emancipatory impulses, present in many forms and processes of modern industrial class society, can gain wide – and murderous – popularity.[98]   'Auschwitz' – as   shorthand   for   Nazi barbarism – would not amount to the whole story. But it would lie inevitably at its centre. For any new synthesis would have to find ways – which in the previous chapter I suggested were possible – of tackling what amounts to a key issue: the relationship of 'normality' and genocide. The methods of a political structural history and the new social history would have to be reconciled in order to bring together in analytical explanation legitimately varying perspectives focusing on the 'banality of evil' as located in everyday 'normality' and the singular motive force of Nazi ideology seen as a highly abnormal 'political religion'.[99]

Finally, the growth and consequences of charismatic rule, incorporated in an analysis of the anti-humanitarian forces of modern society which made Nazi barbarism possible, would only gain their proper perspective through the hard school of comparative method. It is surprising how little rigorous, genuinely comparative analysis of Nazi Germany and Fascist Italy has so far been undertaken.[100] Detailed comparison of charismatic rule and leadership cults in the two systems, of structures of rule, and of social conditions has hardly begun. Comparative exploration of specific social groups or of political structures and political cultures by contrasting Germany with the western democracies also remains more of a rarity than might have been imagined.[101] Yet only through the comparative perspective of analysis of political and social structures can an explanation be offered – far removed from simplistic *Sonderweg* notions of German peculiarities seen in terms of national characteristics and stereotypes – of why Germany alone of

*1933 bis 1945*, München, 1987, which offers a good, succinct survey, incorporating the advances of much recent research on society in the Third Reich.

[97] This is strongly encouraged by Hans-Ulrich Wehler, '30. Januar 1933 – Ein halbes Jahrhundert danach', *APZ* (29 Jan. 1983), pp. 43–54, here p. 50.

[98] See Peukert, *Volksgenossen* (ch.2 note 45), esp. pp. 13–17, 289–96, for stimulating ideas pointing in this direction (drawing on Foucault and Habermas).

[99] See the exchange on this point between Friedländer and Broszat in 'Briefwechsel', pp. 358, 363–5. On Nazism as a secular religion, there is now also Robert A. Pois, *National Socialism and the Religion of Nature*, London/Sydney, 1986. And I am indebted to Karl A. Schleunes for a preview of his as yet unpublished paper. 'Nazism as a Political Religion: The Continuing Search for an Interpretation of National Socialism'.

[100] Important comparative work is a least underway, and is being carried out on the regime phase in both countries by Wolfgang Schieder (Trier) and, on the working class, by Tim Mason (Rome). On Mussolini and Hitler, there is now Knox's essay, referred to in ch.2 note 51.

[101] Kocka, *Angestellte* (ch.2 note 61) set an example which has been insufficiently followed up. See now also Jürgen Kocka's recent article, 'German History before Hitler: The Debate about the German *Sonderweg*', *JCH*, 23 (1988), pp. 3–16.

advanced industrial nations adopted a fascist solution to its problems, and how the German variant of charismatic dictatorship differed in character and consequences from its Italian counterpart.

These problems, and the divides in historical interpretation examined earlier in this book, are not arcane scholarly debates about bygone times. As the *'Historikerstreit'* so plainly demonstrated, changing perspectives of research on the Nazi era have a direct relevance and importance to present-day political awareness, moral sensitivity and democratic consciousness. The past does shape the present – in very obvious ways in Germany, though not by any means always or only in negative fashion. Open, informed, and reasoned confrontation with the past helps to produce historically determined responses to present-day problems. Germany is less able than most other countries to avoid such a continuing confrontation. It is better to accept that, as a positive social and political value, the struggle of the present with the past must go on, rather than cherish the empty illusion that the time is ripe for the line to be drawn under consideration of the Nazi era, or that the Third Reich can be treated as a 'normal' period of history.

The struggle with the past must, however, be a rational, not purely emotional one. The *'Historikerstreit'* demonstrated how little Nazism can be treated simply as an 'ordinary' problem of cold historical scholarship, how strongly passionate feelings of moral denunciation are built into the continuing debate. Yet, as justified and even necessary as such feelings are, moral denunciation in the long run will not suffice and can easily become the stuff of legend and not understanding.[102] In some ways, the *'Historikerstreit'* has been rooted in this point and, from a number of radically different perspectives, there is a broad level of agreement about it.

The moral outrage at Nazism, the revulsion, and the *'nie wieder'* ('never again') determination needs to be constantly reinforced by genuine historical scholarship and understanding. This depends in turn upon the willingness and ability of specialist historians of Nazism to popularize (in the best sense) their findings without doing as injustice to their complexity. It would be easy, of course, to exaggerate the historian's influence, past or future. (Some contributors to the *'Historikerstreit'* seem to have succumbed to this over-estimation of their own importance). The limited democratic and emancipatory sensitivities in current western society are frequently revealed through widespread lack of interest in and ignorance of politics, in a fairly narrow dependence of the social and political tolerance level on material prosperity, and by common authoritarian reactions and forms of behaviour shown in inner fixations with 'law and order' and expressions of racial intolerance and discrimination against ethnic minorities, immigrants and 'guest workers' – present-day manifestations of the 'pathology' of modern

---

[102] See Broszat's pertinent comment ('Briefwechsel', p. 365): 'The danger of the suppression of this era does not in my opinion consist only of the normal forgetting, but in this case, almost paradoxically, because for didactic reasons people are too much "at pains" about this chapter of history. From the original, authentic continuum of this history, an arsenal of teaching sessions and statuesque images are pieced together, which more and more develop an existence of their own, especially then in the second and third generation come to be placed before the original history, and are finally naively misunderstood as the actual history'. See also Broszat, *Nach Hitler*, pp. 114–20.

industrial society. The recent rise of a fascist mass movement of considerable size in France provides an indication of the still existing potential, given opportune circumstances, for the overt political mobilization of these anti-democratic sentiments. Significant forces of fascism can be resurrected, therefore, at least temporarily, even in the heart of civilized western Europe. Yet popular knowledge of what fascism was really like is low. Surveys of knowledge about Hitler and Nazism among young Germans have produced disturbing results; and what 'knowledge' exists is often personalized and sensationalized through information media all too frequently pandering to macabre fascination and a taste for simplistic and superficial explanations.[103] In other countries (such as Britain) it has not been unknown for pop-groups to appear decked with Nazi insignia. And a year or two ago, holiday-makers on the Costa Brava were able to buy tee-shirts printed with a picture of Hitler or a map of his 'European Tour'. However modest his own contribution may be in counteracting the debasement of democratic and humanitarian values which make such obscenities possible, the specialist historian of Nazism has not only the task but also the duty of attempting, through the multiplier effect of publications and teaching, to describe and explain, as clearly and cogently as possible but in balanced and undogmatic fashion, the realities of fascist values, fascist politics and fascist rule. The task is important not because of any – inherently unlikely, despite the recent disturbing events in France – renewed triumph of fascism in the foreseeable future, but in the hope of strengthening the awareness that democratic, humanitarian values are not an inevitable, or necessarily lasting, property of modern industrial society, but that they must constantly and repeatedly be fought for and defended against all inroads – some quite new in form – of modern authoritarianism.

---

[103] See Freimut Duve (ed.), *5 Millionen Deutsche: 'Wir sollten wieder einen Führer haben . . .'. Die SINUS-Studie über rechtsextremistische Einstellungen bei den Deutschen*, Reinbek bei Hamburg, 1981; Peter Meyers, 'Didaktische Aspekte zur Behandlung des Nationalsozialismus in Schule und Erwachsenenbildung', in Peter Meyers and Dieter Riesenberger (ed.). *Der Nationalsozialismus in der historisch-politischen Bildung*, Göttingen, 1979, pp. 8–34, esp. p. 19; and the balanced assessment of Lutz Niethammer, 'Nach dem Dritten Reich ein neuer Faschismus? Zum Wandel der rechtsextremen Szene in der Geschichte der Bundesrepublik', in Paul Lersch (ed.), *Die verkannte Gefahr. Rechtsradikalismus in der Bundesrepublik*, Reinbek bei Hamburg, 1981, pp. 105–27, esp. pp. 121–2.

# Suggestions for Further Reading

Most of the works consulted in the writing of this book are in German, and full references are provided in the relevant footnotes. I have confined suggestions for further reading to a selection of available works in English which have a particular bearing on the debates explored above, and have attempted where possible to include recent publications.

## General Historiographical Surveys

Pierre Ayçoberry, *The Nazi Question* (London, 1981).
John Hiden and John Farquharson, *Explaining Hitler's Germany. Historians and the Third Reich* (London, 1983).
Klaus Hildebrand, *The Third Reich* (London, 1984).
(A selection of documents relating to all the aspects of Nazism dealt with above, and with an admirable commentary by Jeremy Noakes, is available in the new, greatly revised, three-volume edition of Jeremy Noakes and Geoffrey Pridham, *Nazism, 1919–1945. A Documentary Reader* (Exeter Studies in History, Exeter 1983–8).

## 1 Historians and the Problem of Explaining Nazism

Tim Mason, 'Intention and Explanation: A Current Controversy about the Interpretation of National Socialism', in Gerhard Hirschfeld and Lothar Kettenacker, eds., *Der 'Führerstaat': Mythos und Realität* (Stuttgart, 1981), pp. 23–40.
Tim Mason, 'Open Questions on Nazism', in Raphael Samuel, ed., *People's History and Socialist Theory* (London, 1981), pp. 205–10.
Jörn Rüsen, 'Theory of History in the Development of West German Historical Studies: A Reconstruction and Outlook', *German Studies Review* 7 (1984), pp. 14–18.
Hans-Ulrich Wehler, 'Historiography in Germany Today', in Jürgen Habermas, ed., *Observations on 'The Spiritual Situation of the Age'. Contemporary German Perspectives* (Cambridge, Mass./London, 1984), pp. 221–59.

## 2. The Essence of Nazism: Form of Fascism, Brand of Totalitarianism, or Unique Phenomenon?

David Beetham, *Marxists in Face of Fascism* (Manchester, 1983).
Geoff Eley, 'What produces Fascism: Preindustrial Traditions or a Crisis of

the Capitalist State?', *Politics and Society* 12 (1983), pp. 53–82.

Martin Kitchen, *Fascism* (London, 1976).

Stein Ugelvik Larsen *et al.*, *Who were the Fascists? Social Roots of European Fascism* (Bergen, 1980).

Juan J. Linz, 'Some Note towards a Comparative Study of Fascism in Sociological Historical Perspective', in Walter Laqueur, ed., *Fascism. A Reader's Guide* (Harmondsworth, 1979), pp. 13–78.

## 3. Politics and Economics in the Nazi State

Tim Mason, 'The Primacy of Politics – Politics and Economics in National Socialist Germany', in Henry A. Turner, ed., *Nazism and the Third Reich* (New York, 1972), pp. 175–200.

Alan Milward, *The German Economy at War* (London, 1965).

Alan Milward, 'Fascism and the Economy', in Walter Laqueur, ed., *Fascism. A Reader's Guide* (Harmondsworth, 1979), pp. 409–53.

Franz Neumann, *Behemoth. The Structure and Practice of National Socialism* (London, 1942).

Richard J. Overy, 'Hitler's War and the German Economy: A Reinterpretation', *Economic History Review* 35 (1982), pp. 272–91.

Alfred Sohn-Rethel, *The Economy and Class Structure of German Fascism* (London, 1987).

## 4. Hitler: 'Master in the Third Reich', or 'Weak Dictator'?

Karl Dietrich Bracher, 'The Role of Hitler: Perspectives of Interpretation', in Walter Laqueur, ed., *Fascism. A Reader's Guide* (Harmondsworth, 1979), pp. 193–212.

Martin Broszat, *The Hitler State* (London, 1981).

William Carr, *Hitler. A Study in Personality and Politics* (London, 1978).

Eberhard Jäckel, *Hitler in History* (Hanover/London, 1984).

Ian Kershaw, *The 'Hitler Myth'. Image and Reality in the Third Reich* (Oxford, 1987).

Hans Mommsen, 'National Socialism: Continuity and Change', in Walter Laqueur, ed., *Fascism. A Reader's Guide* (Harmondsworth, 1979), pp. 151–92.

Edward N. Peterson, *The Limits of Hitler's Power* (Princeton, 1969).

## 5. Hitler and the Holocaust

David Bankier, 'Hitler and the Policy-Making Process on the Jewish Question', *Holocaust and Genocide Studies* 3 (1988), pp. 1–20.

Martin Broszat, Hitler and the Genesis of the ''Final Solution'' ', *Yad Vashem Studies* 13 (1979), repr. in H. W. Koch, ed., *Aspects of the Third Reich* (London, 1985), pp. 390–429.

Christopher Browning, *Fateful Months* (New York, 1985).

Christopher Browning, 'A Reply to Martin Broszat regarding the Origins of the Final Solution', *Simon Wiesenthal Center Annual* 1 (1984), pp. 113–32.

Gerald Fleming, *Hitler and the Final Solution* (Oxford, 1986).
Gerhard Hirschfeld, ed., *The Policies of Genocide* (London, 1986).
Helmut Krausnick, 'The Persecution of the Jews', in Helmut Krausnick *et al., Anatomy of the SS State* (London, 1968), pp. 1–124.
Otto Dov Kulka, 'Major Trends and Tendencies of German Historiography on National Socialism and the "Jewish Question" (1924–1984)', *Yearbook of the Leo Baeck Institute* 30 (1985), pp. 215–42.
Karl A. Schleunes, *The Twisted Road to Auschwitz. Nazi Policy toward German Jews, 1933–1939* (Urbana/Chicago/London, 1970).

## 6. Nazi Foreign Policy: Hitler's 'Programme' or 'Expansion without Object'?

William Carr, *Arms, Autarky, and Aggression. A Study in German Foreign Policy, 1933–1939* (London, 2nd. edn., 1979).
William Carr, *Poland to Pearl Harbor. The Making of the Second World War* (London, 1985).
Milan Hauner, 'Did Hitler want a World Dominion?', *Journal of Contemporary History* 13 (1978), pp. 15–32.
Klaus Hildebrand, *The Foreign Policy of the Third Reich* (London, 1973).
Konrad H. Jarausch, 'From Second to Third Reich: The Problem of Continuity in German Foreign Policy', *Central European History* 12 (1979), pp. 68–82.
Meir Michaelis, 'World Power Status or World Dominion?', *The Historical Journal* 15 (1972), pp. 331–60.
Gerhard Weinberg, *The Foreign Policy of Hitler's Germany. Diplomatic Revolution in Europe 1933–36* (Chicago/London, 1970).
Gerhard Weinberg, *The Foreign Policy of Hitler's Germany. Starting World War II* (Chicago/London, 1980).

## 7. The Third Reich: 'Social Reaction' or 'Social Revolution'?

Richard Bessel, 'Living with the Nazis: Some Recent Writing on the Social History of the Third Reich', *European History Quarterly* 14 (1984), pp. 211–20.
Richard Bessel, ed, *Life in the Third Reich* (Oxford, 1987).
Ralf Dahrendorf, *Society and Democracy in Germany* (London, 1968).
Richard Grunberger, *A Social History of the Third Reich* (London, 1971).
Ian Kershaw, *Popular Opinion and Political Dissent in the Third Reich. Bavaria 1933–1945* (Oxford, 1983).
Jeremy Noakes, 'Nazism and Revolution', in Noel O'Sullivan, ed., *Revolutionary Theory and Political Reality* (London, 1983), pp. 73–100.
Detlev Peukert, *Inside Nazi Germany. Conformity and Opposition in Everyday Life* (London, 1987).
David Schoenbaum, *Hitler's Social Revolution* (London, 1966).

## 8. 'Normality' and Genocide: the Problem of 'Historicisation'

Saul Friedländer, 'Some Reflections on the Historication of National Socialism', *Tel Aviver Jahrbuch für deutsche Geschichte* 16 (1987), pp. 310–24.
Otto Dov Kulka, 'Singularity and its Relativization. Changing Views in German Historiography on National Socialism and the "Final Solution"', *Yad Vashem Studies* 19 (1988).
The available literature in English on this issue is currently very limited. A forthcoming anthology edited by Peter Baldwin (Harvard) will contain many of the most relevant contributions to the discussion. For material in German, see the notes to Chapter 8.

## 9. Living with the Nazi Past: the 'Historikerstreit' and After

Richard J. Evans, 'The New Nationalism and the Old History: Perspectives on the West German '*Historikerstreit*', *JHM* 59 (1987), pp. 761–97.
Saul Friedländer, 'West Germany and the Burden of the Past: the Ongoing Debate', *Jerusalem Quarterly* 42 (1987), pp. 3–18.
Charles Maier, *The Unmasterable Past: History, Holocaust, and German National Identity*, Cambridge, Mass., 1988.
The article by Otto Dov Kulka, listed above in the reading to Chapter 8, is also of central relevance. A number of further important studies in English, notably by Richard Evans and Geoff Eley, are forthcoming in the near future (see Chapter 9 notes 5–7).

# Index

# Index